MW00582480

Prologue to History

Prologue to History

The Yahwist as
Historian in Genesis

John Van Seters

Westminster/John Knox Press
Louisville, Kentucky

Book design by Kristen Dietrich

First Edition

Published by Westminster/John Knox Press
Louisville, Kentucky

This book is printed on acid-free paper that meets the American National Standards Institute Z39.48 standard. ∞

PRINTED IN THE UNITED STATES OF AMERICA
9 8 7 6 5 4 3 2 1

Library of Congress Cataloging-in-Publication Data

Van Seters, John.
  Prologue to history : the Yahwist as historian in Genesis / John
Van Seters. — 1st ed.
        p.   cm.
  Includes bibliographical references and indexes.
  ISBN 0-664-21967-5
  1. Bible. O.T. Genesis—Historiography.   2. J document (Biblical
criticism)   3. History, Ancient—Historiography.   I. Title.
BS1235.5.V36   1992
222′.11067—dc20   91-45298

To
John W. Wevers

CONTENTS

PREFACE

This study of the Yahwist has been a long time in the making and represents a rather continuous interest since an earlier book, *Abraham in History and Tradition,* which dealt extensively with this Pentateuchal material. Over twenty years ago, when I began to investigate some of the similarities and parallels between the Yahwist (J) and the Deuteronomistic historian (DtrH), I became convinced that the nature of J's composition was not fundamentally different from DtrH — that it reflected a closely related genre of historiography and that it was produced at a time close to, but also later than, that of the national history contained in Deuteronomy to 2 Kings. This position was in opposition to much of the prevailing view (to be treated below) and called for extended reexamination.

Because the subject matter that makes up the Yahwist in Genesis was understood as part of the early evolution of Israelite historiography, I felt obliged to treat at length the question of Israelite historiography in a broad comparative context in *In Search of History,* with primary focus on the Deuteronomistic History as the first national history in Israel. For the last decade I have returned again to the Pentateuch to address, in a more extended form, the nature of the Yahwist as a form of ancient historiography. This present volume should be judged, therefore, as still part of the same discussion undertaken in the previous works. Even so, this will not be the end of it, for I propose to follow soon with another book dealing with the Yahwist in Exodus to Numbers. Nevertheless, I am prepared to let the argument of this book speak for itself.

A major portion of the research for this book was undertaken during a research leave in 1985–86, spent at Oxford University. This was made possible by the generous assistance of research fellowships from the National Endowment for the Humanities and the Kenan Fund of the University of North Carolina. To both I wish to express my sincere thanks. I am also grateful for the hospitality and assistance afforded me at Oxford as a visiting fellow at Oriel College, where Professor Ernest W. Nicholson was my gracious host. He and his family assisted me in many ways during my stay. Thanks are also due to his colleagues John Barton, John Day, Stephanie Dalley, Rex Mason, James Barr, and others, who engaged me in discussion about my work and generally made my year at Oxford a most memorable one.

My visits to a number of other institutions in the United Kingdom, Germany, Switzerland, and Holland during that research year to give lectures and seminars about my work on the Yahwist allowed me to test and improve my views on the subject. It put me in debt to the hospitality of so many that I can scarcely begin to name them all. Special mention, however, should be given to H. H. Schmid and Albert de Pury, who did much to make my European tour possible. They also hosted my lectures in Geneva and Zurich and organized a special session of the Swiss Society for Near Eastern Studies to discuss with me the theme of the "Yahwist as Historian." This "preliminary report" was translated by Schmid and published as *Der Jahwist als Historiker*. De Pury also published, as editor, my two Geneva lectures: "Myth and History: the Problem of Origins" and "Tradition and History: History as National Tradition" in *Histoire et conscience historique dans les civilizations du Proche-Orient ancien*. Much of the content of these lectures appears in revised form in Chapter 2 of this volume. To these two scholars, for their encouragement and support and for their warm friendship, I am deeply grateful. My thanks are also due to Professor Otto Kaiser, editor of *Zeitschrift für die Alttestamentliche Wissenschaft,* and its publisher W. de Gruyter, for permission to use my article, "The Creation of Man and the Creation of the King," in Chapter 3 and to Professor John Emerton, editor of *Vetus Testamentum,* and its publisher E. J. Brill, for the use of my Leuven Congress lecture, "The So-called

Deuteronomistic Redaction of the Pentateuch," in Chapter 13.

Since that year of research in 1985–86, the press of academic duties and the continuous flood of new literature have conspired to delay the appearance of this work. Even so, I am sure that the diligent reviewer will be able to identify some important lacunae in the treatment of this vast topic. This is not intended as the last word or the whole picture on Genesis. It is offered more in the nature of a set of observations and suggestions about the Yahwist. If it stimulates some lively discussion on the nature of J's composition, it will have accomplished its purpose.

I wish here to recognize the continued support of my home institution, the University of North Carolina, and my colleague Jack M. Sasson, who has read part of the manuscript and offered his advice and criticism. Dr. Fred Cryer also made some helpful suggestions during the final stages of editing. The views expressed here, however, are entirely my own. But there is one feature of the book for which I am not entirely responsible. It is the policy of Westminster/John Knox Press to edit for inclusive language and this has introduced into the book such terms as "humankind." When dealing with ancient cultures for whom such notions of "linguistic correctness" were quite foreign and anachronistic, I remain uneasy about the use of inclusive language in this work. Nevertheless, my thanks are due to the staff of Westminster/John Knox Press and its editor Jeffries M. Hamilton for all assistance with the book's publication.

Finally, a word of gratitude to my wife, Elizabeth, for her encouragement and helpfulness in so many ways. The book is dedicated in friendship to a former teacher and colleague, John W. Wevers.

Abbreviations

AB	Analecta Biblica
Ac Ant	*Acta Antiqua*
Ac Or	*Acta Orientalia*
ANET	*Ancient Near Eastern Texts Relating to the Old Testament*, ed. by J. B. Pritchard, 3rd ed., Princeton, 1969
An St	*Anatolian Studies*
AOAT	Alter Orient und Altes Testament
APA MS	American Philological Association, Monograph Series
Ar Or	*Archiv Orientalni*
ASTI	*Annual of the Swedish Theological Institute*
ATANT	Abhandlungen zur Theologie des Alten und Neuen Testaments
ATD	Das Alte Testament Deutsch
BA	*Biblical Archaeologist*
BASOR	*Bulletin of the American Schools of Oriental Research*
BHS	Biblia Hebraica Stuttgartensia
BLit	*Bibel und Liturgie*
BN	*Biblische Notizen*
BS	Biblische Studien
BTS	Biblisch-theologische Studien
BWANT	Beiträge zur Wissenschaft vom Alten und Neuen Testament
BZ	*Biblische Zeitschrift*
BZAW	Beihefte zur Zeitschrift für die Alttestamentliche Wissenschaft

CAD	*The Assyrian Dictionary of the Oriental Institute of the University of Chicago*
CB OTS	Coniectanea Biblica, Old Testament Series
CBQ	*Catholic Biblical Quarterly*
CBQ MS	Catholic Biblical Quarterly, Monograph Series
ETR	*Études Théologiques et Religieuses*
EvT	*Evangelische Theologie*
FOTL	The Forms of the Old Testament Literature
FRLANT	Forschungen zur Religion und Literatur des Alten und Neuen Testaments
FzB	Forschung zur Bibel
HAR	*Hebrew Annual Review*
HKAT	Handkommentar zum Alten Testament
HSM	Harvard Semitic Monographs
HSS	Harvard Semitic Series
HTR	*Harvard Theological Review*
HUCA	*Hebrew Union College Annual*
ICC	The International Critical Commentary
IDB	*The Interpreter's Dictionary of the Bible*, 4 vols. Edited by G. A. Buttrick. New York, 1962
Int	*Interpretation*
JAOS	*Journal of the American Oriental Society*
JBL	*Journal of Biblical Literature*
JCS	*Journal of Cuneiform Studies*
JJS	*Journal of Jewish Studies*
JNES	*Journal of Near Eastern Studies*
JSOT	*Journal for the Study of the Old Testament*
JSOT SS	Journal for the Study of the Old Testament, Supplement Series
JTS	*Journal of Theological Studies*
KuD	*Kerygma und Dogma*
LCL	Loeb Classical Library
MDIK	*Mitteilungen des deutschen archäologischen Instituts, Abt. Kairo*
MDOG	*Mitteilungen der deutschen Orient-Gesellschaft*
OBO	Orbis Biblicus et Orientalis
PBS	Publications of the Babylonian Section, University Museum, University of Pennsylvania
RA	*Revue d'Assyriologie et d'Archéologie Orientale*

RAI	Recontre Assyriologique Internationale
RLA	*Reallexikon für Assyriologie*
SANE	Sources from the Ancient Near East
SANT	Studien zum Alten und Neuen Testament
SBS	Stuttgarter Bibelstudien
SBT	Studies in Biblical Theology
Scrip Hier	*Scripta Hierosolymitana*
SHAW.PH	Sitzungsberichte der Heidelberg Akademie der Wissenschaften, Phil.-hist Klasse
SJOT	*Scandinavian Journal of the Old Testament*
SVT	Supplement to *Vetus Testamentum*
TB	Theologische Bücherei
ThR	*Theologische Rundschau*
ThSt	Theologische Studien
TLZ	*Theologische Literaturzeitung*
TWAT	*Theologische Wörterbuch zum Alten Testament*
UF	*Ugarit-Forschungen*
VT	*Vetus Testamentum*
WMANT	Wissenschaftliche Monographien zum Alten und Neuen Testament
WO	*Die Welt des Orients*
ZA	*Zeitschrift für Assyriologie*
ZAW	*Zeitschrift für die alttestamentliche Wissenschaft*
ZTK	*Zeitschrift für Theologie und Kirche*

INTRODUCTION

The subject that I have undertaken to treat in this book is an investigation into the nature and form of the book of Genesis. To what genre of literature does it belong, and how can we account for its presence within the Hebrew Bible? Is there any reason why it stands at the beginning of a "history" that extends from Genesis to 2 Kings and introduces such a large part of the biblical corpus? Past attitudes and approaches to the study of Genesis have either regarded this question as so self-evident as to be trivial — it begins the story at the beginning — or they have explained the whole book on the basis of its parts, the larger or smaller units within it. Genesis becomes a collection of traditional pieces. I have not been satisfied with either answer. First, the beginning of a national tradition by an account of the primeval origins of peoples and nations, as we have it in Genesis, is rather exceptional in Near Eastern historiography and therefore its form is not so obvious as it may now appear to us by its very familiarity. Second, concerning the view that Genesis is the gradual accumulation of traditions, I would argue that the form of the whole demands as much explanation as that of its parts. My concern is not with "holistic" exegesis or some form of "canon" criticism but rather with the hermeneutical task within the discipline of historical criticism in which it is essential to understand the nature of the literary work before interpretation can properly begin.[1]

In what follows, I will argue that the book of Genesis is a work of ancient history in two senses. First, it is a work about ancient times, an *archaiologia,* a particular genre of early historiography that served as "prologue" to the national traditions of many states

1

and peoples. As such, it shares certain characteristics with these works that must be understood at the outset of any study of the book. Second, it is the work of an ancient historian who shared with antiquity certain understandings about his task that are reflected in the nature of his writing. The notion that Genesis is a "history book" is not new, but in a review of past scholarship on the Pentateuch, I will try to show how this idea was set aside in the interest of emphasizing Genesis's folkloristic origins. In its place, scholars spoke of collections of legends and schools of storytellers. This led to the complete neglect of comparative study of the genre of historiography as it related to the Pentateuch for the last century. Out of a broad interest in ancient historiography that I have pursued for some time through earlier publications, especially in *In Search of History,* it has become clear to me how extensive is the impulse to preserve in "historical" form both the achievements of the present and the traditions of the past through a variety of types and genres of literature, and how these have been combined and developed into more comprehensive treatments of the past. Investigation of the various small units in Genesis, however, has not led to an understanding of the larger form of the book, as it should have done.

Much space and effort could be expended at this point in attempting to define the genres "history" and "historiography," without the hope of gaining any widespread consensus. Such attempts were made in the earlier work, *In Search of History,*[2] evoking a variety of responses from the critics but without offering convincing alternatives. In this work, my approach will be to suggest an understanding of the genre by the association of the Yahwist in Genesis with works from antiquity that have comparable interests and content as well as similar structural and compositional forms and techniques. This is not just a search for parallels to the creation story, for instance, but how comparable subject material fits into the culture's own literary and traditio-historical development and within a body of historiographic literature.[3] It remains to be seen how a proper recognition of genre in Genesis can influence interpretation and an understanding of the Yahwist's literary history.

Cognizance of the form and nature of Genesis and of its "authors" has been very much affected by the presence of myths and legends in it having to do with origins of the cosmos, humanity and culture, and individual nations and tribes. The element of etiology permeates the book in many different forms, and it is this material that has been judged as incompatible with historiography; therefore, the place of myth, legend, and etiology in early history writing will need to be investigated. The confusion between modern historiography and the task and technique of the ancient historian has been a serious detriment to the investigation of the historiography of the Hebrew Bible as a whole and Genesis in particular.[4] Even a casual reading of such classical historians as Herodotus, Dionysius, Livy, and Pausanias would have suggested that the presence of myth and legend within ancient historiography has to be taken seriously.

Likewise affecting the study of the form of Genesis has been the rise and dominance of the tradition-history methodology that holds certain fixed ideas about the creation and transmission of tradition. In my previous study of Abraham (*Abraham in History and Tradition*) I raised questions about this approach. In the present work, I offer reasons from the sociological study of tradition that cast further doubt on the method of tradition-history currently used in biblical studies. What the sociology of tradition says about the creation of national traditions may be confirmed by observations from the literate societies of antiquity and may provide a more secure and controlled basis from which to judge the development of Israel's traditions. Furthermore, the rise of literacy, another major social factor, has been closely associated with the rise of historiography and the coalescing of Israel's national tradition as reflected in the Pentateuch. So this subject will also call for some attention.

There are two other "literate" civilizations in which primeval traditions form an important part of their national "canon" that will serve as the main focus for our comparative investigation. The first, Mesopotamia, is obvious because it has such direct parallels as the flood story and many other alleged similarities to Genesis. It has received most of the attention by scholars in the past. The second civilization to be considered is Greece, which has been given little notice since Near Eastern archaeological discoveries took over the limelight. I have already suggested reasons in previous publications for rectifying this neglect.[5] The concern in this comparative analysis will be not only with the content of the traditions about primeval times but also the historiographic forms that took up these traditions as part of their national traditions.

With the publication of C. Westermann's massive and erudite commentary on Genesis,[6] the question may well be posed as to whether further studies can add much that is new on the nature and compositional development of Genesis. The fact is, however, that monographs have continued to appear, including the major study by E. Blum, *Die Komposition der Vätergeschichte* (1984), which have moved the discussion of the nature of Genesis in quite a new direction different from that of Westermann. The present investigation can, likewise, be understood as a work in dialogue with some of the important assumptions and conclusions of Westermann's commentary, as well as with that of other recent studies. At the same time, I acknowledge the great usefulness of Westermann's surveys of past scholarship, his comprehensive bibliographies, his discussions on the text and on many literary-critical aspects of Genesis. There seems to be little need to repeat this quite prodigious achievement. The emphasis of this book will be upon some fundamental differences in the literary-critical starting point and how this affects the analysis of the whole. The same applies *mutatis mutandus* to the other recent studies that will be considered here.

In this treatment of Genesis, I have also imposed some restrictions that may be controversial or disputed. The first is to assume that there is a comprehensive form of Genesis earlier than the final form whose author I identify as the "Yahwist." I do not recognize the existence of a parallel Elohistic source within the Pentateuch, so that by Yahwist (J) I include all the pre-Priestly material. This is equivalent to the so-called Jehovist (JE), but this terminology has other connotations that I do not want associated with my understanding of this author. Because I have argued these issues of Pentateuchal criticism in other publications, principally in *Abraham in History and Tradition,* I will not take up the matter again here. In the subsequent analysis of certain texts, however, I will make some observations that have a bearing on the problem of the Elohist. Likewise, I will not discuss directly the Priestly Writer's work, which I consider as a secondary supplement to that of J and not an independent composition. This issue will be considered in the context of textual analysis in which there is a mixture of J and P and some need to clarify their relationship. Furthermore, the Priestly corpus does not represent a different genre from that of J, but merely a later stage in the development of the Pentateuch's historiography.

One of the persistent criticisms of my previous work, *Abraham in History and Tradition,* was that the study of only one segment of tradition, the story of Abraham, was too limited to be able to draw conclusions about the nature of the Pentateuch as a whole.[7] This is a valid reservation, and the present study greatly extends the analysis to Genesis as a whole. Thus, in the Jacob traditions I believe it is possible to show that there is the same basic stratification of sources with pre-J materials taken up and expanded by J and further supplemented by P. I do not consider it necessary to debate which of the pre-J materials may reflect oral tradition. In my earlier work I took a "minimalist" view, but even those efforts to identify oral sources have met with criticism.[8] Yet the fact remains that ancient historians by their own testimony made use of oral tradition,[9] and it seems quite reasonable to attribute some of the folkloristic material in Genesis to such sources.

Since my earlier work on the Abraham tradition, there has also been a growing tendency to regard the "final form" as Deuteronomistic in some vague way and to see it as part of the redaction of the whole corpus from Genesis to 2 Kings. This tendency I do not consider helpful, and it is not confirmed by the present analysis. I will continue to argue, instead, that the Yahwist was written as a "prologue," in form and function, to the Deuteronomist's history. The relationship of these two histories will have to be explored, at least as it relates to certain topics or themes. But I will avoid reviewing the past history of Pentateuchal criticism or the current state of the discussion, which has been done so frequently in the past few years.[10] On a few particular issues it will be necessary to review the history of the discussion, and these *Forschungsberichte* already make the study somewhat cumbersome. I have tried, however, to keep them to a minimum.

Another restriction that I have imposed on this study is to confine myself to Genesis, even though my subject is the Yahwist as historian. This does not mean that I agree with those who suggest that there is a firm literary break between Genesis and Exodus and who therefore reject any notion of a Yahwist. The same kind of objections were raised against M. Noth's notion of a Deuteronomistic history that combines everything from Joshua to 2 Kings as one work. My reason for this limitation to Genesis is quite simple. There are enough issues and problems in Genesis to discuss in this volume. The Yahwistic corpus in Exodus–Numbers raises a somewhat different set of questions that are best confined to the focus of a second study. Work on such a book is already well advanced so that it should appear soon after this one. I will, however, within the body of this study touch on the issue of the continuity between the two major parts of the Yahwist's work.

The bulk of this book will focus on the activity of the Yahwist as an antiquarian historian, his use of older source materials, and his shaping of these into a vulgate tradition. I will argue that these materials were made up of elements from both eastern and western antiquarian traditions. This is especially true of the primeval history of Genesis 2–11. For the "patriarchal age" the sources were more local in character, but still they correspond to a clearly discernible pattern of historiography. The Yahwist's theme of the promises to the patriarchs, so decisive for Israel's own identity, is a development of the "land theology" in the Old Testament to which J makes a very important contribution. This theme will need to be investigated in some detail.

The hermeneutical debate between advocates of historical criticism and those who are concerned with the "final form" of the text is given a new twist in this study. The charge against historical criticism is that it engages in almost endless fragmentation of the text in a quest for the original oral and written sources, as if these were the real tradition. This study agrees with the critique that they are not. The countercharge against those advocates of a "canonical" approach to the final form is that they merely disguise their assumptions about the literary nature of the text in some vague notion about a redactor or "canonical process" like a deus ex machina, with the audience and the context scarcely discernible.[11] Here too the interpretive schemes become endless. The present study searches for the final form within the historical literary process, a form that is the *vulgate tradition*[12] for both a specific historical situation, and a tradition that continues to function as vulgate through revision within new successive historical communities in which it became authoritative. If the evidence that follows can support such a construction, it may encourage quite a different kind of hermeneutical dialogue from the one that has been the case for the last few years.

NOTES

1. See the recent discussion of S. Bonner, "The Importance of a Diachronic Approach: The Case of Genesis-Kings," *CBQ* 51 (1989), 195–208.
2. J. Van Seters, *In Search of History* (1983), pp. 1–6.
3. See the recent discussion by T. Longman, *Fictional Akkadian Autobiography: A Genetic and Comparative Study* (1991), pp. 3–36.
4. A recent example of such confusion is the book by B. Halpern, *The First Historians: The Hebrew Bible and History* (1988), in which the comparison is made at the very outset between the modern historian Carlyle and the Deuteronomistic historian of Joshua–2 Kings. Halpern's book offers a major critique to my own work in ancient historiography, so the present work may be viewed as an implicit response to it.
5. See esp. Van Seters, *In Search of History*, pp. 8–18.
6. C. Westermann, *Genesis*, Biblischer Kommentar I/1–3, 1974–82. This will be referred to in this work in the English translation, *Genesis 1–11, 1984; Genesis 12–36*, 1985; *Genesis 37–50*, 1986.
7. See, e.g., the review of J. J. M. Roberts (*JBL* 96 [1977], 112): "In the first place, no analysis restricted to the Abraham material can legitimately claim to replace the documentary analysis which, with all its faults, has been tested in and makes reasonable sense of the whole Tetrateuch." Roberts goes on to state that including the Jacob material would have led to quite different results. The present study may be viewed as a response to this criticism.
8. See R. C. Culley, *Studies in the Structure of Hebrew Narrative* (1976), pp. 27–30; P. G. Kirkpatrick, *The Old Testament and Folklore Study* (1988), pp. 61–64.
9. See W. Aly, *Volksmärchen, Sage und Novelle bei Herodot und seinen Zeitgenossen: Eine Untersuchung über die volkstümlichen Elemente de altgriechischen Prosaerzählung*, 1921.
10. See now the excellent survey by A. de Pury and T. Römer, "Le pentateuque en question: position du problème et brève histoire de la recherche," in *Le pentateuque en question*, ed. A. de Pury (1989), pp. 9–80.
11. See Bonner, "The Importance of a Diachronic Approach."
12. The use of this term will be discussed below.

1
THE PROBLEM
OF FORM

It is not particularly new to describe the Yahwist as a historian. At least since the time of Wellhausen, the J source of the Pentateuch has been characterized as a piece of historiography, *ein Geschichts-werk*. But what is quite remarkable is that in spite of this oft-repeated conviction there has been so very little attention paid to the consequences of such a form-critical classification for the literary and traditio-historical understanding of the Pentateuch and of the Yahwist in particular. Part of the problem for this lies in the history of Pentateuchal research. Therefore, it may be useful just to sketch a few lines of the history of that discussion as it has to do with this one question: Is the Yahwist source a history?

Wellhausen describes his "Jehovistic work (JE)" as "pure history-book," which he contrasted with Deuteronomy as "pure law book."[1] But he was also concerned to assert that JE was a self-contained historical work prior to the Priestly history and was not just filler material. He was willing to grant that this source had a certain fragmentary and disjointed character as compared with P, but that was because it was closer to the sources of origin. When all of it was taken together, however, it represented early Israelite historiography.

At the same time that Wellhausen could speak in this way about the JE work as a whole, he could also describe the nature of the patriarchal stories in quite a different way. He placed particular emphasis on the etiological aspect of these stories, which were "not history proper at all, but folklore." The early process of transmission was oral tradition and "the product of a countless number of narrators, unconsciously modifying each other's work. . . . The whole literary character and loose connection of the Jehovist story of the patriarchs reveals how gradually its different elements were brought together, and how little they have coalesced to a unity. . . . As with the legend of the beginning of things, so with the legend of the patriarchs. What is essential and original is the individual elements in the several stories; the connection is a secondary matter and only introduced on the stories being collected and reduced to writing."[2]

It is easy to see how these statements anticipate the work of H. Gunkel.[3] With Gunkel, however, this whole emphasis on the preliterary stage was taken much further. Having the Genesis narratives primarily in view, Gunkel denied that these stories were history. As preliminary to his discussion of the form of prose narrative in Genesis, Gunkel set forth his criteria of why the material in Genesis could not be history. The thrust of the discussion is to impugn the historicity of the stories of Genesis in order to identify the particular units as legends and the whole as a kind of *Volksbuch*. This was in contrast to Wellhausen, who spoke of a *Geschichtsbuch*, even though Wellhausen had made it quite clear that such a designation did not imply that the traditions used in it were historical by modern standards.[4]

Gunkel classifies the stories of Genesis as *Sagen* (legends) mostly etiological in form and originally individual units of tradition. Gunkel drops the notion of the Pentateuchal sources J and E (or JE) as history books and describes them as collections, part of the process that had already begun on the oral level. Gunkel makes the further statement:

> The writing down of the popular traditions probably took place at a period which was generally disposed to authorship and when there was a fear that the oral traditions might die out if they were not reduced to writing. We may venture to conjecture that the guild of storytellers had ceased to exist at that time, for reasons unknown to us. And in its turn the reduction to writing probably contributed to kill out the remaining remnants of oral tradition, just as the written law destroyed the institution of the priestly Thora.[5]

Gunkel seems to have in mind here the analogy of the Grimm brothers' collections, by which he was so strongly influenced, but it is hardly convincing for antiquity. Furthermore, Gunkel also argues that the process of making collections of legends went on for hundreds of years, because even P is still a collector of legends, which rather contradicts this quoted statement about the sources of legends drying up.

Gunkel takes direct issue with previous literary criticism (indirectly with Wellhausen) over the notion of J and E as authors. The sources are "collections, codification of oral tradition." The primary evidence against J as an author is (1) the heterogeneous nature of the materials used; (2) the relationship of the variants J and E to each other, which suggests collections of pieces, some of which are almost identical; and (3) the fact that J itself appears to be made up of several sources, especially in the primeval history. Gunkel concludes: "From this survey of J's sources we perceive that J is not a primary and definitive collection, but is based upon older collections and is the result of the collaboration of several hands." Gunkel further asserts that what we have preserved in the biblical sources is "but a small portion" of what originally existed. "In olden times there may have been a whole literature of such collections, of which those preserved to us are but the fragments."[6] Finally, Gunkel sums up his position thus:

> But for the complete picture of the history of the formation of the collec-
> tion the most important observation is that with which this section began:
> *the whole process began in the stage of oral tradition.* The first hands which wrote
> down legends probably recorded such connected stories; others then added
> new legends, and thus the whole body of material gradually accumulated.
> And thus, along with others, our collections J and E arose. J and E, then,
> are *not individual authors,* nor are they editors of older and consistent single
> writings, but rather they are *schools of narrators.*[7]

What Gunkel has given to us is a kind of sociology of tradition for ancient Israel, but it is derived entirely from his imagination. He does not adduce a single ancient parallel for such legend collections. In fact, there were no such collections of legends in the libraries of Mesopotamia, although there were copies of individual epics; nor were there such collections in Egypt. The collections of ancient Greece are another matter, and we will return to these below. But if Gunkel cannot prove that the process of collection began at the oral stage, then he has not moved beyond Wellhausen at all.

The impact of Gunkel's work on English-speaking scholarship can be seen in the very influential Genesis commentary by J. Skinner.[8] In his introduction, he freely acknowledges his debt to Gunkel and outlines a view on the nature of Genesis very similar to Gunkel's. This includes the notion that the two sources, J and E, represent two parallel recensions of collections of the national traditions that were preserved by guilds of storytellers. At the same time, however, he suggests that behind these two versions a "popular tradition has been systematised, and a sort of national epic composed, at a time prior to the composition of J and E."[9] This view of a national epic behind the sources, J and E, is put forward in spite of the fact that Skinner does not believe that Genesis reflects an original poetic composition.

The notion that the form of Genesis could best be explained by positing a national epic behind the present prose version of Genesis became a widely accepted view in English and American scholarship, championed by no less a figure than W. F. Albright. The fact that in both Greece and Mesopotamia myths of creation and primeval times and the legends of heroes were presented in epic form seemed to give weight to this position. But Genesis is not written in epic poetry or epic style, and efforts to find an epic original behind it are not convincing. Because I have previously examined this matter, I will not repeat myself here.[10] This position of an original national epic behind Genesis has moved so completely out of the mainstream of discussion on the Pentateuch that it is not involved in the subsequent studies that we will consider.

G. von Rad, for all his emphasis upon the *Sagen* of Genesis, firmly rejects Gunkel's characterization of J as merely the name for a process of story collection.[11] He returns to Wellhausen's characterization of the Yahwist as a *Geschichtsbuch* and asks how this remarkable form came about. The form-critical problem of the Hexateuch is really the form-critical problem of the Yahwist. His answer, by now so familiar, is to suggest that the historical form of narration derives from the ancient cultic salvation-history credo, as illustrated by Deut. 26:5–9. It was this form that the Yahwist combined with the legal tradition of Sinai, expanded in the patriarchal narratives, and to which he affixed the prologue of the primeval history. Von Rad firmly rejects the notion that the Hexateuch could have "developed gradually from that short, ancient creed, through the accretion of layer upon layer of old traditional materials added by the efforts of many generations." Against both Gunkel and the subsequent traditio-historical

schemes, von Rad asks the question: "How could such heterogeneous materials as those embraced by the Yahwist have cast
themselves in this form of their own accord?"[12] It is one thing to
speak of a random collection, a repertoire of ancient stories, that
could have existed at various places throughout Judah and Israel.
It is quite another to think in terms of a deliberate collection, selection, and arrangement in a consistent and continuous historical
framework. For von Rad, it is within and through this structure
that the Yahwist presents his theology.

Likewise of interest is the way in which von Rad modifies
Gunkel's approach to the rise of historiography in ancient Israel.
For Gunkel, the first stage in the development of history writing
was the collection of etiological sagas such as represented by J.
This went through various stages of refinement, with interest focusing more and more on recent political events, until the apex is
reached in the so-called Court History of David (2 Sam. 9–20,
1 Kings 1–2). Von Rad follows this scheme from individual legend
to the almost secular political narrative of the Court History (or
"Succession Story"), but he then develops it further in a remarkable
way. He specifically classifies the Yahwist as a major historical work
along with the History of David's Rise and the Succession Story,
and states:

> The Jahwist's work may be a little later, for it is probably to be assumed
> that the contemporary history was the first to be depicted, and that it was
> only then that the need of a picture of the earliest history grew up. . . . What
> was new was that Israel now found herself able to shape history into great
> complexes; that is, not merely to call to remembrance isolated events basic
> to the history, or to string data more or less connectedly together for the
> purpose of cultic recital, but really to present the history in its broad
> historical connexions, including all the many events which cannot be made
> to fit with complete consistency into any teaching, and taking in also its
> reverses, and, above all, its terrible and splendid humanity.[13]

For von Rad, the Yahwist has become, in form, a historian; in purpose, a theologian; and in social status, a member of the intelli-
gentsia of the court who had a significant "formative effect on the
general public."[14] The distance here from Gunkel on the form of
the Yahwist is decisive and cannot be bridged. Von Rad has come
out on the side of Wellhausen against Gunkel — that the Yahwist
is indeed an author and historian wherever the inspiration for

the work's form and the material for its composition may have come from.

M. Noth, in his work on the Pentateuch, stands much closer to the position of Gunkel, although with some modification toward the position of von Rad.[15] For Noth, the Yahwist is primarily the literary fixation and theological reworking of the received Pentateuchal material that already had a unity and interconnection of its various parts. This form is not so much the elaboration of a cultic credo by one author as it is the development of a set of confessional themes covering all the major parts of the Hexateuch from the patriarchs to the conquest of the land. These confessional themes had their place in the amphictyonic religious community before the rise of the monarchy in preliterate Israelite society. In other words, Noth found a more concrete sociological context than Gunkel had suggested for the development of the Pentateuchal tradition, precisely to answer von Rad's question of form. However, he still had one block of material left over, the primeval history, which he could not make a part of Israel's primitive cultic material. For this part alone he invokes the authorship of J. He states:

> What deserves notice is just the fact itself that J did not present his portrayal of the nature of man in general formulations, but rather through the use of received narrative material of a predominantly popular sort. The result was that his presentation corresponded in character to the ensuing Pentateuchal narrative, except that the latter was already available to him as a compact unit, while the *Urgeschichte* he constructed first on his own from numerous individual elements. For this task the only unit of any sizeable extent given to him was the Flood story, which stemmed from Babylon.[16]

Here is a most curious combination of Gunkel and von Rad. J plays the part of author and historian only for the primeval history and then is merely the faithful scribe for all the rest of the Pentateuch. But if he could have been historian for one part of the work, why not for all? Furthermore, there is a serious contradiction of Gunkel here, for it was especially in the fragmentary character of the primeval history that Gunkel had his strongest argument for J as a mere collection.

Noth's own work on Israelite historiography focused primarily upon the so-called Deuteronomistic historian (DtrH),[17] a work neglected and even belittled by Gunkel. This complex from Deuteronomy to 2 Kings was a *Geschichtswerk,* the product of historical research, collection, arrangement, and theological orientation. But in contrast to von Rad, Noth was not willing to treat the Yahwist in the same way but emphasized that the Pentateuch must be approached methodologically in an entirely different manner. Yet the distinction between the Pentateuch/Hexateuch and DtrH left unresolved the dispute between von Rad and Noth over the relationship between the two, because both von Rad's credo and Noth's confessional themes included the Conquest, which was now such an important part of DtrH. Thus both the beginning and the ending of the Pentateuch created very serious problems for Noth's notions about the form of the Yahwist.[18]

A number of scholars have continued to view the sources of the Pentateuch, J and E, as histories. One inference that they drew from this form-critical identification is that it is inconceivable that J and E should have ended their histories at a point so far in the past. Consequently, scholars like O. Eissfeldt, G. Fohrer, G. Hölscher, and H. Schulte continue to find traces of these historical works in the later biblical books.[19] For the Yahwist, this meant that his work continued from the primeval history up to the time of the United Monarchy. Eissfeldt's comment on this point is significant:

> All the analogies suggest that Israelite historical writing began when Israel had reached or just passed its zenith, i.e., under or soon after David and Solomon; and that it did not restrict itself to the immediate present or to a section of the past closely connected with it, but presented the whole development of the people from its beginnings, linked with the beginning of the world and of mankind, right down to the contemporary scene.[20]

The suggestion of comparative study looks promising here, until one discovers that "all the analogies" in this quotation come down to one, that of the Maccabean period. And his primary concern is to draw some parallel between the achievement of the Maccabees and that of David as a way of dating the J source. On the form-critical issue, it offers no further help.

The approach of S. Mowinckel to the Yahwist's place in Israelite historiography has been quite singular, but at least he raises the form-critical question.[21] For him, the appropriate model for all Israelite historiography is the Norwegian saga, which may include material from oral tradition but also comprises much larger, complex literary works. In this way, both the Yahwist and the Deuteronomist have written sagas. For Mowinckel, the beginning of historiography was the development of the family saga of the Davidic-Solomonic period, written as recent history. Only then did the Yahwist create a great synthesis of earlier traditions in the ninth or early eighth century B.C. (This is a modification of von Rad's position.) The Deuteronomistic saga includes the rest of the material in Kings but also a synthesis of the earlier sagas back to the time of Moses. However, Mowinckel does not make clear the relationship of the Yahwist's saga to the Deuteronomist. The saga as a form of historiography is very vague and never clarified by Mowinckel. In the end, it has not advanced the form-critical discussion at all in the last twenty years.

C. Westermann has tried to find a mediating position between that of Gunkel and von Rad, with special reference to the book of Genesis. He does this by making the following assertion:

> The crucial point is that the written version is the result of an unbroken line from its beginnings in word of mouth, through many stages of oral tradition right up to its fixation in writing. The individual passage passes thereby through contexts that were already there before its insertion into the whole. The traditio-historical method therefore requires an explanation that has equal regard for both the oral and the written stages of the formation of the Pentateuch.

At the preliterary stage, Westermann can affirm that there were many different paths of tradition within the Pentateuch, like Noth's Pentateuchal themes, quite independent from each other. When Westermann comes to deal with the literary stage of the tradition, however, he once again reverts to von Rad's view of the Yahwist as a historian in the Davidic-Solomonic era. He states that the Yahwist's work "is the first, as far as we know, in the history of the world to bring together a historical whole that encompasses several different epocs [sic]."[22] This includes the full extent of the Hexateuch from the primeval story to the settlement in the land. But this recognition of the Yahwist as historian does not lead Westermann to explore the genre of early historiography as a clue to the characteristics of the literary form of the Yahwist. Like von Rad, he is more interested in the theology of the Yahwist than in his historiographic features.

This view by Westermann is presented in a discussion on Pentateuchal research at the conclusion of his treatment of Genesis 1–11, the point at which the Yahwist is regarded as most original

and most like a historian. When Westermann comes to the patriarchal stories (*die Vätergeschichte*), he seems to revert to the position of Gunkel and emphasizes that the sources J, E, and P are
not writers in the modern sense but tradents that merely hand
on traditions.[23] In his view, it is virtually certain that not a single
story in Genesis 12–50 is invented and that many may go back
to the "patriarchal age" itself (which he seems to regard as within
the first half of the second millennium B.C.). Even those texts that
are part of the framework or thematic structure and so often identified with the perspective of the Yahwist himself may only be
modifications of early traditions that derive from the patriarchal
period.

Yet at this point we encounter something of a contradiction
in Westermann. He is eager to assert that J is not an author and
therefore not one who could use his own imagination in telling
his stories. He states: "It is extremely improbable, if not impos-
sible, that all these stories have been invented. Originally only what
happened was narrated."[24] One might reasonably conclude from
this and other similar statements that the patriarchal stories were
a kind of history, but Westermann insists that they are not history
or historiography because they are not the work of authors. In this
he follows Gunkel. Thus Westermann would appear to be saying
that the Yahwist is not a historian because he did not write fiction
but faithfully handed down traditions about things that actually
happened. Stated in this way, such a conclusion appears absurd.
The simple equation that historians are authors and authors write
from their own imagination has completely aborted the form-
critical discussion. What is a historian? What is the historian's relationship to tradition, oral and written?

In an earlier study, Westermann made much of a comparison
between the character of the patriarchal stories as "family" stories
and the so-called family sagas of Iceland, dating to the Middle
Ages, about the twelfth century A.D.[25] This was a significant departure from Gunkel's understanding of *Sagen,* especially of their
etiological character, which had come under some criticism. In
this way, Westermann attempted to introduce new criteria into
explanations of the nature and development of the patriarchal
narratives. I questioned the viability of this comparison in my
earlier work, and my judgment has been largely upheld.[26] Although

the notion of "family stories" is still used in his commentary as a form-critical category to evaluate some of the stories of the patriarchs,[27] Westermann has largely set it aside in his discussion of the form of Genesis as a whole.

G. W. Coats, however, in his form-critical study of Genesis, continues to follow Westermann's earlier study of "sagas" in Genesis, ignoring the criticisms raised against the use of the Icelandic saga model for the patriarchal stories.[28] Coats understands Genesis as a collection or series of sagas, one "primeval" saga and three "family" sagas, corresponding to the three patriarchs: Abraham, Isaac, and Jacob. This leads to the curious designation of the whole of Gen. 25:19–37:2 as the "Isaac saga," although for Westermann this is basically the Jacob tradition, and the "Jacob saga" then becomes the Joseph story. The scheme becomes quite unacceptable. Coats does not address the genre of Genesis as a whole or the work of the Yahwist in particular. In his "introduction" to the narrative literature of the Old Testament, he excludes the Pentateuch from the category of history and reserves that designation for the Deuteronomistic History and Chronicles.[29]

R. Rendtorff follows in the line of Gunkel and Noth.[30] He wants to examine the development of the larger units of tradition as distinguished by Noth, but he has abandoned Noth's sociological basis in the theory of the amphictyony. This means that Rendtorff can now admit the primeval history as such a unit without any need to ascribe it to J, as Noth had done. It is enough simply to identify a major block of traditions that is largely self-contained, such as the patriarchal stories, and then to develop a theory to account for its gradual growth in various stages and especially to account for the eventual formation of its thematic unity. If the promise theme is the result of a complex tradition-history, then there is no need for an author, the Yahwist, to be held responsible for the imposition of such a unity, as von Rad had suggested.

Rendtorff's criticism of the notion of the Yahwist as an author is directed primarily at the Yahwist as theologian. But the problem with this is that "theologian" is not an appropriate form-critical category. There are no formal theologies in the Old Testament. That is not what von Rad had in mind when he spoke of the Yahwist as a theologian. The prior question that must be asked is whether the Yahwist is a historian, that is, whether the features observable in this source of the Pentateuch are compatible with the style and techniques of early historiography. Only after this is established can it be debated as to whether or not this historian can be viewed as a theologian in much the same way that one speaks of the theology of DtrH.

The problem with Rendtorff's position is that it has no system of verification and no sociological model or comparative analogies to which his theory of tradition growth may be related, because he has abandoned Noth's amphictyonic and pre-state milieu of emergent tribes. So Rendtorff has no way of overcoming the criticism that he is quite arbitrary in devising solutions to his own choice of problems. Where does such tradition development take place? Why does it grow in just the way he suggests? Who are responsible for its development and maintenance? In what form is the transmission, written or oral? A theory of tradition-history that does not address these questions cannot hope to replace those like von Rad and Noth, who at least made an attempt to supply such answers.[31]

E. Blum's effort to carry Rendtorff's program forward has led him to revert to specific authors and stages in the composition of the patriarchal narratives and to relate these to concrete situations in order to answer the above set of questions.[32] In doing so, however, he avoids the designation Yahwist. But the form-critical question raised by von Rad for the whole of the Hexateuch is not addressed. Instead, Blum limits himself to the meaning of the patriarchal stories and interprets their form as *Völkergeschichte*.[33] For this purpose he takes the genealogical structure of the stories as primary; and with the use of anthropological models suggested by R. R. Wilson,[34] he regards such a presentation of the people's identity and of their relationship to their neighbors as reflective of a primitive period of Israelite history. It is on the foundation of this primitive historiography that the later amplifications and modifications are built.

Blum has followed Westermann in seeing in the genealogical structure a primitive base for the formation of the patriarchal traditions. But the anthropological material collected by Wilson will hardly account for the stories joined together by the genealogies. Blum's own account would also seem to suggest that the genealogy actually grew and developed along with the expansion of the patriarchal stories themselves. Furthermore, the same meaning of *Völkergeschichte* and its explanation cannot be used for the growth of the primeval history, even though it employs genealogies. But a discussion of the primeval history is studiously avoided by Rendtorff and Blum.[35]

Quite a new possibility has been put forward by my earlier work on Abraham and by the related studies of H. H. Schmid and M. Rose.[36] These have all suggested that the Yahwist source of the Pentateuch is a much later work than Wellhausen advocated and is to be regarded as much closer in time to the DtrH, or even after him. This makes it the same kind of work as DtrH, a history book, but one that could take the presentation of Israel's history from the conquest to the end of the monarchy for granted. Instead, it concentrated on the most ancient period from the creation of humankind to the time of Moses — a *Vorgeschichte* of an established historical tradition. This would solve the form-critical problem of the Hexateuch and clarify the relationship of the Yahwist to the Deuteronomist, especially to the account of the conquest in Joshua, which seems to be a necessary component of the Yahwist's work. Of course, there would be little need any longer for invoking a Dtr redactor as a kind of deus ex machina for every point of contact in the Tetrateuch with the Deuteronomic tradition or for the final form of the Pentateuch.[37]

The task of carrying out an extensive study of the relationship of the Yahwist source to the Deuteronomist has been undertaken in a detailed fashion by Martin Rose,[38] and still there remains much more to be done. But this kind of literary-critical study must now go hand in hand with a form-critical study of the nature of the Yahwist as historian. Only when these two important areas have been investigated can we begin to make some tentative observations about the history of the traditions within the Pentateuchal sources. Our task in the rest of the presentation will be the form-critical one: What does it mean to describe the Yahwist's work as a history? For the purpose of this discussion, I will simply include together all the pre-Priestly material of the Pentateuch, what Wellhausen refers to as the Jehovist. Even the removal of the so-called Elohistic texts from consideration would have little effect on the discussion as a whole.

Conclusion

Let me sum up a number of points that seem to me worthy of further discussion. There are two issues that lie at the basis of so much of the scholarly debate about the question of the form of Genesis. These have to do, first, with whether or not myth and legend (*Sage*), as these were commonly understood, are compatible with the writing of history. And second, if they are not, then how is one to explain the form of the book of Genesis?

Some scholars unjustly regard Wellhausen as suggesting that J was merely an author who invented everything he wrote, with no subtlety about the nature of the materials within J. In fact, Wellhausen seems well aware of the large amount of folklore, both myth and legend, derived from oral tradition within J and has made particular allowance for it. It is hard for me to see that any real advance in the larger form-critical issue—the nature of J's work—has been made since his time.

From the time of Gunkel and Skinner to the present, the identification of myth and legend in Genesis has tended to preclude the possibility of describing the work as history and thus to suggest other models. Gunkel's introduction of the notion of "collector" (*Sammler*) of the myths and legends, even at the preliterate stage, was the real point of departure from Wellhausen and the beginning of the whole development of tradition-history of the Pentateuch, as in the works of Noth, Rendtorff, and others. If that suggestion is to work, one must first establish the activity of the collector or collecting institution in a manner more convincing than has been the case thus far. The British-American notion that the collection was a national epic means that we will have to consider the possible relationship of epic to early historiography.

Von Rad actually returns to Wellhausen, against Gunkel, on the matter of the Yahwist as historian. The Yahwist is the collector of the older legendary traditions. Von Rad's main point, in the form-critical problem of the Hexateuch, is to find the model of historical presentation that inspired the Yahwist's work. Even if his *kleine Credo* did not solve that problem, he still raised the question, How did all this material come together in this particular form? That question will not go away.

Noth's approach is to reconstruct an institutional context, the amphictyony of the pre-state period, as an agency for collecting the Israelite traditions (from the patriarchs to the conquest), but he must revert to a Yahwist as historian for the non-Israelite traditions of the primeval history. With the demise of the theory of an amphictyony, Rendtorff and others who follow Noth leave the collection process in limbo.

The most important criterion for identifying myth and legend in Genesis by Gunkel and those who followed him was etiology. When questions were raised about the appropriateness of this criterion as an adequate explanation for the form of narrative in Genesis, Westermann redefined *Sage* to mean saga and introduced a new possibility for understanding the form of Genesis, particularly as it has to do with the patriarchs. This still maintained the split between the primeval history and the patriarchs with a position similar to that of Noth. But his attempt to find "family sagas" in Genesis corresponding to his Icelandic model must be judged a failure, so that the problem of etiology in Genesis has not been solved, only postponed.

From the above survey, it would appear that there has not been any real advance in the basic form-critical question—the nature of the Yahwist's work in Genesis—since the time of Wellhausen. The only new consideration that has opened up since his literary work on the Pentateuch is the possibility that the Yahwist (or Jehovist) is much later in date than previously thought and therefore part of a larger development of Israelite historiography in the early exilic period.

In the study that follows, I intend to address these issues on a broad comparative basis along the lines of my earlier study *In Search of History*. What is remarkable about the last century of discussion is that no one has attempted to compare Genesis with works of ancient historiography or ask about the *form* in which subjects related to primeval history and origins of peoples and culture are presented. So the first question that must be addressed is the place of myth and legend, especially etiology, in the various forms of ancient historiography. It cannot be assumed that because they are excluded by their very nature from modern history, they are not present in ancient historiographic genre. This preliminary discussion will also address the question of the development of national traditions and the relationship that early historiographic forms have to the rise of literacy and the development of a classical literary tradition.

Once we have established the plausibility that in Genesis we have to do with a type of antiquarian historiography concerned with origins and a national tradition of people and place, we will give special attention to the treatment of similar "primeval" traditions in Mesopotamia and Greece. These will provide a basis for the particular study of the Yahwist as an antiquarian historian who drew upon a range of such primeval and national traditions to create his "prologue" to the history of Israel. The form and character of that work as reflected in Genesis will occupy the major part of this study.

NOTES

1.   J. Wellhausen, *Prolegomena to the History of Ancient Israel* (1885), pp. 295–362.
2.   Ibid., pp. 333, 326f., 335.
3.   H. Gunkel, *Genesis, übersetzt und erklärt*, HKAT I/1, 1901; 3rd ed., 1910. See the introduction in English translation, *The Legends of Genesis*, 1901 (repr., 1964), pp. 123–144. Subsequent quotations are taken from this work.
4.   Wellhausen, *Prolegomena*, pp. 333ff.
5.   Gunkel, *Legends*, pp. 123f.
6.   Ibid., pp. 125, 129.
7.   Ibid., p. 130. See the italics in the commentary.
8.   J. Skinner, *A Critical and Exegetical Commentary on Genesis*, ICC, 2nd ed., 1930.
9.   Ibid., p. xxiii.
10.   See Van Seters, *In Search of History*, pp. 18–31, 224–227, for references to Albright and his "school." Cf. F. M. Cross, "The Epic Traditions of Early Israel: Epic Narrative and the Reconstruction of Early Israelite Institutions," in *The Poet and the Historian*, ed. R. E. Friedman (1983), pp. 13–39.
11.   G. von Rad, "The Form-Critical Problem of the Hexateuch," in *The Problem of the Hexateuch and Other Essays*, trans. E. W. T. Dicken (1966), pp. 1–78.
12.   Ibid., pp. 50–52.
13.   Von Rad, *Old Testament Theology*, vol. 1 (1962), p. 49.
14.   Ibid., p. 56.
15.   M. Noth, *A History of Pentateuchal Traditions*, trans. B. W. Anderson (1972), esp. pp. 228–247.
16.   Ibid., p. 237.
17.   M. Noth, *The Deuteronomistic History*, JSOT SS 15, 1981.
18.   See Noth's commentary on *Exodus* (1962), pp. 12–15, for some modification of his views.
19.   O. Eissfeldt, *The Old Testament: An Introduction* (1965); G. Fohrer, *Introduction to the Old Testament* (1968); G. Hölscher, *Geschichtsschreibung in Israel: Untersuchung*

zum Jahwisten und Elohisten (rev. ed., 1952); H. Schulte, *Die Entstehung der Geschichts-schreibung im alten Israel,* BZAW 128, 1972.

20.   Eissfeldt, *The Old Testament,* p. 247.

21.   S. Mowinckel, "Israelite Historiography," *ASTI* 2 (1963), 4–26.

22.   Westermann, *Genesis 1–11,* pp. 574, 575, 589.

23.   Westermann, *Genesis 12–36,* pp. 23–58.

24.   Ibid., p. 43.

25.   C. Westermann, "Arten der Erzählung in der Genesis," *Forschung am alten Testament,* TBAT 24 (1964), 9–91 = *The Promises to the Fathers* (1980), pp. 1–94.

26.   J. Van Seters, *Abraham in History and Tradition* (1975), pp. 134–138; see R. N. Whybray, *The Making of the Pentateuch,* JSOT SS 53 (1987), 152–158.

27.   Westermann, *Genesis 12–36,* p. 51.

28.   G. W. Coats, *Genesis with an Introduction to Narrative Literature,* FOTL 1, 1983.

29.   Ibid., p. 9.

30.   R. Rendtorff, *Das überlieferungsgeschichtliche Problem des Pentateuch,* BZAW 147, 1977.

31.   See my review, "Recent Studies on the Pentateuch: A Crisis in Method," *JAOS* 99 (1979), 663–673; also W. McKane, in *VT* 28 (1978), 371–382.

32.   E. Blum, *Die Komposition der Vätergeschichte,* WMANT 57, 1984.

33.   Ibid., pp. 478ff.

34.   R. R. Wilson, *Genealogy and History in the Biblical World,* 1977.

35.   This applies to Blum's most recent work as well, *Studien zur Komposition des Pentateuch,* BZAW 189, 1990.

36.   Van Seters, *Abraham;* H. H. Schmid, *Der sogenannte Jahwist,* 1976; M. Rose, *Deuteronomist und Jahwist: Untersuchungen zu den Berührungspunkten beider Literaturwerke,* ATANT 67, 1981.

37.   The recent work by Whybray, *The Making of the Pentateuch,* is primarily a critical appraisal of the current state of Pentateuchal studies. Whybray reviews the present position on the Documentary Hypothesis and agrees with those who no longer find it adequate. He also examines the history of the discussion of oral tradition and its relationship to the methodology of tradition-history and offers his critique of these approaches. Many of his views are similar to those expressed here and in my earlier work. In a short treatment at the end of the book he offers "an alternative approach." This consists of taking my suggestion about the form of the Pentateuch as a history and suggesting that there was only one author/historian who composed the whole of the Pentateuch. His remarks about such a history, however, I regard as too vague and imprecise to add anything further to the discussion.

38.   See Rose, *Deuteronomist und Jahwist.*

2
MYTH AND
TRADITION IN ANCIENT
HISTORIOGRAPHY

Myth and Legend in History

The main stumbling block to considering the Yahwist as a historian is the presence of myth and legend in Genesis.[1] Gunkel went to great lengths to demonstrate that the characteristics exhibited by the stories in Genesis were antithetical to the whole notion of history; therefore, in his view the two could not be brought together. On the surface, myth and history suggest a set of contrasts between fantasy and reality, fiction and fact, the supernatural and the natural, the paradigmatic act and the singular, unrepeatable event. Or one can speak of contrasting modes of consciousness in which the mythological and the historical are set at different poles: the one timeless and otherworldly; the other bound to chronology and to concrete factual experiences. One can point to myth's close association with religion, ritual, and the world of the gods while viewing history as basically secular and political.

This view of the matter, however, is an anachronism when applied to the ancients for whom our modern sense of history and what is appropriate historical research is quite unknown. A little familiarity with ancient texts reveals that these contrasting qualities of myth and history can often be found in the same work, so that in any given instance, such as the *Histories* of Herodotus or the biblical books from Genesis to 2 Kings, there is a mixture that is not easy to categorize. Scholars often explain this mixing of the features of myth and history by such terms as the mythologization of history or the historicization of myth. Perhaps

24

more precise delineation of terminology would be helpful.

In defining the terms *myth* and *history*, it is best for our purposes to keep to a rather broad understanding of these genres. Following the lead of recent discussion, I would suggest that myth is a traditional story about events in which the god or gods are the primary actors, and the action takes place outside of historical time.[2] In addition, myth contains some structure of meaning that is concerned with the deep problems of life and offers explanations for the way things are. Under the category of history are the broad range of historical texts, written records of past events that celebrate the deeds of public figures and important events of communal interest, within a chronological framework. These records reflect the problem of historical change and seek to account for it in political terms within "historical" time.[3]

Coming somewhere between the two is the third category of *Sagen*, or legends about heroes and eponymic forefathers. Because these figures are usually godlike and share the stage with deity, because their actions and activities have a special paradigmatic character, and because they live in a time and place that is essentially unhistorical or prehistorical, they belong more to the realm of myth than they do to history, whether or not they reflect, dimly, some historical event or personage. Myth and legend appear so often together, as they do in Homer, that their combination is not a problem. It is the presence of either myth or legend in a historical work that requires some explanation.

The historicization of myth is a process of rationalization of myths or mythical elements by the use of historical categories of arrangement or explanation, such as the imposition of genealogical or chronological succession on myths and legends. It does not change fancy into fact but transposes a story from one narrative genre to another, reflecting a certain mode of interpretation. This often transforms the individual myth from a traditional story into part of a continuous ordered narration with a larger view of the past.

The mythologization of history is the imposition of mythical motifs and elements onto historical materials and traditions. This gives to the particular historiographic form a more universal and paradigmatic character. This may be done by the use of absolute references: in time—the beginning; in scope—the world;

in ultimate cause—the gods. The historicization of myth or the mythologization of history may be two sides of the same coin, depending on whether the myth or the historical tradition is the primary focus of attention.

To illustrate these principles, I will use some examples from ancient Egypt. Many examples could also be drawn from ancient Greece and Mesopotamia, but these will appear when the primeval traditions of these two civilizations are reviewed in the next two chapters. In ancient Egypt of the third millennium B.C., there is a remarkable historical text, the Palermo Stone, which records in strict annalistic fashion the names of rulers over at least seven centuries from the period before the unification of Upper and Lower Egypt down to the end of the Fifth Dynasty.[4] For each of the dynastic rulers, it also records important annual events. In its present form, it constitutes a form of royal annals that was given some special ceremonial significance, no doubt having to do with the legitimation and perpetuation of royal authority.

The genre of annalistic compilation of royal deeds does not seem to have had any successor in Egypt, except in the listing of kings and their length of reigns, as can be seen in the Turin Canon of Kings, which continues the list down to the Eighteenth Dynasty.[5] What is especially noteworthy, however, is the Turin Canon's treatment of the early predynastic period. Instead of repeating from the Palermo Stone the names of the early kings before Menes, the Turin Canon substitutes the names of gods, demigods, "glorified spirits," and mythical kings, all with very long reigns.

This seems to be a clear case of mythologizing a historical tradition. It obviously linked the royal power and legitimacy with divine and heroic precedent. It gave to the Egyptian empire a central place in the cosmos, a universal and paradigmatic depth that the earlier tradition of the Palermo Stone could not convey. The mythical origins of kingship were of more consequence than the historical ones. The Turin Canon actually sacrificed part of the ancient record, the predynastic kings of the divided monarchies of Upper and Lower Egypt, in order to give to the state a divine origin and unity. Furthermore, it is this mythological form of the historical tradition that becomes the "vulgate" tradition and finds its later continuation in the Hellenistic historian Manetho.

The opposite tendency, that of the historicization of myth, can be seen in a text of the late eighth century B.C., known as the Memphite Theology.[6] The text begins with a rationalization of the myth of the conflict of Horus and Seth in which, under the supreme earth god Geb, the dispute between the two gods is peacefully resolved and the two regions of Upper and Lower Egypt are given to Seth and Horus respectively. Subsequent to this, Horus, the son of Osiris, the firstborn of Geb, is given the whole of Egypt as his inheritance. This act presents the etiology of the united kingship of Upper and Lower Egypt and the establishment of the united monarchy in Memphis. The concern here is not with all the complex details of the myth but with the use of the tradition to legitimate the peaceful unity of Egypt, which was politically expedient for the rulers of the Twenty-Fifth (Nubian) Dynasty.

The claims of Memphis as the appropriate political center of a united Egypt were further enhanced by invoking two other myths in revised form. The one was the Osiris myth in which Memphis was the place where "Osiris had drowned in his water" but had been rescued by Isis and Nepthys and subsequently resides with the rest of the gods in Memphis. This myth is related to the notion of Memphis as the center of the land's fertility. Memphis is also identified as the point at which Ptah, through his divine command, created the whole cosmic and social order and all the gods, their cities, shrines, and offerings, the whole cultic order of the land, including the 'animation' of all cult statues.

The Memphite Theology has thus combined three blocks of mythical tradition from different sources and has historicized them in terms of the beginnings of political and religious life and the political concerns and realities of the time of its authorship. It is a complex etiology that functions as explanation and legitimation of political and religious authority. At the same time, the text pretends to be "historical" by claiming to be derived from a source of great antiquity, even though it has now been demonstrated that the claim is false. As such, it belongs to a number of similar "antiquarian" texts composed in this period that make appeal to the past for propagandistic purposes.[7]

As these Egyptian examples illustrate, the interaction between myth (including legend) and history has its clearest and, for our purposes, most important focus in the problem of origins or etiology. The concept of origin has a twofold aspect. It means both the beginning (*archē*) and also the cause (*aitia*), and both of these play a prominent role in myth and history.[8] In myth, the beginning is essentially timeless and the cause is paradigmatic. What happens at the beginning and what a god or hero does constitutes the basis for the later corresponding reality. Hence the frequent association of myths with rituals: religious, social, and political. In history, the beginning is the chronological starting point, and the cause is an event at a point that is in continuous relationship to a series of events in an unbroken chain down to the reported effect. Herodotus, for instance, knew that the mythical beginning and cause of the hostilities between the barbarians and the Greeks that led to the Persian wars was a series of crimes in the heroic age that culminated in the Trojan War. But because he could not bring that into direct connection with later historical events, he begins at that point in history where he believes that such a continuity of cause and effect is possible.

It would be tempting, on the basis of this observation, to make a clear distinction between primitive mythological thinking and more enlightened historical thinking, and to see these two perspectives on origins as reflective of a cultural and mental dichotomy. Indeed, it is not unusual to find the claim that non-Israelite, or pagan, religion reflects the mythological mode of thinking, whereas Israel made the historical way of thinking decisive for its religion, and whatever non-Israelite myth it inherited it transformed by a process of historicization.[9] This general viewpoint, however, must be firmly rejected as not in keeping with the facts. It can clearly and easily be established that texts reflecting mythical modes of thinking can be found alongside of historical texts in all the ancient civilizations. We have already seen this to be the case in our examples from Egypt in the same document, and others will be given below for Mesopotamia and Greece.

Nevertheless, the subject of etiology deserves some further consideration because of its importance for the book of Genesis. Here I will focus on the views of B. S. Childs, which have had a considerable impact on the study of the Pentateuch.[10] Childs finds that earlier scholars, such as Gunkel, Alt, and Noth, have used the term *etiology* too loosely for almost any form of causation, and he wants to restrict it to a specific genre, a form of mythical story that reflects a metamorphosis in nature in primordial time, to account for present reality. On this basis he criticizes Gunkel's examples of etiologies in Genesis because

> in each case he was forced to reconstruct the original etiological story from a projected *Vorlage* to accord with his *religionsgeschichtliche* pattern. However, in every case the biblical story had been given a different function within the final narrative from that assumed to be the original. The etiological element was either destroyed (Gen. vi 3), robbed of its independence (xxxii 22ff.), subordinated to a theological lesson (iii 14ff.), or historicized (iv 8ff.). The reshaping was so extensive that one could no longer speak meaningfully of an etiological form as a form critical genre without resorting to reconstruction.[11]

Childs contrasts the genre of mythical etiology by the biblical type in which "in a non-mythical story an act in the past simply established a *precedent* which assumed an authority for later generations within a particular community."[12]

There are a number of reasons why Childs's view of etiology is quite unacceptable. First, he has created his own circumscribed genre of etiology, which neither corresponds with the broad range of comparative material in Mesopotamia, Egypt, and Greece, nor with the scholarly treatment of this subject in these related disciplines. Etiology may be in story form, but it can also be anecdotal or a brief etymology. Second, Childs's criticism of Gunkel assumes a number of non-Israelite etiologies that were transformed by the author of Genesis. But there is no evidence for most of these. Their etiological character may be entirely Israelite. Where we have similar stories, such as in the case of the destruction of Sodom and Gomorrah and the Greek story of Philemon and Baucis,[13] the treatment is the same, describing metamorphoses in nature as acts of divine judgment. Very few stories in Genesis can be described as examples of precedent. Third, we have already shown an Egyptian example of the historicization of myth. Many more will be noted below. But the case of Herodotus is noteworthy. Although he prefers to begin with the historical *aitia* of the Persian War, he still cites the heroic examples of hostilities as if they were a series of historically related events, which originally they were not.

Fourth, there are "mythical" etiologies in the Old Testament that are purely Israelite and may even represent the mythologization of "historical" precedent. Thus, whereas Deuteronomy gives the Israelite servitude in Egypt as a precedent for permitting one's servants to rest on the Sabbath (Deut. 5:15), P makes the Sabbath derive from the very structure of creation, which is mythical. I can find no sound reason for treating etiology in Genesis differently from that of the neighboring cultures.

The discussion of myth in biblical studies has long been dominated by the concern to define or understand myth in terms of its mentality and its association with ritual.[14] The "mental" and cult-functional parameters are so tightly circumscribed that it is easy to show how, in the biblical tradition, the mentality of myth has been broken and the mythical fragment transformed to a new purpose. This approach is no longer adequate.

Given the very rich corpus of literary works from the classical world of ancient Greece, it would be helpful to look at the problem of myth in this culture. Here one finds that in the Greeks' understanding of the past there is no decisive break between the mythical mentality of an absolute and timeless beginning and the historical past. Instead, between the two is a large "gray area" that is occupied by etiology. There is little evidence that Greek myth had any ritualistic function.[15] It was basically explanatory in character. As van Groningen asserts: "The myth, which fixes religious speculations in a narrative form, is a philosophy *avant la lettre*. It wishes to explain all sorts of things; in fact, it wishes to explain everything."[16] The form of this explanation is primarily etiological, which may be in terms of a cosmogony or theogony to address questions of cosmology and nature or in terms of stories about gods and heroes in the early heroic age. These could often be "political" in that they related to eponymous ancestors or heroes of particular states, tribes, or regions.

At this point we encounter the problem of the transition between mythical etiology and the earliest antiquarian histories of political states. Concerning this transition to historiography, M. I. Finley states:

> The atmosphere in which the Fathers of History set to work was saturated with myth. Without myth, indeed, they could never have begun their work. The past is an intractable, incomprehensible mass of uncounted and uncountable data. It can be rendered intelligible only if some selection is made, around some focus or foci. In all the endless debate that has been generated by Ranke's *wie es eigentlich gewesen* [sic] ("how things really were"), a first question is often neglected: what "things" merit or require

consideration in order to establish how they "really were"? Long before anyone dreamed of history, myth gave the answer.[17]

Among the earliest historians, the so-called genealogists, myth was the primary source for subject matter about the beginnings of political life. The concern of these historians and mythographers was to assemble, organize, and systematize the vast complex body of myths. One of the primary literary devices for doing so was the use of genealogy. As Hesiod had done for the gods in his *Theogony*, the historians did for the myths of the primeval period from the earliest humans to the heroic age of the Trojan War.[18]

P. Veyne gives an apt description of this genre of antiquarian historiography, which stretches over several centuries from the sixth century B.C. to the Roman era. He states:

> This genealogical literature, in which Pausanius found a historiography, in reality tells of *aitiai*, origins, the establishment of the order of the world. The implicit idea . . . is that our world is finished, formed and complete. . . . By definition, this establishment occurred before the dawn of history, in the mythical time of the hero. Everything focuses on telling how a man, a custom, or a city came into being. Once born, a city has only to live its historic life, which is no longer the concern of etiology.
>
> Etiology . . . was thus limited to explaining a thing by its beginning: a city, by its founder; a rite, by an incident that formed a precedent, for it has been repeated; a people, by a first individual born from earth or a first king. Between this first fact and our historical era, which begins with the Trojan War, stretches the succession of mythical generations. The mythographer reconstitutes — or rather invents — a seamless royal genealogy that spans the whole mythical age. When he has invented it, he feels the satisfaction that comes from complete knowledge. Where does he get the proper names that he affixes to every branch of his genealogical tree? From his imagination, sometimes from allegory, and, more often, from place names. The rivers, mountains, and cities of a country come from the names of the original people who lived there, who were thought to have been the kings of the country rather than its sole inhabitants. The ageless human trail found in toponyms originates in the human onomasticon of mythical times.[19]

I have quoted this description of etiology in Greek literature at length because it is so completely at variance with that of Childs, and it betrays such a close similarity to that of the etiology in Genesis. Etiology as a form of cosmology developed in the direction of philosophy and science, but etiology as it pertains to the beginnings of political, social, and cultic life was the concern of early historians. Both the philosophical and the historical developments were a gradual process.

Even when we come to Herodotus, the father of history, the etiological interest has not been left behind. Van Groningen states: "The quickly flourishing historical science of Herodotus and those who follow his example is particularly rich in aetiological elements."[20] In fact, van Groningen characterizes this early type of historiography as "etiological" because it is concerned with explanations from the past by tracing the cause back to the beginning. Although Herodotus may rationalize or historicize the various traditional "causes," the impulse to such explanation comes from the mythological and genealogical heritage.

Up to this point we have assumed in our discussion of myth and history that myth also includes legend. Most of the discussion about etiology in Genesis has to do with *Sagen*, etiological legends. In fact, it is Gunkel's effort to identify these different etiologies that has led to the complex process of tradition-history to identify the various layers of tradition prior to their collection into their present form. This methodology, with at least implicit notions about the form of Genesis as a slowly accumulating corpus of traditions, has presented no literary model as its explanation. Here I think it would be useful to consider the place of legend in Greek historiography as undertaken in the valuable study of W. Aly.[21]

Aly was a contemporary of Gunkel and Gressmann and was influenced by their work on folk traditions in the Old Testament. He attempted the same kind of form criticism of the early Greek historians, particularly Herodotus. A few observations will indicate the value and relevance of his work to the discussion of Genesis:

1. Aly argues that in Herodotus the individual stories stand at different levels in their distance from the original oral tradition sources. In some cases they represent a rather loose collection of almost unaltered folk traditions close to the original source and hardly integrated into the theme of the larger work. At other points the stories have been thoroughly reworked so that they reflect the skill and seriousness of the author and his concern to create the definitive tradition of an episode and to make clear its meaning for the work as a whole. The "primitive" stories and the

"developed" narratives all come through the same author, who is both collector of traditions and historian.

2. Aly states that, like the Old Testament, Herodotus does not hand on complete *Märchen* but only selections, individual motifs of such stories that have been "historicized" by association with historical names and made into *Sage*. It is in this transformation of *märchen*-like motifs within the history that I think the comparison with the Old Testament would be most helpful. The same could be said for etiological motifs in Herodotus.

3. Aly attempts to classify material in Herodotus into two basic categories, the material in the *logos* form, which corresponds to the historian's activity as storyteller, and his scientific investigations and speculations. In fact, as later scholars have pointed out, there is a large part of Herodotus that is a mixture of the two. Even Aly admitted as much. Aly also emphasized the importance of the *Rahmenerzählung*, and here he sees strong influence from Near Eastern forms of historiography like the chronicles and king lists.

4. Although the emphasis in Aly's work was on the forms of the inherited folk tradition, he was still sensitive to the influence on Herodotus of the Homeric epic tradition, of Greek tragedy, of the sophists and their "wisdom" tradition, and of the rhetorical traditions of public life. In other words, through the medium of his history, with its large amount of traditional material, Herodotus still reflected his own times and their influence on him, so it is quite legitimate to ask what Herodotus was trying to express of his own views in his work.

If early Greek historiography is an appropriate model to understand the work of the Yahwist, as I believe it is, then both the kinds of traditions preserved and the manner of their collection, revision, and arrangement into a larger whole will be greatly clarified. Comparison with Herodotus does not justify the kind of tradition-history that one finds in Noth's work on the Pentateuch and the many scholars that have followed this approach. How could it, because in Herodotus all the levels of development from simple to highly reworked traditions and all the editorial structures and devices are represented in the one work at the same time? Like Herodotus, one can expect the Yahwist to use older legends as sources for his work but also folk motifs as a basis for quite new stories composed to express his thematic purposes. For his framework, the Yahwist may use common historiographic structures, such as genealogies, but also thematic elements that create the larger sense of unity. And like Herodotus, the Yahwist may also reflect the literary, cultural, and religious heritage of his day. If he belongs to the exilic period, as I have long argued, then this heritage will be considerable.

History as National Tradition

I regard it as self-evident that the book of Genesis constitutes, in both its earlier stage of the Yahwist's work and in its final form, the national tradition of Israel's origins. But the question that we want to address is, To whom or to what institution or process should we attribute the origination and development of such a tradition?

Ancient Greece supplies ample testimony, both direct and indirect, as to the importance that similar national traditions held for them. Works that dealt with national traditions, whether of individual states or of the Hellenic peoples in general, were very numerous and popular. The range of historiography includes the genre of recent history, such as the treatment of the great wars in Herodotus, Thucydides, and Polybius, but also works that dealt with ancient times and the founding of various states. There can be no doubt that national traditions in historiographic form were very important in Greek society. Although in Israel they were not as abundant as in Greece, they were no less important, given the amount of space that national historical traditions now occupy in the Bible. How did such traditions arise?

The sociological study of tradition has argued, in recent publications,[22] that the formation of traditions is the activity of an intellectual elite, not the work of the community as a whole. This runs counter to a position often expressed or presumed in biblical studies. Yet S. N. Eisenstadt specifically identifies society's intellectuals as the "creators and carriers of traditions."[23] This is true for many different kinds of tradition, including that of the historical traditions. The historian, as an intellectual, is the creator and maintainer of historical tradition. E. Shils makes the statement:

> Images about the past of one's own society, of other societies, and of mankind as a whole are also traditions. At this point, tradition and

historiography come very close to each other. The establishment and improvement of images of the past are the tasks of historiography. Thus historiography creates images for transmission as tradition.[24]

Of course, there may be a great many inherited images of the past—traditions of almost infinite variety. But their selective collection and organization according to chronological and thematic or "causal" relationships is the intellectual activity of historiography.

The traditions created by historiography are national traditions. Shils points out that the whole development of modern scientific historiography went hand in hand with the promotion and development of national histories that gave legitimation and identity to national societies. These national traditions were incorporated into the educational syllabi as necessary and vital. He further states: "The promotion of a belief in continuity and identity with the national past, reverence for national heroes, the commemoration of founding events . . . were among the tasks laid on the teaching of national history."[25] Such histories did not come to life by themselves. They were written by historians, and only in this way did they become a "classical" tradition of events and personages that formed the basis of all successive rewriting. What was true of the modern period was true of antiquity as well, as I hope to show below.

Although historians are involved in creating traditions in the service of the state, they may at the same time exercise a certain criticism and constant revision of the historical traditions under the impulse of new visions of social relevance or new knowledge and a concern for the tradition's truthfulness.[26] In this capacity, critical historiography has often served as the arbiter and judge over a wide range of traditions, screening what is to be accepted and what is to be rejected. But even later revisionist historiography works largely within the same framework of the national or corporate tradition, always in relationship to the work of earlier historians and what they initially identified as the events, deeds, and persons worthy of commemoration, however much that portrait is changed from one generation to another.

These observations are abundantly confirmed by the historiographic traditions of the ancient Near East and Greece. Let me illustrate with a few examples.[27] In Mesopotamia, one of the most important classics of its historiography is the Sumerian King List.

It is a remarkable literary work of the early second millennium.[28] In its oldest form, it tells how kingship descended from heaven and was established at Kish. It then enumerates the dynasties of various cities given in a single sequence in which the rule over the whole region of Mesopotamia passed from one city to the next over a very long period of time until it is traced down to the first dynasty of Isin, ending about 1800 B.C. This reconstruction of the history of kingship does not square with historical fact, because most of the "dynasties" covered by the list were not successive but contemporaneous with others in the same list. The author, in creating the list, simply collected all the dynastic traditions on earlier kings from the various cities and then put them in artificial sequence in order to suggest, for political purposes of his own time, that there could be, legitimately, only one true kingship. This intellectual and literary construction became a classic tradition in the region. It was not the only one, and it did not go unchallenged. Nevertheless, it was important enough that it was continued and developed by the scholarly scribal tradition for many centuries. It also received an important expansion in the form of a prologue of "primeval history" dealing with the time before the flood.[29] Finally, Berossus, a priest and historian of Babylon living in the third century B.C., created a new national tradition out of the Sumerian King List, the Babylonian chronicles, and a number of myths and legends.[30] His work became an authoritative tradition on Babylonian history for historians of the Greco-Roman world.[31]

A similar historical tradition developed in Egypt with its king-list tradition. The so-called Turin Canon of Kings is a king list composed at the beginning of the Eighteenth Dynasty, ca. 1500 B.C.[32] It begins with the reigns of the gods and demigods who ruled before Menes, all with very long reigns, and then proceeds to list the names of kings and the length of each of their reigns. It also creates the notion of "dynasties" by grouping a number of kings under a common heading and by giving the summation of all their reigns. Occasionally, short pieces of information are included but without extensive historical narrative.

The Turin Canon was not simply the accumulation of bureaucratic records but the product of research and skillful composition with the purpose, perhaps, of reestablishing the sense of royal continuity and authority after the troubles of the Second Intermediate

Period. The fact that our extant text is a copy from about 250 years later is evidence that it became a national historiographic tradition. This same king-list tradition constitutes the framework of Manetho's *Aegyptiaca,* a historical work of the Hellenistic period and an authority for the history of Egypt used by Greco-Roman historians.

In ancient Greece, according to P. Veyne, historians consciously set about to create national traditions, "a vulgate version of the past," whether pan-Hellenic in scope or restricted to the individual *polis*.[33] Veyne further states: "The materials of a national tradition are not the tradition itself, which always emerges as a text, a tale carrying authority. History is born as tradition, not built up from source materials."[34] This observation is very important for this study because the opposite view has long held sway in biblical studies. Since the time of Gunkel, the premise of tradition-history is that the tradition resides in the materials and that the collector or historian, J, is almost incidental to the process of its development. I would argue, however, that following the Greek model, the Yahwist, as historian, created the national tradition as reflected in Genesis.

Once the Greek historian had established the tradition regarding some particular historical period or event, or the origins of a state, then later historians could augment it or attempt to improve it by a rewrite of their own. But the tradition, once established, usually remained the foundation for all later versions of the history. Historians did not document their work and did not appeal to sources or earlier works consulted, except in matters of controversy or as embellishments. Accurate reproduction of the source was not required. When history is the vulgate tradition, then it is more important that each event correspond to type than that it reflect what actually happened or what is contained in a source.[35]

It is primarily in the local histories of the individual states of Greece that the national historical tradition comes to the fore, because it is in this form that "research" into the myths of the past and their associations with peoples and places establishes a continuity with the present historical and political reality. A case in point is a work by Hellanicus called the *Atthis,* that is, the Athenian historical tradition.[36] Hellanicus created, for the first time, the Athenian national tradition from Athens's earliest beginnings in the mythological age through all the successive periods down to his own day. He was the first to develop the complete list of Athens's legendary kings and fix their chronological relationship to the age of the Trojan War. He established Theseus as the real ancestral hero of the Athenian people. He filled the gap between the age of myth and the historical period with etiologies on Athenian customs and institutions. For the latest historical period, he created a firm chronology tied to the yearly office of the archons of Athens. The history of Athens was frequently revised and expanded in subsequent versions, but it did not essentially deviate from the literary form of the classic *Atthis* tradition.

The historiography of the Near East and Greece entirely confirms the sociological observations about the development of historical traditions by intellectuals who are individual authors. For ancient Greece, they organized and rationalized the older individual oral(?) traditions of myths and legends in order to bring them into a greater unity. Later historians continued to create new national histories or revisions appropriate to their own generations. There seems to me to be every good reason to apply these same principles and observations to the historians of ancient Israel, and the Yahwist in particular.

Literacy and History

The rise of historiography in ancient Israel and the earliest written sources of the Pentateuch have been viewed as strongly influenced by the beginnings of literacy. The assumption is that the Davidic-Solomonic period was just such a time in which literacy would have played an important role in the development of the state and the earliest literary works would have been produced for the service of the United Monarchy. The suggestion has a certain degree of plausibility, reinforced by the fact that literacy had for so long been an important part of the great civilizations of Mesopotamia, Egypt, the Hittites, and major cities of Syria-Palestine prior to the rise of the Israelite-Judean state. It is even assumed that when David took over Jerusalem he inherited a complete bureaucracy of scribes with court archives and perhaps even a library.[37]

The evidence for literacy in the United Monarchy, however, is almost nonexistent. The very few early epigraphic finds demonstrate that alphabetic writing was known, but they hardly justify the assumption of widespread literacy or the production of literary works in this period. The study of literacy in ancient Israel is still rather limited and primarily concerned with the adoption, development, and use of the alphabet, and on the question of whether or not there were schools in ancient Israel.[38] In a few brief studies, some comparison has been made with the study of literacy in ancient Greece and its applicability for Israel.[39] Such comparison might be helpful, because both Greeks and Hebrews adopted the same alphabetic Phoenician script, used the same writing medium, and often made very similar use of it. The study of literacy in Greece and Rome has produced a considerable quantity of literature and some degree of sophistication with the subject.[40] This discussion makes clear that it is entirely misleading to argue for extensive literacy on the basis of only a few epigraphic remains.

The date for the beginning of a fully alphabetic script in ancient Greece is disputed, but it was very likely before the mid–eighth century B.C. This does not mean that Greece went from an illiterate to a literate society overnight. For the next three centuries, until the beginning of the fifth century, there were few epigraphic remains and a rather limited number and range of literary works. For a long time, the transmission of information continued by means of oral tradition, and only gradually did written records and literary forms of communication gain a significant place and begin to replace oral methods. R. Thomas states: "The application of writing to certain areas was slow and gradual, and much was left to memory and oral transmission as late as the fourth century."[41] The extant inscriptions from the period before the fifth century are very brief, and many are merely the identification of the owners of ceramic vessels. There is some indication of the promulgation of laws or decrees in the seventh century, but it became a widespread practice by the sixth century to have public displays of laws and treaties written in stone "for eternity." Coinage also came into common use by the end of the century, as well as other commercial uses. This period also saw the introduction of ostracism. Letters are rare before the fifth century, perhaps because papyrus was expensive. In one special case, a private letter written on lead from ca. 500 is actually preserved. It appears to be a "message of desperation" by someone unaccustomed to writing such texts.[42] When letter writing does receive mention by fifth-century authors, letters are "largely reserved for grave occasions or for sensitive secret communications," often with sinister consequences for the bearer.[43] Papyrus was probably used for some legal and other documents as well as literary works. But in this period, administrative and pragmatic applications of literacy predominate.[44]

Concerning the use of writing for literary works, the development was slower. The epic works of Homer and Hesiod were probably put into writing by the seventh century, but the dating is disputed. Poetic works in written form begin to flourish in the sixth century, and some "wisdom" sayings and early philosophic writings were also produced. Collections of oracles were made, as well as inscribed dedications to temples. Works in prose narration did not begin until the end of the sixth century and came into their own only in the fifth century. These were the antiquarian histories of the various states whose substance was very close to the oral traditions of myth and legend. The fifth century became the great classical period of literature in which a number of literary genres blossomed. But it must be emphasized that this did not take place until several centuries after the introduction of writing among the Greeks.[45]

This rather slow development of literacy, in which at least three centuries passed before literary works in prose were produced, has a bearing on the comparable situation in Israel. It may be that by the time of the United Monarchy there was some limited use of writing, especially in the court or administrative circles. There may have been some royal inscriptions of a monumental type, but their number was probably small and their length quite brief. But kings have always wanted to leave a permanent public record of their deeds, their building activity, and their gifts to the deity, even if few could read them. It is not until the eighth century that we begin to get administrative ostraca appearing in excavations, and their number increases greatly in the seventh and sixth centuries. Alongside of this are the *lmlk* seals and those with personal names on ceramics as well as votive inscriptions and graffiti on building walls and other objects. The remarkable

Balaam text of ca. 700 B.C. written on the wall of a Jordan valley sanctuary is an early work in prose narration. Royal inscriptions, such as the Moabite stone from the ninth century and the Saloam tunnel inscription from the end of the eighth century, are rare. Bullae and bullae impressions of the seventh and sixth centuries attest to the use of papyrus for documents, including correspondence.[46] It is such small finds as the bullae that attest to document consciousness from the seventh century onward, so that personal use of writing before this time must have been rare.

In Millard's review of these finds, he acknowledges the preponderance of materials from after 750 B.C. but attempts to account for the scarcity of epigraphic materials from earlier periods by ascribing the lack to the accident of archaeology; that is, the fact that unless there is a substantial destruction level, the debris will be rather sparse.[47] But there are many such debris layers from earlier periods in which ostraca, had they existed, might have appeared. The pattern of epigraphic finds from Israel simply corresponds closely with that of ancient Greece.

Furthermore, Millard attempts to defend the view that writing was widespread and within the competence of every citizen, and for this he invokes the Greek parallel.[48] But in a recent study, W. Harris disputes any extensive literacy in fifth-century Athens, the height of the classical period, and estimates that between 5 percent and 10 percent were literate.[49] The use of "names on vessels and notes on potsherds" does not attest to a high degree of literacy.[50] Millard takes the matter one step further when he assumes that literacy, as attested by the preexilic finds, also means the production of literature. He states: "Where there was writing there was certainly the possibility of literature, and of reading it. We may conclude that few Israelites were out of reach of the written word, a situation certainly facilitated by the simplicity of the alphabet."[51] But we have already indicated above that the development of literature in Greece was much more gradual than that of other uses of writing and of more limited access to the ordinary Greek. Comparison with Greece leads to the opposite conclusion; that is, that there was only a modicum of literacy before the late monarchy period.

Concerning the development of literary works in ancient Israel, matters are more difficult to judge. There may have been some examples of early poetry and some specimens of laws on public display that are now reflected in the law codes of the Pentateuch. But the dating of these is hardly possible. By the eighth century, collections of prophetic oracles were being produced. The Josiah reform would suggest the possibility of the public proclamation of laws and covenants in written form. It is quite possible that foreign stimulus from Egypt and, after the rise of Assyrian domination, from Mesopotamia encouraged the development of wisdom literature and the use of king lists. But it is unlikely that extensive prose literature developed before the late seventh or early sixth centuries, and, like Greece, this early prose was also historiographic in form.[52]

This outline of the rise of literacy in Israel is admittedly brief and tentative. Although it rests heavily on the analogy of the situation in Greece, Israel also shares much more with Greece than it does with Mesopotamia and Egypt. The form of prose historiography, as reflected in the Yahwistic work of the Pentateuch, has within it the same mixture of genres as those of Greece, including traditional materials of myth and legend, with an emphasis on etiology and national origins. It corresponds to the same kind of national tradition at the same stage of literacy. It is hardly reasonable to suppose that such a highly developed work of prose narration would stand at the beginning of Israel's development of literacy. The Greek example speaks strongly against its origin in the Davidic-Solomonic period.

NOTES

1. See my fuller treatment of this subject: "Myth and History: The Problem of Origins," in *Histoire et conscience historique dans les civilizations du Proche-Orient ancien*, Les Cahiers du CEPOA 5, ed. A. de Pury (1989), pp. 49–61.
2. See esp. G. S. Kirk, *Myth: Its Meaning and Function in Ancient and Other Cultures* (1970), ch. 1; see also W. Burkert, *Structure and History in Greek Mythology and Ritual* (1979), pp. 1ff.
3. See Van Seters, *In Search of History*, pp. 1–6.
4. Ibid., pp. 131–134; see also Eberhard Otto, "Geschichtsbild und Geschichtsschreibung in Ägypten," *WO* 3 (1966), 161–176; E. Hornung, *Geschichte als Fest. Zwei Vorträge zum Geschichtsbild der frühen Menschheit* (1966), pp. 21ff.; and most recently, D. B. Redford, *Pharaonic King-Lists, Annals and Day-Books* (1986), pp. 86–90.
5. See Redford, *Pharaonic King-Lists*, pp. 1–18, for discussion and bibliography.
6. For the text, see *ANET*, pp. 4–6; M. Lichtheim, *Ancient Egyptian Literature*, vol. 1, pp. 51–57. This text was long thought to originate in the Old Kingdom, but

a reevaluation of its dating and significance was made by F. Junge, "Zur Früh-datierung," *MDIK* 29 (1973), 195–204. See also Lichtheim, *Ancient Egyptian Literature*, vol. 3, p. 5.

7. See Van Seters, *In Search of History*, pp. 161–163; Lichtheim, *Ancient Egyptian Literature*, vol. 3, p. 5.

8. For this discussion I am much indebted to B. A. van Groningen, *In the Grip of the Past* (1953), pp. 25–34, 82–108.

9. See B. S. Childs, *Myth and Reality in the Old Testament*, SBT 1/27, 1960. The views here are reflected in his other works on etiology; see below.

10. B. S. Childs, "The Etiological Tale Re-examined," *VT* 24 (1974), 387–397. See also B. O. Long, *The Problem of Etiological Narrative in the Old Testament*, BZAW 108, 1968.

11. Childs, "The Etiological Tale Re-examined," *VT* 24:392.

12. Ibid., p. 393.

13. See Ovid, *Metamorphosis*, 8.625ff.

14. See the critical review by J. W. Rogerson, *Myth in Old Testament Interpretation*, BZAW 134, 1974.

15. P. Veyne, *Did the Greeks Believe in Their Myths?* (1988), p. 17 and n. 28. Veyne seems to deny all cult-functional understanding of Greek myths and does not even consider most etiological myths as composed to legitimate religious practice. See the literature he cites for support.

16. Van Groningen, *In the Grip of the Past*, p. 83.

17. M. I. Finley, "Myth, Memory and History," in *The Use and Abuse of History* (1971), p. 13.

18. A more detailed discussion of this will be taken up below.

19. Veyne, *Did the Greeks Believe in Their Myths?* p. 25.

20. Van Groningen, *In the Grip of the Past*, p. 26.

21. Aly, *Volksmärchen, Sage und Novelle bei Herodot und seinen Zeitgenossen*.

22. See S. N. Eisenstadt, "Intellectuals and Tradition," *Daedalus* (1972), 1–20; E. Shils, "Intellectuals, Traditions, and the Traditions of Intellectuals: Some Preliminary Considerations," *Daedalus* (1972), 21–34; and idem, *Tradition*, 1981.

23. Eisenstadt, "Intellectuals and Tradition," p. 1.

24. Shils, *Tradition*, pp. 54f.

25. Ibid., p. 59.

26. However, ancient criteria of a work's truthfulness are somewhat different from those used in modern historiography.

27. More detailed treatment can be found in J. Van Seters, "Tradition and History: History as National Tradition," in *Histoire et conscience historique dans les civilizations du Proche-Orient ancien*, Les Cahiers du CEPOA 5, ed. A. de Pury (1989), pp. 63–74.

28. T. Jacobsen, *The Sumerian King List*, 1939; Van Seters, *In Search of History*, pp. 70–72; P. Michalowski, "History as Charter: Some Observations on the Sumerian King List," *JAOS* 103 (1983), 237–248.

29. This will be treated more fully in chapter 3.

30. S. M. Burstein, *The Babyloniaca of Berossus*, SANE 1/5, 1978; G. Komoroczy, "Berossus and the Mesopotamian Literature," *Ac Ant* 21 (1973), 125–152.

31. The reasons why it was used by Josephus and Eusebius but not by the Greek

historians is explained by E. Bickerman, "Origines Gentium," *Classical Philology* 47 (1952), 72f. The prehistories of Berossus and Manetho, with their very long chronologies, seriously threatened to undermine the Greek national tradition.

32.   A. H. Gardiner, *The Royal Canon of Turin*, 1959; H. W. Helck, *Untersuchungen zu Manetho und den ägyptischen Königslisten*, 1956; Van Seters, *In Search of History*, pp. 135–138; Redford, *Pharaonic King-Lists*, pp. 1–18.

33.   See esp. Veyne, "When Historical Truth Was Tradition and Vulgate," in *Did the Greeks Believe in Their Myths?* pp. 5–15.

34.   Ibid., p. 7.

35.   Veyne's remarks are completely at variance with those presented by Halpern, *The First Historians*, ch. 1. The difference between ancient and modern historians is not understood by him. He simply ignores the whole subject of ancient historiography outside of the Old Testament.

36.   L. Pearson, *The Local Historians of Attica*, APA MS 11, 1942; F. Jacoby, *Atthis: The Local Chronicles of Ancient Athens*, 1949.

37.   See, e.g., S. Yeivin, "Administration," in *World History of the Jewish People*, vol. 4/2, *The Age of the Monarchies: Culture and Society*, ed. A. Malamat (1979), pp. 147–171, esp. pp. 149ff.

38.   See M. Haran, "On the Diffusion of Literacy and Schools in Ancient Israel," SVT 40 (1988), pp. 81–95, for recent discussion and bibliography.

39.   S. Warner, "The Alphabet: An Innovation and Its Diffusion," *VT* 30 (1980), 81–90; A. R. Millard, "An Assessment of the Evidence of Writing in Ancient Israel," in *Biblical Archaeology Today, Proceedings of the International Congress on Biblical Archaeology, Jerusalem, April 1984* (1985), pp. 301–312. Millard's article contains a useful survey of the epigraphic remains from the time of the monarchy.

40.   J. Goody and I. Watt, eds., *Literacy in Traditional Societies*, 1968; J. Goody, *The Interface Between the Written and the Oral*, 1987; R. Thomas, *Oral Tradition and Written Record in Classical Athens*, 1989; W. V. Harris, *Ancient Literacy*, 1989. These works contain extensive bibliographies.

41.   Thomas, *Oral Tradition and Written Record*, p. 16.

42.   See Harris, *Ancient Literacy*, p. 56.

43.   Ibid., p. 88. One is reminded here of David's letter to Joab, carried by the hand of Uriah, which plotted the latter's death (2 Sam. 11:14–15).

44.   For further discussion of this subject, see Harris, *Ancient Literacy*, pp. 45–64.

45.   If one adopts the high chronology for the introduction of the Phoenician script into Greece, then the lag in the production of literary works is even more startling.

46.   On the use of papyrus in the preexilic period in Israel, see M. Haran, "Book-Scrolls in Israel in Pre-Exilic Times," *JJS* 32 (1982), 161–173.

47.   Millard, "An Assessment of the Evidence," p. 305.

48.   Ibid., p. 306.

49.   Harris, *Ancient Literacy*, p. 114.

50.   Haran, "Diffusion of Literacy," pp. 91ff., makes an important distinction between the literate scribe and the craftsman for whom the use of writing, such as inscribing on clay vessels, was rather marginal.

51.   Millard, "An Assessment of the Evidence," p. 307.

52.   The Deir 'Alla text is a kind of hortatory prose that falls between the early prophetic literature and this later prose.

PART ONE

Primeval History
in Antiquity

3
MESOPOTAMIAN TRADITIONS ON THE PRIMEVAL HISTORY

The Mesopotamian traditions dealing with primeval times are numerous, and most of them are by now well known. It is not my intention to present them all here in any detail but instead to give particular attention to those themes and aspects of the Mesopotamian primeval traditions that may have relevance for the Yahwist's primeval history. At the outset of such a survey, it must be emphasized that Mesopotamian culture presents a considerable diversity of traditions about primeval times, and one cannot presume that each myth or motif had its specific place in some ancient preconception of a larger scheme of primeval times.[1] This caution is particularly important when one is faced with the highly fragmentary condition of many of the texts. The temptation to fill in the gaps from the parallel accounts is almost irresistible.

Yet it is the case with many of the texts, which we now regard as Mesopotamian "classics" and which became part of the great scribal tradition, that they began as quite innovative literary works. Although they made use of traditional materials and motifs, they often departed from them in rather new and radical ways.[2] This makes the evolution of Mesopotamian primeval traditions quite complex, so comparison with the biblical traditions must be done with considerable caution.[3]

Creation and the Flood

Atrahasis

The oldest narrative presentation of the combined creation and flood stories is *Atrahasis*.[4] Briefly stated, it tells how a group

47

of second level gods revolted against their superiors in order to escape from doing all the work. The "strike" was settled by means of the creation of humankind out of the flesh and blood of the god who was the leader of the strike, in order that humankind might do the service of the gods. After a lacuna in the text, in which people take over the obligations of civilization from the gods, there follows an account of the flood. This disaster was the last of three attempts to reduce or destroy the human population, because humankind's great proliferation led to too much noise, which disturbed the sleep of Enlil, the chief god. Humankind, however, was saved through the aid that Enki, a rival god, gives to the hero Atrahasis, who built an ark for all the animals and his family. With this simple outline in mind, let us examine some elements of the story in greater detail.

The procedure for the creation of humankind is a rather complicated one. A particular god is chosen, probably the leader of the revolt,[5] and he is slain. His flesh and blood are mixed with clay. The god's spirit or ghost (*ețemmu*) is permitted to remain in the flesh so that this quality is imparted to humankind as a source of life. Then begins a long process of treading the clay, dividing it into fourteen pieces, setting aside seven to be male and seven to be female. A special structure is built, and with the aid of fourteen birth goddesses and an appropriate gestation period, the mother goddess acts as midwife to bring forth the new creatures. All of this is related etiologically to certain birth and marriage rites.

A number of uncertainties in this description remain that lead to quite different interpretations. The name of the god chosen for slaughter is read by W. G. Lambert as *We* or *We-ila,* and most scholars have followed him in this.[6] A. Kilmer has suggested that if read as *Wela,* it could perhaps suggest an etiology for the term man, *awilum.*[7] W. von Soden takes it as Sumerian *gestu'e* and interprets the name to mean "endowed with understanding." This would support von Soden's interpretation of *țemu* as "intelligence" or "the ability to plan" (*Planungsfähigkeit*).[8] The text tells us that this was the god "who had *țemu*" and that this god was slaughtered "together with his *țemu.*" Lambert renders *țemu* as "personality." These interpretations, which see in *țemu* a special quality, also generally believe that through creation of humankind out of this rebellious god this quality was passed on to humankind as well.[9]

But this is nowhere specifically stated. W. Moran interprets *ṭemu* in a more concrete sense of "plan" or "scheme" with the meaning that the god chosen for slaughter was specifically the one who had the scheme to revolt and that this god was slain "together with his scheme."[10] This interpretation would suggest that *ṭemu* was not something passed on to humankind. All this seems like hair-splitting, but it has considerable importance for the interpretation of the epic as a whole and for its comparisons with Genesis.

The understanding of *eṭemmu*, "spirit" or "ghost," is also controversial.[11] It seems preferable to interpret the *eṭemmu* as the spirit or ghost of the slain god, which is permitted to remain in the flesh of the god after it is mixed with clay to produce man. The *eṭemmu* would thus be the source of life for humankind, and as a sign of this life for all time, the gods will hear the "drum" (*uppu*), the human heartbeat. This will also serve as a memorial, for all time, of this act of creation and why it was that humankind was made to serve the gods.[12]

Another line in the creation account calls for special consideration. In a late Assyrian version, S obverse iii. 1–21, which Lambert and Millard associate with the creation of humankind, line iii. 14 reads: *uṣurāte ša nišima uṣar mami*. Lambert translates this line as: "Since Mami (the mother goddess) conceived the regulations for the human race."[13] But this translation is suspect. The *Chicago Assyrian Dictionary* renders the sentence: "Mami draws the figures of mankind."[14] This seems to be confirmed in the parallel passage in I, 288ff., which describes the final act of creation: "She (Mami) drew a pattern in meal (*iṣir qema*) and placed the brick, 'I have created, my hands have made it. Let the midwife rejoice in the prostitute's house.'" Further evidence for the meaning of the line may be seen in another late Assyrian fragment, W 14–16, having to do with Ea's (Enki's) instructions to Atrahasis about building a boat to save himself from the flood. Atrahasis complains that he does not know anything about shipbuilding, so he asks Ea: "Draw the design on the ground (*ina qaqqari eṣir uṣurtu*) that I may see [the design] and [build] the boat." It would appear from this that *CAD* is correct in suggesting that as part of the creative activity of the goddess, she actually sketched the shape that humankind was to have.

In the Mesopotamian tradition represented by the *Enuma Elish* epic, creation is the result of a cosmogonic struggle among the gods out of which comes the whole cosmic order of things. By contrast, *Atrahasis* does not have such a cosmogonic conflict, only the peaceful division of jurisdiction among the principal gods: Anu, Enlil, and Enki.[15] The treatment of the creation of humankind in *Enuma Elish,* however, is much shorter than in *Atrahasis* and is, perhaps, a secondary motif. Humankind is created by Ea (Enki) from the blood of the rebellious god Kingu. No clay is used.[16] Humankind is also required for the service of the gods, although no need for such service has previously been suggested by the story. The fact that humankind is made by Ea, even though the rest of the cosmos is made by Marduk out of the carcass of Tiamat, and the fact that the rebel god Kingu has not much point in the rest of the story apart from providing material for humanity's creation, suggests that the motif of humanity's creation in *Enuma Elish* was probably derived from *Atrahasis* and rather loosely associated with the larger theme of the cosmogony.

Let us return to the text of *Atrahasis.* After the account of the creation of humankind, the text is badly broken so that it is not clear what activity is to be viewed as filling this space. Yet it seems likely to me, given the brief remarks about the building of shrines and canals and providing food for humankind and gods, that this section has to do with the new creatures taking over the responsibilities from the gods who had previously done these tasks.[17] But it is going too far to suggest that these lines contain a full description of the antediluvian period, based on the *Sumerian Flood Story.*[18]

The rest of the epic has to do with the flood story. After several hundred years,[19] humankind becomes very numerous, and this leads to such commotion and noisy activity that the god Enlil, resident on earth, cannot sleep. He summons an assembly of the great gods to inform them that he is going to plague humankind, presumably to diminish their numbers (although the text is broken at this point). Atrahasis, the hero, is then presented, without introduction, in dialogue with his god Enki. Atrahasis is both wise (his name means the "very wise one") and pious, but whether or not he is a king is never made clear, although he apparently has the respect of the elders of the city. Enki suggests to Atrahasis that the plague may be averted by making special offering to the god Namtara, who was responsible for the plague, and to him alone.

The god is shamed by this special attention and puts an end to the plague. The whole process happens again after another lengthy period. This time it is a famine that Enlil demands, and the god who receives special attention is Adad, god of rain and fertility. The offering again has the desired result, and Adad too puts an end to the drought. The third attempt at destruction by Enlil, apparently a more severe famine or series of disasters (the text is badly broken at this point), does not succeed any better.

Finally, a flood is agreed upon under oath by all the gods, which restricts even Enki, the friend of humankind, from giving direct aid. But by means of the ruse of speaking to the hut in which Atrahasis is sitting, and not to the hero directly, Enki is able to inform him of the imminent disaster and to instruct him in the skills of building a boat. Atrahasis builds the boat, supplies it with animals and birds, and sets his family on board. Then the flood comes. For seven days and seven nights the flood rages. At the great devastation the gods are distressed, particularly the mother goddess. How the flood ends is no longer preserved in the text, but the great gods discover that Atrahasis and his family have been saved by means of the boat and come like flies to the sacrifice he offers. Enlil learns that Enki once again has defied the gods to rescue humankind. It also appears that the mother goddess and Enki are obliged to create humankind again (the text is broken at this point). Does this mean that Átrahasis and his family are transported to a distant realm to live forever, as in other versions of the story? The extant text does not say. However, what is clear is that the creator gods, Enki and Mami, must create, in addition to normal males and females, a third group of mortals, namely, childless women. They also create disease demons responsible for infant mortality. At the same time, certain categories of religious orders for women who are not permitted to bear children are established. All these measures are apparently aimed at birth control to counter the overpopulation in the primeval age. At the same time, the story offers an etiology for natural conditions affecting the lot of humankind and for certain religious customs and institutions.

On a number of points in this part of the epic there are also differences of opinion. These have to do primarily with the cause of the flood. The most obvious and straightforward interpretation of the story is the one that sees the cause as the noise that disturbs the chief god Enlil due to the overpopulation of humankind. The plagues all emphasize the ways in which the population is diminished, at least temporarily. The flood, however, was too great a threat of total annihilation. The final measures taken by the creator deities are a means of maintaining a balance by nature and custom in the order of the world.[20] W. L. Moran states: "The origin of this balance is, in our opinion, the central question of the Atrahasis Epic, which accordingly we consider as fundamentally a cosmogonic myth. The answer defines man's established place in the universe."[21] It is on the importance of humanity and its passive role in the struggle of the gods toward the final cosmic order that Moran sees the essential unity between the two parts. Such a reading gives a certain self-contained quality to the flood story but at the same time emphasizes important links with the first half of the epic.

Some scholars, however, have rejected this interpretation and have suggested that there must have been a great crime to bring on such calamities.[22] For this reason, the "noise" (*rigmu*) and "uproar" (*huburu*) are interpreted as having the connotation of rebellious activity. The parallel is drawn between the noise of the rebellious gods of the first part and the noise of humankind in the second. Now it is true that the term *rigmu* is used of the rebelling gods (I, 77) when they raise the battle cry and rouse Enlil out of bed. But this term is used in a variety of ways throughout the epic, so that its use in both parts of the epic counts for little. For the rest, the situations are entirely different. There are no statements or accusations made anywhere that humankind is rebellious and refuses to honor or provide for the gods. It is only Enki who specifically suggests that humankind neglect the personal gods in favor of the one who can end the plague. I cannot believe that the author would depend so entirely upon a very subtle interpretation of two rather ambiguous terms when he could have expressed quite explicitly any rebellious activity by humankind as he did of the gods in part one.

Nor is it possible to accept von Soden's suggestion that the cause of the flood is humanity's attempt through the powers of intellect to overreach its limits and narrow the space between god and humankind.[23] The whole attitude of pious obedience by

Atrahasis, the leader of the people, in his relationship to Enki militates against this interpretation. No specific text is cited by von Soden in explicit support of this interpretation, and as a general inference from the story it seems to me unwarranted.

R. A. Oden attempts to support the positions of both von Soden and Pettinato in combination with yet another argument.[24] He questions the interpretation of overpopulation as the cause of the flood on quite different grounds. In a fragment of a late Assyrian recession (R), which Lambert and Millard place at the end of the flood story, there is a reference to *uṣurat niši,* rendered by Lambert as "regulations for the people."[25] Oden argues that this fragment suggests that there may have been additional regulations or controls placed upon humankind and that "the birth control regulations which remain at the end of Atrahasis are wholly misleading for one interested in the nature of the human crime which brought the flood."[26]

Three things must be said about this late Assyrian fragment. The first is that its placement by Lambert and Millard at the end of the flood story is highly suspect. It should in fact be taken closely with S iii.8–21 as part of the creation of humankind and may even be part of the same late Assyrian text. Note the similarity:

S iii.14, 20	*R 5–7*
uṣurāte ša nišima uṣar mami	uṣurat nisi x [. . .
[z]ikaru ana [ardate]	zikaru [. . .
	ana ardati [. . .

The *uṣurat niši* (R 5) corresponds to the *uṣurāte ša nišima* (S iii.14), and the references to "man" (*zikaru*) and "young woman" (*ardatum*) in R 6–7 seem to be reflected in S iii.20. In the Old Babylonian text at this same point, the subject of man and wife and the whole subject of marriage (I.272–276, 299–305) are brought into connection with the act of creation. Second, as indicated above, *uṣurat niši* does not necessarily mean "regulations for humankind" but can be rendered as the "shapes or figures of the humans" that the mother goddess forms, just as a potter forms clay or an artist draws a picture. But even if one were to render the text to mean "guidelines for humanity," it has more to do with customary behavior than a set of laws. Third, this phrase is found only in late Assyrian versions, which may point to a modification or addition. Consequently, there are no grounds for supposing that the gods established any additional set of regulations or laws limiting humankind as a consequence of the flood. Only those customs and natural causes that have to do with birth control and over-population come at the end of the flood story.

Sumerian Mythology

It is not possible, or even desirable, to deal with the rich variety and complexity of Sumerian mythology for this study of the Yahwist. Its problems are many, not the least of which is the fact that so many of the texts are quite fragmentary. The diversity of Sumerian mythology is not amenable to any systematic or unified presentation of its theology, so myths, taken together, may often be incompatible or contradictory. Even so, we may be sure that we have only a small part of a rich tradition, much of which now lost is presupposed in the myths that are extant.

The primary purpose of looking at Sumerian mythology for this study is to give some traditio-historical perspective to the development of Mesopotamian primeval history.[27] This has to do with such themes as the creation of humanity, the flood, and the antediluvian age of kings and sages as different from historical times. The literary tradition of these themes means that later versions of these themes do not succeed and displace earlier versions but come to stand alongside of them and so increase the complexity and diversity for later ages. Thus Berossus of the third century B.C. still had access to the ancient Sumerian mythological tradition in his attempt to reconstruct the Mesopotamian primeval age.

Yet there is a problem that must be kept in mind while dealing with the Sumerian mythological literature. The extant texts are primarily Old Babylonian in date, so one cannot always assume the priority of the Sumerian tradition over the Akkadian.[28] Nevertheless, the possibility of an older Sumerian tradition that goes back to the Ur III period or earlier is reasonable and is a legitimate starting point for viewing the extant tradition as it has survived.

The description of the creation of humankind in the myth "Enki and Ninmah" provides a precursor for the account in *Atrahasis* with a number of significant points of contact.[29] In the Sumerian myth, also, the reason for humanity's creation is to relieve the gods of their hard labor. But unlike *Atrahasis*, there is only a hint of two classes of deities, those who work and those who do not, with the working class in revolt. The situation in the Sumerian myth seems to arise out of the great proliferation of gods following the course of the theogony. It is all the gods, both major and minor, who complain of the toil; and in this case it is Enki, not Enlil, whom they hold responsible because he is the creator god of deities as well.

In the Sumerian myth, Nammu, the primeval mother goddess, appeals to Enki, the god of wisdom who resides in "the deep," to create humankind. He carries this out with the help of Ninmah, the goddess of birth, and eight assisting deities. At the same time, Enki assists Nammu in fashioning humankind (the fetus?) from clay in the Abzu, a realm of underground watery abyss, which is also the source of fertility. This figure of clay is perhaps implanted in the birth goddess, where it develops and is finally born, according to the design of Nammu. This certainly seems to anticipate the same elaborate arrangement that is set forth in *Atrahasis*, where notions of creation by birth are combined with those of the potter working with clay. But there is no suggestion in this Sumerian myth that any divine blood was used in the mixture, which may be an innovation in *Atrahasis*.

In the second part of the myth there is a banquet celebrating the creation of humankind during which a contest takes place between Enki and Ninmah while the gods are inebriated.[30] Ninmah creates deformed creatures while Enki finds occupations for them in society. The etiological purposes of the myth are obvious, but this part of the myth has no direct parallel in *Atrahasis*, so the latter may have used a somewhat different version of the Sumerian creation myth. Even so, in *Atrahasis*, at the end of the flood narrative there is a sequel to the new creation in which barren women as well as demons of childhood disease are created, which could be viewed as equivalent to the creation of deformed creatures in the Sumerian myth. Still, the motives for the second creation and the addition of an exceptional class of persons or creatures are quite different and may reflect an innovation of the mythographer of *Atrahasis*.

The Sumerian myths have a very diverse series of etiologies to account for the origins of civilization and agriculture and its benefits for humankind. Enki seems to play a major role in many of these myths and is given special prominence in "Enki and the Organization of the Universe," undoubtedly related at least in a general way to his cult in Eridu.[31] Kramer describes the myth as containing "a detailed documentation of Enki's creative and resourceful deeds in providing for man's essential needs related to food, shelter and clothing, including the appointment of quite a number of deities to take charge of and supervise the varied and diverse cultural activities vital for man and his civilization."[32] In these early Sumerian myths, the sages as inventors do not play any role. In the extant portion of *Atrahasis* there is no hint of Enki's role as benefactor of the arts of civilization. In the *Enuma Elish,* Marduk, son of Ea (Enki), does seem to take over this role of organizing the universe after the defeat of Tiamat. But even there, little is said about the gifts of civilization from the gods to humankind.

In the myth "Inanna and Enki: The Transfer of the *Me* from Eridu to Erech,"[33] Enki of Eridu is lord of the *me*'s, the principles of civilized life. The myth deals with the transfer of the *me*'s from one of the primeval cities to another, with the patron god playing a major role in the process. This may be related to the tradition of antediluvian cities; but if so it reflects considerable flexibility at this stage, because Erech is not found in the later lists of the primordial cities.

The Sumerian Flood Story

In its present form, the *Sumerian Flood Story*[34] is late Old Babylonian (ca. 1600 B.C.) in date, and it appears likely that it does not belong to the earlier Sumerian myths that we have been considering as precursors of the Mesopotamian tradition. It is no earlier, and perhaps even later, than *Atrahasis,* but the exact relationship between the two is difficult to say.[35] The text is very fragmentary, which makes interpretation difficult.

The story begins, after a long break, with a reference to some devastation of the human race and the wish for restoration expressed by an unnamed god. This restoration of peoples and animals by the great gods takes place, expressed in the following terms (i.48–50):

After An, Enlil, (and) Ninhursag had created the black-headed people, animals multiplied everywhere, animals of all sizes, the quadrupeds, were placed as a fitting ornament of the plains.[36]

This can hardly be understood as the original creation of humankind, and because it mentions the "black-headed people," that is, the Sumerians, it must refer to the beginnings of this region. Although there is another long gap in the text, it would appear that the account continues with the establishment of various elements of civilization including, in the preserved portion, the descent of kingship from heaven and the founding of five cities with their patron deities. The god also inaugurates the system of irrigation by which the land may flourish. Another gap brings us to the account of the flood. We are introduced to the hero, king Ziusudra, who receives a secret revelation concerning the coming disaster. He presumably builds a boat and supplies it (there is another gap), and then the storm comes for seven days and nights. After this, the sun appears, and he prostrates himself before the Sun-god and makes a sacrifice. He is subsequently granted eternal life, like a god, and settles in Dilmun, a land over the seas.

With so fragmentary a text, it is hazardous to speak of the work's theme and meaning, especially with the beginning and ending both missing. T. Jacobsen wishes to fill in the blanks and understand the text on the basis of similar later creation-flood stories of Mesopotamia as well as the story of the Deluge in Genesis.[37] Yet it is not clear that the text includes a treatment of the creation of humankind in the same way as *Atrahasis* but only a restoration after some great devastation, the nature of which is quite obscure. The descent of kingship and the founding of the five antediluvian cities with divine rulers or patrons are lacking from the extant text of *Atrahasis*.[38] They seem to be particular developments influenced by the Sumerian King List tradition (on this see below). There is also no hint in the present text of the *Sumerian Flood Story* about the cause of the flood, nothing about the rivalry of Enlil and Enki or even that Enki was the god to assist humankind.[39] The gods seem to have had second thoughts about the decision, but they could no longer prevent it from taking place. Ziusudra is presented as a very pious ruler for which in the end he is rewarded with eternal life. All the main points in the flood story seem to be in general agreement with *Atrahasis,* except that *Atrahasis* does not contain any reference to the ultimate fate of the hero, probably due to a lacuna in the text.

The Gilgamesh Epic

The account of the flood in the *Gilgamesh Epic* is a story within a story and belongs to the late version of the epic only.[40] The flood story is a long digression told by Utnapishtim, the survivor of the flood, to Gilgamesh, who came to him in his quest for eternal life. The account is a slightly modified rendering of the flood episode in *Atrahasis.* Many of the lines are virtually identical, and at one point the flood hero is even called Atrahasis rather than Utnapishtim, the name otherwise used in *Gilgamesh.*[41] Comparisons between *Gilgamesh* and *Atrahasis* are generally made with the Old Babylonian version of the latter, because it is by far the most extensive version preserved. Yet the modifications and innovations found in *Gilgamesh* may not all be attributed to the author of *Gilgamesh* but may rest largely upon a post-OB version of *Atrahasis,* as a few late Assyrian fragments would seem to suggest. It would therefore be fairly safe to assume that the *Gilgamesh* flood story is a later version, with little change, of the *Atrahasis* flood story.

One modification, however, that is found in *Gilgamesh* is the name of the flood hero Utnapishtim. This name was already present in the older version of the epic and appears to be an Akkadian equivalent of the name Ziusudra in the *Sumerian Flood Story.* The emphasis in both forms of the name is on the fact that the hero of the flood was granted life like the gods and set apart from the rest of humankind in a distant realm.[42] This ending to the flood story in *Atrahasis* is already found in the Middle Babylonian version that comes from Ugarit.

Thus the *Gilgamesh Epic* ends the account of the flood by describing how Utnapishtim and his wife gained immortality. This is entirely appropriate to the larger theme of the epic, but it does not give any suggestions about the restoration of humankind and civilization after the flood. So we are left in some doubt as to how this matter was handled in the late versions of the *Atrahasis* story.

Assyrian Bilingual Account of Creation

This is a bilingual text in Sumerian and Akkadian of uncertain date (from 11th century to ca. 800 B.C.).[43] It begins with a brief cosmology about the establishment of heaven and earth, the principal gods, and the fixing of the Tigris and Euphrates with their canals. The major gods then hold counsel and decide to make humankind from the blood of some slain craftsman gods. The purpose of their creation is given at length as providing the necessary labor to do the agricultural work, to build sanctuaries, and to render service to the gods. At the end of the decree, there is mention of two persons by name: Ullegarra and Annegarra (l. 52), but their identification is disputed. Heidel regards them as the first human pair,[44] but this is now rejected in favor of regarding them as deities to be worshiped in the sanctuary mentioned in the previous line.[45] In the description of the creation of humankind out of the gods (ll. 60–61), the gods of skilled craftsmen produced the corresponding humans, whereas the unskilled gods' blood gave rise to unskilled workers, "like grain from the ground."

One scholar characterizes this as an aberrant tradition that is not representative of Mesopotamian thought.[46] Yet it seems to be a commentary for the learned[47] on how the blood of the gods produced different types and skills among humankind. They all correspond to divine prototypes, and their skills and nature are inherited. There is nothing in this text of the rebellion of the gods, as in *Atrahasis* and *Enuma Elish*. The whole account has much more the form of speech or plan and corresponding action.

The Erra Epic

The *Erra Epic* was a "classical" Assyrian work of the eighth century B.C. The subject of this epic, that of the exploits of the god of plague, Erra, and how he seriously threatened the destruction of Babylon, is not our concern here.[48] Within the work, however, there is a speech by Marduk, the god of Babylon, which tells about how he once brought a flood upon humankind (I.130–148). Nothing is said about how humanity was saved, only that Marduk spared a small remnant. The text also suggests that the *ummanu* (the sages) were sent down to Apsu (by means of the flood?) so that their special knowledge was lost.[49] Whether these allusions to the flood reflect a modified Babylonian version or the writer's innovation is difficult to say. That Marduk replaces Enlil is not entirely surprising.[50] But nothing is said about any rivalry from Ea (Enki).

Two Neo-Babylonian Creation Myths

A Neo-Babylonian text that deserves some consideration is a bilingual text from Sippar, but it represents a strong Eridu/Babylon tradition.[51] Its late date means that it is neglected as non-traditional,[52] but it contains a number of elements of concern to us here. The mythological text "forms a rather elaborate introduction to an incantation which was recited for the purification of Ezida, the temple of Nabu at Borsippa."[53]

The text begins with a description of the time when conditions of life and civilization, as later known, had not as yet been created. Then Marduk began to create the earth and the dwellings of the gods. Together with the aid of the goddess Aruru, he created humankind. He then produced, in turn, animal life, the Tigris and Euphrates, vegetation, the cities, and civilized life. The text gives a more comprehensive, straightforward account of creation than the older tradition, including the creation of vegetation and animal life along with that of humankind. The episode of the revolt of the gods and the death of one of them as material for the creation has disappeared in this version. Marduk has also replaced Enlil and Ea as sole creator.

In another Neo-Babylonian ritual text, a creation myth is included in which, after Anu created the heavens, Ea alone is the principal creator.[54] The special feature of this text is that Ea creates a number of deities who are the patrons of the arts, crafts, agriculture, and religion. He then creates the king to maintain the temples, and finally humankind to do the service of the gods. Here again nothing is said about humankind's being made from the slain deity. The patron deities are created to anticipate their usefulness for civilization. Even the king is created before the people. This text seems to combine within the acts of creation the theme of the development of civilization. This also has some relevance for the following text about the special creation of the king.

A Myth on the Creation of the King

A recently published Neo-Babylonian mythical text contains a description of the creation of humankind in the tradition of *Atrahasis*.[55] This is the creation of common humanity (*lullu* — men), whose purpose it is to do the labor of the gods. But quite different from these earlier texts, the myth also states that the divine pair of the mother goddess and Ea are to make a king quite distinct from the rest of humanity. The text states the following:

> Ea began to speak, he directed his word to Belet-ili, "Belet-ili, Mistress of the great gods, are you. You have created the common people, now construct the king, i.e., distinctively superior persons. With goodness envelop his entire being. Form his features harmoniously; make his body beautiful!" Thus did Belet-ili construct the king, distinctively superior persons. The great gods gave the king the task of warfare. Anu gave him the crown; Enlil gave him the throne. Nergal gave him weapons; Ninurta gave him glistening splendor. Belet-ili gave him a beautiful appearance. Nusku gave him instruction and counsel and stands at his service.

Much of the language of this part of the text corresponds directly to that found in royal inscriptions, royal hymns, and coronation rituals, which have a long tradition in Mesopotamia.[56] In these texts, the king is often spoken of as created or formed in the womb by the deity and given the various royal attributes of wisdom, strength, and beauty by the different gods of the pantheon.[57] At the king's coronation, the gods are likewise said to participate together in entrusting to the king the various insignia of his royal office: throne, vestments, scepter, and so forth. What is remarkable about this mythical text is that the bestowal of physical endowments at birth and the regalia at the coronation have both been combined and then placed mythologically back into the time of creation itself as a way of expressing the inception of kingship. By the use of such texts in this way, the author of the myth has moved from the particular legitimation of individual kings to the general legitimation of kingship itself. And he has expanded the myth of the creation of humankind to include the special creation of the king.

Evidence that the Babylonian text is a late mythological composition can be seen from the fact that its closest linguistic parallels are to be found in late Neo-Assyrian and Neo-Babylonian texts.[58] In fact, the author of the text clearly indicates his source when he ends with the oath "Whoever speaks falsehood and deceit to the king . . . ," an oath formula that is a direct parallel to a concluding coronation oath in a prayer of Ashurbanipal.[59] This rather firm late dating becomes important when we come to consider the biblical tradition.

The Antediluvian Age

The Sumerian King List

The Sumerian King List (SKL),[60] in its earliest form, set forth the succession of "capital" cities and their rulers in Mesopotamia from the time when kingship descended from heaven to the first dynasty of Isin.[61] There seems to be broad scholarly agreement that only in the latest versions of this text tradition was the list of kings extended back before the flood to include eight to ten antediluvian kings and their cities, each king having a very long reign.[62] Apart from the mention of the flood, this tradition seems quite separate from *Atrahasis,* because in the latter work there is no mention of kingship. Atrahasis is the only leader or sage mentioned as living throughout the successive periods of disaster.

The relationship of SKL to the *Sumerian Flood Story,* however, is more complex. There are three basic similarities between the SKL (in the late WB versions)[63] and the flood epic. The first is the statement at the beginning of the antediluvian section in both texts that "kingship was lowered from heaven." In both cases, this could have been derived from the older version of SKL, which begins the postdiluvian series of kings in this way. What makes this secondary usage particularly obvious in the flood epic is the fact that the story does not proceed to list the kings of the period as one would expect from SKL(WB). Nor is there any justification for thinking that such kings were named in a later part of the text where there is a lacuna.[64]

The second similarity between SKL(WB) and the flood epic is the enumeration of the five antediluvian cities with the same names and in the same order.[65] But there is also a most important difference. The epic indicates that the deity founded the five cities, gave them their names, and apportioned them to patron deities. Yet it nowhere suggests that these cities ruled the region successively, as is explicitly stated by SKL(WB). It is difficult to suppose that the epic eliminated the names of the kings and substituted a series of patron deities instead. The notion of five important antediluvian cities existing side by side is probably the more original version.

Furthermore, the SKL(WB) has a curious way of expressing the transfer of power from one city to another. It does not follow the form used for the dynastic changes of the postdiluvian period but shifts to a first person present-future, which J. J. Finkelstein renders as "I will bring to an end (the ascendency of) city A, etc."[66] He sees this as spoken, not by the author, but by a god such as Enlil. This would suggest that it is a phrase derived from an epic source; but, as we have seen, the cities are not treated individually in this way in the flood epic. Nevertheless, the text does at times have deities speaking in the first person, and it seems highly probable that the text did include a statement by Enlil about bringing to an end humankind, or more specifically bringing to an end the five cities. If this were the case, then it is not too difficult to suppose that the author of SKL(WB) could have adopted this phrase to use as a way of describing the overthrow of the five cities individually and successively instead of all at once. This would further suggest that the author was the one who actually modified the antediluvian tradition by providing it with a series of rulers with long reigns. These kings were then attached to the five cities. Such a modification would represent a secondary historicizing of an earlier mythical tradition.

The third similarity between SKL(WB) and the flood epic has to do with the reference to the flood itself. The two versions read:

SKL(WB)	*Sumerian Flood Story*
The Flood swept over.	The Flood swept over the capitals.
After the Flood swept over,	After the Flood swept over the country for seven days and seven nights ...
when kingship was lowered from heaven.	

The wording is so similar that dependence of SKL(WB) on the *Sumerian Flood Story* seems certain.[67] But the author of SKL(WB) merely uses those parts in his source that would provide a transition to the postdiluvian period.[68]

The relationship of SKL to *Gilgamesh* is of some importance here. Because the flood story in *Gilgamesh* is presented as a first person reminiscence of the hero Utnapishtim, it begins rather abruptly with the revelation of Ea (Enki) to the hero and therefore gives little reference to any context for the story in the primeval age. Yet there is fairly clear indication (in XI.23) that Utnapishtim is regarded as the last of the antediluvian kings, just as Ziusudra is in some versions of the SKL.[69] And also like Ziusudra, he is the son of Ubar-Tutu and the ruler of Shuruppak, the last of the antediluvian cities.

The gods are also said (in XI.13) to be resident in Shuruppak before the flood. This is in contrast to *Atrahasis*, where Enlil alone is said to reside in Nippur, and to the *Sumerian Flood Story*, where the gods have their abode in the various capital cities, including Shuruppak, simultaneously. This placing of all the gods in Shuruppak before the flood is not just a matter of local tradition[70] but a way of adapting the *Atrahasis* story to the antediluvian tradition of SKL in which Shuruppak is the last antediluvian city for both gods and humankind.

A text from the time of Nebuchadnezzar I (late 12th century B.C.) may also be mentioned here. In it a connection by ancestry is made between his kingship and that of the antediluvian period, "seed preserved from before the flood." W. G. Lambert, who published the text, states that it "wedded the Old Babylonian concept of legitimacy to a traditional Sumerian version of the beginning of history."[71]

The Lagash King List

Another text that deserves some consideration here is the Lagash King List, which E. Sollberger interprets as "a politico-satirical work written by a Lagaš scribe in answer to the author(s) of the Sumerian King List who had ignored the rulers of Lagaš, although some of them . . . had certainly been paramount kings of Sumer."[72] He goes on to show that the king list was created by adding to the few known historical kings the names of many fanciful, invented rulers with fantastically long reigns and fictitious biographical notes, often in a style that parodies the Sumerian King List phraseology.

The Lagash text begins with the flood and with a reference to humankind having been spared from destruction. It then recounts a new creation of humankind by An and Enlil, transposing the antediluvian period to the time after the flood before kingship was sent forth from heaven. Thus, in the first postdiluvian period, humankind is presented as being in a primitive state without agriculture and civilized work to do, with the result that the population began steadily to decrease. In dependence only on rain and without the water produced by the construction of canals, there can be little fertility. There were also no offerings for the gods. In this situation, the gods (presumably An and Enlil) give to the people the arts of agriculture. Although there is a break in the text at this point, one may assume that kingship is now given as well, because the text resumes, after the break, with a listing of the kings of Lagash, concluding with Gudea, a historical figure and the last great king of Lagash.

The text itself, and very likely its actual composition, date to the middle Old Babylonian period.[73] This makes it contemporary with the WB version of SKL. As Sollberger points out, "The fact that our text begins with the very line which in WB, and in that manuscript only, introduces the postdiluvian section is certainly more than a coincidence. It is reasonably safe to infer that WB is actually the text which provoked our Lagaš scribe into composing his patriotic satire."[74] But the matter goes considerably beyond this, because Sollberger shows that the Lagash scribe made use of a number of Sumerian literary texts including the *Sumerian Flood Story*. This raises the whole question of the relationship of this text to other Mesopotamian creation and flood traditions. First of all, the motif of overpopulation as the cause of the flood in *Atrahasis* is completely reversed. In this text, after the flood the gods An and Enlil, who create humankind, again come to their aid to increase the population with the arts of civilization in order to provide for the needs of both humankind and the gods. By starting with the flood, the author did not need to say anything about its cause and could represent the high deities in a completely benevolent fashion.[75] The theme of the primeval descent of kingship from heaven and the establishment of agriculture, probably as gifts of An and Enlil, is here presented after the flood and perhaps deliberately in reverse order, because the point seems to be rather strongly emphasized that agriculture and canal building came before kingship.[76]

Here is a case of traditions being combined and rearranged with remarkable flexibility to suit the author's own purposes. The creation-antediluvian traditions are transposed to a point after the flood, and then this epiclike narrative is used as a prologue for a king list. Both parts then serve as a parody or criticism of other Mesopotamian "classical" traditions in the form of a pseudo-historical text. The primeval age has vanished with everything set in "historical" time after the flood, a historicization of the myth. That a Mesopotamian scribe would attempt such a complex and "heterodox" combination should alert us to the fact that reconstructions of this kind were always possible and that there is no such thing as a single Mesopotamian view of creation or primeval history.

The Dynastic Chronicle

The "Dynastic Chronicle" (7th century B.C.) is a descendant of the classical Sumerian King List tradition. Here the king list is extended down to later Assyrian times. It now appears likely that this version of the king-list tradition also contains the name of nine antediluvian kings and a narrative account of the flood, although only a few hints of it remain in the very fragmentary text.[77]

The Sages

In the primeval traditions viewed thus far, the benefits of civilization, including kingship, are gifts from the gods. They are directly involved in imparting the knowledge and skills of society and its institutions to humankind as divine ordinances (Sumerian *me*). In the later Babylonian traditions about primeval times, sages (*apkallu*'s) are thought to arise at the beginning of human history who were both wise and pious, and whose primary role it would appear was to record and preserve special knowledge, mostly of a religious nature, for the good of humankind.[78] The earliest literary reference to them seems to be in the *Erra Epic* (8th century B.C.) I.147, 162, where it is said that the seven sages were sent down to Apsu at the time of the flood, where their knowledge perished with them. On the basis of the cuneiform texts alone, it would be going too far to describe them as inventors of the arts of civilization.[79] Apart from having highly specialized knowledge, very little else is said about them. The classical number of such sages is seven, and in some cases in very late texts they are dated to the reigns of antediluvian kings.[80]

The identity of the sages appears to be derived from quite separate myths and legends. As in the case of the Adapa myth, certain persons are specially created and endowed by Ea with wisdom and other attributes associated with the deity. They are noted for their piety and devotion toward this god and are often associated with the sea or may even have their abode with Ea in Apsu. Some consider the sages as guilty of hubris on account of their wisdom, for which they are made to suffer, but this is probably a misunderstanding of the Adapa myth.[81] Such sages seem to belong primarily to the time before the flood, although they may make an appearance after the flood as well. Their association with a specific ruler as his vizier or counselor is likely a late secondary historicization of these traditions. Apart from the vague allusions in the *Erra Epic*, the sages' traditions had a very loose connection with the other antediluvian traditions until the Hellenistic period. There was considerable flexibility in the names, numbers, and association with ante- and postdiluvian kings.

The Babyloniaca of Berossus

Berossus, a priest of Babylon in the third century B.C., wrote the *Babyloniaca* as a new national tradition in response to the treatment of Babylonian history by the older Greek historians.[82] He reveals the influence of the Greek historiographic tradition by beginning his work with some biographical references as to his time of life, station as a priest of Marduk, and nationality, that is, a Chaldean. He characterizes his work as containing "the histories of heaven (and of earth) and the sea and the first birth and the kings and their deeds."[83] This range of subject matter is not at all exceptional within Hellenistic historiography.[84] Berossus reveals his sources to be texts preserved in Babylon over a very long period of time. In his introduction, he also gives some general remarks on the geography of the region, an obvious concession to the interests of his Greek audience, who would expect such information about a foreign country.

Berossus does not begin his account with the creation of humankind but with the primeval age in which "there was a great crowd of men in Babylon" who "lived without laws just as wild animals" in a "state of nature."[85] This situation is not reflected in the extant text of *Atrahasis,* although there is a lacuna in the text where one might possibly expect it. This idea of primitive people as uncivilized does reflect early Sumerian tradition.[86]

Early in this primeval period,[87] a strange creature, both human and fish, named Oannes appeared to instruct humankind in all the arts of civilization so that nothing remained to be discovered after this time. Berossus indicates that at a somewhat later period, during the time of the kings, similar creatures appeared. Oannes can quite definitely be identified with the sage U'an-adapa of the Adapa myth and the other creatures with the tradition of the antediluvian sages. That these earlier sages also had a fishlike appearance and were associated with the sea is confirmed by a bilingual text published by E. Reiner.[88] In Berossus some of the sages are associated with antediluvian rulers and one with a post-diluvian king, and for this there are also parallels in the late Mesopotamian texts, as noted above.

The way in which Berossus separates Oannes from the rest of the sages and makes him the originator of all civilization, however, goes beyond everything else in the older tradition of the sages. The explanation, proposed by Komoroczy, is that these attributes of Oannes are original to Enki/Ea, and it is only in the close association of Oannes/Adapa in particular with this god that all of these features have been transferred from the god to the first sage. As Komoroczy states: "In Sumerian mythology, as this is shown by the 'Enki and the World Order' . . . , with the culture creating act of the deity the world becomes definitive, that is, it arrives at a state in which more 'inventors' are already not needed, in which there is everything 'required for a civilized life.'"[89] Berossus has combined this tradition of Enki with that of the sages in a partial historicization, but in the process he appears to make the subsequent sages rather superfluous.

Berossus presents a cosmogony and the creation of humankind in the form of a speech by Oannes. In this way, it does not need to be presented as a reported event but as the record of most ancient wisdom.[90] It is now generally recognized that behind the statements on creation attributed to Oannes lies a form of the *Enuma Elish* epic.[91] It is perhaps not surprising that Berossus, a priest of Marduk, should make reference to this most important Babylonian religious tradition and attribute it to the first possible author-sage to give it the greatest antiquity and authority. The creation of humankind in Berossus is related to the death of a god and the mixture of his blood and earth as the necessary components of human life. This is similar to the creation of humankind in *Atrahasis.*[92]

Berossus continues the long tradition of the antediluvian kings that one finds in the later versions of the Sumerian King Lists. In *Babyloniaca,* they are supplemented with some brief anecdotes, and the sages are associated with some of these kings.[93]

For his account of the flood, Berossus seems to have been dependent upon the *Sumerian Flood Story,* because the name of the hero in his version is Xisuthros = Ziusudra.[94] But this would not seem to account for everything in his version, so he may have had access to a later form of *Atrahasis* such as is now found in the *Gilgamesh Epic.* For instance, the *Babyloniaca* contains the episode about the use of birds for reconnaissance at the end of the flood. This is a motif that is, at present, not found in any version of the flood story earlier than the one used in the *Gilgamesh Epic.* The remark about the burying of all writings before the flood at Sippar so that civilization would survive the flood seems to be derived from a local tradition of that place that is not found in the other extant flood stories.[95] The Berossus version of the flood does not seem to reflect the divine rivalry of the older versions but only the one deity, Kronos (Ea). If Marduk/Bel (= Zeus) has replaced Enlil as the one who brought the flood, as in the *Erra Epic,* it creates the strange situation of making Kronos the rival of Zeus's authority. There is also a surviving remnant in addition to the hero, Xisuthros, and his family who go to live with the gods. The surv'vors once more establish Babylon.

It is clear, not only from what Berossus himself says, but from a careful scrutiny of his work, that he had a great variety of different texts, both mythological and historiographic, at his disposal. These were virtually all literary, and many were highly esoteric, at least as far as his day and age was concerned. His literary work, therefore, represents an effort at systematic and highly complex selection and integration of texts, many of which had never been combined in this way before. Especially important is the way in which so much mythology has been incorporated into this "history." The very nature of such historical works with their great diversity of tradition makes it doubtful that one can impose upon them a single theme.

Summary and Conclusion

The tradition-history of the primeval age in Mesopotamia is the complex development of antiquarian scholars and mythographers over a very long period of time. Each treatment of the themes of creation, the antediluvian age, and the flood stands in a certain continuum of development with earlier traditions while introducing, at the same time, innovative combinations and interpretations or entirely new details. In the survey of these traditions, the simplest and oldest(?) form of the creation account is represented by the first part of the *Enki and Ninmah* myth in which the mutual skills of Enki and Ninmah combine to make humankind as a way of relieving the gods of their work. Humankind is made of clay yet engendered by the deity. In *Atrahasis,* the theme of conflict among the gods of those who work and those who do not is introduced, so that humanity's creation not only relieves the lesser gods of their labors and resolves the dispute, but now the leader of the revolt is slain to provide divine flesh and blood as part of the mixture for humanity's creation. This is also reflected in the *Enuma Elish,* where the creation of humankind plays a minor part in a larger cosmogony. The procedure in *Atrahasis* by which several pairs of humans are created at once is also more complicated and associated etiologically with certain rites and customs. Furthermore, *Atrahasis* now combines the creation of humanity with the story of the flood to constitute an extended primeval age. The recreation of humankind as a result of the flood's destruction introduces an additional series of changes in the human condition as etiologies of life as experienced in the "historical" period.

The primeval age of *Atrahasis,* however, does not yet have any connection with historical time as reflected in the historiographic traditions. Atrahasis is not a king of a particular city. This is changed in the *Sumerian Flood Story.* This myth may have followed the pattern of *Atrahasis* and included both creation and the flood together, but its fragmentary character make this quite uncertain. What it adds to the tradition, however, is an elaboration of the antediluvian period to suggest that kingship descended from heaven at this time and that five of the most ancient cities with their cult centers were founded at this time. The hero, Ziusudra, is now a king, most likely associated with one of these cities, Shuruppak. This form of the tradition was historicized in the late versions of the Sumerian King List tradition, which introduced a series of antediluvian kings of great age for the five primeval cities alongside the "historical" king-list series. The flood was used as a boundary between the primeval and historical ages. The flood story in the *Gilgamesh Epic,* which otherwise follows the *Atrahasis* version quite closely, reflects this historicizing innovation, because the hero Utnapishtim is a king of Shuruppak, the son of Ubar-Tutu, as in SKL.

In spite of such heterodox versions of the primeval age as the Lagash King List, the main stream continued as a strong "classical" tradition down to Hellenistic times. Later modifications included the combination of the "sages" tradition with that of the antediluvian rulers and the creation of the king alongside of humankind in general. There were also other myths about the primeval age that were not integrated into the scheme as we know it, and one must resist the temptation to do so.

This sketch of the tradition-history of the primeval age in the Mesopotamian literary tradition is not meant to suggest that the whole development was unilinear or that no variations could be introduced from time to time. Thus, in the *Erra Epic,* Marduk replaces Enlil as the instigator of the flood, but whether that innovation became standard is not at all certain. There also seems to be a tendency, in Neo-Babylonian texts, to play down or suppress the element of divine rivalry and to emphasize the role of one principal deity, Marduk or Ea, with the help of a mother goddess, in the creation of humankind. Nevertheless, in spite of all the variation, by the mid–first millennium B.C. there was something like a classical Mesopotamian scheme for the primeval age, an eastern antiquarian tradition, that could be used by Berossus in his *Babylonian History.* This was a learned literary tradition that maintained and transmitted the older classical works and that created new ones as the need or creative urge to do so arose.

One major theme that we have not included in our review is that of theogony or cosmogony, even though this often plays an important role in some of the texts under consideration, such as *Enuma Elish.* To do so would have greatly extended this survey, but because it does not relate directly to the primeval history of the Yahwist, there is no need to go into this complex stream of tradition.[96]

It is against this background of Mesopotamian tradition that we will view the Yahwist's primeval history in Genesis. The similarity of the Bible to the Babylonian flood story has been obvious for a long time. More recently, the publication of the more complete version of *Atrahasis* has placed an emphasis on the larger scheme of the primeval age from creation to the flood. My view is that any comparison must be made with an understanding of the diversity of the Babylonian tradition and the complexity of the tradition's development. In addition, one must take account of the western antiquarian tradition as a major factor in the biblical tradition. It is to this subject that we now turn.

Notes

1. See W. G. Lambert, "A New Look at the Babylonian Background of Genesis," *JTS* 16 (1965), 288–290.
2. See Lambert on *Enuma Elish,* ibid., p. 291.
3. Cf. P. D. Miller, "Eridu, Dunnu, and Babel: A Study in Comparative Mythology," *HAR* 9 (1985), 227–251. Miller draws his comparisons with the Genesis primeval history from a selection of Mesopotamian texts widely separate in time and provenience that are too easily amalgamated to produce a common Mesopotamian view.
4. For the standard edition, see W. G. Lambert and A. R. Millard, *Atra-Ḫasis: The Babylonian Story of the Flood,* 1969. See also the translation in S. Dalley, *Myths from Mesopotamia* (1989), pp. 1–38.
5. So W. L. Moran, "The Creation of Man in Atrahasis I 192–248," *BASOR* 200 (1970), 52.
6. Lambert and Millard, *Atra-Ḫasis,* p. 153, note on line I, p. 223.
7. A. D. Kilmer, "The Mesopotamian Concept of Overpopulation and Its Solution as Reflected in the Mythology," *Orientalia* 41 (1972), 164.
8. See von Soden's translation in "Die erste Tafel des altbabylonischen Atramhasis-Mythos. 'Haupttext' und Parallelversionen," *ZA* 68 (1978), 50–94, esp. p. 65. See also idem, "Konflikt und ihre Bewaltigung in babylonischen Schöpfungs-

und Fluterzählungen. Mit einer Teil-Übersetzung des Atramhasis-Mythos," *MDOG* 111 (1979), 11. Dalley, *Myths,* p. 15, also follows von Soden here.

9.   See esp. G. Pettinato, *Das altorientalische Menschenbild und die sumerischen und akkadischen Schöpfungsmythen* (1971), p. 45. For a critique of this view, see H. M. Kummel, "Bemerkungen zu den altorientalischen Berichten von der Menschenschöpfung," *WO* 7 (1973–74), 31.

10.   Moran, "The Creation of Man," *BASOR* 200:52.

11.   Von Soden, in works in n. 8 above, reads *edimmu/widimmu* and interprets it as *Urmensch*, a creature without culture; but this does not seem to square with humankind's immediate responsibility to replace the gods in building canals, temples, and so forth.

12.   See Kilmer, *Orientalia* 41:163. Cf. Moran, "The Creation of Man," *BASOR* 200:54–56.

13.   Lambert and Millard, *Atra-Ḥasis,* p. 63; see also Dalley, *Myths,* p. 17.

14.   *CAD* 4:348. See also *ANET,* p. 100: "The forms of the people Mami forms."

15.   For a comparison between *Enuma Elish* and *Atrahasis,* see von Soden, "Konflikte," *MDOG* 111:6–13; also Kummel, *WO* 7:29.

16.   Von Soden, "Konflikte," *MDOG* 111:12, suggests that it is this blood that makes humankind rebellious, a new motif that puts emphasis on the problem of sin, but I do not see any suggestion of this in the text. Against this is Kummel, *WO* 7:31, who emphasizes that the blood merely represents the life principle within the earthly substance.

17.   See T. Jacobsen, *The Treasures of Darkness* (1976), p. 118.

18.   So Kilmer, *Orientalia* 41:166.

19.   Lambert conjectures 1200 years; Dalley reads the text as 600.

20.   See Kilmer, n. 7 above; also W. L. Moran, "Atrahasis: The Babylonian Story of the Flood," *Biblica* 52 (1971), 51–61.

21.   Ibid., p. 58.

22.   See G. Pettinato, "Die Bestrafung des Menschengeschlechts durch die Sinflut: Die erste Tafel des Atramhasis-Epos eröffnet eine neue Einsicht in die Motivation dieser Strafe," *Orientalia* 37 (1968), 165–200.

23.   Von Soden, "Konflikte," *MDOG* 111:12f. This view depends upon his interpretation of *ṭemu* as meaning "intelligence," the special quality derived from the rebellious god, as discussed above.

24.   R. A. Oden, "Divine Aspirations in Atrahasis and in Genesis 1–11," *ZAW* 93 (1981), 197–216.

25.   Lambert and Millard, *Atra-Ḥasis,* p. 105.

26.   Oden, "Divine Aspirations," *ZAW* 93:208; cf. T. Frymer-Kensky, "The Atrahasis Epic and Its Significance for Our Understanding of Genesis 1–9," *BA* 40 (1977), 147–155, esp. pp. 149–150.

27.   This is the concern of Pettinato in *Das altorientalische Menschenbild.*

28.   See the remarks of Kummel in criticism of Pettinato, *WO* 7:27; also S. N. Kramer and J. Maier, *Myths of Enki, the Crafty God* (1989), p. 7.

29.   S. N. Kramer, "Sumerian Mythology Reviewed and Revised," in *Biblical Archaeology Today, Proceedings of the International Congress on Biblical Archaeology, Jerusalem, April 1984* (1985), pp. 286–298. For this text, see esp. pp. 292–293; also

Kramer and Maier, *Myths of Enki,* pp. 31–37; and T. Jacobsen, *The Harps That Once...* (1987), pp. 151–166.

30.   Jacobsen, *The Harps,* pp. 152–153, argues that the second part of the myth did not originally belong with the first half.

31.   Kramer, "Sumerian Mythology," p. 294; Kramer and Maier, *Myths of Enki,* pp. 38–56.

32.   Kramer, "Sumerian Mythology," p. 294.

33.   Ibid., pp. 294–295; Kramer and Maier, *Myths of Enki,* 57–68.

34.   For the publication of the text, see A. Poebel, *Historical and Grammatical Texts,* PBS 5 (1914), no. 1. For translation and discussion, see T. Jacobsen, "The Eridu Genesis," *JBL* 100 (1981), 513–529; idem, *The Harps,* pp. 145–150; S. N. Kramer, "The Sumerian Deluge Myth: Reviewed and Revised," *An St* 33 (1983), 115–121. For the text, see M. Civil, "The Sumerian Flood Story," in Lambert and Millard, *Atra-Ḫasis,* pp. 138–145. See also the discussion by P. D. Miller, *HAR* 9:227–251. Miller follows Jacobsen in his reconstruction and interpretation of the text.

35.   On this dating, see Jacobsen, "The Eridu Genesis," *JBL* 100:513; Kramer and Maier, *Myths of Enki,* p. 246 n. 10. On its relationship to the Sumerian King List tradition, see below.

36.   This translation follows Civil, "The Sumerian Flood Story," p. 141.

37.   See works cited in n. 34 above.

38.   I do not think that Jacobsen is justified in supposing that the gap after the mention of the five cities would have included a list of the antediluvian kings. Because all five cities are named together, it is difficult to see how the various kings of each city would have been given in succession, as they are in SKL.

39.   That may be suggested by iii.142: "Enki took counsel with himself" when the gods had sworn to destroy humankind. The speech to the wall in col. iv is also similar to Enki's speech in *Atrahasis.* Still, the lack of any mention of Enki's role is surprising.

40.   J. Tigay, *The Evolution of the Gilgamesh Epic* (1982), pp. 214–240; A. Heidel, *The Gilgamesh Epic and Old Testament Parallels,* 2nd ed., 1949.

41.   The arguments for literary dependency are given in some detail by Tigay, *The Evolution of the Gilgamesh Epic.*

42.   For a discussion of the names, see ibid., 229–230.

43.   See A. Heidel, *The Babylonian Genesis,* 2nd ed. (1951), pp. 68–71.

44.   Heidel, *The Babylonian Genesis,* pp. 68, 70 n. 56.

45.   Pettinato, *Das altorientalische Menschenbild,* p. 81; M.-J. Seux, *La Création du monde et de l'homme d'après les textes du Proche-Orient ancien* (1981), p. 62.

46.   Seux, *La Création,* pp. 51, 61.

47.   See the last line: "Let the wise teach the mystery to the wise."

48.   On the text, see L. Cagni, *The Poem of Erra,* SANE 1/3, 1977; also Dalley, *Myths,* pp. 282–315. For a discussion on dating, see Cagni, pp. 20–21.

49.   See also ll. 162–163.

50.   IV. 50 refers to the city of Sippar, "which the Lord of Lands did not allow the Flood to overwhelm." This would seem to reflect the tradition of Enlil as responsible for the flood.

51.   See primarily Heidel, *The Babylonian Genesis,* pp. 61–63.

52.   See Seux, *La Création,* p. 51. Cf. P. D. Miller, *HAR* 9:237, who links this text closely with the reference to Eridu in the *Sumerian Flood Story.* If the latter does not contain a reference to creation as he supposes, then the connection is rather weak.

53.   Heidel, *The Babylonian Genesis,* p. 61.

54.   Ibid., pp. 65–66.

55.   W. R. Mayer, "Ein Mythos von der Erschaffung des Menschen und des Königs," *Orientalia* 56 (1987), 55–68. On *Atrahasis,* see above, n. 4. Much of the discussion of this text is drawn from my article "The Creation of Man and the Creation of the King," *ZAW* 101 (1989), 333–342.

56.   Mayer, *Orientalia* 56:63f. For this comparative material, see "Insignien," "Inthronisation," and "Investitur" in *Reallexikon der Assyriologie* V, 1976–80, pp. 109–114, 128–136, 138–144; "Königtum. B" in *Reallexikon der Assyriologie* VI, 1980–83, paras. 89–92, 101, pp. 166–167, 170.

57.   In addition to the sources in n. 56 above, see also M.-J. Seux, *Épithètes royales akkadiennes et sumériennes,* 1967 (see under *banu* B, pp. 51–52, and *saraku,* pp. 291–292); H. Frankfort, *Kingship and the Gods* (1948), pp. 237–240, 299–301; Tigay, *The Evolution of the Gilgamesh Epic,* pp. 153–158, esp. the text of Ashurbanipal on p. 154.

58.   Mayer, *Orientalia* 56:63ff.

59.   Ibid., p. 65.

60.   For the standard edition, see Jacobsen, *The Sumerian King List;* also J. J. Finkelstein, "The Antediluvian Kings," *JCS* 17 (1963), 39–51.

61.   There is considerable debate about the original incipit of the text. Lambert (*Atra-Ḥasis,* pp. 16, 25) believes that it began with a reference to the flood, but W. W. Hallo, in "Beginning and End of the Sumerian King List in the Nippur Recension," *JCS* 17 (1963), 52–57, argues that it opened with the statement about the descent of kingship only.

62.   Of these late versions, the Weld Blundell prism (WB 444) has eight kings ruling five cities, whereas a smaller text (WB 62) has ten kings ruling six cities. On the antediluvian kings, see Jacobsen, *The Sumerian King List,* pp. 55–68; see also Finkelstein and Hallo in *JCS* 17:39–57; W. W. Hallo, "Antediluvian Cities," *JCS* 23 (1970), 57–67; and my earlier treatment in *In Search of History,* pp. 70–72.

63.   See note above. Our primary comparison here is with WB 444, which is closer to the *Sumerian Flood Story.*

64.   So Jacobsen, "The Eridu Genesis," *JBL* 100:513–529; followed by P. D. Miller, *HAR* 9:227–251.

65.   In later exemplars there are some variations. See Finkelstein, "The Antediluvian Kings," *JCS* 17:39–51, esp. pp. 46f.; Hallo, "Antediluvian Cities," *JCS* 23:57–67.

66.   Finkelstein, "The Antediluvian Kings," *JCS* 17:42. A. L. Oppenheim, in *ANET,* p. 265, renders the SKL text, "I drop (the topic) Eridu, etc."

67.   On this, see Jacobsen, *The Sumerian King List,* pp. 58–60.

68.   It would have been inappropriate to repeat a reference to "the capitals" (pl.) in SKL because its author viewed them as destroyed successively and not all at once. It should be noted that the *Sumerian Flood Story* does not seem to recognize

that Sippar was an exception to the destruction. However, Sippar was noted as spared from the flood in the late *Erra Epic*, IV.50. See Hallo, "Antediluvian Cities," *JCS* 23:65.

69.   But see Finkelstein, "The Antediluvian Kings," *JCS* 17:48.

70.   So Lambert and Millard, *Atra-Ḫasis*, p. 19.

71.   W. G. Lambert, "The Seed of Kingship," in *Le palais et la royauté. XXXe recontre assyriologique internationale*, ed. P. Garelli (1974), p. 432.

72.   E. Sollberger, "The Rulers of Lagaš," *JCS* 21 (1967), 279.

73.   On the dating, see ibid., p. 280.

74.   Ibid.

75.   An and Enlil seem to function in a similar fashion at the end of the *Sumerian Flood Story*, vi. 252–260.

76.   Just how much this contrasts with the *Sumerian Flood Story* remains uncertain because of the fragmentary nature of both texts.

77.   On this text, see A. K. Grayson, *Assyrian and Babylonian Chronicles* (1975), pp. 40–42, 139–144; Lambert and Millard, *Atra-Ḫasis*, pp. 17f. It does not seem to me that Jacobsen ("The Eridu Genesis," *JBL* 100: 519–520) and P. D. Miller (*HAR* 9:245–246) are justified in using this very late text to fill a lacuna in the *Sumerian Flood Story*. See above, p. 57.

78.   See Lambert and Millard, *Atra-Ḫasis*, pp. 18–19; W. G. Lambert, "Ancestors, Authors, and Canonicity," *JCS* 11 (1957), 1–14, 112; and E. Reiner, "The Etiological Myth of the 'Seven Sages,'" *Orientalia* 30 (1961), 1–11.

79.   Cf. Wilson, *Genealogy and History*, pp. 149–152. Wilson seems to me to overstate the case for the sake of the biblical parallel. So also Hallo, "Antediluvian Cities," *JCS* 23:62–64.

80.   See I. S. Klotchkoff, "The Late Babylonian List of Scholars," in *Gesellschaft und Kultur im alten Vorderasien*, ed. H. Klengel (1982), pp. 149–154.

81.   See B. Kienast, in "Die Weisheit des Adapa von Eridu," *Symbolae . . . Böhl Dedicatae*, eds. M. A. Beek et al. (1973), pp. 234–239.

82.   See the edition by Burstein, *Babyloniaca;* also Komoroczy, "Berossus."

83.   Burstein, *Babyloniaca*, p. 13.

84.   *Pace* Burstein, *Babyloniaca*, p. 6. Burstein wishes to disqualify the work as history because it contains an account of creation. But for antiquity, that would certainly *not* count against it, and there can be no doubt whatever that Berossus intended his work to be a Hellenistic history.

85.   Ibid., p. 13.

86.   See Komoroczy, "Berossus," *Ac Ant* 21:140–142.

87.   The statement "in the first year" cannot be taken literally and means only "in olden times." See ibid., p. 148.

88.   Reiner, *Orientalia* 30:1–11. See also *Erra Epic* I. 162.

89.   Komoroczy, "Berossus," *Ac Ant* 21:151.

90.   I cannot agree with Burstein (*Babyloniaca*, p. 6), who says that because the first part of Berossus's work can be characterized as "wisdom," it cannot be history as well. Early Greek historiographers also made use of the Hesiodic tradition for the beginnings of their histories, and this too is "wisdom." Also, some of the Greek sophists like Hippias of Elis were likewise historians.

91.   Burstein, *Babyloniaca,* p. 14 n. 10; Komoroczy, "Berossus," *Ac Ant* 21:131–133.
92.   On the significance of the divine blood and clay, see Lambert and Millard, *Atra-Ḥasis,* pp. 21–22. The fact that Berossus suggests that the divine blood is the source of human intelligence and a share of divine wisdom might be taken to support the interpretation of *ṭemu* in *Atrahasis* in a similar way. See also above, pp. 48–49.
93.   A still later Uruk list has a different pairing of the seven sages with seven antediluvian kings. See ibid., p. 25.
94.   On the flood story in Berossus and its parallels, see also ibid., pp. 134–137.
95.   See ibid., p. 137. However, note the statement in *Erra Epic:* "Even Sippar, the eternal city, which the Lord of the Lands (Marduk) did not allow the Flood to overwhelm because it was dear to him . . ." (IV.50f.), which may point to such a Sippar tradition. On this, see Komoroczy, "Berossus," *Ac Ant* 21:137–139. In the Lagash King List tradition, civilization does not survive the flood, and everything must start all over again.
96.   Any consideration of the creation account in Gen. 1:1–2:4a (P), however, would need to examine this tradition.

4

GREEK TRADITIONS ABOUT THE PRIMEVAL AGE

In reviewing the Greek traditions about the primeval age, I will limit this study to the origins and early history of humankind, excluding from consideration any discussion of the origins of the gods and the cosmos. However, it is clear that the birth of the gods and the struggles among them for supremacy, as set forth in Hesiod's *Theogony,* were subjects that were not always so neatly separated from the earliest history of humankind. The result is a rather confused mass of mythical traditions about creation and the primeval times. Thus it would be quite arbitrary to impose a unified system on such traditions. The degree to which efforts at unity and integration were made in antiquity will be noted below. At this point, I will merely indicate the range of themes that appear in Greek sources on the primeval age and then look at the attempts to bring them into some kind of order.

Themes of the Primeval Age

By contrast with Mesopotamia, there is no myth setting forth the creation of humankind in Greece comparable to that of *Atrahasis.* What we have instead are numerous allusions and mythical anecdotes that cannot be fitted into any unified system.[1]

The Creation of Humanity and the Golden Age

One prominent notion in Greek mythology and poetry is that early humanity was "born from the earth" (*gegenes*), just as mother earth was also the ultimate origin for all the gods in the theogony. Furthermore, this early race of humankind was often thought of as a race of giants "larger, fiercer and more uncouth than the present one. . . . Earth bore these huge and violent creatures to her husband Ouranos (heaven)."[2] The parallel to the divine giants and Zeus's struggle for supremacy over them in Hesiod's *Theogony* is obvious. What is not so obvious is whether the human race of giants should be identified with the divine giants or how the two traditions relate to each other. This ancient race of giants seems to belong to the age of Kronos, although remnants of giants could still be found in distant regions in the heroic age, as in the case of Odysseus's encounter with Polyphemus in the *Odyssey*.[3]

Those who were born from the soil, and therefore *autochthones*, could serve as the ancestors of later peoples. Such were the Pelasgians, the original inhabitants of Arcadia. The same was said for the Athenians. This claim to being autochthonous, based upon a genealogical connection with an autochthonous ancestor, became an important political tradition and a matter of prestige and civic pride.[4] Of particular importance was the use of autochthony to express ethnic identity and a close connection with a particular region or territory.

The myths could speak, in a general way, of the gods creating people or a race of people. They could also designate Zeus as the creator of humankind, but not necessarily the first race of humankind. At the same time, the deities Prometheus and Hephaestus could be regarded as the specific creators of man and woman respectively, formed from the earth as potters form clay. But various peoples could originate in extraordinary ways, such as when Deucalion and Pyrrha create the Leleges race by throwing stones.[5] The Greek traditions do not derive all of humankind from a single source or common human pair at the beginning of time. Thus there could be many different beginnings at different places, and this possibility plays havoc with the many later attempts to construct a universal history from primeval times.

The Greek tradition of origins, in fact, seems to focus more on the origins of particular states, tribes, and peoples than on humankind in general. They are in the nature of "charter myths" that legitimate custom, institutions, and territorial claims.[6] These states and tribes it traces back to heroes and eponymous ancestors, many of whom are the offspring of a deity. Subgroups within a larger political or ethnic entity may be represented as descendants or branches in a segmented genealogy. These first ancestors were also frequently regarded as the first rulers of the peoples they represent—a rather contradictory, but still quite persistent, idea.[7]

Notions about the conditions under which earliest mankind lived differ considerably. The oldest age could be represented as the simple rural life of a shepherd without the gifts of civilization or agriculture. A more elaborate view is that of a golden age, the age of Kronos, in which men are superior in strength and pleasures are many without any ills. In this age also, gods and men mingled freely and even ate and drank together.[8]

The termination of the primeval age is represented in various ways. Hesiod, for instance, presents two quite different views. One has to do with the creation of woman.[9] In this account, Zeus is presented as having a rival in the crafty figure of Prometheus, man's champion, who is a god not unlike Enki in the Mesopotamian tradition. When Prometheus tricks Zeus in the matter of the portions of meat for god and mankind in the first "sacrificial" meal, Zeus retaliates by hiding from mankind the means of an easy life. When Prometheus tries to restore something of this to man by the theft of fire, Zeus proceeds to bring evils on man by means of the creation of woman. For although the gods existed in both sexes, it would seem in this view that humanity was originally male. Zeus instructs the divine craftsman, Hephaestus, to create woman from earth, after which she is endowed by the gods and goddesses. In one version of the story, the woman provides an etiology for marriage and procreation that in itself is regarded as the primary source of ill for mankind. In the other version, the woman, Pandora, who was made evil by nature, also brought with her a fateful jar of toil and sickness. This dubious gift from the gods was accepted on behalf of mankind by Epimetheus, "stupidity," and thus the evils were perpetuated by this union.[10]

The myth has obviously been modified by Hesiod for the purpose of his own didactic concerns, as the two different versions make clear. Nevertheless, one can identify in it certain basic features:

1. The creation of woman is separated from that of the general creation of mankind and other creatures.

2. The creation of woman is associated etiologically with the origins of marriage.

3. The origin of evil is in some way associated with the first woman, who perhaps through her curiosity releases evil into the world.

In the second version, Hesiod presents his account of the five races (*gene*) of humanity in which each is brought to an end by the gods or Zeus and is replaced by an inferior one, leading to the present race, which will come to its end as well. This successive degeneration is represented by metals: gold, silver, bronze, and iron.[11] No explanation is given for the degeneration apart from the fact that each race was made that way. Hesiod offers these two versions of the origin of evil as alternatives with no attempt to reconcile them. We will return to the story of the five races below.

The Flood

Another explanation for the end of the primeval age is through a particular disaster that few survived. The clearest example of this is the flood tradition, but its appearance in Greek tradition does not seem to be any earlier than the early fifth century B.C. and was very likely an import from the Near East.[12] More common in the older tradition is the disaster of war, particularly the Trojan War, which brought an end to the heroic age.[13] When the flood tradition does come into Greek mythology, it was associated with Deucalion, which means that because Deucalion stands at the beginning of his line of mortals, it scarcely allows enough time for a primeval age, and it creates great confusion for the other parallel traditions about early ancestors whose descendants remained unaffected by it. Thus the tradition of Phoroneus, "the first man," could be told as it related to the peoples of the Peloponnesus without any reference to the flood.[14]

The classical version of the flood story that is the best known is that from Ovid[15] and Apollodorus.[16] The cause of the flood in Ovid appears to be the proliferation of evil in the Iron Age, the last of Hesiod's four races.[17] But before he recounts the flood, he also mentions the war of Zeus with the Giants and the atrocity of Lycaon as an example of human corruption. Zeus then declares in a council of the gods his intention to end the human race with a flood. One righteous and pious couple, Deucalion and his wife

Pyrrha, are discovered as survivors in a small boat, and Zeus spares them by ending the flood. When dry land is restored, the pair, on the advice of a divine oracle, repopulate the earth by throwing stones over their shoulders. Those thrown by Deucalion become males and those by Pyrrha, females. The animal world is created anew from the earth, not from any taken on board the boat.

In Apollodorus's version, Zeus plans to destroy the people of the Bronze Age. Nothing is said about the other ages or why this one should be destroyed. Prometheus, however, warns Deucalion, his son, who constructs a chest (*larnax*) equipped with provisions and takes on board his wife, Pyrrha. The flood destroys most of the population in Greece, but some escape to the mountains. The flood lasts nine days, after which the floating chest lands on Mount Parnassus, where Deucalion emerges and sacrifices to Zeus. He is given a wish by the deity and chooses to have people as companions. Thus he and Pyrrha throw stones and so produce men and women from the stones. This is followed by the Deucalion genealogy.

Both Ovid and Apollodorus refer to Prometheus as the creator of humankind from water and earth. This follows a theogony, so that creation by Prometheus is an artificial bridge between the accounts. Prometheus is not a creator of humanity in Hesiod, and the fact that Apollodorus follows the old tradition in making Deucalion the son of Prometheus shows how poorly the item fits in the context. The item about the throwing of stones to make people was not original to the flood story, but explained how Deucalion, a king, obtained a people to rule, the Leleges.[18] The notion of a divinely provoked catastrophe as a punishment for human evil is also a very Greek notion. Only the brief reference to a couple who survive a flood by means of a boat (or chest) is an innovation from eastern sources. Although Prometheus may resemble Enki in his role of instructing Deucalion to construct the chest, this may be accidental, because this action is also consistent with his role as savior of humanity in Hesiod.[19] Furthermore, one should not assume that all the details as set forth in these late versions can be read back into references to the flood several centuries earlier.

What should be obvious from this brief review is that the diversity of traditions in the Greek world allowed for so many variations in the presentation of accounts about early times that uniformity and consistency were hardly to be expected. The poets of epic, lyric, and tragedy exercised great freedom in their use of these themes. From Hesiod to Apollodorus there was never a primeval-history tradition comparable to that of Mesopotamia, in which one moved from the creation of humanity to the development of civilization and later history.

Nevertheless, there was a certain intellectual movement that encouraged the systematization and integration of some of the traditions about the beginnings of peoples and primeval times as a way of expressing a unified national "antiquarian" tradition.[20] This leads us to consider that particular development of Greek historiography that made use of primeval myths and legends in presenting its distinctive version of primeval history.

Culture Heroes

The Greeks also had their culture heroes or first inventors that belonged in a vague way to the primeval age. These were primarily gods who were the patrons of certain arts or crafts, or who, in mythology, were associated with the activity or object they were said to have invented.[21] Thus Athena was the inventor of the cultivation of olives, of wifely arts, and of instruments of war, such as the chariot. Demeter invented the cultivation of grain, Dionysus that of viticulture, Apollo the calendar and the lyre, and Hephaestus various crafts and technology. But such inventions were usually mediated through heroes to whom the knowledge was revealed by the deity. Prominent among the culture heroes in the later tradition was Prometheus, who gave humankind fire. In *Prometheus Bound,* Aeschylus makes this gift the basis of civilized life, so that all other gifts of civilization come from him as well. Because Prometheus means "forethought," the god becomes symbolic of the progress of humankind through its own intelligence in spite of the gods.[22]

The early historians paid considerable attention to the question of the first inventors, as they did to the whole subject of etiology, the cause and beginning of things. Herodotus frequently speaks of first inventors, but he never identifies these as deities. He sometimes names historic persons, such as Arion of Corinth, who composed and produced the first dithyramb, Glaucus of Chios, who discovered the welding of iron, and Philon, who established weights and measures for the Peloponnesians. He deliberately replaces the legendary Minos, who was the first to rule the sea, with the historical Polycrates, who was the first historical person to attempt to do so. Many inventions were simply attributed to older foreign nations, such as the Egyptians, the Babylonians, and the Phoenicians, as inventors, rather than to the Greeks and their gods.[23] This historical and ethnographic interest clearly stems from the older mythological tradition in which heroes and ancestors were the originators of culture and custom.

A strong interest in inventions persisted down into the Roman period, as can be seen in "catalogues of inventors" (*Heuremata*) made from gleaning information from older sources. The most comprehensive list is that of Pliny the elder in his *Natural History*.[24] This lists 139 inventors—divine, heroic, and human. Pliny expresses in his catalogue a degree of historical euhemerism through the inclusion of divine and human inventors without distinction and through the suggestion at the outset that some inventors may have been venerated as gods because of their inventions. This reflects a historical and philosophical perspective much older and quite widespread by the Hellenistic period.

It is at this point that something should be said about *The Phoenician History* of Philo Byblius.[25] A large part of the work that is preserved in the quoted excerpts of Eusebius's *Praeparatio Evangelica* is the so-called History of Culture, which deals with the theme of inventions. Because there is no extant Phoenician text that establishes a clear precedent for this work, it is best to study it in the context of the Greco-Roman world to which it dates. The principle of euhemeristic interpretation of myth is strongly emphasized throughout the work, and this applies to the theme of inventions as well. Thus, in the prologue one finds the statement:

> The most ancient of the barbarians, and especially Phoenicians and Egyptians, from whom the rest of mankind received their traditions, considered as greatest gods those men who had made discoveries valuable for life's necessities or those who had in some way benefited their nations. Since they considered these men as benefactors and sources of many blessings, they worshipped them as gods even after they passed on.

It is not difficult to find here the principle, reflected in Herodotus, that the Egyptians and the Phoenicians were the primary benefactors of culture in the Greek world and the euhemerism reflected in Pliny that the divine inventors were originally humans. The philosophical outlook of the work is unquestionably that of the Greco-Roman world.[26] Thus many of the inventors, although presented as among the first of humanity, are demythologized gods, either Greek or Phoenician.

The subject matter of inventions, however, is treated in a manner quite different from any of the Greco-Roman sources. Following the cosmogony and closely tied into it by Philo there begins the history of humankind, apparently deriving from a single pair, Aeon and Protogonos. These are demythologized Greek philosophical "deities" of creation in the cosmologies, but whether they correspond to Phoenician deities is debatable.[27] This is also the beginning of the history of culture, because the oldest discovery begins in the first generation and continues in succeeding ones. The structure for the history is genealogical and includes numerous narrative anecdotes about the occasion of such inventions. Although this structure of genealogy and stories is quite similar to that of the *Catalogue of Women* and the historical *Genealogies* of the Greek tradition, to be considered below, the subject focus of these works is quite otherwise.

It is the differences from the Greek treatment of inventors that point to a particular Phoenician tradition of inventors and primeval age. This section of the history is a mixture of local traditions from the various Phoenician cities, such as Tyre, Beirut, and Byblos. Their combination has produced doublets and parallels, so that there is more than one inventor for some of the cultural achievements.[28] There are also some obvious contradictions. Although the names of gods as inventors are often clearly identifiable, whether Greek or Phoenician, the stories about their inventions are much more appropriate to human inventors and their needs of food, shelter, and occupations. They cannot derive from Phoenician myths. In the Greek tradition, the gods become inventors by bestowing gifts of civilization on humankind, which is altogether different. In some cases, the connection between the inventions and the deity, such as Chousor, is obvious, as it is in the Greek tradition with the corresponding deity Hephaestus. In others it is not. A number of inventors are given names that correspond with their inventions. There is no reason to suppose that these must reflect deities.[29]

These factors make it difficult to unravel all the different traditional materials, foreign influences, and degree of Philo's own ingenuity behind the history. Here we are concerned only with those general observations of form that seem to reflect a genre of primeval history in the western tradition. This includes a history of culture in genealogical form in which the beginnings of civilization are associated with the early generations of humankind.

The closest non-Greek parallel to Philo's history is not the "sages" tradition of Mesopotamia, as is so often suggested.[30] The Mesopotamian tradition does not emphasize "invention," and the Phoenician history says nothing about the flood. It is the actual ancestors of each successive generation who are the inventors. The parallel that comes to mind is the biblical one in the primeval history of Genesis, especially chapter 4.[31] This strongly argues for a "western" antiquarian tradition whose subject was the inventions of civilization in primeval times. Apart from the fact that the gods, such as Enlil or Enki, taught humankind the arts of civilization at the time of their creation, the theme of inventions is not a Mesopotamian tradition, and the effort to find it there is forced and misleading.

Antiquarian Historiography

Let us turn from this discussion of common themes in the Greek primeval tradition to the development of a particular genre of antiquarian literature in the classical world. Although many of the sources for reconstructing such a literature are highly fragmentary, preserved largely in the quotations of later sources,[32] the broad outlines are sufficiently clear to be useful for comparison with the biblical tradition.

The Hesiodic Tradition

There has been some attempt in the past to see in Hesiod's story of the five races "an early piece of Greek historical writing" or "at least a forerunner of the historical perspective."[33] Although the myth is not a parable, it does have a strong moral tone and has a clearly didactic character. At the same time, because it deals with the beginning of things, it is "history at the point where it turns into philosophy,"[34] but in this case that means moral philosophy. Four races have been assigned to metals that are clearly metaphorical of the quality both on the physical and moral levels. A brief summary of the myth will be helpful.

The gods made a golden race (*genos*) of mortal people in the time of Kronos, and this age was one without sorrow or toil and with great abundance. After this generation (*genos*) died, they became the kindly spirits that roam the earth in aid of humankind. Then the gods made a second race of silver, "less noble by far." Children were brought up by their mothers and remained simpletons for one hundred years. After reaching maturity, they lived only for a short time, were guilty of much wrongdoing, and neglected the worship of the gods. This race was removed by Zeus in anger.[35] These became the spirits of the underworld. Zeus made a third race of bronze, which was known for its warlike activity. Yet because of this, these mortals destroyed themselves and became the dwellers of Hades. Zeus then made a fourth race (not associated with any metal), this one more noble and righteous than the previous one. These were the heroes or demigods, "the race before our own." This one includes the heroes involved in the wars of Thebes and Troy. Some of these died in battle; others were transported to the Isles of the Blessed, where Kronos is said to reign. The fifth race, of iron, is the present one, and in it there is much labor and sorrow. It is described as becoming progressively worse in the future until it will be destroyed.

This presentation views history as a series of epochs, but there has been no effort to establish a sense of continuity from one race to the next in the form of a genealogy or other connection.[36] Furthermore, it is clear that the heroic race interrupts the sequence of the metals and of the progressive degeneration, so it provides a problem for the scheme as a whole.[37] Yet it should also be noted that each age/race constitutes an etiology for certain types of spirits of the dead, all of which required some explanation. Again, there are the same qualitative levels of spirits except for the heroes, but the heroes had to be put before the present age because of the many genealogical links in other traditions with the present age.

Even though Hesiod sought to combine a variety of traditions, and even though there is a certain degree of secularization and rationalization reflected in this piece, it is still difficult to characterize it as historiography. This was not the form of the Hesiodic tradition that was taken as a model by later historiography. Instead, the five races story was of more interest to philosophers and theologians. In one respect, there is a clear difference from the Pandora myth that immediately preceded this one. In the five races, there is a strong emphasis on moral evils resulting in destruction. This is especially true in Hesiod's preaching and predictions about the present age, which will receive the divine judgment of Zeus.[38]

The Theogony

The basic form and structure of the *Theogony* would appear to be an initial cosmogony accounting for the creation of the cosmos, combined with a theogonic succession myth into which other Greek traditions about the gods and their relationships to each other have been included. These have all been unified by means of complex segmented genealogies. Although aspects of the *Theogony* bear comparison with Near Eastern materials, particularly the Babylonian *Enuma Elish* and a more recently discovered Babylonian theogony,[39] the one aspect that is neglected in the *Theogony* is the creation of humankind and the beginnings of social and political life. One is, however, left with the impression that the struggles within the ranks of the gods were partly concurrent with the early history of humankind. This is also suggested by the myth of the five races in *Works and Days,* in which the Golden Age is ascribed to the time of Kronos, whereas Zeus does not come to the fore until the end of the Silver Age, which he destroyed.[40] It would appear that the Greek traditions were not cosmogonic in character and were only integrated with such "foreign" materials with some difficulty.

G. S. Kirk has suggested that the aim of Hesiod in the *Theogony* was "to construct a brief history of the earlier generations [of gods] from the very moment when sky and earth first separate down to the firm establishment of Zeus."[41] In this process, "the assignment of divine prerogatives [by Zeus] and the stabilization of the world of nature were the real climax of Hesiod's poem."[42] This treatment of mythology, with all its complex and often conflicting traditions, as a "history" in which all the various aspects of the divine world are accounted for is a major rationalization of the etiological explanation of reality. It also established an authoritative tradition about how the families of the gods were to be understood.

This system of organization and schematization, by genealogies and catalogues interspersed with narratives to produce a "history," was open-ended and could invite additions.[43] At the end of the theogony is a brief catalogue of heroes whose mothers were goddesses. This was an early addition to the work. But of more importance for our discussion is a second major addition to the *Theogony* that comes under the title of the *Catalogue of Women*.

The Catalogue of Women

The *Catalogue of Women* was an anonymous addition made to Hesiod's *Theogony* but was not preserved together with the *Theogony* in our extant texts, although already in antiquity, shortly after it was composed, it was regarded as the work of Hesiod.[44] Nevertheless, much of its content has long been known from a large number of references in ancient authors. Yet it is only with the discovery, publication, and careful study of papyri fragments of the *Catalogue* that its true structure and character have become known.[45]

The *Catalogue* was intended as a continuation of the *Theogony* in the same style of epic poetry; but instead of dealing with the families and exploits of the gods, the subject has now shifted to families of heroes and eponymic ancestors and their extensive genealogies. These genealogies are interspersed with narratives about heroic exploits as well as anecdotes and annotations. As M. L. West states:

> We can see that these narratives were often very summary; but they are there, and are an essential ingredient in the poem. A large number of traditional myths, perhaps the greater part of those familiar to the Greeks of the classical age, were at least touched on and set in their place in the genealogical framework. Thus the poem became something approaching a compendious account of the whole story of the nation from the earliest times to the time of the Trojan War or the generation after it. . . . Its poet had a clearly defined and individual view of the heroic period as a kind of Golden Age in which the human race lived in different conditions from the present and which Zeus terminated as a matter of policy.[46]

This description suggests that the *Catalogue* is a primeval "history" of the nation from its earliest beginnings down to the end of the heroic age, the Trojan War, structured in a way similar to that of the *Theogony* and intended as a counterpart to it.

The composition of the *Catalogue* was not the result of a gradual accumulation of materials but reflects a systematic plan with careful construction of its various parts. The framework of the introductory proem and the concluding narrative represent their own perspective of the heroic age as a period in which gods and humans lived together—an age that was brought to an end by Zeus to make a clear separation between the two realms of human and divine. Into this framework, and somewhat at variance with it, the genealogies and narratives are placed. Among these one can distinguish a number of major independent epic cycles that involved a different set of heroes and were associated with different regions.[47] The author has collected these traditions, reshaped them to suit his pattern, and added a number of bridging blocks to fill in the gaps. The result did not eliminate all the inconsistencies, and later genealogists did much in their works to integrate the various major traditions.

The *Catalogue* was perhaps the original *archaiologia* and the basis for all later attempts at primeval history.[48] This antiquarian tradition became a major preoccupation of many historians from the sixth century B.C. onward as a subject of vital concern to most of the states and communities of the Greco-Roman world.

Early Greek Historiography

With our present knowledge of the *Catalogue of Women,* made possible through the labors of M. L. West, it now becomes clear that the work stands at the beginning of a long and erudite tradition of genealogical literature. Written as a supplement to Hesiod's *Theogony,* it created a new genre that became a national tradition of fundamental importance to later Greek historiography. Even though it makes use of the language and poetic structures of epic, it represents an alternative in form and perspective to that of Homer. Although the latter uses genealogies and catalogues of gods and heroes, these are only digressions and not the means of structuring the work as a whole. Furthermore, the *Iliad* is one story with other stories included as retrospective accounts. Once a work like the *Catalogue* is structured by means of genealogy, the emphasis shifts to a comprehensive "history" of gods and humanity with a genealogical chronology and with all the myths and heroic traditions fitted into that framework in some way or other.

A comparison with Apollodorus's *Bibliotheca* (first or second century A.D.) makes it clear that this later work is heavily dependent upon the Hesiodic tradition of *Theogony* and the *Catalogue of Women* and demonstrates the strong continuity that existed in the genealogical tradition. The *Bibliotheca* also made use of the fifth century B.C. genealogists to develop the synoptic version, but we may assume that these earlier writers were also familiar with the Hesiodic tradition and used it as the basic point of departure for their own writing. This is critical when it comes to assessing their form and structure because they are now so fragmentary.

Acusilaus of Argos, an early fifth-century genealogist, begins with a theogony, following Hesiod, but then proceeds with the development of the line of Phoroneus.[49] This represents a reordering of the material in the *Catalogue*, no doubt to put emphasis upon his native Argos as the place of origin of the first man. Nevertheless, the extensive genealogical tradition of the *Catalogue* allowed him to include the families of central and northern Greece as well as the heroic tales of the Argonaut's voyage and the Trojan War. In form, the work also contained "the same mixture of genealogical framework and plain narrative filling that characterizes the *Catalogue*."[50] Into this scheme, Acusilaus fitted the tradition of the great flood in the time of Deucalion and Pyrrha, but how he synchronized it with the Phoroneus genealogy is not clear because Phoroneus is presented as the "first man." Additional material for this tradition was probably drawn from the epic *Phoronis*.[51]

Pherecydes of Athens, a contemporary of Acusilaus, wrote a *Genealogiai* that did not begin with a cosmogony or the families of the gods,[52] but like the *Catalogue*, dealt with the various genealogies of the ancestors of humankind. An alternative title used for this work, *Autochthones*, is significant because it suggests, by analogy with the *Catalogue*, that a basic organizing principle for his genealogies was to begin each line with an ancestor who was "sprung from earth." The structure and arrangement of the work, with its many parallel genealogies interspersed with stories of the heroes, greatly expanded the content of the *Catalogue* from five books to ten and made this author a mine of useful information for later writers.[53] Pherecydes also makes quite explicit the connection between his eponymic heroes and the peoples and places of his own time, an important feature of later historiography. This connection of the heroic past with the present was further strengthened by the use of the genealogies of noble families to bridge the gap to historic time.[54] For the most part, however, Pherecydes' work must have served as a useful handbook on mythology for poets and playwriters of tragedy[55] as well as later historians.

Hecataeus of Miletus, an earlier writer of the late sixth century B.C., produced works in both geography (*Periegesis*)[56] and history (*Genealogiai* or *Heroologia*).[57] The scientific work on geography, the result of his many travels, had a considerable influence on his other work, the *Genealogiai,* which combined features of both genres. Hecataeus's work also goes back to the Hesiodic tradition, except that he did not begin with a theogony. However, because he regarded the *Catalogue* as part of Hesiod's writings,[58] he may be referring directly to the *Catalogue* when he suggests in his proem that he is going to make some sense out of the tales of the Greeks: "The tales of the Greeks are many and absurd."[59] This probably means that he found many contradictions among the different myths and legends that were created by collections such as that represented by the Hesiodic tradition. His own version was probably an effort at one selective consistent version, "as seems to me to be the truth."[60] He also identified the peoples and places of the legends with place-names and the geography of his own day. Furthermore, it is likely that he used Heracles as a convenient fixed point for making a connection between the heroic age and historic times because, as an aristocrat, he traced his ancestry back sixteen generations to Heracles.

The other interest Hecataeus had was in geography, the *Periegesis,* which L. Pearson characterizes in the following way:

> As a literary form the *Periegesis* is extremely simple: merely a description of different cities and peoples taken in order as they would be passed by someone sailing in a ship along the coast. Such a description would include brief mention of curious customs and *thaumata* and often a remark about the origin of some settlement or the part it played in ancient legend.[61]

In form it is an itinerary used as a literary structure in which it is common to find references to mythology, ethnography, etymologies of place-names, and the etiologies of city foundations. This means that the subject matter of these two types, *Genealogies* and *Itinerary*, was not very distinct.

This form of genealogical history is greatly expanded in the work of Hellanicus of Lesbos, who wrote in the latter part of the fifth century B.C.[62] He produced a large number of works on mythography, ethnography, and chronology, all regarded by ancient scholarship as "histories." The mythographic works appear to have treated the main genealogical branches of the *Catalogue* as separate works.[63] Thus the *Phoronis* dealt with the descendants of Phoroneus, the Argives, the Pelasgians, and the Thebans, whereas the *Deucalioneia* treated the history of the Hellenes in its main branches of the Dorians, Ionians, and Aeolians, just as it appears in the *Catalogue*. His ethnographic works placed considerable emphasis upon the mythological origins and heroic history of the Greek cities and islands. In this they differed little from the genealogical works.[64]

Of special interest for this study is Hellanicus's *Atthis,* which he wrote at the end of the fifth century.[65] Here his concern was to write a history of Athens from its foundations, through the heroic age, the Dark Ages, and the historic period up to the time of the author. About Hellanicus's *Atthis* Pearson writes: "It would not be at all surprising if he was actually invited to Athens by Pericles and engaged to write the first history of the Athenians."[66] For the historical period, there existed only a few disconnected accounts of separate episodes of the Athenian past, whereas for the ancient period there were a few individual tales about the legendary hero, Theseus, and the names of some of the early kings from the mythological age. It was the task of an experienced and erudite historian, such as Hellanicus, to put together all of these traditions into a consistent and continuous arrangement and to fill in the gaps from local lore and from the wider pan-Hellenic mythological traditions.

Concerning Hellanicus's method, Pearson suggests that many of the details on mythology and legend were the historian's own inventions "since considerable ingenuity and originality were necessary if he was to offer a consistent and comprehensive account of heroic genealogy."[67] For the oldest period, Hellanicus is dependent upon the *Catalogue* and Pherecydes, which made use of at least two separate genealogical traditions both with autochthonous ancestors, Cecrops and Erechtheus. Out of this complex and confusing genealogical tangle Hellanicus constructed a continuous list of kings from the first ruler, Cecrops, down to the generation contemporaneous with the Trojan War. In this process he made a number of connections with the broader mythological tradition from the beginning of the heroic age to its end. Yet this attempt to link chronologically (by generations) the Athenian tradition to the Panhellenic heroic tradition left him a few generations short. This meant that he had to supplement his list of Athenian kings drawn from the names of ancestors in the *Catalogue* and Pherecydes. So he mentions a group of kings before Cecrops, beginning with Ogygus, who was contemporary with Deucalion and the time of the great flood at the beginnings of humankind. Still short of kings for his genealogical synchronisms, Hellanicus duplicated the names of two kings in the list to make all the synchronisms come out correctly.[68] This is a case of the imposition of a historiographic form, the king list, upon a quite different kind of genealogical material. In other words, it is the historicization of the mythological tradition. This had implications not only for early Athenian history but also for the whole of the heroic age, and such genealogical chronologies became a standard measure in dealing with "ancient history."

The primary focus of the early period in the *Atthis* was on Theseus, a king of Athens in the generation before the Trojan War. In many respects, he represented the true founding hero of the Athenian state. His exploits were developed in parallel to those of Heracles, who played a similar role for other Greek states.[69] Also belonging to this period were a series of famous trials in the Areopagus, which established the authority and character of this important institution.[70]

The gap between the heroic age and the historical period proper was a problem, because there was no kingship for this period and therefore no chronological scheme that could clearly bridge the gap. There were no historical events, no records or traditions, that could be used to fill in the period. Instead, Hellanicus filled it with material of local interest having to do with topography and religious cults.[71] There was a strong tendency by later writers of Athenian history to follow this same practice in treating religious matters at this point in their accounts. These were generally of a strongly etiological character.

Information from the historical period itself was very sparse. Of particular importance was the constitution of Solon and the reforms of Cleisthenes, but even these events were rather obscure and subject to a great deal of interpretation by Hellanicus and later historians.[72] The period of the tyrants and the events leading up to, and including, the Persian Wars had been dealt with by Herodotus, and Hellanicus probably added little of his own to a summary of these events. He could say very little about the fifty years between the Persian Wars and the outbreak of the Peloponnesian Wars, as Thucydides complained. For the last part of his history, down to his own time at the end of the fifth century, Hellanicus could make use of the annual office of archon in Athens to establish a chronological framework for events, a scheme that gave rise to a subsequent annalistic style for local chronicles.[73]

It is important to emphasize that Hellanicus established a literary tradition of Greek historiography, one "which the local historians kept alive with a certain degree of progress and development."[74] This includes the way in which mythical traditions about Athens's beginning, local lore and religious customs, and political history were combined in a continuous work. These historians often reflected quite different political viewpoints, yet they shared "their concern with religious ritual and the mythological explanations of religious customs with constitutional antiquities and the development of Athenian democratic institutions; their interest in the topography of Athens and Attica and the sacred associations of different Attic sites, and . . . their interest in anecdote and biographical detail."[75]

Our brief survey of the genre of early Greek historiography of the *Genealogies* type, from the *Catalogue of Women* to the works of Hellanicus in the sixth and fifth centuries B.C., reveal the development of a distinctive form of primeval history for ancient Greece. The primary focus of these works is on the origins of the various Greek peoples, tribes, and states as well as some foreign nations, by means of genealogical descent. Into this genealogical structure all major traditions relevant to the particular history were fitted, whether pan-Hellenic in scope or only local. The exploits of heroes and eponymous ancestors and the direct intervention of the deity in the affairs of humankind are common subjects. The origin of peoples is often expressed in terms of birth and association between groups, by family relationships of eponymous ancestors. Tribes and peoples could either be autochthonous to the region they inhabit or they could have migrated, through their ancestor, to their present location from another region. This form of primeval history has almost nothing in common with that of Mesopotamia, where the emphasis is upon the creation of humankind, early universal kingship, and the flood as a marker between the heroic age and historical times.[76]

Another aspect of this early historiographic tradition, emphasized by F. Hartog,[77] is the use and proliferation of etymologies for peoples and places. This becomes a form of primitive philology, an exercise in erudition parallel to that of the genealogy itself. It also allowed for a steady means of expansion of the primeval traditions. In this way, etiology was not restricted to a single point in an oral tale but was a literary technique that was almost unlimited.

The Antiquarian Tradition

When the sophist Hippias of Elis is asked by Socrates on what subject the Spartans like to hear him lecture, Hippias answers: "They delight in genealogies of heroes and of men and in stories of the foundations of cities in olden times, and, to put it briefly, in all forms of antiquarian lore."[78] In other words, the kinds of traditions represented by the *Catalogue of Women* and the early historians and mythographers, such as Acusilaus, Pherecydes, Hecataeus, Hellanicus, and many others, constituted a very strong and popular antiquarian tradition that found a responsive chord in Greek society. A. Momigliano has tried to draw a distinction between the antiquarian (Hippias) and the true historian (Thucydides), but such a separation for antiquity is not so easy to maintain.[79] The difference, for the ancients, was primarily one of subject matter. Although Herodotus appears to dismiss the heroic age quickly when dealing with the theme of rivalry between the Greeks and the barbarians (I. 5), much of the ethnographic material of his history is antiquarian in form and character.[80]

Some remarks by Polybius on this subject are quite illuminating. Although he himself chose to follow Thucydides' style of reporting on contemporary political events, he was aware of the much more popular field of "ancient history" and is rather apologetic about his choice of subject matter. He states:

> Since genealogies, myths, the planting of colonies, the foundation of cities and their ties of kinship have been recounted by many writers and in many different styles, an author who undertakes at the present day to deal with these matters must either represent the work of others as being his own, a most disgraceful proceeding, or if he refuses to do this, must manifestly toil to no purpose, being constrained to avow that the matters on which he writes . . . have been adequately narrated and handed down to posterity by previous authors.[81]

In spite of Polybius's suggestion that the market was already flooded with such antiquarian works, there was always room for more. These were generally of two kinds, those that could serve as handbooks on mythology and those that were more directly related to historiography. In the former category was the *Bibliotheca* of Apollodorus of the first or second century A.D. A direct descendant from the *Catalogue of Women*, Pherecydes, and other such works, it tried to give a comprehensive picture of origins and the deeds of the heroes from the Greek perspective. The other form of antiquarian work is represented by the early history of Rome written by Dionysius of Halicarnassus in the first century B.C. Such works describe the origins of a people or state and its development down to historical times. The model for this type of history was almost certainly the *Atthis* tradition, perhaps specifically that of Hellanicus.[82] Because this form of history is more akin to the biblical "antiquarian tradition" of the Yahwist, it may be useful to look at the work of Dionysius a little more closely.

Dionysius opens his history with a long introduction explaining why he has chosen the early history of Rome as his subject matter. He is interested in demonstrating the worthy and noble origins of the Romans, that is, that they were Greeks, in order to reject the slanderous remarks about them by his Greek fellow countrymen. He wants further to show that the founding of their institutions and customs has led to their present greatness and that Rome is entirely worthy of governing the world, including the Greek peoples. At the same time, his history contains ancient examples of Roman piety, justice, self-control, and valor of the highest order for the admiration of other peoples, especially the Greeks. In other words, such a work was a form of propaganda, a legitimation of claims and rights, a statement of identity and destiny.

Dionysius describes the subject matter of the history as the most ancient legends (*muthoi*), primarily derived from Greek tradition, which he extends down to the Punic Wars. This means that he undertook to write a prologue — an *archaiologia* — for the history of Polybius. The history deals with wars of conquest and internal strife, the primary subjects of classical histories, and how these conflicts were resolved. In addition, it presents the forms of government from the monarchy onward, as well as descriptions of laws and customs — "the whole life of the ancient Romans." Dionysius undertakes to do all this in a variety of styles appropriate to the various subjects for information, edification, and entertainment. The author also claims that he is the first to undertake such a unified work of Rome's early history.[83]

The point of mentioning the work of Dionysius is that the *archaiologia* represents an important branch of ancient historiography. This antiquarian tradition goes back for hundreds of years to the sixth century B.C. at least, but because the earlier examples are so fragmentary, the text of Dionysius provides us with a model of what such *archaiologia* were like. This means that it is appropriate to use such works for comparison with the biblical material, even though they date from a much later period.

Conclusion

I have tried to establish, in this chapter, a basis for the discussion of a "western antiquarian tradition" that is parallel to, but quite distinct from, the eastern antiquarian tradition of Mesopotamia. This western tradition includes within its treatment of the primeval or heroic age quite different themes and concerns, and it structures its presentation in a very different form or genre. The western focus on the origin of peoples and tribes and on the first inventors of culture and the treatment of these by means of genealogical chronology is absent from the eastern tradition. By contrast, the eastern emphasis upon the creation of humankind, universal kingship and the flood as the end of the primeval age, and the structure of a king-list chronology play only a marginal and secondary role in the western tradition as late foreign elements.

In the analysis that follows, I will try to make a number of more specific connections between Genesis and these two anti-quarian traditions on points of particular detail. Our purpose is not merely to search, in a general way, for parallels to the biblical text but to see them in terms of their relationship to these two broad streams of tradition about the primeval age. Our task is to understand the nature of Genesis as "prologue" or *archaiologia* to the history of Israel and what that says about its form and the character of its composition, especially as it has to do with the work of the Yahwist.

NOTES

1.   See esp. the work of W. K. C. Guthrie, *In the Beginning: Some Greek Views on the Origins of Life and the Early State of Man*, 1957; also S. Blundell, *The Origins of Civilization in Greek and Roman Thought*, 1986.

2.   Guthrie, *In the Beginning*, p. 22. Much of what follows is dependent upon this useful collection of materials.

3.   Ibid., pp. 80f.

4.   Van Groningen, *In the Grip of the Past*, p. 9; Guthrie, *In the Beginning*, pp. 22–23; Blundell, *The Origins*, pp. 7–9.

5.   H. G. Evelyn-White, *Hesiod: The Homeric Hymns and Homerica*, LCL (1936), p. 209. The story contains an etiology with the play on the words λᾶας (stone) and λαός (people). Note the comment in Guthrie, *In the Beginning*, p. 27, (based on Ovid) that stones are "the bones of their mother (earth)." Cf. Matt. 3:9; Luke 3:8.

6.   See G. S. Kirk, *The Nature of Greek Myths* (1975), p. 273.

7.   For a useful overview on the great importance of genealogy in Greek thought, see van Groningen, *In the Grip of the Past*, pp. 47–61.

8.   On notions of the Golden Age, see Guthrie, *In the Beginning*, pp. 63–79; also Blundell, *The Origins*, pp. 135–164.

9.   See the two variants in Hesiod's *Works and Days* 42–105 and his *Theogony* 570–612. The latter has the woman as the source of evil without the jar.

10.   For a discussion of the story, see Blundell, *The Origins*, pp. 9–10.

11.   Hesiod, *Works and Days* 106–201. The age of the heroes, placed between the Bronze and Iron Ages, is an obvious misfit. See T. G. Rosenmeyer, "Hesiod and Historiography (Erga 106–201)," *Hermes* 83 (1957), 257–285; also E. R. Dodds, *The Ancient Concept of Progress and Other Essays on Greek Literature and Belief* (1973), pp. 3–4; M. L. West, *Hesiod: Works and Days* (1978), pp. 172–177, and the works cited there.

12.   The earliest reference to the flood is in Pindar, *Olympia* 9.49ff. Here the remark about the flood, referred to as a new song of the Muses, clearly inter-rupts the account of Pyrrha and Deucalion and their offspring, the heroes of the race of Iapetos (Japheth). The relationship of this earlier level, without the flood, seems particularly close to the tradition reflected in the *Catalogue of Women* (see below, n. 18).

13.   More on this below.

14.   Cf. R. S. Hendel, "Of Demigods and the Deluge: Toward an Interpretation of Genesis 6:1–4," *JBL* 106 (1987), 13–26. I cannot agree with Hendel, who wants to date the coming of the flood tradition into Greece in the Late Bronze Age. Its awkward late association with Deucalion speaks against such a suggestion.

15.   Ovid, *Metamorphosis* 1.259–417; Lucian's account (*De Syria Dea* 12) seems heavily influenced by the biblical and Mesopotamian traditions directly. See R. A. Oden, *Studies in Lucian's De Syria Dea* (1977), pp. 24–36.

16.   Apollodorus, *Bibliotheca* 1.7.2.

17.   See Ovid, *Metamorphosis* 1.125ff. Ovid omits any mention of the heroic age. E. G. Kraeling ("Xisouthros, Deucalion and the Flood Traditions," *JAOS* 67 [1944], 183) is in error when he suggests that Ovid places the flood after the Bronze Age.

18.   M. L. West, *The Hesiodic Catalogue of Women: Its Nature, Structure, and Origins* (1985), pp. 55–56. This observation confirms the secondary character of the flood tradition in Pindar, *Olympia* 9.49ff.

19.   The version of the flood in Lucian's *De Syria Dea* 12 should not be considered as reflecting the Greek tradition. It is obviously dependent directly on the Babylonian and biblical sources as well as aspects of the local culture. See Oden, *Studies in Lucian's De Syria Dea,* pp. 24–36.

20.   I am somewhat hesitant in using the term *antiquarian* because it suggests a pursuit that was not quite serious. In fact, it was a subject that was taken very seriously both by those who wrote on these matters and by a rather large public. See the remarks by Polybius, *Histories* 9.1–2, and Plato, *Hippias Major* 285D.

21.   See A. Kleingunther, *Protos Heuretes,* in Supplement to *Philologus* 26, no. 1 (1933), 1–155; and K. Thrade, "Erfinder II," *Reallexikon für Antike und Christentum* (1950), vol. 5, pp. 1191–1278; "Das Lob des Erfinders," *Rheinisches Museum für Philologie* 105 (1962), 158–188. For a brief overview, see van Groningen, *In the Grip of the Past,* pp. 33–34; and Blundell, *The Origins,* pp. 169–171.

22.   See Dodds, *The Ancient Concept of Progress,* pp. 1–25. Note esp. Aeschylus, *Prometheus Bound* 442–506; and discussion by Kleingunther, *Protos Heuretes,* pp. 66–89.

23.   See Kleingunther, *Protos Heuretes,* pp. 43–65; Thrade, "Erfinder II," pp. 1204–1213.

24.   Pliny, *Natural History* 1.7.57–60. See A. O. Lovejoy and G. Boas, *Primitivism and Related Ideas in Antiquity* (1965), pp. 382–388.

25.   I am following the text and study of H. W. Attridge and R. A. Oden, *Philo of Byblos: The Phoenician History,* CBQ MS 9, 1981; see also A. I. Baumgarten, *The Phoenician History of Philo of Byblos: A Commentary,* 1981; and J. Ebach, *Weltentstehung und Kulturentwicklung bei Philo von Byblos,* BWANT 108, 1979 (with a subtitle, "Ein Beitrag zur Überlieferung der biblischen Urgeschichte im Rahmen des altorientalischen und antiken Schöpfungsglaubens," which indicates its special relevance for this study); and my earlier remarks in *In Search of History,* pp. 205–208. The works of Attridge and Oden, Baumgarten, and Ebach have extensive bibliographies.

26.   See the remarks by Attridge and Oden, *Philo of Byblos,* pp. 3–9; Baumgarten, *The Phoenician History,* pp. 38–39; and Ebach, *Weltentstehung,* pp. 393–408.

27. See Baumgarten, *The Phoenician History*, pp. 146–148; cf. Ebach, *Weltentstehung*, pp. 109–115.
28. See esp. Ebach, *Weltentstehung*, pp. 266–270.
29. As Baumgarten does in *The Phoenician History*, p. 140.
30. See Hallo, "Antediluvian Cities," *JCS* 23:62–64; Wilson, *Genealogy and History*, pp. 149–152; and Ebach, *Weltentstehung*, pp. 335–375.
31. I will return to the details below.
32. See the wok of F. Jacoby, *Die Fragmente der griechischen Historiker*, 1923–1958.
33. Rosenmeyer, *Hermes* 83:260.
34. O. Gigon, *Der Ursprung der griechischen Philosophie* (1945), pp. 22–23.
35. This is the only race that is described as ending in this way. What form the wrath of Zeus took is not stated.
36. Yet the account does seem to presuppose the *Theogony* in which the age of Kronos was succeeded by that of Zeus as the transition between the first two races.
37. Ovid simply omitted it.
38. F. Solmsen, *Hesiod and Aeschylus* (1949), p. 86. It might be useful to compare Hesiod with J in the use of the mythological traditions for "wisdom" purposes, both in the story of Pandora and in the story of the five races.
39. W. G. Lambert and P. Walcot, "A New Babylonian Theogony and Hesiod," *Kadmos* 4 (1965), 64–72.
40. Note that Ovid places the struggle against the giants after the four races, a very awkward fit.
41. G. S. Kirk, "The Structure and Aim of the Theogony," *Fondation Hardt pour l'étude de l'antiquité classique* 7 (1962), 93.
42. Ibid., p. 94.
43. See ibid., pp. 63ff., on the problem of additions.
44. It was quoted as such by Hecataeus of Miletus.
45. The discussion that follows is particularly indebted to the recent work of West, *Hesiodic Catalogue of Women*.
46. Ibid., p. 3.
47. Ibid., pp. 137f.
48. See ibid., pp. 6–7. In the past, scholars have not made much of the *Catalogue* in their explanations of the origins of Greek historiography. However, it will certainly deserve more comment in the future. For the present, see Thomas, *Oral Tradition and Written Record*, pp. 173–195; also F. Hartog, "Écriture, généalogies, archives, histoire en Grèce ancienne," in *Histoire et conscience historique dans les civilizations du Proche-Orient ancien*, ed. A. de Pury (1989), pp. 122–125.
49. See my earlier discussion in *In Search of History*, pp. 8–18, with literature cited there. In particular, see K. von Fritz, *Die griechische Geschichtsschreibung*, vol. 1, 1967; L. Pearson, *The Early Ionian Historians*, 1939; and C. W. Fornara, *The Nature of History in Ancient Greece and Rome* (1983), pp. 4–12; also Thomas in n. 48 above.
50. West, *Hesiodic Catalogue of Women*, p. 6.
51. Pearson, *Early Ionian Historians*, pp. 170f.
52. So von Fritz, *Geschichtsschreibung*, p. 83; cf. West, *Hesiodic Catalogue of Women*, p. 6.
53. On the nature of the work, see F. Jacoby, "The First Athenian Prose Writer,"

in *Abhandlungen zur griechischen Geschichtsschreibung von Felix Jacoby* (1956), pp. 100–143.

54. See esp. the discussion of Thomas, *Oral Tradition and Written Record,* pp. 161–167. Note her statement (p. 173): "The construction of a genealogy from an Homeric hero to the recent day was not simply a matter of writing down the oral traditions as they were remembered, nor even a matter of synthesis. It involved manipulation, adding new generations, filling in gaps in the family tradition, incorporating ancestors who were remembered in a vacuum." This is an apt description of the work of ancient antiquarian historians. See also von Fritz, *Geschichtsschreibung,* p. 86.

55. See also Jacoby, "The First Athenian Prose Writer," pp. 124, 126 n. 82.

56. Von Fritz distinguishes two different works in geography: a map of the world (*Periodos Ges*) and a descriptive geography (*Periegesis Ges*). Others regard it as the same work.

57. For an extensive discussion of the fragments, see Pearson, *Early Ionian Historians,* pp. 25–106; see also von Fritz, *Geschichtsschreibung,* pp. 48–76.

58. See West, *Hesiodic Catalogue of Women,* p. 136.

59. On the preface to his *Genealogies,* see Thomas, *Oral Tradition and Written Record,* pp. 183–184; Fornara, *The Nature of History,* pp. 5–7; and Hartog, "Écriture, généalogies, . . . ," pp. 125–127.

60. Von Fritz (*Geschichtsschreibung,* p. 66) interprets the prologue to mean that he rationalized the fabulous elements in the accounts of the heroic exploits. However, there is very little evidence of such an outlook.

61. Pearson, *Early Ionian Historians,* p. 30.

62. See ibid., pp. 152–235; von Fritz, *Geschichtsschreibung,* pp. 476–522.

63. West, *Hesiodic Catalogue of Women,* p. 7. It may be necessary to correct Pearson's view (*Early Ionian Historians,* pp. 170–171) that the two works *Phoronis* and *Deucalioneia* represent a chronological sequence, the first dealing with the first mortal and the beginnings of human life, and the second beginning with the flood and subsequent generations. In fact, the two genealogical lines of Phoroneus and Deucalion were parallel, as the *Catalogue* shows, and never viewed as sequential.

64. Hence the great difficulty in determining from the extant fragments just how many works Hellanicus actually wrote.

65. Pearson, *Local Historians,* pp. 1–26; Jacoby, *Atthis.*

66. Pearson, *Local Historians,* p. 7.

67. Ibid., p. 8.

68. Ibid., pp. 8–12.

69. Ibid., pp. 18f.

70. Ibid., pp. 15–17.

71. Ibid., p. 20.

72. Ibid., p. 24. See also the study of Thomas, *Oral Tradition and Written Record,* as a general discussion of this problem.

73. See Jacoby, *Atthis,* pp. 169–176; von Fritz, *Geschichtsschreibung,* pp. 496ff.

74. Pearson, *Local Historians,* p. 146.

75. Ibid., p. 163.

76. An exception might be the genealogy of the Old Babylonian dynasty, which begins with a series of tribal names. See J. J. Finkelstein, "The Genealogy of the Hammurapi Dynasty," *JCS* 20 (1966), 95–118; Wilson, *Genealogy and History*, pp. 107–114. This was subsequently absorbed into the Assyrian King List. See Van Seters, *In Search of History*, pp. 74–76. The Hammurapi dynasty genealogy is often viewed as "western" in form and origin.

77. Hartog, "Écriture, généalogies, . . . ," p. 128.

78. Plato, *Hippias Major* 285D.

79. A. Momigliano, "Ancient History and the Antiquarian," in *Studies in Historiography* (1966), pp. 1–39.

80. As we have seen above in the discussion of the theme of "first inventors."

81. Polybius, *Histories* 9.2.

82. A. Momigliano, "History and Biography," in *The Legacy of Greece*, ed. M. I. Finley (1981), p. 174.

83. Compare the prologue to Josephus's *Antiquity of the Jews*. It is clear that Josephus modeled his work after that of Dionysius. See Momigliano, "History and Biography," p. 174.

PART TWO

Primeval History
of the Yahwist

5

THE STORY
OF PARADISE

The account of the creation of man and woman and their
life in paradise until their expulsion through disobedience in Gen.
2:4b–3:24 has been the subject of extended literary-critical discussion, much of which bears directly upon the nature of the Yahwistic
work. A review of some of the important issues in this discussion
and the direction of current study is desirable.

Biblical scholarship has identified a number of problems or
tensions within the text of Genesis 2–3 that have given rise to questions of unity or diversity of authorship and/or traditions and
themes behind the present form of the text. Although the list of
such problems may vary somewhat from scholar to scholar, there
are a number that consistently remain the focus of attention and
call for some kind of explanation. These may be set forth in rather
brief compass.

1. First, on the limits of the text there is rather widespread
agreement about the beginning of the paradise story and that of
the Yahwist's work as a whole in Gen. 2:4b: "On the day when
Yahweh God created the earth and the heavens . . ." This represents
a clear introductory statement that sets it off from the previous
account of creation in Gen. 1:1–2:4a. With chapter 4 there is a new
story, and even though there are enough elements in common with
chapters 2–3 that it is generally attributed to the same author, most
scholars do not include it within the discussion of Genesis 2–3.[1]

2. The major difficulty that has stimulated the discussion of
the story's unity has been the presence of doublets and repetition.
Among these is the mention of two special trees in 2:9, both of
which are presumably in the middle of the garden. The "tree of

107

life" is referred to only here and at the end of the story, 3:22, whereas the "tree of knowledge of good and evil" takes on a central role in the story in 2:17 and in 3:1ff. There are two apparent endings, the one having to do with a curse on the nature of man's and woman's life in the world (3:16–19), and the other, their expulsion from the garden (3:22–24). There are two different statements about the expulsion set down side by side (3:22, 24). There is some difference in the terminology used about the garden and man's role in the garden, and repetition about his being placed within it (2:8, 15). There is also the double mention of clothing (3:7, 22). Such doublets have encouraged attempts to identify two separate literary accounts throughout, but such source analysis has not been very convincing.

3. Likewise remarkable for this story is the use of the compound designation for deity: Yahweh God. Because the use of the divine name *Yahweh* or the generic term *Elohim* has been so important for source analysis, some scholars have argued that this designation points to the combination of two relatively fixed and similar sources. But this argument is considerably weakened by the fact that such alleged combinations of J and E elsewhere in the Pentateuch have not produced the same compound designation for deity. So it is more likely that the compound is a deliberate use by one author (or redactor).[2]

4. There are also certain elements in tension within the story that must be accounted for. The prohibition against eating the forbidden fruit is given to the man before the creation of the animals and the woman, and yet both the snake and the woman know of it in 3:1ff. Furthermore, the threat of capital punishment does not seem to correspond with the final judgment given. Related to this problem is the interpretation of the phrase "knowledge of good and evil," which bears on the kind of story being told and therefore the expectations of the reader/audience.

5. Likewise at issue are the narrative structures within the story and the extent to which they may point to, or support, the idea of a plurality of themes or traditions behind the present story, specifically, a creation account and a paradise story. Important in this regard is the role of etiology in 2:24 and 3:14–19 as it relates to such possible preliterary traditions.

6. The character of the "little geography" in 2:10–14 as an

erudite digression or supplement is widely recognized, but how it is related to the work of the Yahwist and the unit as a whole is not clear and has called forth a variety of answers. This also concerns the question of the work's form.

7. How much can comparative material help in uncovering the traditions behind the text? Perhaps nowhere else is there a greater temptation toward fanciful constructions than in the case of Genesis 2–3 in the absence of external accounts that are comparable to the biblical story.

Approaches to the Problem of Literary Unity

A common and long-standing approach to the problems enumerated above is to divide the material in Genesis 2–3 into two or more sources. This is the approach of the influential study of K. Budde in the tradition of Wellhausen and continued by many scholars with considerable variation in the source division down to such recent studies as H. Haag, W. Fuss, and J. Scharbert.[3] Alongside of the source analysis, H. Gunkel introduced the principles of tradition-history which proposed that behind the literary sources of the text was a diversity of traditions, principally a creation tradition and a paradise tradition.[4] J. Begrich built on the traditio-historical approach of Gunkel by deemphasizing the source division (a major strand and a very fragmentary secondary narrative) and put most of the emphasis upon the long process of tradition development behind the literary form. Most of the tensions and contradictions are to be explained in this way.[5]

There has been a fairly strong tendency since Begrich to move away from any source division on the literary level and even to emphasize the literary unity of Genesis 2–3. At the same time, the doublets, points of tension, and other problems of the text have been attributed to the preliterary traditio-historical growth of the tradition.[6] Rather than engage in an extensive review of the many works on the subject, I will focus attention primarily on three scholars: C. Westermann, O. H. Steck, and E. Kutsch.[7]

Westermann stands in the scholarly tradition of Gunkel and Begrich, with his emphasis upon the form-critical and traditio-historical approach. Although he accepts the more recent scholarship that emphasizes the unity of the J account, he argues that the story structure reveals a diversity of tradition used by this author. The tradition that is basic to the whole is the story of the Fall, which, he says, "begins with the command that God gives to his human creatures, and ascends to a climax with the transgression of the command. It then descends from the climax to the consequences of the transgression — the discovery, the trial and the punishment. The conclusion, the expulsion from the garden where God has put the man and woman, calls to mind again the beginning. There is a well-rounded, clear and polished chain of events."[8] Westermann then argues that there are some elements not essential to this story structure that may be isolated and form a complete whole in themselves, for example, 2:4b–8, 18–24, which has its own narrative structure. This structure he compares to that of a workman who, by various attempts or stages, brings his work to completion. Westermann further attempts to support his proposal of two different narrative structures by additional arguments concerning style and manner of presentation.

There are some serious problems with Westermann's separation of the two traditions. These problems surface when one notices the rather loose correspondence that his supposed structures have to the actual text. In the first place, the introduction of 2:4b–6, which indicates the conditions of the cosmos before humanity's creation, clearly seems to anticipate more than just the creation of man and woman. The statement "there was no man to till the ground" suggests the final outcome of man's cultivation of the ground at the end of the paradise story. The lack of vegetation seems to correspond more closely with the statement in v. 9 than in v. 8, and the statement about the subterranean water source in v. 6 also suggests the origin of the river in Eden in v. 10.[9] It also seems rather forced to argue, as Westermann does, that the garden in v. 8 is not paradise but only the location where man is placed and sustained. It hardly represents man's normal condition of life.

The most serious weakness of this reconstruction is Westermann's tendency to follow earlier commentators since Gunkel in identifying the etiological statement of 2:24 as a conclusion to an old tradition. (The fact is that he does not do this in the case of the paradise story with the etiologies of 3:14–19.) Because the family situation reflected in 2:24 does not correspond to the description of the primal pair in the preceding verses, and because the point of the narrative by Westermann's own description is not the origin of love,[10] one must regard 2:24 as a kind of etiological digression or parenthesis.[11] In such a case, v. 25 would naturally follow after v. 23 and lead directly into the following scene.

Furthermore, Westermann does not make a convincing case for the independence of a paradise story that begins with 2:9, 15ff. It is not so easy to attribute all the cross-references between the creation tradition and the paradise story to the redactional process that combined the two. The most serious of these problems is to account for the principal figures, the man/Adam, his wife, and even the snake as one of the animals that Yahweh had made. In most of the previous attempts to identify an earlier paradise tradition, scholars have felt compelled to include some of the material from the creation of man account as part of the paradise story.[12] Westermann is also convinced that the narrative structure that he has discovered, that of the crime-punishment pattern, is evidence for the story's original independence because it recurs throughout the primeval history. But it would seem to me to be much stronger evidence in the opposite direction, as a pattern imposed on the traditional material by the author of the whole because the pattern is not characteristic of any comparative materials dealing with the primeval period.

Westermann reflects some ambiguity about the relationship of the Yahwist to his sources and his creativity. He has considerable difficulty in distinguishing exactly what, in the text, belonged to the older stories and what is an addition by J. He is reluctant to attribute any elaboration to the latter. He states:

> J's art consists rather in this: he made a selection from the many traditional stories about humanity in primal time, chose those passages that suited his story, and fitted them together in such a way as to give the impression of a perfect whole. This view of the origin of Genesis 2–3 gives a simple and natural answer to the difficulties exegetes have found there.[13]

The solution may be satisfying to Westermann as a theoretical possibility, but it is only an artificial construct that has nothing by way of comparative example to commend it. The process he describes suggests the conflation of *written* texts, not oral traditions, and no such texts as he construes them have survived. Rather than speculate about "many traditional stories" that we do not have, it would seem preferable to compare the J account with those texts that we do have and try to make an assessment on J's art and creativity from that comparison.

O. H. Steck follows in the line of Gunkel and Westermann but with a stronger emphasis on the literary unity and creativity of the Yahwist. He asserts that none of the problems and tensions in the text of Genesis 2–3 can be attributed to a division of sources, an approach that through frequent trial and error has become largely bankrupt. The only possibility for him is to explain such tensions in the text as reflecting the preliterary history of the tradition used by the Yahwist in his work.[14]

From this position Steck sets out to show, first, how every part of 2:4b–25 is closely tied to the rest of the story in chapter 3. Thus the introductory words of creation — or what had not yet come into being — and the creation of man, 2:4bf., 7 find their completion in the goal of the story in 3:17–19, 23, even in the use of the same terminology. At the same time, these natural Palestinian conditions of the need for rain and the cultivation of the land by the farmer contrast with the paradise watered by a spring and in which man is set as gardener.

The piece of geographic digression in 2:10–14 is considered by Steck as a piece of older lore that the Yahwist has skillfully worked into his text by the framework of 2:9 and 2:15. He also interprets 2:8 as exhibiting the same kind of geographic interest, with its location of the garden *in* Eden in the east.[15]

The function of 2:16–17 as an anticipation of the story in chapter 3 is widely recognized because it is essential to the paradise story (though some have argued that it anticipates too much and is anticlimactic, at least in its present form). The matter of 2:18–24, however, is much more controversial. Yet Steck insists that it not only creates the necessary background for chapter 3 (cf. 3:1 with 2:19 and 3:12 with 2:20ff.) in explaining the characters of the snake and the woman, but it also establishes a contrast between man, who acts in consort with the deity, and the human pair, who act outside of the deity's will.[16] The violation of the divine command changes the relationship between the sexes and even between the humans and the animals (3:14–16). The notice about nakedness in 2:25, which is part of the innocent delight of the woman's creation in 2:23, contrasts with the clothing scenes in 3:7ff., 21.

Steck concludes this part of his analysis by stating that on the literary level Genesis 2–3 manifests a deliberately constructed narrative throughout in which the Yahwist played a major role in its formation. At the same time, he asserts that the kinds of problems in the text outlined above cannot be entirely dismissed and must be clarified not on the literary level but by means of tradition-history.

Steck interprets the traditio-historical task as that which is related entirely to the oral prehistory, the stage through which the story passes up to the point of its being fixed in writing.[17] He regards as possible a certain degree of flexibility at the oral stage in the way it makes combinations or is limited by other stories and story elements. The traditio-historical task looks specifically for those points of tension or differences of content even in a unified literary work to unravel its previous pieces, and then to explain their synthetic combination.

The basic question since Gunkel is to identify how many different individual stories and how many stages preceded the work of the Yahwist. Steck can distinguish only one older paradise story[18] and expresses great caution in trying to reconstruct its content. The closest comparison he can find is that of Ezek. 28:12ff., which still has many differences, suggesting the range of variation possible in the tradition. The other clue that he depends upon heavily is the fact that in 3:22–24 only the man is mentioned as expelled from the garden, so the woman and the snake belong to another tradition or level in the story's formation.

Without attempting to reconstruct the early paradise story (Pg) from specific language or verses of the text of Genesis 2–3, Steck outlines its basic elements as consisting of the following:

1. A description of paradise as the garden of God, called Eden, in which was an exceptional tree in the midst of the garden. This tree played an important role in the story. The garden also had a guardian.

2. The man was commanded not to eat of the tree (there was no threat of death), and in violation of this command he alone was expelled. This man was also the first one created by God.

Nothing else can with certainty be attributed to this level of the tradition. It is possible that there was a temptation and an interrogation scene involving only man, but if so it did not include the snake. The latter is lacking from Ezekiel 28. Concerning the trees, Steck considers the "tree of life" as a later addition, following earlier scholars, and thus the "tree of knowledge" to be the original one.[19]

Steck does not consider it at all likely that a separate creation tradition can be constructed that was independent from the present material in the paradise narrative (Pe). Nor can one reconstruct a parallel preliterary paradise story. Although some older material existed alongside of Pg, it did not consist of additional story units. Steck concludes: "This means that the extant paradise narrative was constructed by the Yahwist himself using Pg and numerous individual pieces of information."[20] The Yahwist expanded and reworked one story that was handed down to him according to his own understanding and in keeping with his much larger treatment of the primeval history.

This represents a rather major shift in the whole notion of tradition-history, because Steck seems to ascribe to the earliest literary stage the most extensive and most definitive role in the formation of the tradition. The Yahwist is permitted to deal directly with a considerable variety of traditional materials, whether they are in story form or not, in order to construct his own narrative. The Yahwist is not merely a collector but an author and composer of some magnitude.[21] This also seems to go considerably beyond Westermann in the degree of literary creativity attributed to J.

E. Kutsch, in his study of Genesis 2–3,[22] likewise raises the question, To what extent is the Yahwist dependent upon a diversity of previously given themes and sources and to what extent are the various elements of the narrative his own creation? This question Kutsch sees as arising out of the great variety of scholarly opinion about such sources and their pre-Yahwistic form.

Kutsch first of all identifies the "little geography" of 2:10–14 as secondary to the larger context, basing his judgment largely on the tension between an Eden in the east (v. 8) and the river's sources in the north. Yet the vagueness of the geography reflected in 2:10–14 hardly makes that argument very cogent. To exclude it would also mean that 2:15 is secondary as a repetition of 2:8 to incorporate the digression. In addition, v. 6 with the reference to the source of the water (*'ēd*) for the river in Eden becomes suspect on this basis, even though it seems most appropriate to the primeval scene. With Steck I would argue for the retention of 2:10–14 in the Yahwist's work.

Kutsch next turns to the problem of the double ending in 3:23//3:22b, 24 and their relationship to the "tree of life," as well as the reference in 2:9b to the two trees "in the midst of the garden." He rules out as quite unlikely any attempt to construct two parallel stories with the two trees as the essential difference between them. Kutsch further argues that 3:22–24 is a grammatical unity, because the object of the verb *wayyᵉšallᵉhēhu* in v. 23 is the *hā'ādām* of v. 22, and the unstated subject of the verbs in v. 24 is Yahweh Elohim of v. 23. It is true that on the traditio-historical level the two statements on expulsion relate to two different ideas that are set down side by side in Hebrew using the *waw* consecutive imperfects, the one relating to the tilling of the ground as in the curse (3:17–19) and the other to the tree of life. If the second statement were rendered in translation by temporal subordination ("and when he had driven out the man, he set the cherubim . . . ,"), this would eliminate the doublets.

Instead of the story ending pointing to two parallel versions, Kutsch suggests that the narrator felt the need to accommodate in his story a motif about a "tree of life" in paradise. Such a mythological motif of a plant or tree of life is widespread in other cultures and mentioned in the Old Testament in Prov. 13:12b, 15:4a, and 3:18a in a metaphoric, "demythologized" form. So the tree of life is not original with the Yahwist.

Concerning the "tree of knowledge," Kutsch does not find that its mention in 2:7 and 2:17 militates against the development of the story in 3:1ff. but is a necessary anticipation. In contrast to the tree of life, the tree of knowledge of good and evil is not something derived from the surrounding world of ideas. Yet it is so central to J's message and perspective that it must be his own invention. It is precisely for this reason that it gave rise to some confusion with the received tradition of the tree of life.[23]

According to Kutsch, the motif of the "garden" must belong to both trees. For the tree of knowledge this is obvious, but it is equally clear that the tree of life could only exist in a land of the gods guarded by divine beings, as in 3:24. Sacred gardens with special trees are well attested in the Near Eastern world of the

Yahwist's day.[24] The Old Testament also mentions Eden, the garden of God in Gen. 13:10 and in late prophetic texts: Isa. 51:3; Ezek. 31:9, 16, 18; 36:35; 28:13; Joel 2:3. The idea of an expulsion from the garden or mountain of God is given in the prophecy of the king of Tyre in Ezek. 28:12ff., but it is difficult to extract any more helpful details.[25]

Because the paradise story is about the first human pair, the introductory material answers the question of where they came from, their creation. Man first (v. 7) and then his wife (v. 18, 21f.) as well as the animals and birds are created. Into this is woven the references to the garden, the trees, and the prohibition, but it is still a unity. Kutsch rejects any attempt to construct from the creation verses a separate account ending in the etiology of v. 24, which he regards as only a digression.[26] Following Steck's argument that the statement in 2:5, "there was no man to till the ground," makes a connection with 3:17, 19, 23b, Kutsch takes the unit 2:4b–5, 7, 18–23(24), as reflecting the formulation of J and not a prior tradition.

It is commonly noted that the form in which the beginning is described as the time when certain features of life "were not yet present" is a manner of speaking common to Near Eastern accounts of beginnings.[27] In the Old Testament, it is given a specific Palestinian flavor.[28] Kutsch further observes, however, that the Mesopotamian texts speak of people being created in various numbers but never as a primal pair, so that the myths reflect a first generation. This is also the case for the Greek myths.[29] Thus there is no known parallel in antiquity to the Yahwist's creation of the first pair.[30] The purpose of the creation of humans in Mesopotamian myths is in order to serve the gods with physical labor and thus provide for them. In Genesis, the task of man is stated at the outset, to work the ground, but this only comes about at the end of the story when man is expelled from the garden.[31] This explanation of how man's labor came about is an innovation in the Near East and therefore part of J's creativity.

Kutsch argues that the creation account cannot stand alone but only makes sense in the context of the paradise story. Because J created the latter, he also made the introduction with man's creation to fit with it, without the need of drawing material from a specific tradition.[32] Kutsch concludes from this that J did not have

before him in a prearranged form any part of the entire complex—
neither a creation story nor a paradise narrative. What he had were
certain motifs such as the tree of life and the garden. The Yahwist
invented the tree of the knowledge of good and evil, by analogy
with the tree of life, as his way of conceiving and forming the story
of the Fall. For this the author had no *Vorlage.* The garden provided
the scenery and locus for the action, and the tree of life the motivation for expulsion from paradise to normal life and an explanation of why man cannot live forever.[33]

From this survey of past literary study of Genesis 2–3 we may
conclude that the curious combination of creation and paradise
themes in this text is not the result of a conflation of literary
sources. Nor is it the result of a tradition-history in the preliterary
stage of development in which different narratives about creation
and paradise have been combined to produce the present unified
story. This still leaves open for consideration the important matter
of genre of Genesis 2–3 and the implications that this question
has for both the literary unity and tradition-history of the work.

The Problem of Genre

As long as scholars were content to see in Genesis 2–3 a combination of older traditions, they tended to identify the etiological
statements in 2:24 and 3:14–19 as the conclusion to etiological
myths having to do with creation and the fall from paradise respectively. The present text was merely a collection or combination
of such earlier forms, partly through the process of tradition growth
and partly the result of literary activity. Once such a tradition-
history has been seriously called into question, as in the work of
Steck and Kutsch, these genre identifications are no longer
adequate.

Among the recent commentators, Steck has given particular
attention to the question of the *Gattung* of Genesis 2–3.[34] On the
literary level, he recognizes it as part of the larger Yahwistic history,
but the more decisive form-critical question for him is the *Gattung*
of this particular story unit. His conclusion is that it is etiological,
not because it manifests the precise formulas that are often found
with etiological narratives, but because the intention of the whole
story is etiological from its opening statement to its conclusion,

which is to account for the rigorous way of life of the Palestinian peasant and, by extension, that of the rest of humanity. This etiological story is presented with all the narrative characteristics of legend (*Sage*) even in its present literary form.

This conclusion of Steck is surprising in one respect in that it no longer identifies as etiological the preliterary form of the early paradise story (Pg). The etiological legend is entirely the product of the Yahwist's literary creativity.[35] Alongside of the Yahwist's etiological explanation for the origins of agriculture, love and marriage, and the names and classification of animals, is J's interest in geography and in the problems of the tension between wisdom and religion. The Yahwist also deals with this last item by means of etiology with his new myth of the tree of the knowledge of good and evil. This etiology of morality—the development of certain mental states characterized as a "likeness to divinity"—in combination with other etiologies and concerns about origins must be addressed by the question of genre. It is doubtful if that can be done without taking into consideration the larger work of the Yahwist.[36]

Recently, G. W. Coats has attempted to identify Genesis 2–3 as a "tale" within the larger work of the Yahwist's primeval "saga."[37] Whether the designation "saga" for the larger work of the Yahwist is appropriate will be considered later. But the description of Genesis 2–3 as a simple tale is hardly adequate. In the case of a tale, one would expect that the "arc of tension" created by the death threat would be realized at the end, but it is not, and there is no special intervention to prevent it. The story gives way in the end to entirely different concerns.

Another recent work that raises the question of genre is that of H. N. Wallace in which the whole of the J source is interpreted as "traditional literature."[38] This means that it was not primarily the creation of J but the "property or creation . . . of the cultural community in its historical perspective."[39] Thus for Wallace the antecedents of J are oral sources that were "epic" in nature. The witness to this is in the presence of formulaic or poetic language in J, which is thought to reflect the epic original.[40] Although this view of the work's genre relates to J as a whole, its relevance to Genesis 2–3 is to interpret the seams and inconsistencies as "marks of an oral style rather than indicators of reworking and editing."[41]

The question of genre, whether of J as a whole or the unit in particular, seems to rest heavily upon one's understanding of the nature of the traditional material used by the Yahwist in his work. This applies both to the possible foreign influences and the native Israelite tradition, especially as it is preserved in written records.

Tradition-History of Genesis 2–3

There are two ways of approaching the question of the traditional material in Genesis 2–3. The one method is to regard all traditional motifs wherever they might be found in the Bible or comparative literature synchronically as quite undatable and therefore part of an ancient reservoir from which a "tradent" drew his particular stock. This is the method of Wallace and allows for his understanding of the work of J as "traditional literature" and of J's relationship to his "sources." The other method is to view the tradition diachronically in an effort to construct a history of the tradition and to find the Yahwist's place within that historical development. The relationship of the traditional elements in J to particular parallels in written and datable works becomes of primary importance for the understanding of J and his place in Israelite thought and religion as a whole. It is the latter method that will be followed here.

Ezekiel 28

The most important comparative material for trying to reconstruct the history of the tradition of Genesis 2–3 is the oracle against Tyre in Ezek. 28:12–19.[42] Already Gunkel had suggested that the myth behind Ezekiel 28 was older than the Genesis 2–3 account, which represented a somewhat "demythologized" version of the other.[43] The account in Ezekiel 28 presents us with a person who was a special creation by the deity, "the signet of perfection, full of wisdom, and perfect in beauty" (v. 12).[44] The figure was given royal honors, including special vestments with jeweled pectoral or breastplate. The abode of this person was in Eden, the garden of God, on the holy mountain in the company of a guardian cherub and among the mysterious "stones of fire" (minor deities?). He was blameless until sin was discovered in him, that of hubris because of his beauty and wisdom. The consequence of this discovery is expulsion from paradise.[45]

It has been tempting for some scholars to expand greatly on this base in Ezek. 28:12–19 by the association of other texts and themes with it, but this may not be entirely legitimate. The oracle in 28:2–10 is an obvious example of this, because it is easy to see some similarity in the description of the king's wisdom, which leads to hubris and his downfall and destruction. But M. H. Pope has made the case that behind this oracle lies the myth of the fallen god El.[46] Such an association is quite a different one from the creation myth of 28:12–19.

That the figure in Ezek 28:12–19 represents the primeval, and therefore prototypical, king is very likely. But there is nothing in this oracle to suggest that he is divine or that he is the first man (*Urmensch*). The myth used by Ezekiel could have represented an etiology for royalty, but nothing in it suggests that it has to do with humanity in general. It is also not clear that the original myth included the notion of sin and a fall or expulsion from paradise. The discussion of this text as a means of reconstructing the original myth of the primordial king in paradise has engendered considerable literature.[47] There is, however, a text from the eastern antiquarian tradition that may be helpful here.

Earlier, in the discussion of Mesopotamian mythological texts, we mentioned a recently published Neo-Babylonian text that told of the creation of the king alongside of, and distinct from, the rest of humankind.[48] At his creation, the king was endowed with all the appropriate attributes of royalty, as well as the regalia of kingship. In this respect, the myth corresponds rather closely to the statements about the creation of the king in Ezek. 28:12–19. It is quite significant that Ezekiel 28 includes references to both the royal qualities of wisdom and beauty as well as the king's regalia, given to the king at his creation, just as we have it in the Babylonian myth. This makes it most probable that Ezekiel is dependent upon the Babylonian tradition.

The Babylonian myth, however, says nothing about the primeval iniquity or fall of the king from favor. That would go entirely counter to the royal ideology, which the text clearly supports. Nor is anything said about a setting in paradise. Instead, the purpose of the king's creation in the Babylonian myth is to rule the mass of humanity that the gods have previously created. Yet it may be pointed out that in the Babylonian New Year's festival, during which the kingship was renewed, the king had to lay aside his insignia and make a negative confession of sin in the presence of the high priest before he could continue in office.[49] Furthermore, the Babylonian kings had great royal pleasure gardens often resembling mountains, as in the case of Nebuchadrezzar's "hanging gardens," planted with many exotic and fruit-bearing trees from Syria.[50] So it is easy to see how all these ideas could be closely associated from their Babylonian sources.

In his oracle, Ezekiel has combined the myth of the king's creation with the notion about his primordial abode on the divine mountain, represented as a pleasure garden,[51] and the theme of the king's humiliation because of sin. However, there is no evidence of a myth that tells about the expulsion of some primeval being from paradise.[52] This must be explained as Ezekiel's own introduction of a prophetic theme of judgment into the picture, namely, the hubris of kings and nations that leads to their downfall.[53] This theme, cast back into primordial times, creates an antiroyal ideology, suggesting that hubris is the fatal flaw of all kings. Note that precisely at this point Ezekiel shifts from primeval time to talk about the present reality of Tyre's trade, its humiliation before other kings, and the destruction of the city. This is a prophetic transformation of the myth of royalty.

The comparison of Genesis 2–3 with the mythical background of the Ezekiel oracle is significant not only for its similarities but also for its transformations. It is a mistake to try to derive both accounts from a common original. The similarities lie in the fact that in both cases the created being is placed in Eden, the garden of God from which he is expelled after his sin is discovered. As suggested above, this scenario seems to be Ezekiel's own invention, which was taken over by the Yahwist. However, the royal figure of Ezekiel has been transformed by J into the first male human. He has lost all aspects of royalty in Genesis[54] and has become the male member of the first couple. He does not have royal vestments, but he and his wife are naked and clothed by the deity only when they are expelled from the garden.[55] They do not have wisdom until after they disobey the divine command and eat the fruit, and this is not presented as an act of hubris so much as the result of youthful curiosity.[56] The sin itself and its discovery are greatly expanded as a story element in the Genesis account.

It is important to notice that in two important respects the Genesis 2–3 account also resembles the quite separate oracle of Ezek. 28:2–10. The first is in the close association of wisdom with deity. It is on the basis of his wisdom that the king of Tyre makes his claim to divinity. That seems to correspond closely with the fact that the fruit of the tree of knowledge gives the human pair in Genesis a likeness to deity. At the same time, this claim to wisdom in Ezekiel brings with it the judgment of death, which is a negation of the king's divinity. In Genesis, the judgment of death is also associated with eating the fruit of the tree of knowledge, but it is only in the denial of the tree of life that this is carried out. Instead, the punishment of expulsion from the second Ezekiel oracle is used. This seems to be a case in which motifs from two different but closely juxtaposed oracles become the sources for motifs in the Genesis story, even though they cause some tension within the composition of the Yahwist.

In this way, the Yahwist has completely transformed the elements of myth from both Ezekiel oracles for his own purposes. The wisdom that led to sin has become the tree of the knowledge of good and evil and the occasion for disobedience. The royal figure now becomes humanity in general, represented by the first pair. The jeweled vestments are the clothing given after the Fall.[57] The cherub, which has no significance in the garden in Genesis, is retained in the expulsion scene as guardian of the tree of life. The death threat remains in Genesis but not its execution.

Other Foreign Traditions

The search to find Mesopotamian parallels for the Yahwist's creation account has usually focused on *Atrahasis* because of its antiquity and its combination of the creation of humankind with the flood story.[58] But few details from the *Atrahasis* account have any correspondence with the Genesis account. The suggestion that humankind was made to serve the gods may be reflected in Gen. 2:15, where the man is put in the garden of Eden "to till it and to keep it." Creation as an etiology of marriage is also suggested in both *Atrahasis* and Genesis. For the rest, however, the whole manner of presentation with the revolt of the gods and the slaying of a particular deity to provide the substance for human creation is missing from Genesis.

Because of these points of disjunction with *Atrahasis*, we ought, perhaps, to give more attention to later Mesopotamian tradition, especially the Neo-Assyrian and Neo-Babylonian texts of creation. We have noted a strong tendency for Ea and his son Marduk to become the creators, not only of humankind but also of the cosmos and the world order in general. The mother goddess may be called upon to assist the deity in the formation of humanity, as in the older tradition. But the theme of divine rivalry and the slaying of a god is not mentioned in these texts, either with respect to creation or to the flood.[59] The treatment of creation has become more comprehensive and more descriptive of a series of acts by the same deity.

The account of Marduk's creation (MC) deserves closer comparison with J's Genesis.[60] MC begins with a series of negative statements about what was not yet in existence, similar to the remarks in Gen. 2:5 about the time when there were no plants and no man to till the soil.[61] MC likewise speaks of all lands being sea but then mentions a spring (*inu*) of fresh water in the sea as the point at which creation begins; this seems to correspond with the water source (*'ēd*) in Gen. 2:6 that "watered the whole face of the ground."[62] At this point, MC mentions the foundation of the temple Esagila in Babylon before any other act of creation, which is not of any concern to J.[63] Marduk then creates humankind to serve the gods, an ancient theme, and this becomes the first act of creation in J, Gen. 2:7. The creation of humankind is followed in MC by a mixed series of creative acts having to do with animals, the Tigris and Euphrates, and vegetation, including herbs, grass, fruit trees, and forest. Genesis 2:8ff. also deals with these same items in a somewhat different order and arrangement, in keeping with its own story. MC returns to the theme of the building of cities and temples by Marduk in the Mesopotamian plain, at which point the text breaks off. For the Yahwist, these are the products of human culture and not part of his creation account.

Line 21 in MC, however, calls for further comment. As if to recognize an old tradition, MC follows the remark about Marduk's creation of humankind by the almost parenthetical statement: "The goddess Aruru created the seed of mankind together with him (i.e.

Marduk)," *daruru zēr amēlūti ittišu ibtanû*.[64] This recalls two statements in Genesis. In the first, Gen. 3:20: "The man called his wife's name Eve, because she was the mother of all living," it would appear that the concept of a mother goddess, responsible for the creation of humankind, has been "demythologized" in the figure of Eve.[65] This statement is also in the nature of a parenthetical digression having little connection with the larger account. The second statement, in 4:1b, seems directly related to the other. Eve, having given birth to Cain, makes the statement: "I have created a man together with Yahweh," *qānîtî 'îš 'et yhwh*.[66] When this statement is set beside that of MC, cited above, the meaning is obvious. The verb *qnh*, "create," can have the same sense as Babylonian *banu*. The object "man," *'îš*, is most curious in this birth notice but is here the direct equivalent of "seed of humankind," *zēr amēlūti*. Finally, the puzzling phrase "together with Yahweh" (*'et yhwh*) corresponds directly with the phrase in MC "together with him" (*ittišu*).

From these observations, it would appear that there is a direct literary relationship between the Genesis account and a form of the Babylonian tradition very similar to this late MC version of the creation myth. This can be seen in the fact that the greatest similarity between the two traditions is with the latest versions of the Babylonian myths and in the close linguistic usage, discussed above. In particular, the Yahwist has reinterpreted the part of the goddess in creation by identifying it with the role of the progenitress, the first mother, even to the point of trying to use the same terminology. This attempt at interpretation of an eastern mythical tradition is a kind of rationalization or "euhemerism" before its time.

Furthermore, the Yahwist in Genesis 2–3 has combined the theme of the creation of humankind derived from the late Babylonian tradition with the fall from paradise theme taken from Ezekiel's king in the garden of God (Ezekiel 28). As I have argued above, the paradise setting in Ezekiel 28 does not reflect a particular myth but only an elaboration of the myth about the creation of the king. So J's use of the paradise setting is derived from Ezekiel and not from a myth common to both. Since the expulsion because of sin in Ezekiel is limited to a single figure, the king, it has led to a corresponding modification of the Mesopotamian tradition whereby the creation of humankind as a larger population mass in the Mesopotamian tradition has become a single pair in Genesis.[67] Such a combination of creation and paradise themes in J from late Babylonian and prophetic sources can only mean that Genesis 2–3 is a rather late exilic text.

There is nothing, however, in this eastern tradition that would account for the separate creation of the woman in the Yahwist's story and her role in the downfall of humanity. For this we may find some clues in the western traditions. From the side of the Greek traditions, there is a certain similarity between the figure of Eve and that of Pandora in Hesiod.[68] Pandora is made by the gods as the first woman after man was already in existence and is brought as a gift. This is made the etiology of married life, on the one hand, and the beginning of trouble for the human race, on the other. If there is a connection between traditions, however, it is certainly very indirect.

The Phoenician tradition, reflected in Philo Byblius, suggests another possibility. Following his cosmogony, Philo gives an account of the first human pair, Aeon and Protogonos, who have been equated by some with Eve (*hawwa*) and Adam.[69] This, however, is disputed because both names in Philo are masculine. So it is usual to understand the pair as divine epithets that have been euhemerized.[70] It is said of Aeon that he discovered the nourishment of trees. This, in Philo, is the beginning of a "history of culture," and the fact that a similar history of culture follows in Genesis makes the connection between the first woman and the discovery of fruit an intriguing possibility.

It is, of course, methodologically unsound to try to reconstruct a common myth behind these western traditions and the biblical account. But there is sufficient similarity to suggest that in addition to those elements that we have identified as eastern there were likely some western traditions that may have been used, and it is from these traditio-historical ingredients that the Yahwist created his ingenious combination. At the same time, it left a number of points of unevenness in the account, which we have noted in our earlier discussion.

The Tree of the Knowledge of Good and Evil

If it is the case that this tree is the invention of the Yahwist to explain how it is that wisdom was the origin and cause of humanity's sin and fall, then this motif more than any other aspect of the story defines its genre. Its very centrality in the whole account has persuaded many scholars that it must derive from an earlier primitive myth, and this has often influenced its interpretation. The tree with its fruit is certainly an etiology of sorts, because it brings about a radical transformation in humankind from a primordial state to one in which humankind now exists. On the mythical level, this is in the pair's awareness of their state of nakedness. But this is peripheral to a change that cannot be observed, that is, that humankind is like divinity with respect to this new knowledge. That is a theological affirmation.

What is this knowledge of good and evil? We need not rehearse all the proposals put forward but will defend the view that it represents the ability to make judgments and decisions about what is right, appropriate, and pleasing for one's life and what is not, entirely from one's own wisdom and experience.[71] Over against this is the life of complete innocence and dependence upon the absolute command of religion concerning what is good for one's life. The author pits two ways of life or viewpoints against each other, that of wisdom embodied in the cunning snake, and that of religion represented by the divine command. The temptation is the dilemma of maturity, and the moment of enlightenment becomes also the moment of a sense of guilt and shame. Humanity becomes godlike in its freedom to choose its own destiny, a freedom taken by breaking the bounds of the divine command. It is this freedom and this ability to make choices for one's life that is the heart and substance of "wisdom."

Moreover, the command had to be stated in the most absolute terms, because it represents the religious demand upon one's life and thus provides the case for the snake (wisdom) against its claims.[72] The mitigation of the death sentence actually lies in the process of hearing the case of the defendants and of passing sentence accordingly. Because the snake also received a sentence as party to the crime, even though it did not eat the fruit, the fruit is not itself endowed with mythical powers.

N. Lohfink has drawn special attention to J's emphasis upon freedom of choice by making a comparison between the motif of the tree of life and a plant of life in the Gilgamesh Epic (XI, 263–289).[73] In the latter account, Gilgamesh is able to acquire with great difficulty and pain the plant of life only to have it stolen from him in an unguarded moment by a snake who eats it himself.[74] Lohfink observes that in both the Bible and the myth, humankind is deprived of the tree/plant of life by a snake. In the myth, the loss of the plant of life is entirely accidental and irrational, whereas in the Bible it is due to an act of humankind's freedom.

Whether or not Lohfink is justified in seeing in J's story a deliberate attempt to "demythologize" the myth by replacing the irrational or fatal element with the idea of humanity's freedom remains debatable. It may be noted that in Hesiod's myth of the origin of evil Pandora also seems to act in freedom. What Lohfink has not sufficiently accounted for is the complete shift from the "tree of life" to the "tree of the knowledge of good and evil," which makes Gilgamesh's quest for eternal life quite different from the temptation for knowledge and less likely that J is directly addressing the issue of the myth.

Furthermore, Lohfink seeks to find the origin for this under-standing of the relationship between sin/evil and freedom in the notion of covenant. The basic elements of this covenant theology are these:[75]

1. Yahweh found/created/chose Israel outside of Canaan.
2. Yahweh brought Israel into a wonderful land.
3. Yahweh gave Israel the law as covenant obligations.
4. If Israel observed the covenant law, things would be well and they would live long in the land.
5. If Israel did not observe the law, then the curse of the covenant would come on them and they would die = go into exile.

This structure, largely reflected in Deuteronomy, is worked out on the historical level in the Deuteronomistic history. According to Lohfink, "This series of propositions of the covenant theology is now likewise the key to the course of the narrative in the Yahwist's story of the fall."[76]

Lohfink is able to draw the obvious parallels with the story of Genesis 2–3: the creation of humankind, humankind's being placed in the garden, the giving of the divine command, life in the garden in cooperation with the deity, the violation of the com-mand with its curse, and expulsion from the garden. Lofink con-cludes from this that it was Israel's basic covenant tradition, with its emphasis on humankind's freedom and responsibility, that lay behind the transformations of the mythical traditions. However, it is possible to draw quite different traditio-historical conclusions from this comparison. If one views the covenant theology as largely the creation of the Deuteronomic tradition,[77] then the Yahwist must be understood as subsequent and indebted to this theological tradition. It would appear that he has given to this national covenant theology a universal dimension.

Conclusion

Having surveyed the literary, form-critical, and traditio-historical problems of the paradise narrative in some detail, it is now possible to make some general remarks about the nature of the Yahwist's work in Genesis 2–3. The literary complexity that was observed at the outset, with doublets and other signs of disunity, can best be explained as resulting from the variety and diversity of "traditional" material (*Wissensstoff*). They are not evidence for a combination of sources or a redaction of literary works in the Israelite scribal tradition. The Yahwist's account of creation and the paradise story is the product of research (*historia*) that includes both biblical and foreign sources. If I have identified these sources correctly, their differences from one another easily account for the lack of unity within the Yahwist's work, even though he has gone to great lengths to integrate the various elements with each other.

The biblical source, Ezekiel, and the Babylonian myths reflect the same milieu of the exile in the Neo-Babylonian period. The degree of literary dependence on these sources speaks against a long tradition-history and in favor of an author living and working at this time. It likewise suggests that no Israelite creation tradition existed prior to this time until the Yahwist composed this work and set it down as the "vulgate" tradition. Not only did he carry out his task of antiquarian research into the sources of primeval history available to him; he also integrated these myths into an Israelite theological perspective and thereby "historicized" them. In the interests of the religion of Yahweh, he has rationalized the role of the mother goddess by replacing her with the first woman/ mother, Eve, "the mother of all living." By restricting the creation of humanity to a single pair, he has also created a "historical" beginning from which a genealogical chronology could be developed. This is a "western" innovation not reflected in the eastern tradition.

The Yahwist's presentation is etiological, as is much of early historiography, in the treatment of the origins of humanity and of the reasons for its difficult plight of toil, hardship, and pain. It is likewise etiological on the philosophical/religious level of accounting for how humankind is like the deity in humankind's attainment of knowledge through a loss of innocence and how this constitutes a fundamental religious problem. This concern for etiology, which the Yahwist shares with the western antiquarian tradition, is so pervasive in the Yahwist's primeval history that it is misleading to try to relegate it to a few formulas or to see it as a residue of an older stage in the tradition. It is fundamental to the historiographic genre in which the author is writing.

The theology of the Yahwist is conditioned to a large extent by what is reflected in the Deuteronomic covenantal tradition, but he also wished to address the new situation of his own day, the exile. What has been presented in the national Deuteronomistic tradition as a matter of loyalty to Yahweh, expressed through obedience to a specific set of laws and a covenant, resulting in the blessing of the good land and long life, has been given universal dimensions by J. The simple act of obedience could ensure life in the garden in a blessed state. In Deuteronomy, violation of the covenant by the people would lead to the curses of innumerable hardships and ultimate exile. Similarly, in J, violation of the prohibition by eating the forbidden fruit leads to a series of curses and expulsion from the garden. In this way, the national religious perspective of DtrH has been universalized under the impact of life in the exile.

These literary, historiographic, and theological characteristics of the Yahwist are not unique to the paradise narrative. What I hope to show in what follows is that they are typical of his writing about the primeval history as a whole.

NOTES

1.   Some scholars feel that Genesis 2–3 and 4 should be considered together in order to reach the proper literary solution to the whole. See recently J. Scharbert, "Quellen und Redaktion in Gen. 2,4b–14,16," *BZ* 18 (1974), 45–64.

Consequently, Scharbert has his own somewhat different list of problems.

2.   For a summary on the various views concerning this issue, see Skinner, *Genesis,* p. 53; also Westermann, *Genesis 1-11,* pp. 198-199. The combination Yahweh God occurs elsewhere in Hebrew only in Ex. 9:30.

3.   K. Budde, *Die biblische Paradiesgeschichte,* BZAW 60 (1932), pp. 1-91; E. Haag, *Der Mensch am Anfang. Die alttestamentliche Paradiesvorstellung nach Genesis 2-3,* Trierer Theol. Studien 24 (1970); W. Fuss, *Die sogenannte Paradieserzählung. Aufbau, Herkunft und Theologische Bedeutung* (1968); see Scharbert, n. 1 above.

4.   Gunkel, *Genesis,* pp. 4-40.

5.   J. Begrich, "Die Paradieserzählung. Eine literargeschichtliche Studie," ZAW 50 (1932), 93-116.

6.   So G. von Rad, *Genesis: A Commentary,* rev. ed., trans. J. H. Marks (1972), pp. 73-102; J. L. McKenzie, "The Literary Characteristics of Genesis 2-3," in *Myths and Realities* (1963), pp. 146-181.

7.   Westermann, *Genesis 1-11,* pp. 178-278; O. H. Steck, "Die Paradieserzählung: Eine Auslegung von Genesis 2,4b-3,24," in *Wahrnehmungen Gottes im Alten Testament* (1982), 9-116 [taken from *Biblische Studien* 60 (1970), 11-131]; E. Kutsch, "Die Paradieserzählung Genesis 2-3 und ihr Verfasser," in *Studien zum Pentateuch* (1977), pp. 9-24.

8.   Westermann, *Genesis 1-11,* p. 190.

9.   On the understanding of *'ēd* in v. 6, see most recently P. K. McCarter, "The River Ordeal in Israelite Literature," HTR 66 (1973), 403-412, esp. p. 403.

10.   Compare Plato's *Symposium.*

11.   The same is perhaps true of the connection between creation of humankind and marriage in *Atrahasis.* See above, chapter 3, under *Atrahasis.*

12.   Gunkel, *Genesis,* pp. 26-27; Begrich, ZAW 50:104ff.

13.   Westermann, *Genesis 1-11,* p. 195.

14.   Steck, "Die Paradieserzählung," esp. pp. 21-35.

15.   Ibid., pp. 28, 53f., and n. 103.

16.   See esp. Steck's note on the meaning of the knowledge of good and evil, "Die Paradieserzählung," pp. 29ff., n. 43.

17.   Here the influence of Gunkel has been too strong.

18.   Steck follows a convention in the terminology of German biblical scholarship in which he distinguishes the present "paradise narrative" *Paradieserzählung* (Pe) of Genesis 2-3 from the original "paradise story" *Paradiesgeschichte* (Pg). There is no counterpart to this usage in English.

19.   According to Steck, the phrase "of good and evil" is a later J addition.

20.   Steck, "Die Paradieserzählung," p. 47.

21.   See esp. ibid., pp. 49-51. Steck goes on to spell out the Yahwist's contributions to the narrative in pp. 51-58.

22.   See n. 7 above.

23.   In Prov. 3:18a, it is stated that "wisdom is a tree of life." This may suggest that the tree of the knowledge of good and evil was created by analogy with the tree of life in the wisdom tradition.

24.   See A. L. Oppenheim, "On Royal Gardens in Mesopotamia," *JNES* 24 (1965), 328-333; D. J. Wiseman, "Mesopotamian Gardens," *An St* 33 (1983), 137-144; and

M. Hutter, "Adam als Gärtner und König (Gen. 2, 8.15)," *BZ* 30 (1986), 258–262.
25. The location of the garden in Ezekiel seems to be on a mountain in the Lebanon region famous for its trees. The royal gardens in Mesopotamia often attempt to imitate the Lebanon region.
26. Cf. Westermann, *Genesis 1–11*.
27. See examples in ibid., pp. 43–47.
28. Steck, "Die Paradieserzählung," p. 52.
29. See above, p. 79.
30. Philo Byblius may be an exception (see above, p. 125), but his euhemerism makes this difficult to judge.
31. See also Steck, "Die Paradieserzählung." Kutsch regards 2:15bβ as a secondary addition ("Die Paradieserzählung," p. 21, n. 63).
32. Kutsch ("Die Paradieserzählung," pp. 21–22) disputes the idea that the references to man in the singular, especially in the section 3:22–24, mean that there was an original version in which man was alone in the garden. He points to the fact that man is often addressed in the story in chapter 3 when both the man and wife are intended. Thus the writer can presuppose that the woman was aware of the command and that she also was expelled with the man from the garden. If this is accepted, then the grounds for an early paradise story as suggested by Steck no longer exist.
33. Kutsch's remarks on the significance of this explanation of the Fall for the rest of the primeval history will be taken up below.
34. Steck, "Die Paradieserzählung," pp. 58–65.
35. This is also confirmed by Kutsch's study, even though he does not specifically address the problem of genre.
36. Note the way in which myth, etiology, and wisdom may be combined in a primitive philosophy in the story of Pandora and the myth of the five races in Hesiod's *Works and Days*.
37. Coats, *Genesis*, pp. 58–59.
38. H. N. Wallace, *The Eden Narrative*, HSM 32 (1985). See esp. pp. 29–34.
39. Ibid., p. 29. What Wallace means by this statement is not entirely clear, although the jargon is familiar. See above (pp. 34–35), where I have criticized the notion that communities "create" tradition. Wallace has also completely ignored the discussion by Steck and Kutsch to which I have referred above.
40. This is the position of his mentor, F. M. Cross, and has been discussed above, pp. 10–11.
41. Wallace, *The Eden Narrative*, p. 55.
42. For a recent review of scholarship, see R. R. Wilson, "The Death of the King of Tyre: The Editorial History of Ezekiel 28," in *Love and Death in the Ancient Near East: Essays in Honor of Marvin H. Pope* (1987), pp. 211–218.
43. This is a position that McKenzie found difficult to explain ("The Literary Characteristics," pp. 154f.). See further his discussion, "Note on the Mythological Allusions in Ezek. 28:12–18," pp. 175–181.
44. On the problems of translation, see Wilson, "Death of the King of Tyre," pp. 214–215.
45. See ibid., pp. 211–218. Wilson notes that in Ezek. 28:12–19 the king of Tyre

has certain features in common with the high priest of Jerusalem, and that the passage contains themes that occur in some of Ezekiel's earlier oracles against the temple. Thus the pectoral with precious stones (v. 13) resembles that of the high priest (Ex. 28:17–20; 39:10–13). The "holy mountain" is also a term used for the temple. The "stones of fire" may refer to the "coals of fire" on the altar. The charge of corruption of the sanctuaries (v. 18) is a common accusation Ezekiel makes against the priesthood (5:11; 21:7; 23:38, 39; 25:3). On this basis, Wilson suggests that the oracle was originally directed at the priesthood (in which case the references to trade in vs. 16 and 18 would have been later additions supplied from the oracles against Tyre in chapter 27), or at least he had the high priest in mind in the guise of an oracle against the king of Tyre. Although the proposal is persuasive, it nevertheless has some serious problems. First, it is hard to tie the high priest to the mythological figure in Eden and to his creation in primeval times. This primeval myth is closely associated with the other elements that Wilson links to the priesthood. Furthermore, it seems quite likely that it was only with the demise of kingship that the high priest became clothed with royal regalia, so it is doubtful that the jeweled pectoral could be part of the priestly apparel in Ezekiel's day.

46.   M. H. Pope, *El in the Ugaritic Texts* (1955), pp. 97–103.

47.   For a bibliography of relevant works, see Wilson, "Death of the King of Tyre," p. 213, n. 10. See esp. the discussions by H. G. May, "The King in the Garden of Eden: A Study of Ezekiel 28:12–19," in *Israel's Prophetic Heritage: Essays in Honor of James Muilenburg,* ed. B. W. Anderson and W. Harrelson (1962), pp. 166–176; and McKenzie, n. 43 above.

48.   See above, pp. 61–62. See my earlier treatment, "The Creation of Man" *ZAW* 101:333–342.

49.   *RLA* V, 112; Frankfort, *Kingship,* pp. 320–349.

50.   See works in n. 24 above, esp. Hutter, *BZ* 30:258–262.

51.   On the meaning of Eden, see A. R. Millard, "The Etymology of Eden," *VT* 34 (1984), 103–106.

52.   Some, like Westermann (*Genesis 1–11,* pp. 246f.), see such a parallel in the Adapa myth. The similarity, however, must be viewed as very weak. Cf. Kienast, "Die Weisheit des Adapa von Eridu."

53.   Isaiah 10:5–19; 14:5–20. This is also the dominant theme in the oracles against Pharaoh and Egypt in Ezekiel 29–32.

54.   Except perhaps in his naming of the animals; see Solomon in 1 Kings 4:33.

55.   For a quite different interpretation of the clothing of humankind, see R. A. Oden, *The Bible Without Theology* (1987), pp. 94–105. However, it is debatable whether his parallels from Near Eastern sources are relevant or whether clothing is ever used to distinguish humankind from deity as he suggests.

56.   It is possible to see in the invitation of the snake to become like gods a suggestion of hubris and a reflection of the Ezekiel tradition. But there is nothing in the activity of the woman or her husband that suggests such an attitude.

57.   Perhaps the precious metals and gems are reflected in the little geography, Gen. 2:10–14.

58. See Oden, "Divine Aspirations," *ZAW* 93:197–216, esp. the literature cited in n. 1; *IDB*, supp. vol., pp. 357–358.

59. As in the *Erra Epic*.

60. See above, p. 60. Many of the elements in the Marduk creation story are traditional, but it is their use and how they are brought together in one text that is significant.

61. In MC the emphasis is upon the lack of any cities and temple—not a concern for J—but l. 2 states: "a reed had not come forth, a tree had not been created" (trans. A. Heidel).

62. See E. A. Speiser, *Genesis* (1964), p. 16, who associates the Hebrew *'ēd* with Akkadian *edu*, the underground cosmic waters. Also most recently, McCarter, *HTR* 66:403.

63. The Yahwist presents a different explanation for the origin of Babylon in Genesis 11. On this, see below, pp. 180–187.

64. For the text, see Pettinato, *Das altorientalische Menschenbild*, p. 41.

65. Wallace, *The Eden Narrative*, pp. 157–158, suggests that Hebrew *hawwa* should be identified with Ugaritic *hwt*, "life," used as an epithet for the goddess Asherah. Because Asherah played a role in Israel as a consort of Yahweh, the connection is attractive.

66. On the various possibilities for rendering this verse, see Westermann, *Genesis 1–11*, pp. 288–292. See Skinner, *Genesis*, p. 102, who uses this same Babylonian text to support the interpretation adopted here.

67. As Kutsch has observed ("Die Paradieserzählung," p. 20), the Mesopotamian texts speak of people being created in various numbers but never of a single pair.

68. See above, p. 80.

69. Quoted in Eusebius, *Praeparatio Evangelica* 1.10.7. See the discussion in Attridge and Oden, *Philo of Byblos*, p. 80 n. 44.

70. See Ebach, *Weltentstehung*, pp. 109–115; also Baumgarten, *The Phoenician History*, pp. 146–148.

71. For a full review of the various proposals and support for the view suggested here, see W. M. Clark, "A Legal Background to the Yahwist's Use of 'Good and Evil' in Genesis 2–3," *JBL* 88 (1969), 266–278. Note his statement: "Applied to Gen. 2f., I think this investigation strengthens the position of those who say that the J emphasis is not on the content of knowledge but on man's moral autonomy. Man takes upon himself the responsibility of trying apart from God to determine whether something is good for himself or not. . . . J's emphasis is on the commandment, whether man will indeed listen to the voice of Yahweh" (p. 277).

72. We also saw above that in Ezek. 28:2–10 wisdom's claim to divinity does not prevent the judgment of death.

73. N. Lohfink, "Die Erzählung vom Sündenfall," in *Das Siegeslied am Schilfmeer* (1965), pp. 81–101.

74. Note that here an etiology on the ability of a snake to shed its skin is used as an element in a larger story. The same is true of the etiological elements in Genesis 2–3.

75. Ibid., pp. 91–92.

76. Ibid., p. 92.
77. L. Perlitt, *Bundestheologie im Alten Testament* (1969); E. Kutsch, *Verheissung und Gesetz*, BZAW 131 (1972); E. W. Nicholson, *God and His People: Covenant and Theology in the Old Testament* (1986). Although Nicholson (ibid., pp. 179–188) argues for the origins of covenant theology in Hosea, it is fundamentally nationalistic from the beginning and does not alter the tradition-history suggested here.

6

THE STORY
OF CAIN AND ABEL

The Problem of Unity

As in the case of Genesis 2–3, the first issue to confront the critical scholar in an analysis of Genesis 4 is the problem of its unity and its relationship to Genesis 2–3. Most scholars treating Genesis 4 regard it as a continuation, in some sense, of the same source as in Genesis 2–3, to which they give the name Yahwist. But that does not immediately resolve the literary question of its unity. Literary unity in Genesis 4 is very much a question of genre. The chapter in its present form suggests a division between the story of the two brothers, 4:1–16, the genealogy of Cain, vs. 17–24, and the genealogy of Seth, vs. 25–26. Among these smaller units there are tensions and interconnections. The Cain who is a nomadic fugitive expelled from the arable land hardly seems a likely city builder. On the other hand, the initial genealogical notice of 4:1 seems to be closely connected in form and substance with 4:17, and many take this initial notice as original to the Cain genealogy. But the birth notice of Abel does not represent the beginning of a collateral line and is of a somewhat different form with no name explanation. It clearly has reference only to the story of the two brothers. Scholars are divided on what to do about the references to occupations because they seem to duplicate those in the Cain genealogy. But Gunkel already drew attention to the fact that both Abel's name and his occupation are duplicated by that of Jabal, "the father of those who dwell in tents and keep cattle" (4:20). Cain is less conspicuously paralleled by Jabal's brother Tubal-cain—

135

the smith. The Song of Lamech in 4:23–24, which some regard as secondary to the genealogy, contains a reference back to the Cain and Abel story, thereby providing another link between the two sections.

The genealogy of Seth in 4:25–26 (5:29) has its closest connections in form with the Cain genealogy, including 4:1. But it also alludes directly to the content of the Cain and Abel story. Yet it suggests in 4:26 that the name of Yahweh was not known previous to the time of Enosh, Seth's son, and so creates some difficulties with the use of the divine name in both earlier units.

It is likewise not clear how chapter 4 fits into its larger context. The story of Cain and Abel does not seem to reflect the stage of a second generation of humankind but an earth well populated with other peoples. This is especially clear in the threat to Cain's life after his murder. The occupations of the two sons are also treated as typical and not as initial inventions. The sense of origins and primeval time is rather absent by contrast with Genesis 2–3. The genealogy in 4:1, 17ff. has a greater sense of continuity with the Adam and Eve story, especially with its connection in 3:20 to the naming of Eve, "the mother of all living." But in form it is entirely different. The Seth genealogy also makes its connection with the primal pair, but the name of Seth's son, Enosh, looks like a doublet of Adam, though the former now belongs to the third generation. Most scholars also regard 5:29 as belonging to the Seth genealogy of J. This text has a reference back to the cursing of the ground by Yahweh in 3:17, but the reference to Noah does not tie the genealogy to the following flood story. Instead, it seems to recognize Noah's discovery of wine—a notation within another genealogy.

These clues suggested to some a complicated picture of sources and literary composition that has not been solved by past efforts at literary division of documents. Proposals having to do with separation of sources, whether on the literary or preliterary level, rest upon notions about the themes or subject matter of the texts. The question that these observations pose is, How can the present text of Genesis 4, in spite of its problems, still be understood as a unified literary work within the larger Yahwistic corpus?[1]

The Two Brothers

The story of Cain and Abel opens with an introduction giving the birth of the two brothers and their chosen occupations. It is true that more is made of the naming of Cain than of Abel, but the significance of Abel's name, "futility," lies in the story itself and cannot derive from any other source, such as a genealogy. The shift from nominal description to verbal action by the rather vague temporal statement in v. 3a, "It happened after sometime . . . ," should not be viewed as a radical break in which an earlier series of events has been lost.[2] The same sequence of themes, expressed in a little different way, can be seen in the Jacob and Esau story of Gen. 25:21–34. Note the following sequence:

a. Birth and naming of children: Gen. 4:1–2a   Gen. 25:21–26
b. Occupations of brothers: 4:2b   25:27[3]
c. Rivalry between the two: 4:3–8   25:29–34

This suggests that we have to do with a basic story form or model and not the happenstance accumulation of traditions.[4]

The reason for the divine preference of Abel's sacrifice and the rejection of Cain's offering has led to considerable speculation, often of a religio-historical or a theological nature. But a reading of the story as it stands may simply suggest that deity in general has a preference for meat over vegetables! It implies that there is something of a contest between the two brothers for divine attention and blessing, and Abel, the shepherd, has the clear advantage. This is not construed as an etiology for any particular form of sacrifice[5] but an observation of a universal fact—at least from the author's point of view. Nor is it a case of rivalry between two different occupations or ways of life.[6]

This raises the question of the relation of vs. 3–5 to the divine statements in vs. 6–7. The latter verses appear to move the whole matter to a quite different level, so that many commentators wish to regard all or part of them as secondary. The reasons for doing so, however, seem to me to be rather spurious. One can hardly fault the author for the repetition in v. 6 of 5b in the form of the divine question: "Why are you angry?" This introduces the divine warning in v. 7. This is a difficult text and calls for some discussion.

In the first part, v. 7aα, the meaning rests on the interpreting of the verb *nāśā'*, which can best be understood in the sense of divine favor.[7] This offers a parallel to the statements about God's preference, *ša'āh*, in vs. 4, 5 and a contrast to Cain's downcast appearance in vs. 5, 6. The general sense seems to be that the important thing from the divine perspective is not the form of sacrifice but "doing good," which will result in divine favor, "things looking up."[8] The comparison between sacrifice and doing good as a means of winning divine favor, with emphasis on the latter, has a strong prophetic note.[9]

In the next part of the statement, v. 7aβ, there is a grammatical problem in the lack of agreement of *rōbēṣ* with *ḥaṭṭā't*, which is most easily dealt with by making the final *t* of the noun part of the verb and construing it as an imperfect *tirbaṣ* with the rest of the verbs.[10] The meaning of the verb *rbṣ* is much discussed, as is the significance of the "door" (door to what?). The verb *rbṣ* is never used in a threatening sense, even for wild animals, and it is often applied to domestic animals. So it is best to understand the metaphor in the sense of sin as a domestic animal that lies in repose at the door of one's dwelling, an animal that has attraction for its owner but must be mastered and constantly kept in check. This makes the comparison with the woman in chapter 3 not so very different.[11]

W. M. Clark[12] has drawn attention to some similarities between Gen. 4:7 and Job 11:13–15. This can be seen in two respects. The first is the positive one:

Gen. 4:7a: "If you do well, will there not be a lifting up?"	Job 11:13a, 15a: "If you set your heart aright . . . surely you will lift up your face without blemish."

The second similarity has to do with the negative and the metaphoric image of evil:

Gen. 4:7b: "If you do not do well, sin lies at the door; its desire is for you, but you must master it."	Job 11:14: "If iniquity is in your hand, put it far away and let not wickedness dwell in your tents."

In both cases, sin/wickedness is represented as something belonging to the domestic scene "at the door," "in your tents." In the one case, the advice is to master it as one would a domestic animal; in the other, it is to refuse to have wickedness as guest in the home. Just as Zophar gives advice to Job in his despondency as to how to regain divine favor, so Yahweh acts as a wise counselor to Cain for the same purpose. The personification of evil in this way and the role of Yahweh as counselor are most similar to the wisdom tradition. But the lateness suggested by these parallels to both prophecy and wisdom does not disqualify it in any way as part of the literary work.

The text of v. 8 is certainly corrupt in its present form and should very likely be emended with the versions to include a short speech by Cain to Abel. There is no reason to believe that a speech was consciously omitted in the course of the composition's development, or even, as some have suggested, at the oral level of the tradition. That would hardly account for the present awkwardness of the use of *wy'mr* without direct speech to follow.

The rest of the story (vs. 9–16) is made up almost entirely of dialogue between Yahweh and Cain. Only in v. 16 is there a final narration of the consequences of Cain's action, and this presupposes the scene of vs. 9–15. Many attempts have been made to separate various sources, layers, or additions within the dialogue passage, but these have all been strongly influenced by notions about the meaning of the text or its earlier forms or traditions. The fact that particularly in the dialogue there are strong similarities between Genesis 4 and Genesis 2–3 means that decisions about the comparison of Genesis 2–3 must have their consequences for the analysis of chapter 4 as well. To this matter we must now turn.

It has often been noted that the structure and language of the two stories are very similar.[13] A simple chart will illustrate this:

a. Divine command or warning	Gen. 2:17; (3:1–5)	Gen. 4:6–7
b. The act/crime	3:6–7	4:8
c. Discovery and interrogation	3:8–13	4:9–10
d. Pronouncement of punishment	3:14–19	4:11–12
e. Mitigation of sentence	3:14–19 (21)	4:13–15
f. Expulsion	3:23, 24	4:16

The similarities between the two stories exist in spite of the fact that the content and situation are remarkably different in either case. So the introduction and setting of the two units bear little resemblance to each other up to the point of the commission of the crime. In both cases, the crime is anticipated by a divine warning. In the case of Genesis 2–3, this is in the form of a divine prohibition and threat, 2:17, which is recapitulated within the context of the temptation by the snake, 3:1–5. In Genesis 4, the warning comes when Cain appears most vulnerable to the temptation; and it comes as wise counsel, 4:6–7, in contrast to the snake's bad advice. In both cases, a brief account of the crime follows, 3:6–7; 4:8. This in turn is followed by two very similar trial scenes in which God acts as prosecutor and judge. There is first the interrogation with a similar set of questions: "Where are you?" "Where is your brother?" "What have you done?" The evidence of a misdeed is cited — the nakedness of the pair, the brother's blood crying from the ground — which leads to admission of guilt in the first case and silence in the second. The pronouncement of punishment in both is in the form of a curse. In the case of both Adam and Cain, it affects their relationship to the soil (*'ădāmâ*). In both stories there is some divine mitigation of the sentence. In the case of Adam and Eve, the sentence itself is made less severe than the threatened death penalty.[14] In Cain's case, the mitigation of the death threat to the fugitive comes as a response to his complaint and is in the form of the sign. Finally, both are expelled, the one from the garden and the other from the arable land.

In addition to this similarity of structure, there is also a considerable correspondence in language. The most notable instance is that of 4:7b with 3:16b. This cannot be explained as just an expansion or later overlay,[15] because such an exercise seems rather pointless. To remove all of these resemblances means that one is not left with a story but at most with a rather trivial anecdote. But if J is the creator of Genesis 2–3 and its basic structure, there is no reason to deny him the authorship of this story as well.

Some attempt has been made to compare this part of the story of Cain with part of Philo's "history of culture."[16] Philo describes the birth of two brothers — Samemroumos (= Hypsouranios) and Ousoos — and states that "they took their names from their mothers, since women at that time mated indiscriminately with whomever they chanced to meet." These two brothers quarreled, but nothing is said of the outcome. Both were inventors and were honored after their deaths. Of Hypsouranios a further line of inventors was produced. It is tempting to see some connection with the biblical account because of the brothers' quarrel, but that motif is common in other traditions, especially if Hypsouranios and Ousoos can be associated with the rival cities of Tyre and Sidon, as some have tried to do. How their names are to be associated with their mothers is not clear. In Genesis, Cain is named by Eve, but it is common in J for the mother to name the child. The apparent promiscuity of the women suggests some connection with Gen. 6:1–4 but not this episode. At most, one can say that there is some similarity of motifs in the two traditions for this part of the story, but little more.[17]

The Genealogy of Cain: Gen. 4:17–24

There has been a strong tendency in the past to see in the genealogy of Cain an originally separate tribal genealogy[18] or primeval tradition[19] and to make this the basis of analysis for this chapter as a whole.[20] But as R. R. Wilson has argued,[21] the unit does not have the characteristics of a tribal genealogy developed and transmitted by oral tradition. Instead, it has all the marks of literary contrivance, pieced together from various kinds of materials. Apart from the connections with the previous story of Cain and Abel (v. 17a), there is in vs. 17–18 a linear genealogy from Enoch to Lamech. In the middle are three names that seem to serve primarily as a bridge: Irad, Mehujael, and Methushael. The last two are a rhyming pair, but Irad seems to belong more closely with Enoch and the previous names. Scholars have often noted a certain grammatical difficulty in v. 17. According to the usual rules of Hebrew syntax, the antecedent for *bōneh*, "builder," should be Enoch. In that case, the city named after Enoch's son would be Irad. This would make good sense if Irad could be identified with Babylonian Eridu, which in some Mesopotamian traditions was viewed as the first primeval city. The reference to Enoch at the end of v. 17 would then be understood as a misplaced gloss.[22]

Lamech seems to be the subject of a separate tradition, which is reflected in v. 19 and the Song of Lamech in v. 23. This has been combined with the three sons of Lamech — rhyming triplets — divided between the two wives.[23] These three are all inventors of culture with some connection between their names and their achievements.[24] This is similar in style to Philo's history, in which inventors often give their names to their inventions. In Genesis, however, these culture heroes each become the ancestors (*'ab*) of the occupations they represent. The statement in v. 24 on the vengeance of Lamech compared with Cain serves to make another connection with the Cain and Abel story, although it is a curious twist to the statement in 4:15.

The Genealogy of Seth: Gen. 4:25–26 (5:29)

This genealogy is also regarded as an originally separate tradition parallel to that of the Cain genealogy because it is represented as such in the P tradition in 5:3ff.[25] But even if one eliminates the obvious "redactional" connections in 4:25 (*'ôd* "again," *'aḥēr* "another") and 25bβ, γ, the similarity in structure of the genealogy following the patterns in 4:1 and 4:17 makes it very likely that we are dealing with a common author. This genealogy does appear to be preserved in a rather fragmentary fashion, because one would expect a series of generations parallel to that of the Cain genealogy. This seems to be borne out in 5:29, which follows the etiological form of 4:1 and 4:25 (except for the change to a masculine subject). Here the connection with the curse in 3:17ff. is inescapable and hardly a gloss.[26]

The remark about the beginning of the worship of Yahweh (4:26) in the time of Enosh is interesting in the light of the remark in Philo's history that Genos and Genea, the first human couple after Aeon and Protogonos, "were the first to raise their hands to heaven" in worship of Beelsamen— "Lord of Heaven" — whom they considered to be the only god. It is likely that in the tradition used by Philo, Genos and Genea, generic terms for humanity, were viewed as the original human pair. They also are said to have settled Phoenicia as the ancestors of the people. In this way, the Canaanites/Phoenicians are autochthonous. The possibility of a similar tradition of the worship of one god at the beginning is suggestive, because Enosh, the "inventor" of religion in Genesis, has a name that is also generic for humanity.

If 5:29 has its original connection with the Seth genealogy, then it is likewise the case that the story of Noah in 9:20ff., which continues the theme of Noah as an inventor of culture, has its original connection with the Seth genealogy. The notice of Noah's discovery is followed by a story in much the same way that the story of Cain and Abel begins with Cain's birth and naming, the birth of Abel, and the statement about their occupations. However, there is some tension in the fact that both Cain and Noah are given the same occupation of farmer. Noah could therefore hardly be the first, unless Cain's beginning is disqualified by his being driven from the land. However, on the literary level at least, the units all belong together.[27]

The Tradition-History of Genesis 4

Evidence for the diversity of traditions behind the literary composition of Genesis 4 seems fairly substantial, because such diversity would appear to be the only way left to account for the tensions and inconsistencies between the various pieces. But any effort to reconstruct the various separate traditions from the present compositional mixture must be viewed as rather speculative. It seems likely that there was a genealogy representing primeval times in two variants, now reflected in the Cain and Seth genealogies. They were not tribal or ethnographic, even though a few of the names may represent eponyms, but learned constructions including some anecdotes and remarks about inventors. Two etymologies are attached to two primitive peoples, Cain and Seth, whereas the etymology associated with Noah marks him as a culture hero. The Song of Lamech may have been incorporated into the Cain genealogy in a pre-J form, in which case 4:24 is probably a J addition. The remark in 4:26 that Enosh was the first to invoke the name of Yahweh is not easy to reconcile with the rest of J's account. However, if Elohim is read for Yahweh in 4:1 in the speech of Eve,[28] on the model of 4:25 and of the dialogue between the woman and the serpent in 3:1–5, this would suggest that according to J humankind did not actually use the divine name Yahweh until the time of Enosh.

It is hard to find any extensive tradition behind the Cain and Abel story in spite of all efforts to do so. Like the story of Adam and Eve, it is more a question of an author combining folklore motifs. There is the motif of sibling and occupational rivalry similar to that of the Jacob/Esau story. The second motif is the etiology of ethnographic characteristics among the Kenites, a nomadic group of Yahweh worshipers quite familiar to the Israelites. This motif does not make the whole story an ethnographic etiology but only a useful "witness" to the truth of the larger story. The universal scope of the theme and the ethnographic aspect are not mutually exclusive, nor are they the result of one type of story being overlaid by another. They are simply the "traditional" elements from which J developed his narrative. But that itself was quite enough to produce the type of inconsistencies that appear in the present text.

The Problem of Genre: Genesis 4

Genesis 4 raises the question of the relationship of narrative to genealogy. This has been dealt with by scholars in various ways. Gunkel thought that genealogy was derived from the remnants of legends that were loosely joined together. Only pieces of the narrative elements remained.[29] Westermann disputed this view by asserting that the genealogy is "an independent genre whose specific function and history can be proved."[30] At the same time, he was aware of the fact that this linear genealogy did not quite fit the type of tribal, segmented genealogy, so he proposed to distinguish between tribal genealogies found elsewhere in the Old Testament and primeval genealogies. But such a distinction is hard to maintain on the basis of the comparative material. In Mesopotamian sources, the linear primeval genealogy has the same form as subsequent historical king-list genealogies, whereas in Greece both linear and segmented genealogies, but especially the latter, may be used for the primeval period from the first ancestors onward.[31]

R. R. Wilson, in his study of biblical genealogies, makes a special point of investigating the problem of the relationship of narrative to genealogy and uses Gen. 4:17–26 as a test case.[32] His own literary analysis of Genesis 4 suggests that it is a "literary unity" and that none of the genealogical components "in their present form ever circulated separately,"[33] although they may have existed separately in a different form. Furthermore, the present form of the Cain genealogy does not, according to Wilson, give any evidence of having been derived from an orally transmitted tribal genealogy. Wilson concludes that Genesis 4 is the literary creation of J from various traditions and pieces of lore, a confirmation of our own analysis. For Wilson, this is a negative conclusion in his comparison with types of *orally* transmitted genealogies. But the question remains as to whether there are sufficient literary models that can be used to explain the genre as a whole.

The one literary tradition that seems most relevant to the Cain genealogy, and which has been used by Wilson and others,[34] is that of the inventors of culture. In the Mesopotamian tradition, this has to do with the sages (*apkallus*) who lived before the flood and who taught humankind civilization. But as we have seen above,[35] this tradition, although having a little similarity in subject matter, is construed in an entirely different way in the Mesopotamian tradition. Its influence on the formation of Genesis 4 can only have been minimal.[36] Perhaps more relevant is the late Babylonian text in which Ea creates a series of deities who are patrons of the arts and crafts, of agriculture, and even of prayer.[37] These are all created before humankind as an anticipation of the needs of civilization. This myth clearly goes back to the old Sumerian tradition about the role of Ea (Enki) in the establishment of the arts of civilization.[38] It also has some similarity to the Greek tradition of patron deities as culture heroes. The Babylonian text seems to include specifically those items that are also covered in the history of culture in Genesis. Does the Yahwist's version represent a "demythologization" of that tradition into historiographic form with human inventors as the "fathers" of these crafts and occupations?

Another possibility is the tradition in Philo Byblius, which gives a history of technology from the earliest cosmogonic beginnings through several generations, with each successive stage in the genealogy contributing various inventions of civilization. Although the Phoenician tradition in Philo is much more extensive, it is also of much later date. Yet in form it is closer to the biblical traditions than the Mesopotamian account and belongs to the same cultural milieu. Furthermore, the Phoenician tradition of the history of culture appears to have been originally separate from other primeval traditions and knows nothing of the flood and an antediluvian period. In similar fashion, the tradition of inventions in Genesis 4 seems to ignore completely the fact that the flood would have wiped out these cultural lineages, so that the inventors of Genesis come from a western antiquarian tradition that does not know of a flood.

It should likewise be emphasized that the *apkallu*-tradition and the myth of Ea's creation of culture from Mesopotamia, the Phoenician history of technology, and the Israelite account of inventors are all learned antiquarian traditions. Furthermore, this linear genealogy of inventors, with some limited segmentation, as in the Phoenician tradition, provided the structure and continuity for the earliest period of the Yahwist's history from the first pair to the time of the flood. At the same time, the Yahwist seems to have deliberately created a two-branched genealogy of Cain and Seth, with both branches containing inventors. Noah, as the inventor of agriculture, is also the son of Lamech in the line of Seth. But if all the sons of Lamech had originally belonged to the same tradition of inventions, then there would have been a complete balance of trades: shepherd, musician and metal-worker, agriculturalist. Perhaps the addition of Naamah, the sister, was a substitute for Noah, who was shifted to the other genealogy.

Conclusion

The story of Cain and Abel is not just a tale but a myth in the sense that it deals with an event in primeval time that is meant to have universal significance. It is another stage in the introduction of evil into the world. But the story has been influenced by wisdom and prophetic traditions, as seen most clearly in 4:7. This treatment in turn has been combined with antiquarian interest in social/tribal origins of the nomadic Yahwists, the Kenites, and all of this is structured in a recurring crime-punishment scheme. The story of Cain and Abel is then set within a genealogical structure that includes a tradition of inventors modified by other materials as well, all in a literary unity.

It would be easy to misunderstand the nature of this unity by not recognizing the genre to which it belongs. Such a complex combination of intellectual traditions with only slight efforts to integrate them belongs to the very character of ancient antiquarian historiography. This is quite evident in Philo's *Phoenician History.*

Although comparisons are often made between various items in Genesis and Philo's history, it is equally important to recognize the similarity of form of the primeval traditions. In this part of Genesis, the Yahwist stands primarily in the western antiquarian tradition.

NOTES

1.   G. W. Coats's category of "primeval saga" (*Genesis,* p. 66) does not help as an explanation because it is presented without any form-critical comparison.

2.   So Westermann, *Genesis 1–11,* p. 294.

3.   Verse 28 is an addition meant to anticipate chapter 27; see below.

4.   I will argue below that in the case of the Jacob-Esau story this episode of rivalry is a pre-J story. In the Cain and Abel story, it is merely a motif that has been used by J, but the story is basically his own.

5.   See Westermann, *Genesis 1–11,* pp. 294–297. Westermann's own explanation, that there is no explanation, becomes perhaps a little too subtle. This means that Westermann must regard vs. 6–7 as a later addition, because it clearly does not fit with his understanding of vs. 4–5 (p. 300).

6.   So J. M. Miller, "The Descendants of Cain: Notes on Genesis 4," *ZAW* 86 (1974), 164–174; cf. Ebach, *Weltentstehung,* pp. 331–332.

7.   As in Gen. 19:21; 2 Kings 3:14; Mal. 1:8, 9.

8.   See esp. Skinner, *Genesis,* p. 106n.

9.   See Amos 5:4–5, 14–15, 21–24; Hos. 6:6; Isa. 1:10–20.

10.   See G. von Rad, *Genesis,* p. 105.

11.   Note also in Plato's *Republic* IX the use of the imagery of passion as a wild beast that must be domesticated.

12.   W. M. Clark, "The Flood and the Structure of the Pre-patriarchal History," *ZAW* 83 (1971), p. 199 n. 66.

13.   Westermann, *Genesis 1–11,* p. 303; Clark, "The Flood," *ZAW* 83:195–200.

14.   Some regard 3:21 as also mitigation, but I do not think that that is its function.

15.   So Westermann, *Genesis 1–11,* pp. 298–300; W. Dietrich, "'Wo ist Dein Bruder?' Zu Tradition und Intention von Genesis 4," in *Beiträge zur Alttestamenlichen Theologie: Festschrift für W. Zimmerli* (1977), pp. 94–111, esp. pp. 98–100.

16.   U. Rüterswörden, "Kanaanäisch-städtische Mythologie im Werk des Jahwisten. Eine Notiz zu Genesis 4," *BN* 1 (1976), 19–23.

17.   Rüterswörden's thesis is that the similarity is sufficient to suggest that the J tradition is a city tradition, not nomadic, and is similar to the city traditions of Tyre and Byblos in Philo. That is why Cain becomes the founder of a city. Yet it may be doubted that the Hebrew text actually makes Cain the builder of a city.

18.   So Gunkel, *Genesis,* pp. 47–49.

19.   Westermann, *Genesis 1–11,* pp. 323–325. Note his distinction between primeval and tribal genealogies.

20.   See also Dietrich, "'Wo ist Dein Bruder?'"

21.   Wilson, *Genealogy and History,* pp. 138–158, esp. pp. 156ff.

22.   See the discussion in ibid., p. 139f. n. 5. Ebach, *Weltentstehung,* pp. 335–338, argues for Cain as the city builder but without facing the grammatical difficulty.

23.   So Wilson, who suggests that the daughter Naamah was added for a balance but has no other function in the series; cf. also Dinah, sister of the twelve tribes.

24.   See the discussion in Ebach, *Weltentstehung,* pp. 340–350.

25.   Ibid., pp. 350–352.

26.   It also appears that the remark about Enoch in 5:24 originally derives from this source as well. This suggests that the P genealogy of Seth was largely taken from the Seth genealogy of J, which it replaced. On this problem, see Ebach, *Weltentstehung,* pp. 325–329.

27.   See below, pp. 178–179.

28.   See the versions.

29.   Gunkel, *Genesis,* p. 49.

30.   Westermann, *Genesis 1–11,* p. 325.

31.   See above, pp. 62–64; 89–90.

32.   Wilson, *Genealogy and History,* pp. 138–158.

33.   Ibid., p. 157.

34.   Ibid., pp. 149ff.; Westermann, *Genesis 1–11,* pp. 325, 329f.; Ebach, *Weltentstehung.*

35.   See above, pp. 66–67.

36.   This is greatly overstated by Westermann, *Genesis 1–11,* p. 325.

37.   See above, p. 60.

38.   See above, pp. 54–56.

7

THE MARRIAGE OF THE SONS OF GOD

The Limits of the Text

The first step in any analysis of Gen. 6:1–4 is to deal with it as it stands, to identify any grammatical and linguistic problems, and to discuss the problems of its literary unity. Above all, what must be established are the limits of the J text. Among scholars, however, a certain diversity of opinion exists on these questions that is based largely on assumptions about the text's preliterary form and tradition-history that are disputed in this study as a whole. So some of the observations on the text that follow must be tentative until the whole picture in this discussion is complete.[1]

There is little problem grammatically with 6:1–2. Its meaning seems clear enough: "It happened when humanity ($h\bar{a}$'$\bar{a}d\bar{a}m$) began to increase upon the surface of the earth and daughters were born to them that the divinities ($b\check{e}n\bar{e}$ $h\bar{a}$'$\check{e}l\bar{o}h\hat{i}m$) saw that the mortal women were beautiful. So they took wives for themselves from whomever they chose." The time referred to is the beginning of humankind after creation, and the focus is the first few generations of mortal women. The "sons of god" are attracted to them because they are beautiful and sexually desirable,[2] and they choose some of them as their mates. There seems little doubt among scholars that the "sons of god" are to be identified as deities, members of the divine council, though inferior in some sense to Yahweh himself.[3] But there is no implication in the wording of v. 2 that the activity of the divinities was particularly promiscuous or that anyone had violated the divine order or commands.[4] It is

149

easy to read into these verses too much from other contexts or traditions.

Verse 3 may be rendered in the following way: "And God said, 'My spirit will not remain within humanity forever because he is also mortal. His lifespan will be 120 years.'" This verse raises a series of problems. First, there is little agreement on the exact meaning of the verb *yādôn,* but it seems to me that the strongest case can be made for rendering it "will abide/remain" and that fits the sense of the verse as a whole very well.[5] The group of consonants בשׁגם has also received some consideration, but the most likely possibility here is to take it as the combination of the preposition בְּ with the relative particle שׁ = בַּאֲשֶׁר: "because" + the adverbial particle גַם, "also, likewise." This kind of construction is characteristic of late prose, especially in the book of Ecclesiastes. In spite of these philological problems, the sense of the verse seems fairly clear, as rendered above.

The real difficulty comes when one tries to relate this verse to the preceding verse. It would seem most reasonable to view this limitation on humankind's lifespan as connected with the offspring of the immortals and mortal women. These offspring, however, are not mentioned until v. 4, so that one solution has been to reverse the order of vs. 3 and 4. This would make for a rather awkward juxtaposition of the divine statement in v. 3 directly before a quite different divine statement in vs. 5–7, especially if v. 3 and vs. 5–7 are considered as stemming from the same source, J. In the one, God merely limits the lifespan to the ideal 120 years; in the other, God declares that he will destroy all humanity at once. Other explanations have been proposed for the unusual placement of v. 3. They rest largely on decisions about the unit's form and tradition-history, which will be considered below.

The unit ends with the statement: "[The giants were on the earth in those days as well as later when] the divinities had sexual union with mortal women and they bore them offspring. These were heroes who in ancient times were famous men."

In its present form, v. 4 is a rather curious construction, with its introductory and concluding nominal clauses sandwiching a subordinated verbal clause between them. Even if one brackets the phrase *wĕgam 'aḥărēy-kēn,* "and also afterwards," as a later addition, this does not help the sense very much. It is the subordination of the verbal clause into a temporal statement dependent upon the nominal clause about the "giants" (Nephilim) that does not follow from the action in v. 2. The temporal clause of v. 4 assumes that the sexual union and the birth of offspring have previously been mentioned as fact. It is also curious after a series of narrative consecutive imperfects in vs. 1–2 to have the nonconsecutive imperfect, suggesting habitual action, used in the verbal clause of v. 4. The most satisfactory grammatical solution to these problems would be to regard the whole statement about the Nephilim as secondary, in which case the אשר was used to make the connection to the existing verbal sentence. This changed the verbs in the process from their original consecutive imperfect form: ויבאו and ויולידו,[6] following directly on v. 2. In that case, the appropriate climax would have come in v. 4b in the nominal statement about the *gibbōrîm*, "heroes." Even as the text now stands, it does not identify the Nephilim with the heroes. This could have been done in a quite simple, unambiguous way in the concluding nominal clause. If anything, v. 4aα seems to suggest the juxtaposition of two distinct groups, the Nephilim and the heroes, but in doing so the flow of the narrative has been seriously disrupted. These observations suggest that the original literary unit consisted of Gen. 6:1–2, 4aβ,b (beginning with ויבאו). To this two additions were made, v. 3 and v. 4aα (as far as אשר), but it is not clear on grammatical or philological grounds that they were both made by the same hand.

Form and Tradition-History of Gen. 6:1–4

The text's form and tradition-history have become virtually inseparable, so the two issues must now go hand in hand. And because the text has been regarded by most critical scholars as fragmentary, the comparative religio-historical background of the ancient Near East and Greece have often been used in the text's interpretation to fill in the gaps. The dangers in filling perceived lacunae or unfinished tales is quite considerable, so simplicity of form and directness of corresponding comparative material will obviously be an asset.

The form of the text, without v. 3, has most often been characterized as a mythical etiology.[7] It is mythical in that it deals with gods and heroes in primeval times, and it is etiological in that it accounts for the origins of a group or class, the heroes. There are some features of this unit, however, even without v. 3, that create some problems for this form-critical definition. First, the remark about the Nephilim clearly disturbs the narrative because it does not account for where they came from. If one insists that they are identical with the *gibbōrîm,* then the remark about the Nephilim is also anticlimactic in its present position, even though giants are mythical creatures who existed in primeval times, as attested by comparative materials.

A second difficulty is that Gen. 6:1–2, 4 is not a tale but a report of the course of events in a very summary fashion and seems to introduce a larger narrative. This has led to a number of conjectures as to how it is to be continued. R. Bartelmus regards it as the introduction to an account of the primeval struggle of the heroes with the giants for which there is ample evidence both from comparative literature and also from the "historical" tales of Israel, such as the story of David and Goliath.[8] But this explanation ignores the grammatical difficulty of the remark about the Nephilim in v. 4a, and the tale as a whole would hardly be etiological any longer. The etiological form of the text does not support, but rather goes against, such a reconstruction.

A third difficulty is that the etiology does not seem complete because it does not explain any origin of a class or group in the narrator's present. If the text had suggested that from these heroes the kings of the nations were descended, then this would correspond more directly to the other etiologies in form. As it is, the point of this introductory narrative with its hint of etiology remains somewhat obscure. Before attempting to clarify this form and its function in the present context, let me discuss two other issues: the place of v. 3 in the whole and the relationship of the Nephilim to the heroes.

A number of scholars have suggested that the pre-Israelite mythical fragment of Gen. 6:1–2, 4 has been incorporated into the Israelite tradition by means of the inclusion of v. 3 to give it a distinctively Israelite interpretation;[9] or it was added to make the whole correspond to the "crime/punishment" model of the stories in Genesis 2–3 and 4;[10] or it was a conscious ironic inversion of that form.[11] What makes all these suggestions less than convincing is the awkwardness of the literary addition of v. 3 and the fact that it cannot easily be associated with either J or P, the literary strata of the primeval history. A very strong argument put forward by Bartelmus for the lateness of v. 3 as an addition to the text is the fact that an allusion or reference to it is completely missing from Enoch 6–11 and shows up only in Jubilees 5:6ff.[12] However, Enoch 12–16, which J. C. VanderKam regards as a later elaboration of 6–11,[13] seems to contain in 15–16 an expanded midrash on Gen. 6:3. In it the "spirits" (pl.) are identified with the heavenly beings, and "flesh" with humankind. This could hardly have been the original intention of Gen. 6:3.

The Old Testament itself may reflect a tradition of humankind's makeup of spirit and flesh in Eccl. 3:18–21. Here Qoheleth compares the fate of humankind, *běnē-hā'ādām,* with that of the animals and observes that both the human and the beast have the same breath, *rûaḥ,* and both come from dust, *'āpār,* reflecting J's story of creation. But Qoheleth suggests that J's "breath of life," *nišmat ḥayyîm* (Gen. 2:7), has become identified by some circles with the divine spirit. Ecclesiastes 3:21, however, questions whether the spirit of humankind has a different origin and destiny from that of the animals. The tradition in Eccl. 12:7, on the other hand, seems to present the more "orthodox" view in which at death "dust returns to the earth as it was, and the spirit returns to God who gave it." It would appear from this that Gen. 6:3 reflects this development in the understanding of humankind's makeup in which humanity combines the divine *rûaḥ* within the earthly "flesh" for a limited period of time, after which the spirit returns to its heavenly source. The comment may have been inspired by the narrative about the sexual union of divinity with humanity, but the connection is a very loose one because the idea is really based upon Gen. 2:7 and therefore applies to all of humankind and not just to the special offspring of Gen. 6:4. Perhaps it was added to emphasize the point that the union did not produce demigods, though the limit of 120 years may reflect a tradition that heroes did live for three generations of humankind.[14]

All of this suggests that the addition was very late, that it did not belong to J, and that it was not a way of accommodating the tradition of Gen. 6:1–2, 4 to Israelite thought. It did not owe anything to the crime-punishment pattern but was secondary to the whole structure and obscured the form of the author rather than clarified it. For our purposes, it may be safely bracketed as a later interpretation of the episode.

There remains the matter of the giants — Nephilim. Here two different possibilities have been recently put forward. On the one hand, it is suggested that the tradition reflects two groups in opposition to each other. On the other hand, the giants and heroes are identified with each other. In both cases, the Nephilim are regarded as belonging to the original account in spite of the textual difficulties cited earlier. Much of the discussion on these matters goes back to the suggestions of E. G. Kraeling, so his study provides a useful point of departure.[15]

Kraeling calls attention to the traditions about primeval times that seem to be reflected in Ezek. 26:19-20 and 32:26-27.[16] In the first reference, 26:19-20, the city of Tyre is compared with "those who descend into the Pit, to the ancient race (*'am 'ôlām*) . . . in the nether world, among the ancient ruins."[17] The author uses the metaphor of a great flood in which God causes the "deep," *tĕhôm*, to come up over the city and the great waters, *hammayim hārabbîm*, to cover them, just as God did to the ancient race who now dwell in the underworld.

The other reference, Ezek. 32:26-27, has to do with the "fallen heroes of antiquity," *gibbôrîm nōpĕlîm mē'ôlām*,[18] who have earlier descended into Sheol in full warrior panoply and who have an honored place there.[19] In the larger context of vs. 17-32, a number of national armies are described as having descended into Sheol and as having been received by the ancient heroes. In each case, it is the result of military activity, and the dead are frequently described as those "fallen by the sword," *nōpĕlîm baḥereb* (vs. 22-24; cf. v. 20). Because in v. 27 the ancient heroes are also described as "fallen," *nōpĕlîm*, Kraeling is inclined to associate this term with the *nĕpîlîm* by explaining the etymology of the term as meaning the famous ones "fallen" in battle. This etymology is quite unconvincing because it does not explain why the Nephilim were consistently regarded as giants. Nor can this passage, by itself, be used to make any such connection, because the same terminology is used throughout for the armies of recent historical times as well, so it seems to carry no special mythological association.

What we seem to have in Ezekiel are two distinct primeval traditions,[20] one in which an ancient people or race is destroyed by the divine judgment of a flood, and one in which the heroes reach Sheol as a result of military conflicts. Kraeling would like to identify the "ancient race," *'am 'ōlām,* with the "heroes," *gibbōrîm,* but this hardly seems likely in Ezekiel. Furthermore, because there is no basis in Ezekiel for any tradition about giants (Nephilim), such a connection with the *gibbōrîm*[21] was a later midrashic inter-pretation based upon a subsequent development of the tradition about the *gibbōrîm.* So there is nothing to suggest that Ezekiel is dependent upon Gen. 6:1–4 or that any of his primeval traditions could be derived from Genesis. The reverse, however, is entirely possible, because Genesis seems to combine a number of themes and traditions that are otherwise quite separate in Ezekiel.[22]

Gen. 6:1–4 and the Antiquarian Tradition

Up to this point, I have attempted to develop the thesis that there were distinct eastern and western antiquarian traditions, that they were erudite constructions and part of the historiographic intellectual tradition. In its early Greek form, the western tradi-tion combines an extensive genealogical framework with quite diverse mythological and legendary narratives, a form that strongly suggests comparison with Genesis. This is particularly true of the Hesiodic *Catalogue of Women,* which throws light on the form and content of Gen. 6:1–4 and on its relationship to the larger context.[23]

The poet of the *Catalogue* begins with a proem in which he summons the Muses to sing of "the women . . . who were the finest in those times . . . and unfastened their waistbands . . . in union with the gods."[24] This statement does not introduce a particular mythical tale or series of stories, as one might expect, but is the beginning of an elaborate genealogy. In it, successive references to such sexual union between gods and mortal women become the starting point for extensive heroic genealogies. These women were presented as the actual ancestresses of the various Greek peoples, whereas their human husbands were merely the putative heads of such lines.

The end of the proem returns to the theme of the sexual union of gods with mortals. After listing the suitors of Helen and giving the account of Helen's marriage to Menelaus together with the arrival of the first child, as a prelude to the account of the Trojan War, there is an interruption in the narrative in which the scene shifts to the realm of the gods. The text states:

> Now all the gods were divided through strife; for at that time Zeus who thunders on high was meditating marvellous deeds, even to mingle storm and tempest over the boundless earth, and already he was hastening to make an utter end of the race of mortal men, declaring that he would destroy the lives of the demigods that the children of the gods (*tékna theōn*) should not mate with wretched mortals, seeing their fate with their own eyes: but that the blessed gods henceforth even as aforetime should have their living and their habitation apart from men. But on those who were born of immortals and of mankind verily Zeus laid toil and sorrow upon sorrow.[25]

This passage is followed by a broken text that seems to identify the disaster inflicted by Zeus as the Trojan War. But before the war itself is described, there is a reference to changes in nature that produce hardships and starvation and that seem to explain a change to a maritime economy. This change is perhaps also understood as an etiology for present human conditions and the "material" cause of the Trojan War.

There are some obvious similarities between the *Catalogue* and Gen. 6:1–4. First, the principal actors are the same, that is, mortal women and the gods. Here *tekna theōn* in the *Catalogue* is the direct equivalent of *bĕnē hā'ĕlōhîm* in the Hebrew text.[26] It is specifically noted in the Bible that the women were beautiful, that the gods had sexual union with them, and that the offspring of the unions were the heroes of the heroic age. This interpretation is certainly borne out by the content of the *Catalogue*.

Regarding the reference to the giants in Gen. 6:4, the *Catalogue* does not support the notion that the heroes were giants, and the mention of giants at all in the *Catalogue* is very rare. They have a much more prominent role in the *Theogony*, and it is only much later that that tradition comes to be combined with the other, as it does in Enoch 6–11.[27] On the evidence of the *Catalogue*, it would be best to view the reference to the Nephilim in Gen. 6:4 as secondary.

Superficially, the statement in Gen. 6:3 does look as if it could be understood to mean that the deity was about to inaugurate a separation between the divine and human realms.[28] But if our earlier interpretation of this verse is correct, then the statement about the limit set on human life is secondary and not related to the divine judgment theme. This makes it all the more likely that Gen. 6:1–4 was followed by an account of a divinely instituted disaster, although the nature of that calamity differs in the two forms of the tradition.

There is some similarity between Genesis and the *Phoenician History*, but its significance is not easy to assess. Philo mentions the birth of giants in the third (or fourth) generation of humankind, the eponyms of four famous mountains. These probably do not correspond to any particular myth about giants, as they do in the Greek theogonies. After these come two important culture heroes who are not giants, Samemroumos and Ousoos, whose mother was said to belong to those women who "at that time mated indiscriminately with whomever they chanced to meet." Considering Philo's euhemerism, this brief remark could reflect the tradition in the *Catalogue* and the Bible about sexual relations between gods and mortal women. The giants are part of this age but are not identified with any other heroes. There is no violent termination of the period and no flood story, but the heroes quarreled with each other.

One cannot reconstruct from these elements a single myth behind Gen. 6:1–4. There was a notion that in the early history of humankind gods mated with mortal women at will to produce heroes. The age was a violent one with great deeds of war, resulting in the heroes' destruction. There was also a separate tradition about a great disaster on humankind in general, reflecting a divine judgment. Ezekiel, as we saw, seems to preserve both of these separately. But the combination of these primeval traditions with the flood story is very loose in the western tradition and does not come into the Greek tradition until the late sixth century B.C.

A further comparison between the *Catalogue* and Gen. 6:1–4 on the question of form is in order here. In neither case can there be any question of reconstructing a specific mythical tale. In both the *Catalogue* and Genesis, the tradition about the union of gods and mortal women is construed as an introduction and interpretive prologue to other materials.[29] This common antiquarian use of tradition makes it quite misleading to speak in either case of mythical "fragments." This would confirm our earlier analysis of

Gen. 6:1–2, 4aβ,b as an introductory prologue to the larger flood story.

At the same time, this brief prologue in Gen. 6:1–2, 4 has close connections with what precedes it. It depends directly upon the story of the creation of humankind, *hā'ādām*, and the proliferation of humankind in the first few generations. In the preceding material, the genealogy focused primarily upon the male offspring. This is balanced by the reference here to the "daughters of humanity." The etiological form within the Cain genealogy also has some similarity here to the form in which this union gives rise to a special class of persons. All of this suggests the authorship of the Yahwist and his considerable freedom in the use of his traditional material.

NOTES

1. For a survey of earlier discussion and literature, see Westermann, *Genesis 1–11*, pp. 363–383; see also the monograph by R. Bartelmus, *Heroentum in Israel und seine Umwelt*, ATANT 65 (1979), pp. 9–78. In addition, see Hendel, "Of Demigods and Deluge"; and J. Van Seters, "The Primeval Histories of Greece and Israel Compared," *ZAW* 100 (1988), 1–22.

2. See Bartelmus, *Heroentum*, p. 18, for the meaning "sexually mature."

3. For the various opinions on the "sons of god," see Westermann, *Genesis 1–11*, pp. 371–373.

4. Cf. P. D. Hanson, "Rebellion in Heaven, Azazel, and Euhemeristic Heroes in 1 Enoch 6–11," *JBL* 96 (1977), 195–233, esp. pp. 210f.; Oden, "Divine Aspirations," *ZAW* 93:213–214.

5. See Westermann, *Genesis 1–11*, p. 375, where he lists the possibilities. See also Bartelmus (*Heroentum*, pp. 18f.) and Hendel ("Of Demigods and Deluge," *JBL* 106:15 n. 10), who propose the meaning "will be strong," but the basis for this interpretation is rather strained. On grammatical observations, see U. Cassuto, *Genesis I*, pp. 290–301.

6. See Samaritan Pentateuch (second verb) in BHS.

7. Westermann, *Genesis 1–11*, pp. 365–368; Coats, *Genesis*, p. 86; Bartelmus, *Heroentum*, p. 22; see also Childs, *Myth and Reality*, pp. 49–57, esp. p. 55.

8. Bartelmus, *Heroentum*, pp. 22–24.

9. So Childs, *Myth and Reality*, p. 56; followed by Coats, *Genesis*, pp. 85–86.

10. Westermann, *Genesis 1–11*, pp. 373ff. Bartelmus, *Heroentum*, p. 23f., disputes that Westermann's scheme works here.

11. D. L. Petersen, "Genesis 6:1–4: Yahweh and the Organization of the Cosmos," *JSOT* 13 (1979), 47–64.

12. Bartelmus, *Heroentum*, p. 28. Cf. J. T. Milik's remarks on the relationship of Genesis to Enoch in *The Book of Enoch: Aramaic Fragments of Qumran Cave 4* (1976), pp. 30ff. See also J. C. VanderKam, *Enoch and the Growth of the Apocalyptic Tradition*, CBQ MS 16 (1984), esp. pp. 122–135.

13. VanderKam, *Enoch*, pp. 129–130.

14. In one fragment of the *Catalogue* (fr. 19a in Evelyn-White, *Hesiod*, p. 603), the hero Sarpedon, son of Zeus, is granted a lifespan of "three generations of mortal man," that is, 120 years.

15. E. G. Kraeling, "The Significance and Origin of Gen. 6:1–4," *JNES* 6 (1947), 193–208. See most recently Hendel, "Of Demigods and Deluge," *JBL* 106:21ff. See also the earlier critical review of Kraeling and others by Petersen, "Genesis 6:1–4."

16. Kraeling, "The Significance," *JNES* 6:196f., 202f.

17. Reading *bhrbwt* with BHS.

18. Reading with the Greek ἀπ᾽ αἰωνος.

19. See also v. 21.

20. In addition to the paradise tradition of Ezek. 28:12–19.

21. As reflected in the Greek of Ezek. 32:27.

22. All the material collected by Bartelmus concerning the stories of heroes both in the Old Testament and elsewhere, particularly in the Greek traditions, may be useful in tracing the broader development of the heroes-giants traditions, but it cannot prove that the original text of Gen. 6:1–4 included the story of such a primeval struggle. At the most, it can help account for why the reference to the giants may have been added to the text.

23. For what follows, see my earlier study "The Primeval Histories."

24. West, *Hesiodic Catalogue of Women*, p. 2.

25. Translation from Evelyn-White, *Hesiod*, pp. 199f. See also the treatment by Hendel, "Of Demigods and Deluge," *JBL* 106:18–20.

26. West (*Hesiodic Catalogue of Women*, p. 119) gives a somewhat different understanding of this text in which he interprets the *tekna theōn* as heroes and thus suggests that it was Zeus's plan to remove the heroes from the human realm to the Isle of the Blessed, in agreement with the remark in the myth of the five races (so in agreement with Apollodorus's *Bibliotheca*, Epitome 3.1.1). But this seems to me an unlikely interpretation. Elsewhere in Hesiod, the "children of the gods and goddesses" are gods, whereas the heroes are characterized as "godlike," *theoeikelos*. The text also reads: πρόφασιν μεν ὀλέσσαι ψυχὰς ἡμιθεῶν, "declaring that he (Zeus) would put an end to the lives of the demigods," and that seems clear enough as a reference to the heroes. So the "children of the gods" must mean the gods themselves, and it is the domain of the gods that is to be forever separate from that of humankind. In that case, the divine judgment falls on both demigods and humans alike.

27. See Milik, *The Book of Enoch*, pp. 30ff.; and Bartelmus, *Heroentum*, pp. 151–190.

28. This is what I suggested in "The Primeval Histories," *ZAW* 100:8.

29. It is altogether possible that the Yahwist knew of traditions in which there were specific stories about the actual union of deity with mortals.

8

THE STORY
OF THE FLOOD

The Source-Critical Analysis

The analysis of this unit must proceed somewhat differently from the preceding because in this case the two primary sources, J and P, have been combined; therefore, the first task is to separate the two and to discuss their relationship to each other. On the identification of the J source, there has been rather broad agreement, already established by the time of Wellhausen, so only minor variations in its designation now exist among modern exegetes.[1] This may be set down as follows, with some doubtful texts set in parentheses: Gen. 6:5–8; 7:1–5, 7, 16b, 10, 12, 17b, 22, 23; 8:(1b), 2b, 3a, (4), 6–12, 13b, 20–22. There is a general consensus that the combination of sources has created some dislocation in the elements of the text represented by 7:7, 10, 12, 16b, but the order of their placement differs among various scholars. Some have suggested that the temporal statement "At the end of forty days" (8:6a) should stand before the section beginning with 8:2b (or 1b), because the account would otherwise have nothing to mark this important transition in the course of the flood.

In this version by the Yahwist, as reconstructed, there is a rather serious lacuna that has to do with the divine instructions to Noah to build the ark. Because this detail has a prominent place in P and because certain other important transitions in the story, such as the ending of the flood (8:1) and the departure from the ark (8:18), are also attributed to P, many scholars have suggested that the P version of the flood story formed the basic account that was then supplemented by details drawn from J. This viewpoint

160

has so completely dominated the many discussions of the flood narrative that few other possibilities have been seriously considered. Even when the proposal has been made to view P as directly dependent upon J in his construction of the final form of the flood story, there has been little discussion about what constitutes the relationship between J and P in particular.[2] This issue is now in need of serious reconsideration.[3]

There are two features of the flood story that make its analysis and separation into two distinct sources rather difficult. The first of these is the strict adherence to the difference in the divine name Yahweh/Elohim as a clue to the division of sources. This may not be altogether reliable, for we have already seen a few instances where J has used Elohim alone instead of Yahweh. If there are other reasons to suspect the presence of J in a text where Elohim is used, then such a possibility must be seriously considered.

The second feature that I wish to point out is that sometimes P appears to take up J's own special terminology. This can be illustrated here by a few examples but will be spelled out in greater detail in the subsequent analysis. The most striking example is in the declaration by the deity in the J source concerning Noah: "For I have observed that you are righteous before me in this generation" (7:1b). This is to be compared with P's statement in 6:10aβ: "Noah was a righteous man, blameless in his generations."[4] The similarity of these two remarks convinced Wellhausen that P must be directly dependent upon the J version.[5] The Yahwist lists the survivors that entered the ark as "Noah, his sons, his wife, his daughters-in-law" (7:7), probably as an explication of "his household" in 7:1. P spells this out even further by naming the three sons along with the mention of Noah's wife and the three daughters-in-law (7:13), whereas the more summary statement of the occupants is given in 8:16, 18.[6] The Yahwist uses the special term for the flood, *mabbûl* (7:7, 10), and this term is also used by P (6:17; 7:6, [17?]; 9:11, 15).[7]

Once it is recognized that Elohim can be used by the Yahwist and that there is considerable imitation of J's terminology by P, then the analysis of the flood story must proceed along quite different lines from those in the past. We must look again at the supposed lacunae in the Yahwist account. First, one would expect to find a reference to the construction of the ark before 7:1 in the form of divine instructions, such as appears in 6:14–16, but this is attributed to P. There is nothing in the description of the ark's construction that is especially characteristic of P.[8] The attribution to P is based upon the introductory statement in 6:13, but this too requires a reappraisal. Genesis 6:13 may be rendered as follows: "And God said to Noah, 'The end of all flesh has come before me for the earth is full of violence because of them. So I will certainly destroy them from [reading *mē'ēt*, BHS] the earth.'" This verse has been universally assigned to P because the divine subject is designated Elohim and because the language is characteristic of other P passages[9] and actually contains three clauses that correspond closely, but in reverse order, with those in vs. 11, 12. But this strong similarity has obscured the fact that v. 13 is saying something quite different from vs. 11–12, even though it uses much the same words. The two verbs in v. 11 are in the *niphal,* which may be either passive or, more likely here, reflexive: "The earth had corrupted itself in the sight of God and had filled itself with violence" in view of v. 12: "God saw that the earth was indeed corrupt because all flesh had corrupted its way upon the earth." What is emphasized is the universal corruption (*šḥt*) of the world without any agency. In this it parallels, but goes beyond, what is suggested in 6:5 to include all living things and not just humankind. But 6:13 goes back to the more restrictive sense of the earth becoming full of violence "because of *them*," so that it is God who will destroy (*šḥt*) *them* from the earth. It is the result of the actions of a certain group that the "prophetic" judgment will come upon "all flesh."

To whom does the "them" of v. 13 refer? It cannot refer to "all flesh" because that is treated in v. 12 as a singular, "its way." There is nothing in the previous P statements that can serve as the antecedent for the third plural suffix. If we refer back to the previous J statement, then the "them" refers to humankind (*hā'ādām*), which is reflected in the plural suffix of *'āśîtîm*, "I made them," which, taken with v. 6, must refer to humankind specifically and not the other creatures.[10] It is precisely this kind of violent activity that has nowhere been mentioned earlier by P.[11] So it is out of this rather specific allusion to earlier actions leading to judgment that P has constructed his own vague statement about the general corruption of all creation.[12]

In 6:13 (J), a prophetic judgment is announced against a particular group: "The end of all flesh has come before me." The prophetic character of this statement has often been recognized because of the use of "end," *qēṣ,* as in Amos 8:2 and Ezekiel 7. But it is also true of the phrase "all flesh" in the meaning of humanity, which is frequently found in prophetic literature, especially in statements of divine judgment.[13] It is therefore the semantic equivalent of *'ādām.* But in P, the term has been broadened to include animal life as well and is used particularly in this sense in the flood story.

Once it is recognized that 6:13 belongs to J in spite of the use of Elohim, then the description of the ark in vs. 14–16 follows directly from this. With vs. 17–21, P introduces his own elaboration anticipating the covenant theme of 9:1–17. The first unit of action concludes with the statement (v. 22): "And Noah did according to all that God had commanded him, so he did." Apart from the additional last two words, *kēn 'āśāh,* and the difference in the divine name, the statement is identical to that of 7:5 (J), so both belong to J. The Priestly Writer's modification of this terminology is found in 7:9, 16.[14] This makes the beginning of the flood story in the J version entirely complete and without any breaks.

The second unit of action in 7:1–5, 7, 16b, 10 is also quite complete, with the only question being whether v. 16b should come after v. 7 or v. 10. It is clearly out of place in its present position. It is also not entirely clear whether the additional clean animals and birds were meant to anticipate the use of some for the sacrifice in 8:20 or as food during the course of the voyage. What is noteworthy is that P combines his statement about the preservation of animals, birds, and reptiles with J's instructions about the building of the ark and then repeats, after J's account of gathering the animals, the fact that Noah brought on board only a pair of each, the clean as well as unclean. This repetition and the need to mention both clean and unclean animals can be explained only as a deliberate attempt by P to modify the statement made by J. The course of events during the flood is briefly stated by J in 7:12, 17b, 22–23. The P version adds nothing to this but elaboration of detail and a different chronology.

The next unit concerning the end of the flood contains a number of problems about which there is some difference of opinion. Many have suggested that the statement in 8:6, "at the end of forty days," is more appropriate at the beginning of this unit, and it may have been displaced because of P's statement about the 150 days' duration of the flood in 7:24. The statement in 8:1, "And God remembered Noah and all the wild and domestic animals that were with him in the ark . . . ," marks the real transition in the story. This is regularly attributed to P on the strength of the use of Elohim, although the phrase 'ăšer ittô battēbâ is the same as that used in 7:23 (J). The closest parallel to this is found in Gen. 19:29, also attributed to P because of the use of Elohim; but it is so obviously dependent upon the J version of the story and the dialogue between Abraham and Yahweh in 18:16ff. that its attribution to J makes much better sense. Another instance is found in Gen. 30:22; and even though Elohim is used here as well, it is scarcely attributed to P. The second half of 8:1 does not fit very well with P's conception of the flood or with P's statements in v. 2a, but it does agree well with J and is similar to J's treatment of the Red Sea episode in Ex. 14:21bβ. Genesis 8:2b, 3a also belongs to J. The statement that the ark came to rest on the mountains of Ararat (v. 4) does not fit with the viewpoint of v. 5, as Skinner has observed,[15] and thus, apart from P's statement of chronology, v. 4 also belongs to J. It fits very well with his interest in geography. Consequently, it would appear that once again the basic account of this part of the story (8:6a, 1, 2b, 3a, 4*) belongs to the Yahwist with only a few P embellishments.

The episode with the birds in 8:6b–12 is entirely the work of the Yahwist, with no additions by P. It presents few problems except that one should probably assume an additional wait of seven days between the sending of the raven and the dove. This is indicated by the statement in v. 10: "Again he waited seven more days." Skinner has pointed out that the two-month time lapse between v. 5 and v. 13 corresponds to the forty days + three weeks in vs. 6–12.[16] This is another clear indication that P is entirely dependent upon the J account.

It has often been observed that there is a lacuna in J between the sending forth of the birds in 8:12 and the building of the altar in 8:20.[17] But the gap may be more imagined than real. In J, God commands Noah and his family to enter the ark, and he does so (7:1a, 7). Except for the change from Yahweh to Elohim, the same command to leave the ark with his family is given together with Noah's compliance, in 8:15–16, 18, and there is no other reason apart from the divine name in v. 15 to deny them to J. The additional remarks about the animals in vs. 17 and 19 would then be P embellishments similar to those in 6:18b–20 and 7:8–9. The final scene in 8:20–22 is from J and links up with the special instructions about the extra clean animals and birds in 7:2–3.

This reconstruction gives to us the complete story of the flood in J: 6:5–8, 13–16, 22*; 7:1–5, 7, 16b, 10, 12, 17b, 22–23; 8:6a, 1, 2b, 3a, 4*, 6b–12, 15–16, 18, 20–22. Once this is recognized, then P appears in an entirely different light. It now seems that P was no more than a series of embellishments, modifications, and supplements having to do with the chronology of the flood, its nature and relationship to all of the cosmos, the numbers and types of creatures taken into the ark, and so forth. There are no new story elements introduced apart from the idea of the covenant with Noah in chapter 9, so there is no reason to believe that P had access to any other source or tradition apart from J. P did not even give the present story its shape, as B. W. Anderson has suggested.[18] That credit belongs to the Yahwist, whose clear and forceful narrative has been somewhat obscured by P's ideological and chronographic concerns.

The Tradition-History of the Flood Story

It has long been recognized that the flood story of Genesis corresponds rather closely to the Mesopotamian flood tradition, especially that version that was preserved in the *Gilgamesh Epic*.[19] If we now compare our reconstructed Yahwist account with this Babylonian version of the flood, the results are quite significant.

Gilgamesh XI	*Genesis 6–8 J*
1. Divine warning and instruction to build the boat followed by detailed description: size of boat, seven levels, nine compartments each level, much pitch to secure the boat.	1. Divine warning is given about the destruction of humankind. Command is given to build the ark of gopher wood with compartments, to cover with pitch, to have a roof and door and three levels. Size of ark is given.
2. Animals brought to the boat to preserve "the seed of all living	2. Animals and birds are brought on board "to keep alive seed upon

creatures." (A-h III i.37—seven days respite before the flood.) Family and animals enter the boat, and Utnapishtim shuts the door.

the face of the earth." Noah brings his family on board, and God shuts the door. Then after seven days' wait the flood comes.

3. Emphasis is on a great storm of wind and rain for seven days. Flood destroys humankind.

3. Rain for forty days produces the flood with the destruction of all life.

4. The storm subsides. Utnapishtim opens the window. The boat lands on Mt. Nisir. After seven days birds are sent out: dove, swallow, raven.

4. The flood subsides and the ark lands on Mt. Ararat. Noah opens the window and releases birds: raven and dove, with seven-day intervals.

5. Utnapishtim leaves the boat and all with him. He offers a sacrifice to the gods, who smell the sweet savor and decide never to bring another flood.

5. Noah and his family leave the ark and offer sacrifice. God smells the pleasing odor and promises never to bring another flood.

6. Utnapishtim is granted eternal life.

6. Noah becomes the new founder of the human race.

Leaving aside for the moment the matter of the motive for the flood, which is not directly addressed in *Gilgamesh*,[20] the Babylonian account begins with divine warning and instructions on building of the boat to the hero Utnapishtim in order to preserve "the seed of all living creatures." This is followed by the actual construction given in greater detail, including the boat's size, the fact that it had seven levels each with nine compartments, and that it was covered with a great deal of pitch. This corresponds very closely to the details of Gen. 6:13–16, even if not all of the elements are in the same order. The seven days' pause before the beginning of the flood does not seem to be in the *Gilgamesh* version, but it is mentioned in *Atrahasis* III i.37. Noah does not attempt any deception of his contemporaries who might ask about the ark's construction, as does Utnapishtim. He simply collects the animals and his family and puts all on board, as in *Gilgamesh*. But nothing is said in either account about provisions of food, although in *Gilgamesh* other possessions are also put on board.[21]

All the basic components of the Babylonian flood story are represented in the biblical account, with the notable exception of the rivalry among the gods, especially Enlil and Ea (Enki), and the fate of the hero. This has led the Yahwist to modify the beginning and the ending and to put his own distinctive stamp upon the tradition at these two points.

E. G. Kraeling, however, has raised the possibility that the biblical tradition may have been influenced by the western transmission of this tradition as it is reflected in the Lucian work, *The Syrian Goddess*.[22] In this version, the race destroyed by the flood was violent and lawless, and the flood came as punishment for these offenses. Few details are given, but the flood hero, Deucalion/Sisythes, because of his piety, is spared by putting himself, his family, and all the animals who came to him *in pairs* on board an *ark*. The fate of the hero, Deucalion, is that he becomes the founder of a new race of men.

The use of Lucian's *Syrian Goddess* for comparison as a witness to an old western version of the flood, however, is suspect. At certain points, the language is very close to that of the biblical account in its P form. This could indicate direct access to the Greek Bible or indirectly through a number of other sources. Lucian clearly made use of Greek versions as well, so he is not an independent witness to any ancient version in the western tradition.

Westermann, in his comparison of the various flood traditions with the biblical account, endeavors to use the Greek versions of the flood to establish a "premythical form" that is older than any Mesopotamian version and that is shared by the biblical account. He does this by calling attention to the fact that in the Greek traditions of Ovid and Apollodorus there is no rivalry between the gods over the flood, as there is in the Mesopotamian version, so that the deity (Zeus) who brings the flood is also the one who ends it and saves the hero (Deucalion). This is similar to the biblical account. The theme of rivalry between Enlil and Enki (Ea) reflect a "steady progression towards a marked mythological shaping."[23] On this basis, he regards the Greek and biblical versions as the more ancient.

This position is untenable. His notions that a less mythical form preceded the more mythical version suggest "romantic" perceptions of *Religionsgeschichte* that can be set aside here. Ovid and Apollodorus are hardly less mythical than the Mesopotamian stories. But there are a number of other points that must be made:

1. It is incorrect to say that there is no divine rivalry in Apollodorus. Prometheus plays the role of Enki in warning Deucalion. This is in keeping with the god's role in Hesiod, but it also may reflect some eastern influence similar to that in Lucian.

Ovid's account does not have such a rivalry because he has combined it with the quite different tradition about the divine visitation and inhospitality theme so that Zeus's judgment is just, not capricious. One late Mesopotamian version of the flood, in the *Erra Epic,* mentions only Marduk (= Zeus?) as the one responsible for the flood and says nothing about a divine rivalry.

2. As indicated earlier,[24] Ovid has combined a number of separate traditions that had no original connection with each other: the use of Hesiod's "iron age" as the evil generation, the episode of throwing stones to produce people, and the hospitality motif. One cannot ignore the Greek history of traditions as Westermann does in order to use these as evidence of his "pre-mythical" form. Ovid, Apollodorus, and Lucian are all antiquarian collectors of traditions that exercised considerable freedom in their arrangements and the use of their sources.

3. It is certainly best to deal with the biblical flood story in the context of its Near Eastern antecedents to which it is most closely related. To use versions of the flood from Roman times as a way of reconstructing some universal theological flood story is highly suspect. The amount of "foreign" literature in circulation was rather high, and Apollodorus and Lucian show every evidence of using it.

Much discussion by scholars dealing with the flood story centers on the divine motivation for the disaster. As noted earlier, the motivation reflected in the *Atrahasis* version of the flood was overpopulation, and efforts to find in this story a different motive akin to rebellion against the gods is unwarranted. The *Gilgamesh Epic* does not state directly why the gods brought the flood, only that "their heart prompted the great gods to bring the deluge" (XI.14). But at the end of the flood, Ea remonstrates with Enlil that he could have used other means to decrease the population of humankind (XI.181–185), which supports the motive of over-population.[25] Ea's statement: "On the sinner lay his sin; on the transgressor his transgression" (180), has often been taken to mean that some perhaps sinned, for which all were made to suffer. But this is only stated as a general principle governing divine acts of judgment and says nothing directly about any specific motive.

It seems likely that the Yahwist, instead of focusing on the theme of overpopulation, took up the principle of the disaster as a direct response to human sinfulness and specific violent actions, sparing the righteous one, Noah, and his family. This would be quite similar to the story of the destruction of Sodom and Gomorrah, with the righteous also spared from the disaster (Genesis 18–19).[26] The notion of great disasters as a result of special lawlessness and inhospitality is also common in Greek tradition. The conclusion from this consideration of the tradition behind the Yahwist is that very little of his flood story is original with him.

The Yahwist's creativity is seen primarily in his formulation of the motivation for the flood (Gen. 6:5–8) and in its conclusion (8:20–22), which reflects on the nature of humankind as sinner and the deity's dealings with them.[27] This can best be understood in the light of the larger context of his work.

The Form and Context of the Flood Story

The story's form and its relationship to the larger context of the J source are inseparable. The previous discussion of the flood tradition has made it clear that the primary imprint of the Yahwist upon the traditional material was in the opening and closing scenes as they have to do with the deity. In its present form, the flood narrative in J is yet another crime and punishment story.[28] The link in the opening passage in 6:5–7 indicates the magnitude of the offense and suggests that ever since the beginning of creation until the time of Yahweh's scrutiny humanity has pursued a continuous evil course of action. The connection with the themes of creation in vs. 6–7 is quite explicit; and the story of the Fall in chapter 3, Cain's murder in chapter 4, and the Song of Lamech in 4:23–24 all seem to reinforce the connection between the flood story and that of the earlier material. It is quite possible that a connection between the creation of humankind and the flood tradition was already suggested by the Mesopotamian primeval traditions as found in *Atrahasis*, but the fact that J's creation story and his antediluvian tradition seem to owe nothing to the *Atrahasis* epic suggests that this connection by J was largely his own work.

The story of paradise and the Fall deals with the universal problem of sin and suffering, and therefore the reason for J's use of a single human pair. It is this that allows the Yahwist to continue the theme of universal wickedness by emphasizing "humankind," *hā'ādām,* as the initial subject of the flood story.

In contrast to this generalization on the state of human evil, the statement in 6:13 is a much more specific indictment on violent actions perpetrated by those on earth who are to be dealt with directly. This may have in mind the violent actions mentioned in the story of Cain and Abel and in the Song of Lamech, but its more immediate connection would seem to be with the heroes of Gen. 6:1–4. It is the heroic age that was especially known as a violent and warlike age and prototypical of such activity in later ages.[29] If, as I have argued, 6:13 belongs to J, then 6:1–2, 4* serves as a direct narrative prologue to the flood story, which also tells how this ancient race of demigods came to an end.

R. S. Hendel has recently argued that the connection between the tradition in 6:1–4 and the flood story belongs to a pre-Yahwistic level of the tradition that J has obscured by his addition of the motive in 6:5–7.[30] But against this are two important considerations. First, every essential element of the flood tradition in J seems to correspond to that of the Mesopotamian tradition, and yet the latter does not suggest that the flood was an end to a heroic age, nor that it was the consequence of judgment on human wickedness. Second, the flood tradition only comes into the Greek primeval traditions at a rather late stage, and then it is associated with Deucalion, the first human of his genealogical line. All of the heroes in the heroic age, the demigods, come *after* him and only come to an end in the Trojan War. The idea that the gods bring about great disasters for many different reasons, one of which may be the violent or sinful activity of men, is a very common theme and reason enough for the Yahwist to formulate his own cause of the flood without any dependence upon a specific form of the flood tradition that included such a motivation.

The two levels of divine motivation for the flood in J, the general and the particular, are represented in two different forms. The one is that of a divine soliloquy (6:5–7) on the nature of God's creation and God's judgment on it. The other is a prophetic judgment speech directed to Noah on the specific activity of those in his own time.[31] This permitted the Yahwist to make a connection with the universal theme of the creation tradition while at the same time incorporating a specific theme about the heroic age. The sense of disjunction between 6:4 and 6:5 was then inevitable, especially when scholars relegated 6:13 to the P source. Once 6:13 is seen as following directly on 6:8, the sense of discontinuity is much less apparent.

Furthermore, the fact that Noah was seen by God to be righteous *in his generation* (7:1) suggests that his salvation in the flood was a mitigation of the specific judgment in 6:13. Although all of his wicked contemporaries were destroyed, he was saved and his household. The same theme is raised again in the story of Sodom and Gomorrah in which Lot and his household are also saved from similar divine judgment (Genesis 19).

The end of the flood story has likewise been changed by the Yahwist. Immediately following the traditional scene of the flood-hero's sacrifice, there is a concluding divine soliloquy that balances, in form and content, the initial statement of 6:5–7 in its universal dimensions. The judgment on Noah's contemporaries, the heroes, cannot be changed, and so it obviously does not come into consideration here. But the judgment on humankind as a whole is mitigated by a vow never to curse the ground again, that is, to destroy all life by means of a flood. To call the flood a curse of the ground, *hā'ădāmâ,* is to deliberately parallel it with the curse of the fall story.[32] This mitigation of divine judgment is given in spite of the fact that humankind has not changed in character from what it was before the flood. Genesis 8:22 also emphasizes the theme of creation and the order of life, just as the flood in 6:7 was regarded as an interruption in the order of creation. The divine guarantee of the regular rotation of the seasons may suggest an etiology for seasonal change, instituted at this time.

NOTES

1.   J. Wellhausen, *Die Composition* (1899), pp. 2–14; Gunkel, *Genesis,* pp. 59–60, 137–138; Skinner, *Genesis,* p. 148; von Rad, *Genesis,* pp. 116, 118, 121, 125; Westermann, *Genesis 1–11,* pp. 395–398; Coats, *Genesis,* pp. 75-82. For an extensive bibliography, see Westermann, *Genesis 1–11,* pp. 384–387.

2.   See F. M. Cross, *Canaanite Myth and Hebrew Epic* (1973), p. 306; and B. W. Anderson, "From Analysis to Synthesis: The Interpretation of Genesis 1–11," *JBL* 97 (1978), 28–39.

3. For J. A. Emerton ("The Priestly Writer in Genesis," *JTS* 39 [1988], 381–400),
the flood story is a test case for the independence of P.
4. See Skinner, *Genesis,* pp. 158–159.
5. Wellhausen, *Prolegomena,* p. 390.
6. On v. 18, see below.
7. Compare also the following: 7:22, "in whose nostrile was the breath of life
(*nišmat ḥayyîm*)," which reflects the Yahwist creation story, with the statement in
P, 7:15, "in which was the breath of life (*rûaḥ ḥayyîm*)." Another phrase from the
J creation story but not used by J in the flood story is "living creature," *nepheš
ḥayyîm,* which P used several times (9:10, 12, 15, 16) in the account of the covenant with Noah. See also "all life," *kol ḥay,* 8:21 (J), and *kol hāḥay,* 6:19 (P).
8. Cf. the description of the temple and palace construction in 1 Kings 6–7 (Dtr).
9. See 6:11, 12, 17, 19; 7:15, 21; 9:2b, 11, 15–17.
10. See also the plural suffix *lāhem* in 6:1.
11. This lack is regularly acknowledged by commentators, following Wellhausen,
Prolegomena, p. 310, but nothing is made of it.
12. The inclusion of 6:13 in J makes the parallel of J's flood story with Sodom
and Gomorrah in Genesis 18–19 all the more pertinent. In both cases, there is
a divine soliloquy followed by the divine sentence and the sparing of the righteous
one and his family.
13. Isaiah 40:5, 6; 49:26; 66:16, 23, 24; Jer. 25:31; 32:27; 45:5; Ezek. 21:4, 9, 10;
Joel 3:1; Zech. 2:17.
14. Cf. also Ex. 12:28.
15. Skinner, *Genesis,* p. 167.
16. Skinner, *Genesis,* pp. 167f. This assumes that the forty days of v. 6a is in its
original place or more likely that it was moved to this location by P.
17. See commentaries in n. 1 above.
18. See work in n. 2 above.
19. For comparison of the other flood traditions, see Westermann, *Genesis 1–11,*
pp. 399–406 ; see also V. Fritz, "'Solange die Erde steht' —vom Sinn der
jahwistischen Fluterzählung in Gen. 6–8," *ZAW* 94 (1982), 599–614.
20. V. Fritz, ibid., pp. 604f., argues on the basis of XI. 182–185 that it is the
same as that of *Atrahasis,* namely, overpopulation.
21. In Berossus, according to Polyhistor, there is some mention of putting food
and drink on board as well. See Lambert and Millard, *Atra-Ḥasis,* p. 135.
22. Kraeling, "Xisouthros, Deucalion and the Flood Traditions." See also the
remarks by Oden, *Studies in Lucian's De Syria Dea,* pp. 24–36.
23. Westermann, *Genesis 1–11,* p. 401.
24. See pp. 81–83 above.
25. So also V. Fritz, *ZAW* 94:604ff.
26. See Clark, "The Flood," *ZAW* 83:193–195, for a comparison between these
stories.
27. This matter has generated considerable discussion in recent years. See R.
Rendtorff, "Genesis 8:21 und die Urgeschichte des Jahwisten," *KuD* 7 (1961), 69–78;
and critiques by O. H. Steck, "Genesis 12,1–3 und die Urgeschichte des Jahwisten,"
(1971) in *Wahrnehmungen Gottes im Alten Testament* (1982), pp. 119–124; and D. L.

Petersen, "The Yahwist on the Flood," *VT* 26 (1976), 440–446. See also V. Fritz, *ZAW* 94:608–612.
28. Westermann, *Genesis 1–11*, p. 48.
29. See Ezek. 32:27–28.
30. Hendel, "Of Demigods and Deluge."
31. Note this same combination of divine soliloquy and judgment speech in Gen. 18:16ff.
32. This does not mean that the curse of creation in Gen. 3:17–18 has been lifted, as Rendtorff suggests (n. 27 above). The curse clearly continues as a part of the experience of life. The curse in 8:21 has reference only to the destruction of the flood, as v. 21b makes quite clear.

9
THE TABLE
OF NATIONS

The flood story in J is followed by a statement about the three sons of Noah who went forth from the ark: Shem, Ham, and Japheth. "And from these the whole earth was peopled" (9:18–19). This introduces the so-called Table of Nations, which must be considered at this point. How the narrative about Noah's drunkenness relates to the Table will be discussed below, but the form and nature of the larger framework in which the narrative unit is now fitted must be taken up first.

The Source Analysis of Genesis 10

The source division of the Table in Gen. 10:1–32 has by now become fairly well established.[1] The usual source distribution is as follows:

J 9:18–19; 10:1b, 8–19, 21, (24) 25–30.
P 10:1a, 2–7, 20, 22–23, 31–32.

The combination of the two sources is very similar to that of the flood story, and our understanding of the nature of the Yahwist depends very much upon how the relationship between J and P is construed. In the older view of the documentary hypothesis, it was suggested that the P version formed the basis of the Table and that a redactor used parts of a J version to fill it out with more detail. This view has been challenged by S. Tengström, who argues that P cannot be understood as an independent document because it presupposes the work of the Yahwist and builds directly upon it.[2] This can be seen, first of all, in the basic structure of the Table, which consists of two elements: (1) the enumeration of the various peoples, and (2) their geographic extension. P emphasizes this twofold scheme in his concluding summary in v. 32, but the scheme in the P source is only complete in vs. 2–5, for the line of Japheth. For the lines of both Ham and Shem, the territorial extension is contained only in the J source (vs. 10–12, 18b–19, 30), so the P source actually requires the J material in order for the concluding statement in v. 32 to be a real summary. If one assigns the summary statements, such as vs. 5, 20, 31, and 32, to a redactor, then the P source could not be used as the basis for the structure of the whole.

Furthermore, Gen 10:1 has troubled scholars greatly. It may be rendered: "These are the genealogies of the sons of Noah, Shem, Ham, and Japheth, and to them were born sons after the flood." J is credited with v. 1b because it is a verbal sentence that breaks the pattern of nominal sentences in P. However, the statement in v. 1b cannot stand by itself and cannot easily be associated with what has preceded it in J. It does, in fact, fit very smoothly with v. 1a, but this half verse is assigned to P because of the reference to "genealogy/ies," *tôlĕdôt*. This use of *tôlĕdôt*, however, is somewhat exceptional for P in that it does not deal with a specific line of descendants but begins a segmented genealogy of the three sons. P has actually created a parallel alternative to it with the *tôlĕdôt* of Shem in Gen. 11:10–26, which continues directly from the *tôlĕdôt* of Noah (Gen. 6:9–10).[3] This means that it is quite likely that the whole of 10:1 belongs to J and provides a kind of recapitulation of 9:18–19 after the inclusion of the story of the curse of Canaan, 9:20–26 (27), as well as a heading for what follows. P would then have adopted this terminology from J for his conclusion in v. 32a (and for his use of the *tôlĕdôt* formula generally), just as he used J's phraseology from 9:19 and 10:1b for his concluding statement in v. 32b to form an inclusio:[4] "These are the families of the sons of Noah according to their genealogies by their nationalities, and from these the nations spread throughout the earth after the flood."

Concerning the content of the genealogies, it would also appear to be the case, as Tengström points out,[5] that among the sons of Ham P has dealt only with Cush and his more obscure offspring. This is because both Egypt and Canaan were already treated by J, which P had in front of him. J's treatment of Cush was to make him the father of a hero who was the founder of nations and not the progenitor of eponyms. Because in this case J's genealogy of Cush did not fit P's scheme, he developed his own (10:7). In the Shem genealogy (10:21–31), the primary line of Eber-Peleg is strangely stunted. This can only be because P has deliberately used the rest of J's genealogy to construct his special linear genealogy of Shem in 11:10–26.[6] This strongly suggests that other materials derived from J were used by P in the Table of Nations, which he reworked into his own style.[7] This treatment also seems likely for the descendants of Japheth, which may have been augmented by some new additions. It seems certain that J had a Japheth genealogy, and there is no reason to suppose that the descendants in his list were markedly different from the list in P.[8]

It is safe to say that the Yahwist had a Table of Nations containing a tripartite genealogical *stemma* with a story of a hero embedded in it. It is this J version that formed the basis for the present Table and not P as commonly suggested. P's only contribution was to make additions of names within the Ham and Shem lines, to modify the whole of the Japheth line in his own style, and to furnish a few summary statements. It remains now to investigate the form and literary tradition that lies behind the Yahwist's Table of Nations.

Form and Tradition

In his recent Genesis commentary, C. Westermann makes the statement that "the table of nations is unique and has no parallel either inside or outside the Old Testament."[9] For Westermann, its composition is a special inner biblical development. The original setting in life of the genealogies is the patriarchal history that reflects a tribal way of life in which genealogies play a major role. It is primarily a genre of oral tradition. Therefore, the presentation of the primeval history in J by means of genealogies "has been taken over from the patriarchal history and applied to the primeval story."[10] Thus, for Westermann, the real genealogies in the Table of Nations are those that reflect descent from persons, and eponyms that represent peoples and places are secondary developments. Westermann further suggests that "J's table of nations is an extension of the conclusion of the flood narrative,"[11] and that the repopulation of the earth by the survivors of the flood is a common conclusion to the flood tradition.

Regarding this last assertion by Westermann, I can find no hint in the Babylonian flood tradition of any scheme of the repopulation of humankind by the flood survivors. What is suggested, in the fragmentary remains that we have, is something like a second creation of humankind by the mother goddess. The flood survivors are, in fact, removed from any further contact with normal life and are given immortality in a realm apart from the rest of humanity.[12] In the Greek tradition, the flood story is put in a rather awkward place within the time of Deucalion at the beginning of the human race before the proliferation of humankind. It is clearly secondary to the genealogies as a whole because it is absent from the earliest versions.[13] So the Table of Nations is not a logical extension of the end of the flood story. It is therefore necessary to offer a more plausible explanation of its form and tradition history.

Contradicting Westermann's claim about the uniqueness of the Table of Nations is the example of the Hesiodic *Catalogue of Women,* which was referred to above.[14] The main body of this work contains an elaborate series of segmented genealogies consisting primarily of the eponyms of Greek-speaking peoples, nations, tribes, and geographical place names. Some foreign nations well known to the Greeks are also included. Mixed with these eponyms are the personal names of heroes and primeval kings.[15] These have been fitted into the segmented genealogies of tribes and states, often with great ingenuity. Also included within the main body of the text are shorter or longer accounts or summaries of heroic legends. This makes it remarkably like J's Table of Nations, which also includes the story of the hero Nimrod within its structure. The *Catalogue,* on the other hand, does not begin with an account of the flood but with a remark about the union of the gods with mortal women to produce the heroes who are the subject of the *Catalogue.* This strongly suggests that the Yahwist has combined this western genealogical tradition and the tradition of the heroes with the eastern tradition of the flood story.

The Story of Nimrod

The story of Nimrod, Gen. 10:8–12, is given in short anecdotal form in which the hero is linked with an eponymic ancestor and accounts for the founding of various city-states and kingdoms. This combination of narrative with genealogy is typical of the western antiquarian tradition. The fact that Nimrod's ancestor Cush (v. 8), who probably stands for the Kassites,[16] is identified with the Cush (v. 6) that represents Ethiopia should come as no surprise. This kind of identity that is based merely upon the similarity of names led the Greeks to identify the Greek heroine Medea as the mother of the Medes, and Perseus as the father of the Persians.

Nimrod is characterized as "the first on earth to become a hero," הוא החל להיות גבר בארץ. In this regard, he belongs both to those who are inventors of culture (4:20–22; 9:20) and to the heroes of 6:1–4. The fact that he is not explicitly given divine parentage does not militate against this connection, because heroes regularly have a human patronymic or ethnic genealogical connection as well. His exploits as a hunter, גבר־ציד, are said to be "before Yahweh," לפני יהוה, setting him apart from mere mortals. Like Heracles, he was known both for his deeds and his founding of kingdoms and cities.[17] There is no need to suppose that the listing of cities in a series, as in vs. 10–11, is a secondary expansion of the tradition, as Westermann suggests.[18] It is just as likely that the Yahwist selected a "heroic" royal figure of Assyria and made him into the founder of both the Babylonian and Assyrian kingdoms and some of their great cities.

This story of Nimrod within the Table of Nations raises questions about the relationship of the Table to the stories that immediately precede and follow. The story of Noah's drunkenness is in fact preceded by the statement that makes the transition from the flood account to the proliferation of humankind. Yet the author has put this story about Noah and his sons at the beginning of his genealogical table because it belongs before the enumeration of the rest of the descendants. So in J's account, the story of Noah's drunkenness also belongs within his Table of Nations.

The Story of Noah's Drunkenness: Gen. 9:20–27

The story opens with the statement about the beginning of agriculture and immediately recalls the contributions to civilization in 4:20–22, 26, although in form it stands closer to the statement about Nimrod in 10:8. The statement that Noah was "the first man of the soil" also recalls his naming in 5:29: "Out of the ground which Yahweh has cursed this one shall bring us relief from our work and from the toil of our hands." The "consolation" would seem to refer more directly to his discovery of wine through the cultivation of the grape than to the flood story. The fact that the remark in 5:29 has the story of the Fall and the curse in 3:17–18 so clearly in mind indicates that the link with the earlier story and the anticipation of the later drunkenness episode are the work of the Yahwist.

In the original story, Canaan was the son of Noah who disgraced his father and thus was cursed, so the reference to Ham as the father of Canaan in v. 22 is an obvious secondary modification.[19] It has also been cogently argued by J. Herrmann that there was only one other brother and that this was Shem.[20] But even the pair, Canaan–Shem, looks problematic to me as hardly constituting an appropriate balance. The gloss in 10:21, "he (Shem) was the father of all the sons of Eber, the elder brother of Japheth," almost certainly refers back to 9:20ff. and suggests that Shem has displaced Eber in the same way that Ham displaced Canaan. The oldest form of the story was about Noah and his two sons Canaan and Eber. Because Eber is simply the eponym for the Hebrews, *'ibrî*, it is the more obvious parallel to Canaan. The story only contained a curse by Noah against Canaan condemning him to lowest servitude among his "brethren." The latter term is used in quite a general way for neighboring peoples, as it is elsewhere in Genesis.[21]

It was the Yahwist who took this rather limited local tradition and fitted it into his more universal perspective by making it the story of Noah and his three sons, Shem, Ham, and Japheth, instead of Canaan and Eber. He retained the Curse of Canaan but added a blessing for Shem (or the God of Shem) to make it match. The model here was obviously the blessing of the sons of Jacob by their father. The statement in Gen. 9:27, which reinterprets the whole curse-blessing as a future prediction, looks like a very late expansion from Hellenistic times.[22] The story has thus been modified in order to fit into the larger scheme of the Table of Nations by making the necessary genealogical adjustments. This technique is fairly standard for Greek genealogists.

The Tower of Babel

The relationship of the Tower of Babel story to the Table of Nations is more difficult to judge. The story in Gen. 11:1–9 appears to stand in some tension to that of the Table, both in terms of the explanation of the different national origins, specifically Babylon (cf. 10:10), and in the chronological location of the episode. But we must not be too hasty in drawing literary conclusions from this for the following reasons:[23]

1. It is quite possible for an ancient author to set down side by side two quite different explanations for the same thing, as Hesiod does on the origin of evil in *Works and Days*.

2. The theme of the Babel story has to do with the migration and settlement of peoples and the building of a city. Such a theme is also prominent within the *Catalogue* and antiquarian histories as an explanation of national origins, and this can stand side by side with genealogical origins from eponymic ancestors or the founding of cities by heroes.

3. The sense of discontinuity between the Table and the Tower of Babel story is reflected primarily in the phraseology of P in 10:5b, 20, 31–32, which makes specific mention of the division by languages and lands and suggests that the dispersal took place after the flood.

Furthermore, when one compares the Yahwist version of the Table with the Tower of Babel story, a number of interconnections become apparent. The one theme in the Babel story, that of Yahweh scattering (*pwṣ*, vs. 4, 8, 9) humankind (*'ādām*, v. 5) over the surface of the earth, reiterates the theme of 9:19, that the descendants of Noah were dispersed (*npṣ*) over the whole earth.[24] In fact, the mere division of humankind into genealogical families in the Table is not incompatible with an account of God's dispersal of the families into the various regions where they were "afterwards" located (10:18). This seems deliberately to allow for such a dispersal in the Tower of Babel story. The remark in 10:25 that in the days of Peleg the earth was divided may also be an anticipation of the Tower of Babel story and a way of locating it within the genealogical structure.[25] The idea that the "sons of men" (*běnē hā'ādām*, v. 5) wish to make a name for themselves (v. 4) relates the story of Babel to Gen. 6:1–4, whereas the statement that the city and the tower are "just the beginning of their deeds" (*haḥillām la ʿăśôt*, v. 6) recalls the theme of "beginnings" in 9:20 and 10:8. All of these indicators point to the common author of the Yahwist for this unit.[26]

Westermann has also argued for the literary unity of the work based on the structure of composition.[27] The beginning, v. 1, with its statement about one language for the whole earth, is contrasted with the end in which there are several languages for all the earth, v. 9. The human activity of vs. 2–4 is paralleled by the divine response in vs. 5–8, often with similar use of language. This means that any analysis of this unit must begin with this literary unity for which the Yahwist is responsible.

In spite of these marks of literary unity, the theme of the dispersal of peoples is often viewed as a variant or a secondary modification of an older story.[28] The motif of the confusion of languages is, in the first place, the divine means for bringing the building activity to an end and provides an etiology for the name of the city, Babel. To this has been added the notion that the confusion of languages also produced the variety of foreign tongues that led to the corresponding dispersion of peoples into their various homelands, each with a unique language. This double etiology had the effect of encouraging scholars such as Gunkel and Skinner to suggest a separation of the account into two variants, a city story and a tower story.[29] Attempts at literary division, however, have recently met with strong criticism.[30]

Westermann, although recognizing the literary unity of the Genesis story, agrees with the view that some tensions remain within the story and attempts to explain these on the basis of a preliterary tradition-history. He argues that the association with Babylon is secondary because it connects a historical place with the primordial situation of the origin of languages that is mythic and ahistorical. He then identifies three motifs—a dispersion of peoples, a confusion of languages, and a tower-building story—that all came together at the preliterary stage of development, as proven by the present narrative's unity. He offers evidence that all three motifs are known in folklore and that they may be independent or associated with each other in various combinations. Thus it is possible that all three individual motifs *could have been* combined on the level of oral tradition.

The weaknesses of this approach are many and amount to

much special pleading. One can almost always drum up parallels from folklore for any biblical story. Such parallels cannot be used to prove an oral prehistory to the Genesis Tower of Babel story. Westermann's denial of a primary connection between the story and Babylon is incomprehensible. His argument for regarding the connection as secondary is spurious. It is a rather common characteristic of Near Eastern primeval traditions that historical places are given their origins in primeval times, and Babylon with its temples was no exception.

By making the references to Babylon a secondary modification, Westermann tries to get by without explaining how such a story about Babylon found its place in the primeval history. Thus he states:

> The motif of the building of the tower is independent and stands on its own feet without being tied to any place. The story, which was alive in the oral tradition in Israel, was localized in Babylon in the land of Shinar. Such a localization in one of the great empires was necessary because the gigantic buildings there were well known. . . . Israel knew of the huge towers in Mesopotamia, especially in the city of Babylon. The material used in construction was also known, 11:3, but the function of these enormous ziggurats was not.[31]

This vague statement avoids saying when it was that "Israel" could have made an imperial Babylon with its famous tower built of special materials the object of this story. The time of Babylon's greatness, the most active period of its tower construction and the time when Israel was in contact with Babylon such that it would be aware of these things, is the exilic period.[32]

I can see no reason to doubt that the story was *originally* told about the ziggurat, Etemenanki, in Babylon. The earliest reference to Etemenanki is in the *Erra Epic* (I, 128) to be dated ca. 765 B.C., according to W. von Soden.[33] When one compares the numerous references to Marduk's temple, Esagila, from the Old Babylonian period onward, this silence about Etemenanki can only mean that it probably did not predate the eighth century B.C. Nor is it likely that it was an exceptional structure in its early stages, given the fortunes of Babylon though this period. The temples of Babylon were destroyed by Sennacherib. It was left to Esarhaddon to restore these sacred buildings, and he attempted to do so in style.[34] It appears that he was responsible for a massive rebuilding of the ziggurat over several years, making it the largest in the Near East. It again suffered destruction in the time of Ashurbanipal and was rebuilt in the time of Nabopolassar and Nebuchadnezzar. This time span of the seventh and sixth centuries B.C. constitutes the most appropriate setting for the Tower of Babel story.

It has likewise been acknowledged that Mesopotamia had its own mythic tradition about how at one time in the beginning all peoples worshiped Enlil with one language.[35] But Enki, for some undisclosed reason and as a habitual rival to the king of the gods, created confusion of languages, an obvious etiology for foreign speech. As in the case of the flood story, this motif of the rivalry between gods has been abandoned, and a new explanation for the cause of the "confusion of tongues" has been sought in the arrogant activity of humankind. P. Jansen has pointed out that in Nebuchadnezzar's inscriptions referring to his construction of Etemenanki he claims to have employed peoples from every part of his realm.[36] This labor force undoubtedly consisted of corvée workers from the various exiled groups, including the Jews. Such a cosmopolitan labor force, speaking many tongues, might have encouraged the association of the tradition about the development of languages with the construction of this tower.

In another late source, Berossus makes a connection between the survivors of the flood, excluding the flood hero and his family, and the building of Babylon after the flood.[37] This may be Berossus's own modification of the tradition, but it could reflect a Babylonian version of the flood story from Babylon's heyday in Nebuchadnezzar's time. In the restoration of religious structures, it was common to associate their origins with primeval times, especially the time of the flood. There is, in fact, a Neo-Babylonian text that tells about the first building of Babylon (= Eridu) and its temple Esagila by the gods before the building of any other city or sanctuary, at the time of creation.[38]

The Tower of Babel story thus reflects materials drawn from the eastern antiquarian traditions as well as more immediate experience of life in that region. Prior to the composition by the Yahwist, there may have been a popular etymology on the name of Babel reflecting exilic attitudes toward the city with its cosmopolitan mixture of peoples. It seems reasonable to suppose that the author, J, developed the story at the time of Etemenanki's restoration as a parody of the real significance of the tower as the "foundation of earth and heaven."[39] The biblical story of the origins of Babylon and its tower is meant to lampoon the efforts of the Babylonian kings to complete it. It is not an etiology of a ruin. The story sets forth the building of the tower as an example of great hubris that can only result in the same kind of response from the deity again. The etiology of the name Babel is meant as a kind of "historical evidence" that divine judgment was passed on the city in primeval times and could perhaps happen again. The confusion of tongues in contemporary Babylon could also suggest the same correspondence with the past.

The idea that a writer of the exilic period would parody Babylonian origins and important sacred structures should come as no surprise. There is a very similar attitude reflected in the prophecy of Second Isaiah. In Isa. 46:1–2, the Babylonian gods are dismissed as impotent idols, and their display in religious processions is described as a portent of their exile. Chapter 47 is a long oracle of doom whose chief theme is the future humiliation of Babylon because of its hubris: "Who say in your heart, 'I am, and there is no one besides me.'" The attitudes reflected in J and Second Isaiah toward Babylon are the same. Likewise, in Daniel 4 there is the recollection of Nebuchadnezzar's greatness, both in terms of his empire and his building activity. This led to his hubris, which brought about his humbling by the deity. The parallel to the Genesis story is clear and suggests a strong tradition about the hubris of Babylon in its time of greatness.[40]

The fact that the Genesis text does not actually specify why God considered the building of the tower and city to be wrong has sometimes been felt to be a problem.[41] Yet when it is seen in the context of the prophetic judgments against Assyria and Babylonia and their principal cities, Nineveh and Babylon, then there can be no doubt that any attempt to become the "navel of the earth" was viewed in just such a negative way.

The Yahwist modified the various elements of this tower story to fit his crime-punishment model for the primeval period. This is reflected in v. 6, in the divine soliloquy, which parallels J's use of the deity's monologue in the beginning of the flood story with the same kind of observations about the intentions of humankind. This element of divine reflection, however, cannot be regarded as a secondary modification of an earlier form of the story in its Israelite form.[42] It is the only motivation for the divine action that follows. But the Yahwist makes the motif of the origin of language do double duty by serving as a parody on the name and reputation of Babylon and as motivation for the broader theme of the dispersion and origins of the various peoples. The dispersion theme belongs to the western tradition as reflected in the Table of Nations, but it has been amalgamated in this story with an eastern city foundation tradition. The result has created some tensions and duplication. Yet the end product is typical of antiquarian historiography.[43]

NOTES

1. See the commentaries, esp. Westermann, *Genesis 1–11*, pp. 495–530. He basically follows Gunkel. So also Skinner, *Genesis*, pp. 187–223.

2. S. Tengström, *Die Toledotformel und die literarische Struktur der priesterlichen Erweiterungsgeschichte im Pentateuch*, CB OTS 17, (1982), 21–25.

3. The use of the plural *dōrōtāyw* by P, in 6:9, is rather curious. J, in 7:1, has the singular, "in this generation." P does not mean that Noah was righteous among his contemporaries but that his lineage was correct and untainted. It is a mistake to interpret 6:9 by 7:1, as Skinner does (*Genesis*, p. 159).

4. One may compare ‏ומאלה נפרדה הגוים בארץ‎ 9:19b (J) with ‏ומאלה נפצה כל הארץ‎ 10:32b (P). Further, both 10:1b and 10:32b end with the phrase ‏אחר המבול‎.

5. Tengström, *Die Toledotformel*, pp. 23f.

6. Genesis 10:24 has been modified to conform with the linear pattern in 11:12–14.

7. The same literary process seems to have been used by P in the case of the Seth genealogy in Genesis 5.

8. The reason given for excluding all these names from J has to do with the early dating of J, which I cannot accept. The alternative often suggested is to place the Philistines under J's Japheth line, but this is clearly contradicted by 10:14. In the Hesiodic tradition, Iapetos is in the direct line of Greek ancestry: Iapetos–Prometheus–Deucalion–Hellen.

9. Westermann, *Genesis 1–11*, p. 501; see also p. 6. It is remarkable that R. R. Wilson does not treat the Table in his book *Genealogy and History in the Biblical World*, because it is so crucial to the subject he discusses.

10. Westermann, *Genesis 1–11*, p. 502.

11. Ibid.

12. See above.

13. As previously noted, Westermann's use of the late versions of Lucian and Apollodorus to reconstruct the earliest form of the flood narrative is quite untenable and not supported by the evidence. The idea of dispersion of peoples after the flood is not attested in any early source.

14.   See the discussion on pp. 89–90.

15.   Because it is also possible for early kings and heroes to become eponyms or for eponymic ancestors to take on heroic characteristics, the distinction of real genealogies as only containing personal names, as suggested by Westermann, should be abandoned.

16.   The identity with the city of Kish seems less likely; see Speiser, *Genesis*, pp. 67, 72; and Skinner, *Genesis*, pp. 207–208.

17.   If the name is to be associated with Tukulti-Ninurta I (so Speiser, *Genesis*, pp. 72–73), about whom an epic exists, then it is slightly ironic because this ruler, an Assyrian, defeated the Kassites of Babylonia and began Assyria's climb as a world power.

18.   Westermann, *Genesis 1–11*, p. 514.

19.   Scandalous stories about heroes and ancestors that often lead to curses or judgments of servitude are commonplace in such works as the *Catalogue*.

20.   J. Herrmann, "Zu Genesis 9:18–27," *ZAW* 30 (1910), 127–131.

21.   Note the use of "brethren" elsewhere in similar contexts where it does not have reference to specific brothers: Gen. 16:12; 25:17; 27:29 (cf v. 40).

22.   A similar expansion may be noted in the fourth Balaam oracle, Num. 24:23–24.

23.   See also von Rad, *Genesis*, p. 144.

24.   See also Steck, "Genesis 12:1–3," pp. 117–148, esp. pp. 128f. Steck regards all the references to scattering as secondary and the work of J.

25.   Another possibility for interpretation of this remark will be proposed below.

26.   Cf. Zenger ("Beobachtungen zur Komposition und Theologie der jahwistischen Urgeschichte," in *Dynamik im Wort* [1983], pp. 35–54), who wants to separate chapters 9–11 from what precedes as a later supplement. His argument rests upon the parallel with *Atrahasis* and the view of Rendtorff that the flood story concludes the primeval age. This might be convincing if the eastern tradition was the only consideration for the form of the primeval history in Genesis. But it is the thesis of this study that J has brought together a wider range of material for his history. Thus the view that the flood is the end of the primeval age must be rejected as inadequate.

27.   Westermann, *Genesis 1–11*, p. 534.

28.   So Steck, n. 24 above.

29.   Gunkel, *Genesis*, pp. 94–97; Skinner, *Genesis*, pp. 223–224. See recently K. Seybold, "Der Turmbau zu Babel. Zur Entstehung von Genesis 11,1–9," *VT* 26 (1976), 453–479; H. Bost, "La tour de Babel. Gen. 11,1–9," in *La ville dans le Proche-Orient ancien*, Les Cahiers du CEPOA 1 (1983), pp. 231–238.

30.   See Steck, "Genesis 12:1–3," p. 128 n. 32; and Westermann, *Genesis 1–11*, pp. 534–537.

31.   Westermann, *Genesis 1–11*, pp. 541–542.

32.   Attempts by W. von Soden ("Verschlüsselte Kritik an Salomo in der Urgeschichte des Jahwisten?" *WO* 7 [1974], 228–240) and by Seybold and Bost (n. 29 above) to make a connection with the Solomonic age as a critique of his temple building seem very farfetched. There is no evidence to date the construction of Etemenanki to the time of Nebuchadnezzar I, as von Soden suggests.

33.   W. von Soden, "Etemenanki von Asarhaddon; Nach der Erzählung vom Turmbau zu Babel und dem Erra-Mythos," *UF* 3 (1971) 253–264.

34.   See the summary of the tower's history by E. Unger in *RLA* I, pp. 364–366; and *Babylon, Die heilige Stadt nach der Beschreibung der Babylonier* (1931), pp. 191–200. See also E. Klengel-Brandt, *Der Turm von Babylon. Legende und Geschichte eines Bauwerks*, 1982; and D. J. Wiseman, *Nebuchadrezzar and Babylon* (1985), pp. 68–73. There is no reason to conjecture, as Wiseman does, that the oldest level of the ziggurat was Old Babylonian in date.

35.   S. N. Kramer, "The 'Babel of Tongues': A Sumerian Version," *JAOS* 88 (1968), 108–111; and Jacobsen, *The Harps*, pp. 289–290 and n. 25. There is only a brief allusion to the myth within the body of the epic *Enmerkar and the Lord of Aratta*, so the details are not known.

36.   P. Jansen, "Babylonischer Turm," *RLA*, I, 385. See also Wiseman, *Nebuchadrezzar*, p. 69.

37.   Lambert and Millard, *Atra-Ḫasis*, p. 136.

38.   Unger, *Babylon*, pp. 263–264.

39.   Contra Westermann (see quote above), who says that the author does not understand the significance of the ziggurat. But that is the whole point of a parody, to say just the opposite.

40.   See also Isaiah 13–14; Jeremiah 50–51.

41.   See Bost, "La tour de Babel," p. 232.

42.   Cf. Westermann, *Genesis 1–11*, p. 551.

43.   The work of C. Uhlinger, *Weltreich und "eine Rede": Eine neue Deutung der sogenannten Turmbauerzählung (Gen 11,1–9)* (1990), has come to my attention too late to be included in the discussion here. It arrives at very similar conclusions about the lateness of the Tower of Babel story, drawing on an even broader range of Mesopotamian material, and confirms my own analysis of this narrative unit.

10
THE PRIMEVAL HISTORY AS A WHOLE

The Structure

Essential to the structure of the primeval history is the genealogy. All the stories are made to stand within this genealogical framework, and yet it is clearly more than a late secondary device for linking traditions together. It contains its own anecdotal traditions about the founders of culture, such as those within the Cain genealogy or that of Noah, the viticulturalist in the line of Seth. It accounts for the origins of the heroes of old in the marriage of gods and mortal women and in the hero Nimrod, the founder of empires. It also includes the Table of Nations as the ancestors of humankind. To this collection likewise belong the stories of Cain and Abel and the drunkenness of Noah. These are all part of the western antiquarian traditions that the Yahwist took up as the foundation for his primeval history.

Into this body of western tradition the Yahwist integrated the eastern antiquarian traditions. The creation story, although containing eastern elements as we have seen, was largely his own hybrid composition. But the flood story was borrowed substantially as it was, with some theological modification, and fitted into the other narratives with some awkwardness by making the semidivine heroes the object of divine judgment and Noah the flood hero. The Tower of Babel story was also worked into the Table of Nations to account for the divine dispersion of the peoples, but at the cost of producing some tension with the Nimrod anecdote.

There is a certain similarity between the use of a generational chronology by the historian of Judges for the purpose of organizing his "savior" stories and J's use of the genealogical structure in Genesis. Thus the Yahwist has been careful to give to each of the primary figures in the stories a clear genealogical connection. In some cases, this has produced some tension between the nature of the story itself, as with Cain and Abel, and the chronological context. The curse of Canaan, a local tradition, has also been given a more universal scope. The Tower of Babel story provides a problem for linkage because it does not have one figure who could serve as a connection in the genealogy. So it is placed in a general chronological context before the time of Abraham, just as the generation of heroes comes before the flood. As I will show below, the place of the Tower story is quite significant for what follows.

The primeval history has the appearance of being a collection of traditional material, but it is far from being just a *Sammlung* in the sense in which Gunkel understood and used this term.[1] This collection has been edited and fitted together into a larger whole. The attitude toward the material varies from fairly close adherence to the earlier source to J's taking considerable liberties in the construction of a new form of the tradition. The traditions reflect a wide range of both eastern and western influences, and although the task of reconciling all the differences and inconsistencies has not been complete, the result has all the marks of an ancient historian, an antiquarian in classical parlance. The task of such a historian was to preserve a record of the past from tradition while at the same time making a unified account out of it. It is my view that nothing else can explain the form of the primeval history better than to view it as the work of a historian of "antiquities" in precisely this sense.

The Thematic Unity

Following the lead of Westermann, I have also identified the main narrative blocks in the primeval history of J as stories of crime and punishment. My one exception to Westermann's list of such stories is that I do not regard Gen. 6:1–4 as such a story but as part of the prologue to the flood. This leaves five examples: the creation and Fall, Cain and Abel, the flood, the drunkenness of Noah, and the Tower of Babel. The precise form of the stories varies because the traditional material taken up by the Yahwist was often amenable to only slight modification. Thus the story of Noah's drunkenness does not introduce the deity into the story at all but allows the father's curse to serve as the punishment. The cause of the flood and perhaps also the etiology of diverse languages have been changed from the Mesopotamian tradition, which attributed them to rivalry among the gods, into punishment for crimes against the deity.

As Westermann has pointed out (contra von Rad), the stories are a simple series that do not reach a crescendo of wickedness but represent a series of different individual or community crimes. It is a mistake to try to identify one type of offense, such as the overstepping of the limits of humanity, as applying to all or most of the stories.[2] The crime or sin of hubris in fact seems to come to the fore only in the case of the Tower of Babel story. The other crimes have to do with disobedience to a divine command (2:17; 3:6, 11–12), the murder of a brother (4:8), widespread violence (6:13), and sexual taboo (9:22, 24). To these crimes there are various divine responses. That of the flood is dictated by the nature of the tradition itself. The divine curses also reflect, to a large degree, the etiological concerns of the various stories, and that is typical of traditions that explain how evils and imperfections came into the world.[3] However, quite apart from these traditional elements there is another set of themes that the Yahwist emphasizes, and these have to do with exile from the land and from the presence of the deity, with wandering and dispersement over the earth, and with servitude to other nations. All these themes seem to point very clearly to the concerns of the exilic community. Even the catastrophe of the flood and the salvation of the righteous remnant are examples that come to the fore in exilic prophecy (Ezek. 14:12–20; Isa. 54:9).

The idea of presenting a series of offenses and their punishment as a way of ordering diverse traditions is not exceptional in the Old Testament. The most notable example outside the Pentateuch is the series of stories in the book of Judges. There the pattern has been established with much greater uniformity, where disobedience to God's laws and commandments is followed by defeat and servitude to a foreign power, followed in turn by salvation through a divinely appointed deliverer. A similar pattern has been discerned in the wilderness rebellions tradition where H. H. Schmid has argued that the pattern in J corresponds to, and is dependent upon, that of the book of Judges.[4] So it is not so remarkable that the primeval history should be organized in a similar fashion. In comparison with the other series, however, the Yahwist has allowed greater diversity of theme and a greater scope in shaping the stories themselves in order to present his series of crimes and punishments.

What has, likewise, become clear in our study of the primeval history is its prophetic character. In the story of the Fall, the emphasis is upon strict obedience to the word of God, with death or exile from God's land as the result of disobedience. This word stands in opposition to the wisdom of the wisest counselors. In the Cain and Abel story, the deity's advice to Cain is that "doing good" will result in acceptance by the deity and is more important than any form of sacrifice. The flood story shows that violence and continuous evil bring down divine judgment on "all flesh." But in judgment there is also mercy for the righteous remnant. The Tower of Babel is about the hubris of the nations that will experience humiliation by the deity. These are all themes familiar from the prophets, usually directed quite specifically at Israel/Judah or one of the imperial powers. By incorporating them into the crime-punishment scheme in the primeval history, they have become universal principles applicable to humankind in general. In this way, the national religion of the prophets is given universal scope.

The Problem of Connection

In a recent article, F. Crüsemann has tried to make the case against von Rad and Steck that the primeval history is a self-contained unit and not part of the literary work of the Yahwist that only begins with Gen. 12:1–3.[5] Much of the case for or against this proposition depends upon the subsequent analysis of the Yahwist's work. Here I want to examine a few of his arguments that form the basis of his larger view. The first is that although there are a number of cross-references within the primeval history that fairly well bind them together, there are virtually no cross-references between the patriarchal stories and the primeval history. He excludes the references to the blessing of the families/nations of the earth in 12:3; 18:18; 22:18; 26:4; and 28:14, as well as the specific reference in 13:10 to the "garden of God." But this kind of argument is part of a larger issue, because the same thing is true of other parts of the Pentateuch and the so-called Deuteronomistic history. For instance, the period of the Judges is mentioned only once during the whole time of the monarchy in the book of Kings (2 Kings 23:22). So that kind of argument may not count for much.[6]

Crüsemann further argues that both the form of the divine speech in Gen. 12:1–3 and the particular use of language is different from that found in the primeval history. Much of the force of this argument depends upon the exclusive focus on 12:1–3, which he views as standing outside of any story context with all the divine speeches in the primeval history that are embedded in stories. But it must be objected that most of the divine speeches in the patriarchal narratives are part of narratives, and it may be that 12:1–3 only seems to be without a narrative context and may not be so isolated as Crüsemann suggests.

It is on the matter of language comparison, however, that Crüsemann's case is particularly weak. He observes that within 12:1–3, the word ארץ means a particular country, whereas the term אדמה means the earth in general. He then asserts that in the primeval history ארץ means the whole earth and אדמה means the arable land. Of course, he must exclude several references (2:11–13; 10:11f.; 11:2; and 4:16) where ארץ means country by suggesting that they derive from the traditional material. In only one case, 6:1, he argues, does אדמה clearly mean the earth as in 12:3. But in a footnote[7] he equivocates on the references in 6:7; 7:4, 23; 8:13. Yet in all these cases it is quite clear that אדמה is directly paralleled by ארץ and must mean the earth as a whole. Furthermore, in the texts directly parallel to 12:3 one finds אדמה used in 28:14 but ארץ used in 18:18; 22:18; and 26:4. Likewise in 18:25, ארץ clearly means the whole earth. Many additional examples could be given to show that the distinction in terminology between the patriarchal stories and the primeval history is completely forced.[8]

Crüsemann likewise exaggerates the difference in perspective between the primeval history as reflecting the agricultural, settled life and the wandering, nomadic life of the patriarchs. Although agriculture is an important subject of the primeval history, it is certainly not idealized. The shepherd Abel has divine favor over the farmer Cain. Nor can Cain's type of nomadic life be compared with that of the patriarchs, except perhaps Ishmael, the outcast. The patriarchs are pastoralists, and as in the case of Isaac they may also farm and be quite productive and prosperous. Yet there may be particular reasons for portraying the patriarchs as wandering pastoralists rather than landowners that has nothing to do with the author's viewpoint of the ideal or model way of life. If we take as an example the exodus-conquest traditions and use the same principle, we would have to regard the traditions about the sojourn in Egypt as deriving from a source with a settled slave outlook, that of the wilderness traditions as reflecting a nomadic source, and that of the conquest as the viewpoint of the settled urban population of Israel. Such an approach carries little conviction.

The proposal of Crüsemann is the legacy of a form-critical method that has split up all the narrative units in the first place, whether into individual stories with Gunkel or larger thematic blocks with Noth. But it is precisely the question of the form of Genesis and the Yahwist's work as a whole that once again raises a caveat against this division in order to restore the scope and unity of that work throughout the Pentateuch.[9]

NOTES

1. See above, pp. 9–10.
2. See, e.g., Oden, "Divine Aspirations."
3. Cf. Westermann, *Genesis 1–11,* pp. 53–56. Westermann states (p. 54): "It is no accident that this group of stories about crime and punishment (apart from the flood story) has practically no prehistory in the myths of Egypt or Mesopotamia, but finds a striking counterpart in the stories of the primitive cultures." This statement, however, overlooks Greece, which certainly did have such accounts.
4. See Schmid, *Der sogenannte Jahwist,* pp. 61–82.
5. F. Crüsemann, "Die Eigenständigkeit der Urgeschichte," in *Die Botschaft und die Boten, Festschrift für H. W. Wolff,* ed. J. Jeremias and L. Perlitt (1981), pp. 11–29.
6. Crüsemann next argues that there is no literary bridge between the primeval history and Genesis 12 (ibid., p. 16). To this issue I will return below.
7. Ibid., p. 17 n. 34.
8. On the use of these terms in Deuteronomy and DtrH as synonymous, see P. Diepold, *Israels Land,* BWANT 95 (1972), p. 152; and T. Römer, *Israels Väter,* OBO 99 (1990), p. 175.
9. This applies also to the latest work by Blum, *Studien zur Komposition des Pentateuch,* pp. 106–108. Blum relies entirely upon Crüsemann to exclude the pre-P primeval history, as a separate work, from the major pre-P composition of the Pentateuch (his KD) extending from Abraham to the death of Moses.

PART THREE

The Patriarchs

11
GENEALOGIES AND ITINERARIES

Genealogy and Literacy

The genealogical statements and the itinerary notices throughout the patriarchal stories have long been recognized as forming a certain structure and framework for the successive narratives found in them.[1] For this reason they were considered as secondary literary creations used to bind together the disparate stories or traditions. Westermann disputed this and sought to trace both genealogies and itineraries back to the level of oral tradition and the primitive pre-state conditions in which, as he saw it, the patriarchal traditions arose.[2]

Westermann bases himself rather heavily upon the work of R. R. Wilson[3] in his assertion that the genealogies are primary to the patriarchal traditions because they are based upon oral tradition and "cannot be understood apart from their oral prehistory." They must go back to a particular function in patriarchal society. Yet it is to be seriously doubted whether Wilson's study actually demonstrates and supports Westermann's position. Wilson's investigation, as it has to do with Genesis, is flawed from the start because of the nature of his comparative material. On the one hand, his Near Eastern linear genealogies, which derive from highly structured literate societies, bear little resemblance to the segmented genealogies found in the book of Genesis. On the other hand, his discussion of segmented genealogies and their comparison with Genesis is based upon anthropological studies of oral tradition in illiterate societies, and this has created an artificial social and form-critical dichotomy between the two types of

197

genealogies upon which Westermann places so much weight. Yet Wilson himself admits that neither the anthropological data nor the Near Eastern material have shed much light upon the particular form, in Genesis, of the combination of narrative within a genealogical structure, whether segmented or otherwise.[4] The fact is, however, that a very prominent *literary* tradition developed in ancient Greece that exhibited precisely this combination of genealogy and narrative, and that must become the basis for any future form-critical comparison of this issue.[5]

The earliest example of this literary form that is extant, even if it is in rather fragmentary form, is the *Catalogue of Women*. This is certainly a well-ordered work, as West has demonstrated,[6] and it contains a series of segmented genealogies interspersed with narrative.[7] It is true that the work may ultimately rest on a number of local oral genealogical traditions,[8] but even between such oral forms and the *Catalogue* there may have been written versions of the major *stemmata* that made up the basis of the final work. But the whole has been shaped and reordered so completely by the final author that it is not easy to discern where he may have borrowed or included earlier written material verbatim into his work. The combination of genealogy and narrative mixed together is so ubiquitous in all the later *Genealogiai* that one can only assume that the *Catalogue* was characteristic of the earliest examples of such genealogies and was the model upon which the later, more extensive, prose works are based.

It is, of course, entirely true that segmented genealogies had an important place in primitive illiterate societies in representing the status and role of social and ethnic groups. But it is not true to say that such genealogies can have no place in the settled, literate, and highly developed society and that therefore one can only date the patriarchal genealogies to the pre-state period. The whole antiquarian tradition of Greece and Rome completely undermines such a contention.[9] If anything, literacy greatly encourages both their preservation and elaboration. Furthermore, the scope of the genealogies in the patriarchal narratives, taken as a whole, is not local but national and international, which tends to point to the later stages of any such development.

It is also quite misleading to suggest that a segmented "tribal" genealogy can only reflect a tribal political structure.[10] Tribes and clans can so easily be used as traditional terms for quite fictional or artificially created groups, as was the case in Athens, and their importance in a literary genealogical tradition does not diminish with changing political structures.[11] Nor is it possible to characterize the genealogies of Genesis as primarily tribal. Apart from the twelve tribes of Israel, J is much more concerned with national states and geographic entities. It is in P and the latest levels of the material that the most attention is given to tribes and clans within Israel and its neighbors.

Itineraries and Literacy

In a similar fashion, Westermann also treats the problem of the itinerary notices in Genesis.[12] These he associates with the constant migrating life of the nomad, and therefore he finds the itineraries arising out of the "patriarchal age." This leads him to dispute the contention of Noth that they are secondary constructions. Instead, Westermann sees both genealogies and itineraries, but especially the latter, as belonging to the early stage of Israel's existence. For this reason he wishes to distinguish them from the itineraries of the sedentary societies, which he regards as of only marginal importance to such states. But at this point Westermann's argument becomes quite forced. In order to explain the form of the itinerary in Genesis, he refers to the studies of G. I. Davies on Near Eastern and classical itineraries, who concludes: "The itinerary is certainly a literary genre which has its *Sitz im Leben* in administrative circles."[13] Yet he must, at the same time, deny that the itineraries of the patriarchal stories are the same because they derive from fundamentally different social contexts even though form-critically they are the same. It would be much easier and more consistent to suppose that the patriarchal itineraries were modeled by the author on the literary itineraries than to propose a purely hypothetical itinerary tradition of great antiquity for which there is no evidence whatever.

The matter, however, can be pursued a step further. Davies investigated only official, administrative itineraries, so Westermann interpreted Davies's claim that none of his examples were invented to mean that those of the patriarchal stories could not, therefore, be "fictional."[14] But there was a large category of itineraries that

Davies did not consider. This category is the group that has to do with journeys in the works of ethnography and travel, the *Periegesis,* and their corresponding "fictional" counterparts, the wanderings of heroes and eponyms or the early migrations of peoples in primeval times.[15] From the earliest mythological sources of the classical world come numerous accounts of the wanderings of heroes and eponyms, during the course of which they found cities, establish sacred places, and settle new peoples in their final homeland. The presentation of such accounts is made to resemble more and more the form of actual voyages of exploration or the journeys of merchants of historical times, the kind of literary itinerary to which Davies made reference.

Such wanderings occur in combination with genealogies in the *Catalogue of Women* as an important theme of the work.[16] And this combination is also found in the subsequent literary tradition of the *Genealogies.* Contrary to the assertion by Westermann that the two forms, genealogy and itinerary, "have little in common and must be dealt with separately," the Greek tradition shows that they must be taken together as the framework of the patriarchal stories.

Furthermore, it is the theme of wandering from one distant place to another that explains the nomadic or pastoral mode of life of the patriarchs and not the other way around. Only by depicting the ancestors in this way could one present the wandering forefathers as migrating with all of their possessions from one distant land to settle eventually in another. In the Greek tradition, by contrast, the same theme of ancestral wanderings results in the migration and colonization of other regions by means of ships so that the ancestors and heroes become sailors.[17] The itineraries are naval expeditions with occasional pauses for temporary settlement and agriculture. In both cases, the antiquarian historians combine observations of contemporary life and current practice with the belief that the ancestors also migrated from various regions and founded cities and nations.

Genealogy of Abraham

The task before us is to trace this basic combined structure of genealogy and itinerary throughout the patriarchal stories. But first we must deal with the question of the relationship and continuity between the primeval history and the patriarchal stories. The continuity has been argued by von Rad on the basis of the perceived theology of the Yahwist, which sees the emphasis upon curse and the negative judgment of God on humankind in general as a contrast and suitable background for the call and blessing of Abraham through whom the nations may also find a blessing.[18] This position has subsequently been supported by O. H. Steck.[19] In opposition to this is the traditio-historical approach of M. Noth, who sees the patriarchal traditions as developing to their present extent almost entirely independently of the primeval history with only a rather late redactional link in 12:1–3. A number of scholars have recently followed this line.[20] The question calls for quite a different approach, because some important lines of continuity have been entirely ignored in the discussion.

The first observation to make is that both the primeval history and the patriarchal age are structured genealogically with the successive periods and passage of time represented by the linear succession of generations. This fact may seem so obvious and natural that it is easily overlooked. However, the primeval history in Mesopotamia as reflected in *Atrahasis* is not treated this way, and only when this period is brought into some connection with the Sumerian King List is a succession of rulers, but not generations in the strict sense, applied to this earlier period. Furthermore, not only do we have a main line of genealogical succession in Genesis but there are also secondary lineages of the segmented variety included. In the primeval history, they occur in the Table of Nations in Gen. 10:13–14, 15–18a, 26–29, and these may be compared with the sons of Nahor in 22:20–24 and the sons of Keturah in 25:2–4. Although the latter could be dismissed as secondary, that of 22:20–24 seems to be important for the subsequent stories of the patriarchs.[21]

The real stumbling block for many is the apparent break in this genealogical continuity by the Yahwist between Noah and Abraham, which is supplied by the Priestly Writer by means of his genealogy of Shem with its chronology. There are two pieces of evidence that make it likely that J also had a linear genealogy from Shem to Abraham. The first is the fact that P repeats the series: Shem–Arpachshad–Shelah–Eber–Peleg of 10:21, 24–25 in

11:10–19. The rest of the genealogy is now preserved only in its P form. Yet scholars have long felt the need to extract a J text from the genealogy of Terah in 11:27–32. This seems entirely reasonable, because it accounts for Abraham's lineage and origins in Mesopotamia and gives the collateral line of Haran–Lot, which is immediately picked up in chapters 12–13, and the line of Nahor–Bethuel–Rebekah, which is dealt with in 22:20–24. The fact that the genealogy in 11:27–30 is so completely worked into P's account of the Shem–Terah genealogy suggests that P was reusing and supplementing J's material for the rest of the genealogy. Whether or not the three intervening figures of Reu, Serug, and Nahor I were derived from J is difficult to say. Wellhausen restores a Jehovist genealogy to Abraham by eliminating Arpachshad and Shelah, making Shem the father of Eber directly. He also regards Nahor I, grandfather of Abraham, as secondary in order to arrive at a sevenfold genealogy.[22] In other places, J works with a series of seven generations ending in a triad (see Gen. 4:17–22), whereas P prefers ten generations (Genesis 5). J's genealogy of Shem was not a separate linear genealogy in the style of P, who had to construct this type of genealogy to accommodate his chronology, but was just part of the larger segmented genealogy of the Table of Nations. This same combination, in which a segmented genealogy also moves from Nahor to Rebekah, the ancestress, is present in Gen. 22:20–24. Thus, the story of the Tower of Babel was included within the genealogy of Shem as a digression after the lineage of Joktan (10:30) but before the connection was made from Peleg to Terah and Abraham. It seems to me difficult to draw any other conclusion.

This means that I must retract my earlier discussion[23] and regard the material in 11:28–31 as belonging to J even though it has been reworked into its present P form. There is no other way to explain the casual reference to Lot in 12:4a; 13:1, 5 as well as the starting point for Abraham's travels as a whole. The unit in 11:28–31 portrays a migration of ancestors, with a first stage from Ur of the Chaldeans to Haran. This would fit well with J's theme of dispersion of peoples following the Tower of Babel story, since Ur is in the region of Shinar (= Babylonia).[24] It is no argument to suggest that because J otherwise associates the family of Abraham with an origin in Haran it is unlikely that Ur of the Chaldeans could also belong in this source.[25] The reference to Ur in 15:7 speaks in favor of this name being in the J source. It is a common feature of such ancestors to achieve their final destination in stages.

This means that we must look again at the Lot narratives in the light of the beginning and the ending. Lot fits into the same family tree with Abraham (as his nephew), and he travels with Abraham to the land of Canaan. Genealogy and itinerary are so closely bound together that, contrary to Westermann, they cannot be separated. Now the purpose of such travels, using the *Catalogue* and the classical antiquarian tradition as guide, is the quest by the ancestors for a land in which their offspring eventually reside. Because Abraham and Lot represent the forefathers of different peoples, they must "separate." This separation (13:11) takes up the same theme that was dominant in the Table of Nations and in the story of the Tower of Babel.

Some scholars have argued that the episode dealing with this separation in 13:5–12 is a self-contained tradition unit that was only secondarily attached to the larger Abraham-Lot story.[26] But this is hardly likely. The whole point of the episode is that the magnanimous Abraham allows Lot first choice of the region he wishes to inhabit. He chooses the southern region of the Jordan valley. This is a strange choice, as any Israelite reader would realize, were he not informed otherwise that it was an extremely attractive region, "like the garden of God," before the subsequent destruction. This means that it is simply an introduction to, and anticipation of, the story of Sodom and Gomorrah in chapter 19.

The story of the destruction of the cities of the plain by divine judgment strongly resembles one of those mythical stories accounting for the existence of utterly barren and desolate regions as based upon an event in primeval times. So it has been considered as resembling more closely the primeval history than the patriarchal stories.[27] And yet it is an event in the life of Lot, who through these circumstances was forced to give up his residence in the plain and move to the eastern high plateau. Here in this deserted region his two daughters have incestuous relations with him and produce the eponymic ancestors of the Ammonites and the Moabites, born precisely in the region they later inhabit. Both genealogy and itinerary come together again in the conclusion of this family line.

Genealogy and itinerary are not independent elements in the tradition; nor do they make up an incidental framework to some otherwise independent Lot stories. On the contrary, the combined ethnography of genealogy and itinerary—an etiology of Israel's neighbors—is the indispensable basis for the whole. All of the various scenes and episodes are composed and fitted into this larger scheme with this ethnographic purpose in mind.

The case of the collateral line of Nahor, brother of Abraham, is similar. Both are mentioned together, with their wives, in 11:29, and one would certainly expect them to be mentioned together in v. 31, as the Samaritan Pentateuch has it.[28] This would represent the first stage in the family migration from Lower to Upper Mesopotamia and locate one branch of the family, the line of Nahor, in that region. That is their final settlement, and no further itinerary for this part of the family is mentioned.

The family tree for the line of Nahor is given in Gen. 22:20–24 as a parallel to that of Abraham. It presents twelve sons, eight by the principal wife and four by the concubine, a pattern that is similar to the twelve sons of Jacob. The line contains the names of eponyms, like the ancestor Nahor himself, but also personal names like that of Bethuel. The remark that Bethuel is the father of Rebekah (22:23a) may well be a later addition and is not necessary to the whole. Even without it, this genealogy plays an important function as an introduction to the story of Rebekah's marriage in chapter 24. The unit may be based upon older ethnographic traditions, but in its present form, with the connection it makes between Nahor through Bethuel to Rebekah and Laban, it is not a self-contained genealogy but part of a larger framework.

This genealogical connection of Nahor's line is made quite explicit in 24:15, 24, 47 (the reference to Bethuel in v. 50 is suspect), and the whole framework of the two branches of the family in two different regions is taken for granted throughout. The notion of marital interconnections between major lineages is a feature of genealogical histories, as is evident also in the *Catalogue*. The fact that the generations in the two lines do not synchronize is dealt with by the fact that Isaac was born to Abraham and Sarah in their old age.

Genealogy of Jacob

This framework of genealogy again plays a role in the Jacob story by emphasizing Laban's relationship to Rebekah as brother and his continuous residence in Haran. It is quite possible that an earlier form of the story placed Laban, the Aramean, closer to the borders of Israel. But the ethnographic genealogy does not relate to that level of the tradition. The shortened genealogical designation "Laban, the son of Nahor" (29:5), even though it leaves out Bethuel, must have this larger framework in mind and merely anticipates the later oath "The God of Abraham and the God of Nahor judge between us" (31:53). The family tree of Nahor ends in the two daughters of Laban, Leah and Rachel, who become through marriage part of the line of Abraham, and nothing is said about the sons of Laban, who are not even named.

The story of Jacob and Laban also settles the territorial boundary between the Arameans and Israelites, so the story becomes an ethnographic etiology (31:51–54). There is no reason to suppose that an old tradition lies behind the remarks[29] or that it reflects a particular political situation. It merely reflects a long-standing political and ethnographic fact in the form of an agreement between the ancestors. As such it is quite appropriate to this genre of ethnographic history.

The unit of Gen. 29:30–30:24 is best described as a genealogical narrative, dealing with the origins of the twelve tribes of Israel as the sons of Jacob. Efforts to divide it into two different sources, J and E, are hardly convincing and have been rightly rejected.[30] Westermann, however, attempts to divide the text on the basis of an older narrative layer and genealogical additions made by a reviser.[31] His reason for doing so rests largely upon his understanding of the patriarchal narratives as family stories and the genealogy as quite a distinct genre. But such an attempt at separation is entirely forced, especially when there is abundant form-critical justification for just this combination of genealogy and narrative episodes and anecdotes, as in the Greek *Genealogiai*. Westermann also insists that the names in the genealogy are to be understood as personal names and not as tribal. But such a distinction in an ethnographic genealogy has little meaning.

The relationship of this unit to the larger context of the Jacob-Laban story is more difficult to answer. As it stands, it clearly represents a long digression and is in some tension with this larger context, because only a space of seven years is given to the birth of twelve children, who are regarded as born in a sequence where even the pregnancies of the various women did not overlap. Jacob's mode of life as shepherd and his place within Laban's family are also nowhere reflected in this unit. On the contrary, the statements in 30:14f. reflect a quite different setting and way of life. It is safe to say that the unit reflects an older tradition about the origin of the various tribes that did not know of the story of Jacob's sojourn and marriages in Mesopotamia.

Nevertheless, the unit 29:30–30:24 has not just been inserted into the other account by a redactor. The author of the Laban-Jacob story clearly uses the theme of Jacob's love for Rachel and the rivalry between the two women as a basis for his own story. Not only does the author account for the two marriages in this way but also adds the necessary details about the two maids, Zilpah and Bilhah. In this way also, the larger story is made to accommodate the earlier narrative with very few tensions. However, once the unit has been fitted in, there is no further reflection of this rivalry in the following narratives (although some preference for Rachel is still reflected in 33:2). Chapter 34, the story of the rape of Dinah, would originally have gone with the genealogical narrative following 30:24.

The one obvious deficiency of 29:30–30:24 is an account of the birth of Benjamin. This is given in 35:16–20 in the context of an itinerary. There is some hint, in the naming of Joseph in 30:24 ("May Yahweh add to me another son"), of an expectation of this birth of Benjamin. This is made explicit in the words of the midwife: "Fear not, you will have yet another son" (35:17). Perhaps the itinerary in 35:16–22a is related to the events recorded in chapter 34. In any event, the oldest form is very likely intended to relate Benjamin to the region that the tribe later settled.[32] The short episode in v. 22a could also be related to the previous unit in which Reuben plays a role in 30:14.

There have, in the past, been various attempts to see in the lists of the twelve sons of Jacob and their groupings according to the wives and maids of Jacob a reflection of political realities in the early history of Israel. The impetus for this was M. Noth's theory of an amphictyonic league in the premonarchy period, which rested heavily upon a certain political and sociological interpretation of these lists. Recently, however, this view has come under considerable attack, so that efforts to identify in these lists a particular historical period have become problematic.[33] But even if one concedes that the twelve-tribe grouping might be based on an older tradition,[34] this particular form of it has been so transformed by the narration of the theme of rivalry between the two principal wives that it can scarcely be taken to reflect any historical reality. As von Rad states:

> It would be wrong, therefore, if one were to consider this narrative about the birth of Jacob's twelve sons simply as a literarily disguised tribal history and accordingly were to explain it historically. On the contrary, it is not about tribes, even personified tribes, but about men. It tells of women and their struggle for husbands and for descendants.[35]

Consequently, one cannot use a political interpretation of this story in order to establish a time frame for the tradition-history of this part of the Jacob story.

Genealogy of Judah: Genesis 38

There seems to be little dispute among biblical exegetes that this chapter represents such an awkward digression within the Joseph story that it cannot have been original to it. Nor does it fit easily with the Jacob story, although it is possible that 38:1 is meant as a continuation of 35:16–22a, the general region from which Judah "went down" toward the Shephelah region. But it seems preferable to regard this chapter as a pre-Yahwistic narrative similar to a number of others that deal with the ethnography and genealogy of ancient Israel.[36]

The chapter has the function of a genealogy of the ancestors of Judah in a narrative form not unlike the birth stories of the twelve sons of Jacob. The fact that the offspring of Judah are three sons, two of whom are killed without heir only to be replaced at the end by two others, cannot be accidental, because the tripartite division of descendants is a very common motif in such genealogical traditions. The whole chapter is best described as a "genealogical story," and it seems to me a mistake to extract part of it in vs. 12–26, as Westermann has done, in order to make it correspond with his category of "family tales."[37] The chapter is a closely integrated whole, and the genealogical and ethnological aspect cannot be viewed as in any way secondary.[38]

This story also envisages the settlement of Judah in the region where the story takes place. Judah has now arrived within his homeland and has established amicable relations with the original inhabitants of the land, the Canaanites. This is such a different ethnographic view from that of the larger work of the Yahwist that it must reflect an older tradition in which this separation and antagonism had not yet become an issue. It is also clear that the whole exodus tradition of migration and settlement is not envisaged in this ethnography and clearly competes with it.

The resemblance in form to the combination of genealogy, ethnography, and story in 25:21–34 is clear, and this is made all the more evident by the resemblance between 38:27–30 and 25:21–26a. In both of these cases, the struggle of the twins in childbirth is meant to reflect a foreshadowing of future rivalry or claim on precedence. Yet Westermann is overstating the matter when he says on the basis of 25:21–26 that such a story "was always the occasion for a new narrative" and therefore regards the ending to chapter 38 as incomplete.[39] Because the entities in both cases were ancestors of future peoples, no further narrative was strictly necessary for its understanding.[40] It is because Westermann does not wish to interpret either story as ethnographic in origin that he insists on such a form-critical evaluation.

Although G. W. Coats recognizes the ethnographic and etiological aspects of the narrative and finds Westermann's genre designation inappropriate, he nevertheless regards vs. 27–30 as an appendix.[41] But v. 26 does not provide an adequate conclusion to the story if it is about how Tamar's cause was adequately resolved.[42] It is in fact the ethnographic and genealogical concern that is primary, and the story is made to serve that purpose. Indeed, if the story were to make Tamar the wife of Shelah, that would greatly complicate the tribal genealogy.

Whether there were other such ethnographic genealogies for the other tribes can no longer be answered, although it is possible that sources for the tribal genealogies exist in later works. The Joseph story served in some way as such a form for the Yahwist, even though it was hardly this in origin. He seems more concerned to focus on Judah and Joseph as the tribes from which the monarchies came and to regard the other tribes as somewhat subsidiary.

Itineraries of the Patriarchs

There are no itineraries in the primeval history, and only genealogies with their generational chronology give some structure to the narrative. In this it contrasts with the patriarchal narratives in which both genealogy and itinerary may be used together to suggest structure. Nevertheless, in the Tower of Babel story there is some suggestion of a migration of peoples to account for national origins, which provides both a background and a connection with the patriarchs. The story begins with the statement about humanity's common language and then continues with the statement: "When they migrated (*ns'*) from the east, they discovered a plain in the land of Shinar and settled (*yšb*) there" (11:2). This establishes a pattern in which a group migrates from one region (here vaguely "from the east") to settle in another region in order to found a city or nation. This pattern is evident in a number of cases in the patriarchal narratives. In all cases, the itinerary is not an independent form but merely a motif or element within the larger story.

The end of the Babel story in the J version recounts humanity's dispersion as a consequence of the proliferation of languages, and this sets the stage for the migration of Abraham's family from this same region. After setting out Abraham's broad genealogical connections, the author describes the movement of this family unit from Ur to Haran, where they settle (11:27–31*). This is meant to account for the origins of this related Aramean people in the region of Upper Mesopotamia.

Then begins the itinerary of Abraham and Lot from this region of origin to their respective lands of settlement. The itinerary statements are concentrated primarily in chapters 12 and 13, accounting for the movement from Upper Mesopotamia to

Canaan, and within Canaan to such important places as Shechem, Bethel, and Hebron. It is noted that the Canaanites and Perizzites were then living in the land (Gen. 12:6; 13:7). The itinerary is also made to accommodate the episode in Egypt (12:10–20) and the separation from Lot, who moves to his own land of destiny. This latter migration by Lot, however, is not completed until after the Sodom story (19:30), where the land of settlement becomes the future homeland of his offspring, the nations of Ammon and Moab. Here too, itinerary and genealogy are firmly linked within the narrative account. Only one other itinerary notice occurs in the Abraham story: "Abraham migrated (*ns'*) from there (Hebron?) to the region of the Negeb and settled (*yšb*) between Kadesh and Shur, and he sojourned in Gerar" (20:1). This is used, presumably, to accommodate the episodes that take place in this region. There is no reason to suppose, however, that "in an earlier stage of the tradition the itinerary formed the frame for a group of Abraham narratives,"[43] because it does not occur in all of the stories. Like genealogy, it is a historiographic structuring device.

The itinerary notices in the Isaac story, in Genesis 26, are used to string together a number of episodes in the life of the patriarch. They have to do with movement in a rather circumscribed region in the Negeb, and the itinerary notices constitute part of the episodes and anecdotes narrated. As I have indicated elsewhere,[44] they are in imitation of episodes in the Abraham story. Nevertheless, the author is able to use the language and formulas of itinerary for his own narrative purposes.

The Jacob story shows an interesting use of the itinerary pattern. Although the Abraham story has the itinerary notices primarily at the beginning, the Jacob story has them at the end, and for good reason.[45] Jacob's travels to Mesopotamia from Canaan are in the nature of a flight by a single individual. Consequently, apart from accommodating the Bethel episode in Gen. 28:10–22, the journey focuses entirely on Jacob's departure, 28:10, and his arrival, 29:1. But when Jacob departs from Laban, he has now become a migrating group, the future people moving from their point of origin in Mesopotamia to Canaan. Into this itinerary a number of different episodes are built: the divine encounters at Mahanaim and Penuel, the reconciliation with Esau, and the rape of Dinah at Shechem, all within the framework of an itinerary (Gen.

32–34). Genesis 35 completes the sequence of moves from Shechem to the Negeb, by way of Bethel, to provide the final context for the move to Egypt (46:1–7).

The itinerary is closely tied to a series of place etiologies in the Jacob story (28:10–22; 32:2–3, 23–33; 33:17; 35:6–7), which is also a feature of the Isaac story in Genesis 26.[46] The itinerary is likewise combined with the genealogical narrative of Benjamin's birth (35:16–21), such that the two elements are here quite inseparable. This episode also contains an etiology of the tribal name and a reference to an "archaeological" marker, the pillar of Rachel's tomb. All these features reflect the basic stock-in-trade of antiquarian historiography.

The reason for the lack of itinerary notices in the Joseph story is obvious. Only the story of Judah (Gen. 38) briefly suggests a migration into the region in which his offspring become a nation. For the rest, the family of Jacob remains settled in one place in Canaan until their movement to Egypt (Gen. 46:1–7). Yet in both Gen. 42:3–4 and 50:24–25 there is in view the later national itinerary from Egypt to Canaan. This is here linked firmly, by the Yahwist, to the itinerary of Jacob and his family and thus forms part of the larger whole.

Just how itineraries work within ancient historiography may be illustrated by reference to Dionysius's *Antiquities of Rome*.[47] Although this work is admittedly several centuries later than the Yahwist, Dionysius refers to older authorities for this information, and, as I indicated earlier, his genre of "antiquities" goes back to early Greek historiography. Dionysius indicates that the original inhabitants of Italy were a barbarian, uncivilized people, the Sicels, but they were displaced by a group called Aborigines. The Aborigines were the founders of Roman families, their descendants being the firstborn or forefathers. The Aborigines migrated to Italy from Arcadia in the fifth generation as descendants of Phoroneus, the first man. Dionysius gives the genealogy of this line down to the first Aborigines, two brothers, who left Greece because there was not enough inheritance for them in the family portion. These two brothers divided Italy between themselves and gave their names to various places when they arrived. They were later called Aborigines on the basis of an etiology, "from the mountains," which was understood to refer to their origins in Arcadia.

Dionysius also lists "archaeological" evidence pointing to their early settlement in unwalled villages.

Dionysius goes on to mention a second migration of Pelasgians, who make up the other component of the Roman peoples. These were descended from another primeval ancestor, Pelasgus, whose genealogy is also given. The migration of the Pelasgians is given in an itinerary with many stopping places to reflect the rather widely dispersed connections of this group's descendants. Eventually, they migrated to Italy at the command of an oracle and joined forces with the Aborigines to defeat the local inhabitants and establish the Roman people.

This example from Dionysius makes it quite clear that we are dealing with a western form of tradition accounting for national origins that includes the notion of ancestors migrating from places of older and higher civilization to new regions, there eventually to displace the unworthy native population. The Greek tradition also combines itinerary with genealogies and etiologies in a complex narrative structure. Migrations by founders or ancestors are often undertaken at the command of a deity or in response to an oracle. All of these features have direct and obvious parallels in the patriarchal stories. The biblical stories of Abraham and Jacob follow this same pattern. They both migrate from Mesopotamia at the urging of a divine oracle and live among a native population whom they eventually displace. Itinerary, genealogy, and etiology are likewise mixed in the narrative to the same degree.

Furthermore, the historian may need to devise various strategies to resolve conflicting traditions of origin. Dionysius was faced with two traditions of ancestral origin, the Aborigines and the Pelasgians. He solves the problem by constructing two different, successive migrations that unite to become the one people. Livy's version of origin concentrates only on the migration of Aeneas from Troy to Italy (another complex itinerary) who joins forces with the Aborigines and settles in the land. The Abraham and Jacob traditions may have reflected southern and northern versions of origins that were integrated by a generational sequence. Israel also seems to have had conflicting or competing origin traditions represented by the patriarchs and the exodus themes. How the Yahwist dealt with this problem will be taken up below.

Conclusion

Genealogy and itinerary do not necessarily reflect early pre-state nomadic traditions, as Westermann has suggested. They are the basic components of a western antiquarian tradition of national origins. The genealogies and migrations of heroes and ancestors together form a basic framework in a literary presentation of such traditions into which stories, anecdotes, and etiologies are fitted. For the patriarchal stories, nothing else points more clearly and unequivocally to the nature of the Yahwist's work as historiography than his use of genealogy and itinerary as the framework for his collection of ancestral traditions. Although there is little in the patriarchal stories that corresponds to any eastern antiquarian traditions, in spite of Abraham's association with Mesopotamia in the tradition, the parallels with the western traditions are extensive and have been neglected for too long.

NOTES

1. On genealogies, see Wellhausen, *Prolegomena*, pp. 319f., 332–333; Gunkel, *Genesis*, pp. 49f.; Noth, *A History of Pentateuchal Traditions*, pp. 214–219. On itineraries, see Noth, ibid., pp. 220–227.
2. Westermann, *Genesis 12–36*, pp. 54–58.
3. Wilson, *Genealogy and History*.
4. Ibid., p. 137.
5. This criticism also applies to Blum (*Die Komposition*, pp. 485–490), who follows Wilson's treatment of genealogy.
6. See West, *Hesiodic Catalogue of Women*.
7. See above, pp. 89–90.
8. See West, *Hesiodic Catalogue of Women*, ch. 3.
9. See van Groningen, *In the Grip of the Past*, pp. 47–61; and Thomas, *Oral Tradition and Written Record*, ch. 3.
10. See Blum, *Die Komposition*, pp. 487f.
11. See van Groningen, *In the Grip of the Past*, pp. 56ff.
12. Westermann, *Genesis 12–36*, pp. 56–58.
13. G. I. Davies, "The Wilderness Itineraries: A Comparative Study," *Tyndale Bulletin* 25 (1974), pp. 80f.
14. Westermann, *Genesis 12–36*, p. 57.
15. See above, pp. 92–93.
16. See West, *Hesiodic Catalogue of Women*, pp. 58–59.
17. See Dionysius, *The Antiquities of Rome*, esp. book 1, for the persistence of this form into Roman times.
18. Von Rad, *Genesis*, pp. 158–161.

19. Steck, "Genesis 12,1–3."

20. Rendtorff, *Das überlieferungsgeschichtliche Problem des Pentateuch*, pp. 154–155; idem, *The Old Testament: An Introduction* (1985); Blum, *Die Komposition*, pp. 467–468. See also the discussion of Crüsemann above.

21. On the Arabian genealogies of Genesis, see F. V. Winnett, "The Arabian Genealogies in the Book of Genesis," in *Translating and Understanding the Old Testament*, ed. H. T. Frank and W. L. Reed (1970), pp. 171–196. Winnett regards 25:2–4 as belonging to J_2 (= my Yahwist).

22. See Wellhausen, *Die Composition*, p. 7.

23. Van Seters, *Abraham*, p. 225.

24. The fact that Ur also comes into prominence again in the Neo-Babylonian period after a long quiescence fits very well with our observations about the Tower of Babel. See Van Seters, *Abraham*, pp. 23–26.

25. See the discussion in Skinner, *Genesis*, p. 239; and Westermann, *Genesis 12–36*, p. 135.

26. See Van Seters, *Abraham*, pp. 221–226; Westermann, *Genesis 12–36*, pp. 171–173; and Blum, *Die Komposition*, pp. 271–289.

27. W. M. Clark, "The Flood," *ZAW* 83: 193–195.

28. See BHS.

29. So Noth, *A History of Pentateuchal Traditions*, pp. 91ff.

30. See recently Blum, *Die Komposition*, pp. 105–111, where he argues cogently against dividing it into J and E sources and presents a case for its structural unity.

31. Westermann, *Genesis 12–36*, pp. 471–472.

32. The identification of Ephratha with Bethlehem is clearly secondary.

33. See C. H. J. de Geus, *The Tribes of Israel: An Investigation Into Some of the Presuppositions of Martin Noth's Amphictyony Hypothesis* (1976), SSN 18; see also N. P. Lemche, *Early Israel*, SVT 37 (1985), pp. 66–76.

34. Herodotus frequently cites groupings of twelve states or kings in primordial times as a literary convention similar to what we have in Genesis. See Van Seters, *In Search of History*, p. 46.

35. Von Rad, *Genesis*, p. 297. This statement is made even though von Rad subscribes to Noth's thesis about an amphictyony, as he states on p. 296.

36. See Westermann, *Genesis 37–50*, pp. 46–50. Cf. Blum, *Die Komposition*, pp. 224–227.

37. Westermann, *Genesis 37–50*, p. 49.

38. Blum regards it as an etiology not just of the tribe of Judah but specifically of the preeminence of David's clan.

39. Westermann, *Genesis 37–50*, p. 55.

40. There is no evidence that the motif had any such introductory function in the *Catalogue*. See West, *Hesiodic Catalogue of Women*, p. 68.

41. Coats, *Genesis*, pp. 274–275. He has some trouble identifying the genre.

42. See von Rad, *Genesis*, p. 361; cf. Blum, *Die Komposition*, pp. 225f.

43. Westermann, *Genesis 12–36*, p. 58.

44. Van Seters, *Abraham*, pp. 175–191.

45. Contra Westermann, *Genesis 12–36*, p. 58, who describes them as "on the periphery."

46. See also the wilderness itinerary in Exodus-Numbers.

47. Dionysius, *Antiquities of Rome*. See especially book 1.9–20.

12
THE THEME OF
THE PATRIARCHAL
PROMISES

Introduction: A History of the Discussion

The theme of the patriarchal promises has received a lot of attention in biblical studies, and it is often regarded as the key to understanding the Pentateuch, or at least the development of the book of Genesis. It is not necessary for our purposes to survey all of the literature in this discussion but only to highlight some of the issues involved that will be central to the pursuit of this discussion.

There are two fundamentally different approaches to the theme of the promises. The one stresses the basic unity of the promises theme, at least within a particular source, and the impact that the theme has upon the shape of the literature as a whole. The other looks for the origin and growth of the promises theme by separating it into distinct entities and by viewing the growth of the patriarchal tradition as directly related to the many-staged growth of the promises theme. In the first approach, the role of an author is quite important, if not paramount. In the second, the hand of an author is of little or no consequence. The possibility of any compatibility between these approaches is very small, so that what is primarily at issue between them is the kind of justification and persuasiveness that can be put forward for the one or the other approach.

In 1928, K. Galling published his *Die Erwählungstraditionen Israels* in which he suggested that there were two important traditions concerning the divine election of Israel: the exodus-settlement tradition and the patriarchal tradition. The former he

215

. and self-contained election tradition,
econdary and dependent upon the other.[1]
texts he deemed early, such as the little credo
ich does not seem to recognize any sojourn
n the Promised Land. He could also point to
phetic tradition, which reflects on the election
e exodus but not of the fathers. When it came to
of the patriarchal promises, Galling, following
Eissi ource division, reviewed the treatment of the promises theme in the Pentateuch[2] and regarded it as "the red thread
through the whole work."[3] Yet he had difficulty in explaining why
such early sources should present a unity of the two themes,
whereas outside the Pentateuch the presentation of the patriarchs
as the elect comes into view only in the latest literature. Even within
the Pentateuch in the early sources of Exodus 3 and in the P source
of Exodus 6 there is preserved a tension between the exodus and
fathers traditions.

Galling describes his approach as a tradition-history and not
as the treatment of abstract theological concepts. But his discussion is limited to the *literary* presentation of the traditions and
not to possible oral forms of the tradition. In other words, for the
Pentateuch he is basically concerned with its authors. In the following year, however, A. Alt, with his study *Der Gott der Väter* (1929),[4]
inspired an entirely different form of traditio-historical approach
to the promises tradition. He suggested that the literary sources
of the patriarchal stories still reflected an older oral level of the
tradition that contained the remnants of a "god of the fathers"
religion of the nomadic presettlement tribes. Essential to this
religion were the promises made by the personal deity to a leader
or founder of the cult, especially the promise of land. In the discussion that followed, attempts were made to recover this preliterary
promises tradition and to account for the various literary forms
of it on the basis of a conjectured tradition-history.

G. von Rad tried to combine these two approaches. He
accepted the priority of the exodus tradition and the antiquity
of the witness to it in Deut. 26:5–9 as an ancient liturgy.[5] And he
ascribed to the Yahwist the expansion of the *Heilsgeschichte* with
the inclusion of the patriarchal traditions and the development
of the promises theme as the unifying element in the whole work.

Yet he acknowledged the origins of the theme in the preliterary traditions about the god of the fathers and the theme of land-promise to the nomadic group as a limited element within these stories. But von Rad went on to assert:

> There is cause to believe that the actual prominence of the promise of the land in the patriarchal sagas in J is attributable to the Yahwist's free treatment of the material; for the original promise . . . is actually broken in a remarkable way by its later inclusion in the Settlement tradition.[6]

For von Rad, the land promise originated in the patriarchal tradition and was secondarily extended to the settlement tradition. Von Rad gives a major role to the *literary* level, the Yahwist, in the tradition-history of the Pentateuch and of the patriarchal promises.

M. Noth placed the emphasis in quite the opposite direction.[7] He builds directly upon the work of Alt and sees the narrative tradition about the patriarchs as arising independent of the Penta-teuchal tradition. Intrinsic in this development is the promise theme. The combination of this patriarchal theme of land posses-sion with that of the exodus-settlement traditions is explained in terms of a vague process at the preliterary level and through several stages. The patriarchal genealogy follows a similar parallel process of development and integration. Noth is very vague in his discus-sion about the specific texts of the promise theme and makes no attempt to identify the older and younger layers or to compare the various forms and subjects of the promise theme. Only with respect to Genesis 15, following Alt, is he willing to recognize, behind "a very complicated history of tradition," "*the* authentic basic element of the 'patriarchal' tradition in general"[8] that included both the promise of posterity and the possession of arable land.

J. Hoftijzer, in his study *Die Verheissungen an die drei Erzväter* (1956), challenged the whole basis for the traditio-historical treat-ment of the promise theme by Alt and Noth by suggesting that there was insufficient evidence for Alt's "god of the fathers" thesis. Thus there was no warrant for regarding the promise theme as of any great antiquity. Hoftijzer then discusses all of the texts, which he assigns to two groups, those associated with Genesis 15 and those associated with Genesis 17. The last group are regularly viewed as P texts and need concern us no further. But Hoftijzer insisted that all of the others be viewed as having common author-ship. He also claimed that all the texts of this group, with the exception of Genesis 15, are secondary additions or interpolations in the contexts in which they are found. Only in Genesis 15 is the promise theme an integral part of the narrative itself. This text he regarded as a unity and the whole promise theme as a late redactional development of the patriarchal tradition.

Hoftijzer's challenge was taken up by Westermann.[9] The latter concedes to Hoftijzer the secondary character of many of the references to promises. But Westermann begins with the assumption that there is in the patriarchal tradition much that reflects a nomadic patriarchal age, and this applies to the promise theme as well. In order to find this promise theme within the old stories, he broadens the range and differentiation of promise motifs to include, among others, the promise of a son. In this way he can identify this motif in two stories for certain, Genesis 16 and 18:1–15, and the possibility of ancient promises in some other places. Westermann then conjectures an elaborate tradition-history for the various promise motifs extending over a very long period of time.

It must be stated at this point, however, that Westermann has greatly muddled the issue rather than clarified it. The category that he introduces, the promise of a son, is clearly not of the same kind as that of the other promises. In the first story, Genesis 16, it is misleading to speak of the promise of a son, because to promise offspring to a pregnant woman would be rather pointless. The divine announcement has to do with the destiny of the child and his descendants. The whole thrust of the story is elsewhere. The story in 18:1–15 is part of a birth story that goes together with 21:1–2, 6–7 and as such stands alongside of other birth stories of childless women both in Genesis 25:19–26 and 30:1–24 and in other parts of the Old Testament. The element of promise is rather incidental, because the deity can also respond to a lament or prayer without a specific promise being involved. If we set aside these birth stories for the moment, we are left with all the texts suggested by Hoftijzer, and the issue of their relationship to the rest of the patriarchal tradition remains.

R. Rendtorff builds directly upon the work of Westermann.[10] He first of all accepts the form-critical work of Gunkel on Genesis that holds that the patriarchal stories consist of numerous originally independent story units. He also accepts the position of Noth that the patriarchal history developed as a self-contained unit independent from the other major themes of the Pentateuch, with the focus being the promises to the fathers of land and offspring. This theme belongs itself to the oldest level of the tradition — to the religion of the fathers, as Alt had argued. Although Westermann, among others, attempted to discover where the oldest level of this promise theme lay, Rendtorff saw in the variety of formulas used to express the various promises the clue to tracing the development of the composition of the forefathers' tradition. For him it appeared likely that one could decide how the parts of the tradition came together by identifying the "relative chronology" of the various promises that constituted the connective links between them.

If one accepts the traditio-historical basis of Alt, Noth, and Westermann that the patriarchal stories reflect a long history of multilayered development to which the promise theme was integral, then such a scheme might very well appear persuasive. But so drastically has the traditio-historical presupposition been undermined by recent research that such an approach becomes problematic. There is no longer any clear starting point because there is no way of proving the antiquity of the divine promises of land and numerous offspring. The antiquity of the patriarchal traditions in general can no longer be asserted with any confidence.

There is also a rather objective test that can be made of Rendtorff's approach. His scheme of the development of the promises is based only upon a consideration of their form in Genesis and the application of a certain logical argument. Thus he holds for the land-promise theme that there are three basic forms: (1) God gives the land to the fathers, (2) God gives the land to both the fathers and the descendants, (3) God gives the land to the descendants only. Rendtorff argues that the development of this form was from 1 to 3. But if we survey the use of such formulas outside of Genesis, this approach becomes very doubtful. In the texts in Exodus and Numbers, which Rendtorff would assign to a Dtr editor, all three forms can be found in the recapitulation of the oath to the fathers, that is:

1. God swore to give the land to the fathers (Num. 11:12; 14:23; 32:11).
2. God swore to the fathers to give them and their descendants the land (Ex. 13:11).

3. God swore to the fathers to give the descendants the land (Ex. 13:5; 32:13; 33:1).

Furthermore, if we include the numerous texts from Deuteronomy that Rendtorff completely ignores, then this indiscriminate distribution makes it even more apparent that the statement that "the land that God swore/promised to the fathers" means exactly the same as "the land that God swore/promised the fathers to give to you/descendants."[11] If in a corpus as homogeneous in language and outlook as Deuteronomy one finds a variety of formulaic expression, there is no need to deny the same possibility to an author of Genesis, especially when Deuteronomy may already constitute a precedent for such expression.

In the same way, Rendtorff also argues that formulas having to do with the forefathers and/or their offspring being a means of blessing to the nations exhibit this same development. These forms are:

Gen. 12:3; 28:14   ונברכו בך כל משפחת האדמה
Gen. 22:18; 26:4   והתברכו בזרעך כל גויי הארץ

Primarily on the basis of the distinction between *bk* "by you," and *bzr'k,* "by your seed," Rendtorff sees an evolution from the earlier form to the later, reflected in the other differences in terminology as well. However, compare:

Ps. 72:17   ויתברכו בו כל משפחת האדמה כל גוים יאשרוהו

Here the *hithpael* of *brk* is used together with "all the families of the earth," which is parallel to "all nations." And this formula is more original to the ideology of monarchy and therefore more likely to be older than any of those used in Genesis.

E. Blum follows the same line as Rendtorff in his program to present the compositional history of the patriarchal traditions in complete detail from the simplest forms to the final product.[12] To do this, Blum broadens the base of his discussion to include the various stories and their relationship with the promise theme to discern the compositional layers so that there is a much greater emphasis upon literary composition. But Blum's dependence upon Rendtorff's analysis of the relative dating of the various forms of the promises has a decisive, and to my mind detrimental, effect upon the reconstruction of how the development of the patriarchal traditions came about.

This criticism of Rendtorff and Blum does not deny that there are layers or stages in the development of the patriarchal traditions, as I have also tried to show,[13] only that the promise theme does not provide the best clue to the identification of those layers. Because Rendtorff found multiple stages in the development of the promise theme, Blum had to find a corresponding number of stages in the related story material. The result, it seems to me, is hopelessly complicated and scarcely convincing. Yet, to their credit it must be said that their attempt to understand the growth of the patriarchal traditions apart from the old source divisions of J and E is commendable. What is needed is to find the right key, which means the right structure or genre of the earlier material, in order to unlock the code to the tradition's development. Such a genre I believe exists in the form of antiquarian historiography to which the themes of new lands and the origins of nationhood are very much related.

One recent author who has rejected Rendtorff's approach is J. A. Emerton.[14] He returns to the older documentary hypothesis of two early sources for Genesis, J and E, but with the critical difference that along with Hoftijzer he regards the references to the patriarchal promises, except for the promise of a son in 18:10, 14 and 16:11, as secondary to the contexts in which they are found. They have all been added to JE in the late monarchy about the time of Josiah and contemporary with the Deuteronomic reform. Emerton does not make clear what a JE text would be like if all the promises were abstracted from it. What was the nature of its coherence? Emerton's approach also demands some account of the relationship of the promise theme and the patriarchal covenant to that of Deuteronomy.

In his major study of the Jacob story, A. de Pury dealt extensively with the theme of the patriarchal promises.[15] Like many of the earlier tradition critics, he assigned different types of promises to different stages or periods of development, considering the promise of land to be older than that of the promise of numerous offspring. This judgment was based upon what he felt to be the appropriate sociological context for such promises, a position similar to that of Noth and others. However, what is new is his attempt in the case of the Jacob story to find a narrative genre that included divine promise as an essential element and that had within it a far wider scope of actions and scenes than Gunkel had been willing to recognize in his small units of tradition. The suggestion that form-criticism ought to function as an important control on literary and traditio-historical analysis is a significant contribution.

More closely akin to the position of Hoftijzer is that of my own work on the Abraham tradition[16] and that of H. H. Schmid on the Yahwist as a whole.[17] In both of these studies, Schmid and I regarded Hoftijzer's "redactional" stratum, which he identified in the Genesis 15 group of promises, as belonging to a much more extensive literary composition of the Pentateuch in the late monarchy or exilic period, to which we gave the label "late" or "sogenannte" Yahwist. Because our studies appeared before Rendtorff's extensive treatment of the patriarchal promises, we did not address directly the question of a multiplicity of layers in the promises.[18] Nevertheless, because we found in all the basic forms of the promises — land, numerous progeny, and blessing — evidence of lateness throughout, there seems little room for any multilayered development over a long period of time. This position seems to have influenced the views of Rendtorff and Blum to the extent that they now compress most of the stages of the development of the promises into a rather short period in the late monarchy and exilic periods.

By contrast, S. Tengström, who published his study of the Hexateuch about the same time as the works of Schmid, Rendtorff, and myself, maintained an early date for the Yahwist.[19] He starts from a position of seeing the promise theme as unified and central to the Pentateuch as a whole and places great weight on the Yahwist as a literary work. Returning to the work of Galling, he states:

> The promises to the patriarchs are to be regarded as no less than the *original primary theme* of a literary epic whose two major divisions, the story of the patriarchs and the exodus/settlement narrative, correspond to each other as promise corresponds to its fulfillment. In all its components from the beginning onward the epic work is marked by this red thread going through it.[20]

Because the promise theme constitutes the original unity of the

Pentateuch, he does not recognize the problem first posed by Galling, much less the radical separation of the two traditions of patriarchs and exodus as suggested by Rendtorff.[21]

A scholar who has recently taken up the challenge of a late dating of the Yahwist by Schmid and myself is K. Berge.[22] He advocates a return to the Solomonic dating of the Yahwist based upon a reexamination of the promise theme. Although he accepts the position that some of the divine promises, such as those of Genesis 15; 18:18f.; 22:15–18; 26:3b–5, 24; 46:1–5, and 50:24 are secondary and late, those of Gen. 12:1–3, 7 and 28:13–15 belong to J and directly reflect the political and sociological character of the Davidic-Solomonic era. The particulars of this thesis will be examined below. What is remarkable about this thesis, however, is that Berge is no longer willing to defend the notion that there was any divine promise to Isaac in J, or even in E. They did not enter the tradition before a very late Dtr redaction. This makes it difficult to understand how Isaac could be viewed as empowered to bless Jacob as he did in Genesis 27, why J would identify Yahweh as "the God of Isaac" to introduce the blessing themes in 28:13, and how the title "God of Abraham, Isaac, and Jacob" could be used so often in references to the promises in the rest of the Pentateuch.

The scope of the Yahwist has drastically shrunk in Berge's study so that it raises questions about its shape and character. Berge gives little attention to such issues and declines to give any opinion about J's historiographic character or literary genre. Yet, as we have seen above, genre dictates the scope and structure of a work, so it matters that Berge regards the whole of Genesis 26, the "life of Isaac," as secondary to J. If we are dealing with a form of antiquarian history, it would be strange to have nothing to say about a whole generation of the first forefathers.

The latest work to appear on the promise theme is that by T. Römer, *Israels Väter*.[23] This is an exhaustive examination of all the references to the "fathers" in the Deuteronomistic corpus and related material in the prophets, especially Jeremiah and Ezekiel. Within this broad investigation is an extensive discussion of the promises to the "fathers." At issue is the question of the extent to which the "fathers" in all of this Old Testament literature can be identified with the patriarchs or whether they merely reflect Israel's forebears in a much vaguer sense. Although some comparison is made with the use of "fathers" in the Tetrateuch (Exodus-Numbers), the theme of the promises to the patriarchs in Genesis is not discussed. Nevertheless, the study has a major bearing upon a discussion of the development of the patriarchal promises and will be taken up in the next chapter.

Summary

This survey does not exhaust the recent discussion of the promises theme by any means, and additional views will be presented in the subsequent discussion. Let me attempt to summarize a series of questions or issues that arise out of the above survey and need to be addressed in this study:

1. The question still remains since the time of Galling concerning what the relationship is between the patriarchal tradition, with its election of the fathers and the promises, and the exodus tradition, with its election of Israel through divine deliverance from Egypt and the gift of the land through the conquest. This is the larger question that the study as a whole attempts to address.

2. How did the patriarchal promises and blessing themes develop in Israel? If some aspect of the promises proves to be "late" in date, that does not justify treating it as secondary or in isolation from the other aspects on the presupposition that some aspects must be traditio-historically or literarily early. There is no compelling reason any longer (such as offered by Alt or Noth or Westermann) for considering any form of patriarchal promise as early.

3. Is there any way of introducing some control into the discussion about the levels of the traditional material in the patriarchal stories apart from the history of the promise form as represented by Westermann and Rendtorff? Neither Westermann's category of family sagas and the stories of the promise of a son[24] nor Rendtorff's treatment of the land-promise (from direct gift to the fathers to indirect gift to the offspring) will work. In their place we propose to consider the model of antiquarian traditions such as those taken up and used by the western tradition of historiography. If we have demonstrated its usefulness in the primeval history, it may prove equally useful for the patriarchal stories, because national

and tribal ancestors play a major role in such materials.

4. What is the relationship of the narrative stories or individual tradition units to the promises? In some cases, the promises may appear to have no connection with the stories in which they occur and so be regarded as secondary and redactional. But those cases should not rule out the possibility that the promise theme can belong to some of the stories as a necessary component. A third possibility is that the author J may have taken up an older tradition and reworked it rather freely to make it fit with the promise theme. Each case will have to be considered individually.

5. What is the relationship of the framework of genealogy and itinerary to the promises themes, because together they provide the individual traditions with unity? This question should have appeared obvious because genealogy seems to relate so directly to the promise of progeny, and that of movement from one region to another to that of the promise of land. Earlier attempts from Alt to Westermann have sought their common roots in the concerns of a seminomadic patriarchal society and so avoided the literary question of the tradition's form. However, the modern myth of the patriarchal society we may set aside as of little concern in the present discussion and focus on how these elements together reflect the form of antiquarian historiography.

In the primeval history, we were aware of the fact that the Yahwist seems to have combined eastern and western antiquarian traditions. In the patriarchal stories, the possibilities for such a combination seem much more limited. Concerning the eastern tradition, in spite of the fact that the forefathers are said to come from Mesopotamia and to continue close relations with the region, Mesopotamian historiography is focused so heavily on the king as to give virtually no place to the forefathers.[25] Yet it is possible, precisely within the theme of the promises, to discern some "royal" eastern influences in the particular shaping of the tradition. As we have seen above, the western antiquarian tradition uses itinerary and genealogy as major structuring techniques in its treatment of national origins, so it is in this combination with the promises that the amalgamation of eastern and western is to be seen. Before taking up this study in detail, it is necessary first to consider the development of the land-promise theme in the rest of the Old Testament.

226   THE PATRIARCHS

NOTES

1. The Sinai covenant tradition was also not a necessary part of the exodus tradition.
2. K. Galling, *Die Erwählungstraditionen Israels,* BZAW 48 (1928), pp. 37–56.
3. Ibid., p. 56.
4. A. Alt, *Der Gott der Väter,* 1929 = *Kleine Schriften zur Geschichte des Volkes Israel,* vol. 1 (1953), pp. 1–78.
5. Von Rad, "The Form-Critical Problem of the Hexateuch," pp. 1–78.
6. Ibid., p. 61.
7. Noth, *A History of Pentateuchal Traditions.*
8. Ibid., p. 111.
9. Westermann, *The Promises to the Fathers.*
10. Rendtorff, *Das überlieferungsgeschichtliche Problem des Pentateuch.*
11. See now the study by Römer, *Israels Väter,* pp. 173–251. Even if one can detect some development of the land theology in Deuteronomy, this usage would be earlier than that of Genesis-Numbers. On the tradition-history of the land-promise, see below, chapter 13.
12. See Blum, *Die Komposition,* a doctoral dissertation that was done under Rendtorff's direction.
13. See Van Seters, *Abraham.*
14. J. A. Emerton, "The Origin of the Promises to the Patriarchs in the Older Sources of the Book of Genesis," *VT* 32 (1982), 14–32.
15. A. de Pury, *Promesse divine et légende culturelle dans le cycle de Jacob: Genese 28 et les traditions patriarchales,* 2 vols., 1975.
16. Van Seters, *Abraham.*
17. Schmid, *Der sogenannte Jahwist.*
18. But see the article by Rendtorff, "The 'Yahwist' as Theologian? The Dilemma of Pentateuchal Criticism," *JSOT* 3 (1977), 2–10, and the responses by Schmid and myself among others in the same issue, pp. 11–45. See also my review of Rendtorff, "Recent Studies on the Pentateuch: A Crisis in Method."
19. S. Tengström, *Die Hexateucherzählung. Eine literaturgeschichtliche Studie,* CBOT 7, 1976.
20. Ibid., p. 110.
21. See also D. J. A. Clines, *The Theme of the Pentateuch,* JSOT SS 10, 1978. Clines's treatment of the promise theme is similar to that of Tengström except that he does not deal with it in terms of a diachronic development, so his views do not come into discussion here.
22. K. Berge, *Die Zeit des Jahwisten, Ein Beitrag zur Datierung jahwistischer Vätertexte,* BZAW 186, 1990.
23. Römer, *Israels Väter.*
24. See Whybray, *The Making of the Pentateuch,* JSOT SS 53:154–158, for a critique of Westermann. See also pp. 205–213 for his critique of Rendtorff and Blum.
25. But see Hammurapi's dynastic genealogy and the Assyrian King List. For a discussion, see Van Seters, *In Search of History,* pp. 72–76.

13

THE LAND-PROMISE
THEME IN THE
OLD TESTAMENT

The So-called Deuteronomistic Redaction of the Pentateuch

I want to take up at this point the question of the nature and extent of the so-called Dtr redaction within the pre-Priestly corpus of the Pentateuch and its relationship to Deuteronomy and the Dtr tradition in the rest of the Old Testament. These texts have been treated in a variety of ways by scholars. Some have regarded them as belonging to a redaction that is earlier than Deuteronomy and characterize them as "proto-" or "early" Deuteronomic, often identified with the redactor of the older sources known as the "Jehovist."[1] Others have considered them as part of a late Dtr redaction of the Pentateuch as a whole, the same as, or later than, those responsible for the corpus from Deuteronomy to 2 Kings.[2] A third possibility is to consider the composition of the Tetrateuch in its Yahwistic form as quite late and therefore to view the Dtr elements not as redactional but as reflecting an author contemporary with, or later than, the DtrH.[3]

This represents such a variety of viewpoints and possibilities that the question arises how to make any progress in the debate. One way is to do close comparisons between similar or parallel texts in the Tetrateuch and Dtn/Dtr,[4] but the strong prejudice for an early date for the Yahwist makes it difficult to demonstrate the priority of Deuteronomy in any such comparison. I believe it is possible to address the comparison between the Yahwist and the Dtn tradition on a much broader scale, dealing with a theme that is basic to both.[5] But before I take up this question I want to discuss briefly the issue of how to decide whether a text is proto-Deutero-nomic, Dtr, or even post-Dtr.

It seems to me methodologically dubious to use the language and terminology of Dtn/Dtr to identify a group of texts as "proto-D" simply because they are embedded within that part of the Pentateuch that has been considered by the documentary hypothesis as earlier than Dtn. The only way that one can properly make such judgments would be to see how the Pentateuchal texts fit into a stream of development or history of tradition in non-Pentateuchal texts that clearly begins before Deuteronomy and proceeds beyond Dtr into the exilic and postexilic periods. The controlling framework of texts by which to construct the history of tradition must have the support of a broad consensus of scholarship. I have in mind the use of Hosea as a starting point, for many would regard this prophet as proto-D, indeed even the originator of much of the D tradition.[6] But equally important would be a comparison with the prophets from the late monarchy into the exilic period: Jeremiah, Ezekiel, and Second Isaiah.

What I propose to do is to take the theology of the land as the theme to be examined and investigate the history of its develop-ment. It is certainly central to the Yahwist in Genesis, and it is often found in those texts in Exodus and Numbers that are frequently considered as Dtr or proto-Dtn. It is also very promi-nent throughout Deuteronomy as a major theological concern, as many studies have pointed out. But our present task will be to look at this theme in both J and D within the controlling framework of the prophetic texts.

The Promise of Land in Deuteronomy: The Law

As L. Perlitt has recently pointed out,[7] the theology of the land permeates the whole of Deuteronomy, and because many regard that book as developing over a period of two hundred years, the land-theology in it may likewise reflect such a history of development. Perlitt suggests that within the law book of chapters 12–26, and therefore reflecting the oldest level of the book as a whole, the land is viewed as the pure gift of God. "The land which Yahweh your God is giving us/you" or its equivalent is frequently used to introduce laws or provide a motivation for legal, ethical, or religious behavior. The function of the law is to regulate and protect life and blessing within the land. Perlitt argues that this understanding of the relationship of law to land means that at the oldest level of the tradition the land is the unconditional gift of God. By implication, therefore, all texts that speak of land-promise, whether in Dtn or in the rest of the Pentateuch, belong to this oldest level of the land-theology tradition, including the land-promise theme in the Yahwist. Only in the later Dtr texts in Dtn did the law serve as a condition to the reception and retention of the land.

This thesis, however, deserves closer inspection. First, it is true that the divine gift of the land introduces a number of laws having to do with the establishment of certain institutions, such as the local law courts, 16:18–20, the monarchy, 17:14–20, the cities of refuge, 19:1–13, and even the temple cultus, as in the law of the altar, chapter 12. In another set of texts, however, the land as divine gift is used as motivation for maintaining the purity of the land against foreign religious practices or unethical activity. Here the theme of defiling the land is often related to the conquest and extermination of the original nations who did such abominations, so anyone who repeated such things would become an abomination too. The implication from the texts on the defilement of the land is clearly conditional. This is spelled out in some of the parenetic texts of the prologue that suggest that the same fate could overtake the Israelites as overtook the previous inhabitants.

Some laws that are of a general ethical nature are qualified by the condition "that you may live long on the land which Yahweh your God gives you," as we find it in the Decalogue concerning the honoring of one's parents (v. 16; cf. 25:15). In the law on just weights and measures (25:13–16), the motivation of living long in the land is combined with the theme of avoiding abominations: "For all who do such things, all who act dishonestly, are an abomination to Yahweh your God," which is the language used of the dispossessed nations. The regulations on the institution of the law-courts concludes with the words: "Justice and only justice (*sedeq*) you shall follow that you may live and maintain possession (*yrš*) of the land which Yahweh your God gives you." Here *sedeq* in a general sense is surely viewed as a *condition* of retaining the land. Contrary to Perlitt, it would appear that the laws of Deuteronomy do suggest that a condition of maintaining possession of the land that Yahweh had given to Israel was loyalty to Yahweh and his laws.

Furthermore, if an oath or promise to the fathers concerning the land is the basis for an unconditional gift of the land, then it is noteworthy that only in three places in the law code is such a promise mentioned. The first of these is in the law having to do with the cities of refuge, which states (19:8f.):

> If Yahweh your God enlarges your border, as he has sworn to your fathers, and gives you all the land which he promised to give to your fathers — provided you are careful to keep all this commandment, which I command you this day . . . — then you shall add three other cities to these three.

This text, which spells out the conditional nature of the *gaining* of new land, has in view the finished corpus of Deuteronomy and must be regarded as a late addition, even later than Josh. 20:7, which still reckons with only three cities of refuge in Cis-Jordan.[8]

The second text that mentions the promise to the fathers in the law code is the law of the firstfruits. The divine gift of the land is mentioned in 26:1 and 26:2, "the land which Yahweh your God gives you," but v. 3 changes to "the land which Yahweh swore to your fathers to give us." However, it has been observed that vs. 3–4 introduce a priest as an intermediary who is otherwise not present in v. 10f., so the verses are suspect of being later (priestly?) additions.[9] The third instance of the promise to the fathers in the law is perhaps closely related to it and occurs in the following law of the tithe. The law consists primarily of a negative confession about not breaking any of the commandments and an affirmation of obeying God's law, and this is followed by a prayer for blessing: "Bless thy people Israel and the ground/land which thou hast given, as thou didst swear to our fathers, a land flowing with milk and honey" (v. 15). The language here is strongly reminiscent of the prayer of Solomon in 1 Kings 8 and is generally regarded as Dtr.[10]

What we can conclude so far is that in the code of Dtn the divine gift of land is not associated with the promise to the fathers (whoever they might be)[11] and that continued possession of the land was in some way contingent upon loyalty to Yahweh and moral living. The divine gift also seems to be connected with the conquest of the land and not with any other tradition.

Land in Hosea and Jeremiah

Let us now turn for a moment to Hosea to ask about any possible proto-Deuteronomic land-theology in this source.[12] Direct statements about God's gift of the land and about the conquest do not appear in this prophet, but the use of the exodus and wilderness themes surely makes a land-theology implicit. In Hosea, Yahweh is the owner of the land and the giver of its fruitfulness, not Baal, the god of the indigenous population. To forget God is to jeopardize those gifts (2:4–15). Indeed, Hosea suggests the possibility of a return to the wilderness and then a new entrance into the land linked with absolute religious loyalty (2:16–17). In 4:1–3, Hosea makes a very strong connection between the keeping of the law, understood as basic ethical principles similar to the Decalogue, and the fertility and prosperity of the land. Land and law are already interrelated in Hosea. This is taken one step further in 9:1–6, where Hosea makes the threat of exile and loss of the land a result of the people's religious pollution and the forsaking of Yahweh: "They shall not remain in Yahweh's land; but Ephraim shall return to Egypt, and they shall eat unclean food in Assyria" (v. 3). As a result of their departure, "Nettles shall dispossess them (*yrš*) and thorns in their tents (v. 6)." The allusion to the land-conquest pattern is clear.

It is not too difficult to see how Hosea anticipates a close association between religious purity and a claim upon the land and its benefits, as found in Dtn. Hosea also broadens this religious concern to include general ethical principles so that the connection between land and law (*tôrāh*) with obedience to the latter as a condition for life on the land is in direct continuity with Dtn. This view is strengthened when we look at Jeremiah and those texts from his early period thought to be most influenced by Hosea.[13] In Jer. 2:4–8, we have a complaint by God against Israel's infidelity, followed by a recital of the sacred history of deliverance from Egypt, guidance through the wilderness, and entrance into the land: "I brought you into a plentiful land to enjoy its fruits and its good things. But when you came in you defiled my land, and you made my heritage an abomination" (v. 7).[14] In a second text, 3:1–5, 19–20, which is reminiscent of Hosea's images of marital infidelity and of parental love, Jeremiah makes direct reference to the land-gift theme.[15] He states as the words of deity: "I thought how I would set you among my sons, and give you a pleasant land, a heritage most beauteous of all the nations" (v. 19a). Jeremiah confirms the land-theology that we found in Hosea and in the earliest level of Deuteronomy and merely makes it more explicit. What is lacking from Hosea and the poetic oracles of Jeremiah and the code of Dtn is any reference to an oath or promise to the fathers.[16] Even when Hosea does mention the forefather Jacob, he has quite different themes in mind. So it is hard to see how the theme of the land as an unconditional gift to the ancestors can be regarded as proto-Dtn, because our best witnesses to proto-Dtn know nothing of this tradition.

Land in Deuteronomic Parenesis

In the parenetic introduction to the law in Deuteronomy 5–11, the theme of the land is dominant so that the law is viewed throughout as directly related to possession of the land. In 5:31ff., the law code as a whole is interpreted as a preparation and anticipation of the people's life in the land. The conquest theme is invoked in terms of the extermination of the original inhabitants of the land as a basis for maintaining the purity of worship and religious devotion to Yahweh alone. Through the conquest, Yahweh is the giver of the land and all the good things in it, and fertility and blessing can come about only by obedience to the law. None of this is new; it merely strengthens what is said in the code and raises it to a fundamental principle.

What is new is that the law, which was thought of as given in the wilderness, could also be the condition for gaining possession of the land in the first place (ch. 8).[17] The wilderness becomes a preparation for entrance into the land. This has some affinities with Hosea's notion of the wilderness as a place in which Israel can learn exclusive and complete dependence upon Yahweh: "As a man disciplines his son, Yahweh your God disciplines you" (v. 5). Yet the positive evaluation of the wilderness experience, derived from Hosea and Jeremiah and expressed in terms of obedience to the law, was counterbalanced by a quite different treatment in 9:6ff. by the presentation of a disobedient Israel in the wilderness. It is explicitly stated that it was not because of Israel's righteousness that they gained possession of the land, for they were obstinate and rebellious, and the author goes on to recount major breaches in the covenant, especially the making of the molten calf. This raises the question of the relationship of the positive wilderness tradition of chapter 8 to the negative tradition of chapter 9, and ultimately to the presentation of the wilderness in the Tetrateuch (J) as well.

A second new element is the emphasis upon the oath to the fathers as the motivation for the gift of the land. The statement of direct gift: "the land that Yahweh gave to you" becomes: "the land that Yahweh swore to your fathers to give to you."[18] It is generally assumed that the reference to the "fathers" is to the patriarchs, but some years ago I offered reasons for questioning that assumption and suggested that the "fathers" referred to the generation of the exodus.[19] Since then it has been argued that in most instances where the "fathers" are mentioned they refer to a group who are prior to the exodus-Horeb generation and that the people from the exodus to the conquest are all treated as belonging to the same group, even though two different generations are involved if all the old exodus generation died in the wilderness.[20]

Most recently, T. Römer has challenged this view. He has examined all the references to the "fathers" in detail in the Dtn/Dtr tradition and in Jeremiah and Ezekiel, and found that apart from a few late additions the "fathers" do not refer to the patriarchs and should be regarded as originally distinct. They may refer to a vaguely defined group that includes those who migrated into Egypt, sojourned there, experienced the exodus and Sinai/Horeb revelation. They are continuous with the later people of Israel. This represents a confirmation of my earlier position.[21]

In the light of Römer's study, it is not necessary to review here all the texts that refer to the land-promise theme. The issue can be addressed by turning first to some prophetic texts as a guide to the theme's development.

Land in Ezekiel and Jeremiah

At this point, the remarkable text in Ezekiel 20 must be given its due in the traditio-historical discussion.[22] The elders of Israel have come to the prophet to inquire of Yahweh, and he responds by reciting to them their sacred history, but in an entirely negative fashion (vs. 4b–6):

> "Let them know the abominations of their fathers, and say to them, Thus says the Lord Yahweh: On the day when I chose Israel, I swore to the seed of the house of Jacob, making myself known to them in the land of Egypt, I swore to them, saying, I am Yahweh your God. On that day I swore to them that I would bring them out of the land of Egypt into a land that I had searched out for them, a land flowing with milk and honey, the most glorious of all lands."

This statement is followed by an account of the "fathers'" rebellion in Egypt, in the wilderness, and in the land of Canaan through successive generations.

Now, concerning the land-theology in this text, there is simply no place for a prior revelation, covenant, and land-promise to the patriarchs. What we have here is an oath to the fathers added to the theme of the gift of the land. This is emphasized in a negative statement in v. 15: "Moreover, I swore to them in the wilderness that I would not bring them into the land which I had given them." This is still addressed to the fathers of the exodus generation. But in speaking about the children of the next generation, Ezekiel states in v. 28: "I brought them into the land which I swore to give them." Here the generation of the fathers who actually received the oath and the offspring have become identical because they are all fathers of the past.

When we compare Ezekiel 20 with Hosea, Jeremiah (poetic oracles), and the Dtn code, what we have is the addition of an oath to the "fathers," the wilderness treated as a condition of entry and retention of the land, and the wilderness as a time of rebellion (as well as Egypt itself). At the same time, Ezekiel continues to put great stress on the theme of the defilement of the land. This seems to parallel the same development that is evident in the parenetic prologue in Dtn.

When we turn to the prose of Jeremiah, the divine gift of land is regularly expressed as "the land that I gave to you and your fathers."[23] In this phrase, the "fathers" simply means the previous generations of Israelites in continuity with the audience in Jeremiah's day. One text, however, is particularly instructive. Jeremiah 11:3–5 states:

"You shall say to them [the inhabitants of Jerusalem], Thus says Yahweh, the God of Israel: Cursed be the one who does not heed the words of this covenant which I commanded your fathers when I brought them out of the land of Egypt, from the iron furnace, saying, Listen to my voice, and do all that I command you. So shall you be my people, and I will be your God, that I may perform the oath which I swore to your fathers, to give them a land flowing with milk and honey, as at this day."

In this text we have a reference to the "fathers" of the exodus generation and a covenant that was made with them, and this is repeated a number of times in the subsequent text (vs. 7–8, 10). This is just as we have it in Ezekiel 20. But in quoting the divine address to the exodus generation, the Dtr author refers to an oath to the fathers that suggests a previous generation. Yet apart from this nothing in this text indicates that he has the patriarchs in mind.[24] It is in fact the same oath of a gift of land, as in Ezekiel 20. So it is merely an inadvertent confusion of generations, and it actually means the exodus generation itself. To suppose that in this one case the "fathers" means something different from all the other uses in the Dtr prose is hardly reasonable.[25] This means that the introduction of the fathers as the recipient of the divine gift of land and the oath to the fathers in Deuteronomy reflects the same development that we have seen in the successive levels of the prophetic materials. Thus the oath to the fathers represents the divine promise to the exodus generation, *even when this appears to contradict the sequence of generations between those addressed in the second person and the fathers.* Furthermore, whatever God is said to have sworn to the fathers in Deuteronomy: a covenant, the gift of land, great increase, to become God's people, deliverance from Egypt, increase of territory—all these things are also said to have been promised directly to Israel, the people, as well.[26]

Holiness Code

It is a simple fact that the land-theology in the laws of the Holiness Code corresponds very closely to that of the Dtn Code in emphasizing the direct divine gift to the people (Lev. 20:22–26; 23:10; 25:2, 38; cf. 18:24–30). There is the same motivation for religious institutions and the same close association between a claim on the land and defilement of the land. There is no mention whatever of the "fathers" in these laws.

However, when we come to chapter 26 there is much more parenetic material in the blessing and curses, and here the parallels are more closely drawn with Dtr's parenetic prologue of Dtn. HC introduces the "fathers" in vs. 39ff. in the same sense as that in Dtr and Ezekiel.[27] It presents the people of Israel in exile as experiencing the ultimate punishment for breaking the law, but then asserts the possibility of restoration, vs. 44f.:

> "Yet for all that, when they are in the land of their enemies, I will not spurn them . . . and break my covenant with them; for I am Yahweh their God; but I will for their sake remember the covenant with the forefathers (rī'šōnîm), whom I brought forth out of the land of Egypt in the sight of the nations in order to be their God. I am Yahweh."

The covenant with the forefathers (rī'šōnîm) of the exodus genera-tion hardly seems to allow for a prior covenant with the patriarchs.[28] Yet in v. 42 we have the rather strange construction:

> "then I will remember my covenant with Jacob, and also my covenant with Isaac, and also my covenant with Abraham I will remember, and I will remember the land."

The first peculiarity about this text is the remarkable reverse order that is not easily explained as original. The second problem is the mention of three covenants when Genesis speaks only of one, that with Abraham. Finally, it is odd that God's motivation for turning again to his people is based upon two different covenants with two different sets of forefathers, the patriarchs and the exodus generation.

If, however, we look at the text in Ezek. 20:5, similar to Lev. 26:44–45,[29] the oath is said to have been made with the "descend-ants (zera') of the house of Jacob." This suggests that originally the text in Lev. 26:42 stated that God remembered his covenant with "Jacob," meaning the people and not the patriarch, and the two covenants in vs. 42 and 45 would be identical.[30] It was only later that Jacob was understood as the patriarch, and then the text had to be extended back successively to Abraham in agreement with Genesis. If this is so, then HC did not know of any land-promise to the patriarchs.

This further calls to mind those texts in Deuteronomy in which the references to the patriarchs—Abraham, Isaac, and Jacob—appear in apposition to the "fathers" as the recipients of the divine promise of land. As I have argued previously, these names were added to adjust the one land tradition with the other.[31]

Land in the Dtr Framework: Deuteronomy 1–4, 29–31

The Dtr historical prologue in Deuteronomy 1–3 is dominated by the theme of the divine gift of land, first by an account of the abortive attempt at settlement from the south, then by the report of Moses' campaign in Transjordan, and finally by the preparations for Moses' replacement by Joshua to lead the assault on Canaan, which is taken up again in the epilogue, especially in chapter 31. Now what we have in the prologue is a specific way of understanding the divine gift of the land not only to Israel but also to its neighbors, the Edomites, the Moabites, and the Ammonites. This gift of the land was in each case by means of conquest of the previous inhabitants of the land, for example: "The sons of Esau dispossessed [the Horites], and destroyed them from before them, and settled in their stead, as Israel did to the land of their possession, which Yahweh gave to them" (Deut. 2:12).

This pattern of migration and conquest of the indigenous population by each of Israel's neighbors is not the ingenious invention of the Dtr historian by analogy with Israel's own tradition. Because he cites the names that these peoples themselves give in their traditions to the original populations and then tries to find the equivalent in his own tradition, he is surely drawing upon extra-Israelite materials. In such traditions it is, of course, the national deities of these countries who gave the land to them, as is clear from Jephthah's message to the king of Ammon: "Will you not possess what Chemosh your god gives you to possess? And all that Yahweh our God has dispossessed before us, we will possess (Judg. 11:24)." Furthermore, Amos points in the same direction by paralleling Israel's migration from Egypt with the Philistines' origins from Caphtor and the Arameans from Kir (9:7). Only the Canaanites apparently considered themselves as indigenous.

Now, as we have seen above, in the antiquarian traditions of Greece and subsequently of Rome, one way of accounting for the origin of nations was frequently to speak of the migration of a people or group from an ancient culture to a new land, often to defeat and displace the original population of primitive peoples by the more noble population.[32] Whether or not this reflected some element of historical reality need not concern us here. What is important is to see that this pattern of migration and settlement as a tradition of national origin was very common and widespread in the Levant and the Aegean region in the first millennium B.C.

Land and Origin Traditions in Genesis

Let us turn now to Genesis and compare the origin traditions of Israel's neighbors presented there. Here we are told that Lot, the father of the Ammonites and Moabites, migrated with Abraham and separated from him, choosing the Jordan valley only to end up, after the Sodom and Gomorrah misadventure, in the eastern highlands. There his daughters produced male offspring for him.[33] This is how, according to this tradition, the Ammonites and the Moabites obtained their land, not by the conquest of a migrating group. It is specifically stated that the land was empty of any other inhabitants, hence the extremity of incest by the daughters of Lot to produce the fathers of the two peoples.[34] Nothing is said about Yahweh or any other deity giving or promising this land to Lot. This directly conflicts with the migration/conquest tradition in Deut. 2:9–10, 17–21.

The same may be said of Esau, the father of Edom. Entirely on his own and without any divine command or impulse, he settles in the hill country of Seir. There is no indication of any conquest of that region, and in the traditions of Genesis 36 (P) he is pictured as intermarrying with the local population. Indeed, the original Horites are viewed as part of the ancestral population of the later Edomite nation and not as a displaced or eradicated group. This constitutes a problem for the migration/conquest of Edom in Deut. 2:4–5, 12, 22, similar to that for Ammon and Moab.

Likewise in the case of Judah, Genesis 38 preserves the tradition of how he migrated and settled alongside the original population and intermarried with them, precisely in the region where the tribe of Judah is to be located. This is clearly an alternate land-settlement tradition that is not connected with the tradition about the migration from Egypt and the conquest under Joshua. This tension has not gone unnoticed in the past, but it has been used to try to reconstruct alternate histories of settlement for the Joseph tribes in the north and Judah in the south. I do not believe that such origin traditions can be used to reconstruct history. But my primary concern at the moment is a literary and traditio-historical one—how to account for the juxtaposition of these conflicting traditions.

What we have here is the possibility of two different kinds of origin traditions that could exist side by side, even though in complete contradiction to each other. The one has to do with eponymous ancestors or heroes as founding fathers; the other concerns groups migrating from one region to another, conquering the local inhabitants. Such was certainly the case in the classical antiquarian traditions of Greece and Rome, and I believe in ancient Israel also. Thus I think that it is entirely correct to suggest that originally the oldest level of the patriarchal traditions was quite separate from the exodus tradition.

But at some point, a historian, the Yahwist, did for Israel what also became a dominant historiographic technique in the classical world, that of the integration of conflicting origin traditions with each other.[35] The method used by the Yahwist was quite simple. Instead of the fathers' actually possessing the land, as Lot and Esau did, they were viewed as gaining it by promise. The "promises to the fathers" that originally applied to the exodus generation were now shifted back to the patriarchs. The crucial question is, When did this happen? When did the historian J make this connection? The answer to this question lies in Ezek. 33:23ff.:

> The word of Yahweh came to me saying: "Son of man, the inhabitants of these wastelands throughout the land of Israel say, 'Abraham was only one when he took possession of the land, but we are numerous. To us the land has been given as a possession.'"

The implication of this text is clear. In this form of the Abraham tradition, he is not just promised the land, but as the ancestor he immediately took possession of it. Those who view themselves as his offspring are using this tradition to assert their claim to the land. But Ezekiel rejects this tradition in favor of the exodus-settlement (= migration-conquest) tradition because, as we have seen, in the whole tradition as he knows it from Hosea onward, the claim to the land is conditional, and he accuses Abraham's offspring of violating those conditions of purity and morality (vs. 25–26). This means that these two streams of land-theology had not yet been integrated as late as the exilic period![36] All the texts that deal with the *promise* of land to the patriarchs are part of this integration of the two bodies of tradition and must be later than Ezekiel.

For those scholars who hold the view that the oath sworn to the fathers in Deuteronomy refers specifically to the promise theme in Genesis, the text of Genesis 15 is of central concern because only in this text, or those dependent upon it (26:3), can such an oath be found.[37] But what has become increasingly evident in biblical scholarship is that this text must be late. It is usually characterized as Deuteronomistic.[38] If Genesis 15 is so late, then it can hardly be the origin of the statements in Deuteronomy, and they must mean something else. They must refer to the exodus generation and not the patriarchs. So the dating and relationship of Genesis 15 to Dtr/Dtn is crucial.

Several years ago I suggested that the statement in 15:7: "I am Yahweh your God who brought you from Ur of the Chaldeans to give you this land to possess it," represents the transformation of a very common formula: "I am Yahweh your God who brought you up out of Egypt to give you this land to possess it," or the like.[39] There can scarcely be any question about the direction of the dependence of the former on the latter. Although the language is Deuteronomistic, the replacing of "Egypt" by "Ur" as the point of origin and the exodus/wilderness generation by the patriarchs is a quite new outlook and is therefore *post*-Deuteronomistic.[40]

The land promise as a solemn covenant, which is really a one-sided oath in Gen. 15:17ff., suggests that the gift of land has become unconditional. And this raises the question of its relationship to law. Did this revision of the land-theology simply set aside obedience to the law as a condition for possession of the land? The answer to this comes in Gen. 15:6, the verse immediately preceding the section dealing with the land-promise: "And he believed Yahweh and he reckoned it to him as righteousness." It was Abraham's righteousness, through his faith in the promise of an heir, that qualified him and his descendants to receive the land. This same point is made again in 22:16–18, where it is stated that the promise to Abraham would come to his descendants because he was obedient to the command of Yahweh: "Because you have

obeyed my voice." This oath involving both the land-promise and
the other blessings is repeated to Isaac (26:3–5) with the assurance
of fulfillment, "because Abraham obeyed my voice, and kept my
charge, my commandments, my statutes and my laws." Scholars have
been too quick to identify these words as a Dtr gloss, although
the influence of Deuteronomy is indisputable. However, in Dtr
these terms always refer to Deuteronomic Code, but that is hardly
possible in the case of Abraham. Again it is an example of a post-
Dtr Yahwist who is transferring the whole of the land-theology's
conditionality of obedience and righteousness to father Abraham,
and that is a radically new position.

Another text in Genesis that is often identified as Dtr is the
divine soliloquy in Gen. 18:17ff., where God contemplates disclosing to Abraham his judgment upon Sodom. The reason for doing
so is that God has chosen Abraham "that he may charge his
children and his household after him to keep the way of Yahweh
by doing what is right and just, so that Yahweh may bring to
Abraham what he has promised him." Again it is the role of the
fathers in Deuteronomy who are to teach their children the law
of Deuteronomy that is transferred to Abraham. When the children
of Abraham heed the lesson of his life, rather than the law of Dtn,
and do what is right and just in a general way, then they can bring
in and enhance the promises. But there is no suggestion that the
promises can be abrogated.

Second Isaiah

The land-theology in Second Isaiah is no longer expressed
in the language of Dtn/Dtr. And yet it is clear that the deliverance
being proclaimed is in the form of a second exodus and wilderness
trek to the Promised Land. But now the patriarchal tradition has
become fully integrated with the other, so that the patriarch's call
from the distant land of Mesopotamia also becomes part of the
model and hope of deliverance (41:8–10, cf. 51:1–3). The resettle-
ment and broad expansion in the land (54:1–3) is described in
terms of the great fruitfulness of the barren woman, with details
that are reminiscent of the patriarchal stories: "'Enlarge the place
of your tent, and let the curtains of your habitations be stretched
out; . . . For you will spread abroad to the right and to the left, and

your descendants will possess the nations and will people the desolate cities.'" Second Isaiah thus shows a movement from antagonism toward the Abraham tradition, as in Ezekiel, to its complete integration, which also corresponds to the shift from the absence of the patriarchal tradition in Dtr to its dominance in the Yahwist.[41]

Conclusion

We are now in a position to summarize the various stages in the evolution of the Old Testament's land-theology from the proto-D form in Hosea to the post-Dtr form in J.

1. First, the land was thought to be Yahweh's land, his inheritance, so that loyalty to him alone and obedience to his laws were the conditions for prosperity and possession of the land.

2. The land was given to Israel after the exodus from Egypt and through conquest of the ancient inhabitants. The wilderness became a preparation for life in the Promised Land.

3. Loss of the land in the exile confirmed the prophetic judgment based on the land's conditionality. Any subsequent right to the land was jeopardized.

4. An alternative tradition of national origin, based upon the eponymous ancestors, allowed for a prior unconditional claim to the land that could be interpreted as the promise to the fathers *before* the generations in Egypt — the patriarchs — and so permitted a new possibility of continued association and claim upon the land.

5. I attribute this daring combination of antiquarian traditions to the Yahwist in the exilic period. It is this combination that is fully affirmed by the Priestly Writer as well (see esp. Ex. 6:2ff.).

K. Galling, in his 1928 study of the "election traditions of Israel,"[42] amassed a considerable body of evidence to show that the two election traditions of the exodus-conquest and the patriarchs were originally quite distinct and remained separate, outside the Pentateuch, until quite late. It was only his early dating of the Pentateuchal sources that prevented him from drawing the conclusion that their integration did not take place until the exilic period. If, as we propose, this was carried out by a post-Dtr author, the Yahwist, in a major supplement to the DtrH, then all the evidence of the so-called Dtr redaction in the Pentateuch can be accounted for.[43]

NOTES

1. N. Lohfink, *Das Hauptgebot. Eine Untersuchung literarischer Einleitungsfragen zu Dtn 5–11* (1963), pp. 121–124; C. H. W. Brekelmans, "Die sogenannten deuteronomistischen Elemente in Gen.–Num. Ein Beitrag zur Vorgeschichte des Deuteronomiums," *SVT* 15 (1966), pp. 90–96.

2. Rendtorff, *Das überlieferungsgeschichtliche Problem des Pentateuch*, BZAW 147 (1977), pp. 158–173; idem, *The Old Testament: An Introduction*, pp. 162–163.

3. Schmid, *Der sogenannte Jahwist;* Rose, *Deuteronomist und Jahwist;* Van Seters, *Abraham;* A. D. H. Mayes, *The Story of Israel Between Settlement and Exile* (1983), pp. 139–149.

4. See the work of Rose in n. 3 above. Among my recent studies, see "'Comparing Scripture with Scripture': Some Observations on the Sinai Pericope of Exodus 19–24," in *Canon, Theology and Old Testament Interpretation*, ed. G. M. Tucker, D. L. Petersen, and R. R. Wilson (1988), pp. 111–130.

5. See now the work by Römer, *Israels Väter.* This work was not available to me for an earlier version of this chapter. It greatly expands the documentation and supporting argument for the position presented here.

6. E. W. Nicholson, *Deuteronomy and Tradition* (1967), pp. 70ff.; W. Zimmerli, "Das Gottesrecht bei den Propheten Amos, Hosea und Jesaja," in *Werden und Wirken des Alten Testaments, Festschrift für C. Westermann*, ed. R. Albertz (1980), pp. 220–228.

7. L. Perlitt, "Motive und Schichten der Landtheologie im Deuteronomium," in *Das Land Israel in biblischer Zeit*, ed. G. Strecker (1983), pp. 46–58.

8. See A. D. H. Mayes, *Deuteronomy: New Century Bible Commentary* (1979), pp. 284f.; idem, *The Story of Israel*, p. 54; A. Rofé, "The History of the Cities of Refuge in Biblical Law," *Studies in Bible, Scrip Hier* 21 (1986), 205–239, esp. pp. 222–224; Römer, *Israels Väter*, pp. 188–194.

9. Mayes, *Deuteronomy*, p. 332; Römer, *Israels Väter*, pp. 57–70, 125–128, 240–241.

10. Mayes, *Deuteronomy*, p. 337; Römer, *Israels Väter*, pp. 242–245. Römer charts and discusses these parallels in detail.

11. See Römer, *Israels Väter*, pp. 192–193, for his comments on the scarcity of the references to the "fathers" in the code in general. Apart from the framing chapters of 12 and 26, only in 13:18 and 19:8 are there any references to the "fathers," and both texts are probably post-Dtr.

12. See W. Zimmerli, "The 'Land' in the Pre-Exilic and Early Post-Exilic Prophets," in *Understanding the Word: Essays in Honor of B. W. Anderson*, ed. J. T. Butler et al., JSOT SS 37 (1985), pp. 245–262, esp. pp. 251f.

13. Ibid., pp. 252–255. For a new analysis of these texts, see M. E. Biddle, *A Redaction History of Jeremiah 2:1–4:2*, ATANT 77 (1990).

14. Biddle argues (ibid., pp. 122–158) that this text belongs to a late Dtr "generations" redaction in 2:4–32. Römer, *Israels Väter*, pp. 403–406, also regards Jer. 2:5ff. as belonging to the later Dtr redaction of Jeremiah. So the text of Jer. 2:5–9 may reflect more of a late commentary on Hosea than an early phase of the land tradition.

15. In a detailed analysis of these texts, Biddle, *A Redaction History*, pp. 83–121, views these texts as redactional and not Jeremiah. But he regards them as earlier than the late Dtr redaction of 2:5ff. See also Römer, *Israels Väter*, pp. 472–473.
16. This is true even if these texts in Jeremiah 2–3 are viewed as primarily Dtr redaction. In Jer. 3:18, the land-promise to the fathers is a postexilic modification of the land-theology in 3:19f. See W. McKane, *Jeremiah*, ICC, vol. 1 (1986), pp. 72–77.
17. See also Perlitt, "Motive und Schichten," p. 54.
18. See Römer, *Israels Väter*, pp. 171–251, where he deals with all the texts in Dtn that mention the land-promise to the fathers.
19. J. Van Seters, "Confessional Reformulation in the Exilic Period," *VT* 22 (1972), 448–459.
20. See D. E. Skweres, *Die Rückverweise im Buch Deuteronomium*, AB 79 (1979); also Diepold, *Israels Land*.
21. The thesis of Römer (*Israels Väter*) is a detailed refutation of Skweres and is in support of my position of 1972 (n. 19 above).
22. Zimmerli, "The 'Land,'" pp. 255ff.; Römer, *Israels Väter*, pp. 495–506.
23. For a discussion of the relevant texts, see Diepold, *Israels Land*, pp. 158ff.; also Römer, *Israels Väter*, pp. 441–475.
24. So also Diepold, *Israels Land*, p. 158; Skweres, *Die Rückverweise*, p. 160; Römer, *Israels Väter*, pp. 475–481.
25. Cf. McKane, *Jeremiah*, p. 238, who takes the meaning of "fathers" in the divine oath to refer to the patriarchs on the basis of Deuteronomy. The only way that that is possible would be to consider this part of the verse as a later addition, but that does not seem to me very likely.
26. See all the references collected by Skweres, *Die Rückverweise*, pp. 86–180.
27. See also Römer, *Israels Väter*, pp. 548–550.
28. Cf. the use of *'ăbôtām hārī'šōnîm* in Jer. 11:10.
29. See also P in Ex. 6:2–8, where the language from both texts is combined.
30. See also Römer, *Israels Väter*, p. 548 n. 367.
31. Van Seters, "Confessional Reformulation," *VT* 22:451f.; see also Römer, *Israels Väter*, pp. 161–167, 222.
32. Such accounts in Herodotus are numerous. See also the account of the founding of Rome in Dionysius, *Antiquities of Rome*, book 1.
33. Gen. 12:4–5; 13:1–13; 19:1–38.
34. Is this a rationalization of local tradition in which the national god had sexual union with the women to produce the ancestors, as in the Greek pattern?
35. Dionysius is a good example of this process. See above, pp. 211–212.
36. On Ezek. 33:23–29, see now Römer, *Israels Väter*, pp. 513–517.
37. This is the basis of Skweres's thesis in the work cited above, n. 20.
38. See R. Rendtorff, "Genesis 15 im Rahmen der theologischen Bearbeitung der Vätergeschichten," in *Werden und Wirken des Alten Testaments, Festschrift für C. Westermann*, ed. R. Albertz (1980), pp. 74–81; and Blum, *Die Komposition*, pp. 362–383. Cf. Emerton, "The Origin of the Promises to the Patriarchs," esp. 30ff.; and Römer, *Israels Väter*, pp. 515–516.
39. Van Seters, "Confessional Reformulation," *VT* 22:454f.

40.   J. Ha (*Genesis 15,* BZAW 181 [1989], pp. 100–103) has recently argued that because the wording of Gen. 15:7 is closest to that of Lev. 25:38, which uses the exodus terminology, then Genesis 15 must be dependent upon P and belong to the final redaction of the Pentateuch. This confuses HC with P, which is not legitimate. As I have already suggested above, J could be post-HC even though HC was incorporated into P. Furthermore, the formula in Lev. 25:38 is clearly Deuteronomistic and reflects this tradition.

41.   There are a number of texts in Exodus to Numbers that have been attributed either to J or to a Dtr redaction that refer to the land-promise theme. Because I am treating only the Yahwist in Genesis, I will leave a further discussion of these to a subsequent volume. In the meantime, see my remarks in the earlier version of this discussion in a supplement to *VT,* forthcoming.

42.   Galling, *Die Erwählungstraditionen Israels,* BZAW 48 (1928).

43.   See the similar conclusions of Römer, *Israels Väter,* pp. 568–575, for the late displacement of the "fathers" by the three patriarchs.

14

THE PROMISE THEME WITHIN THE ABRAHAM-ISAAC STORIES

The Pre-Yahwist Tradition

This investigation must depend heavily upon my previous literary analysis of the Abraham story, which will not be repeated here.[1] Excluded from consideration are the Priestly texts of Genesis 17 and 23, as well as the late text of Genesis 14, which does not contain any reference to the promises theme. The earlier study identified two pre-Yahwistic strata of the Abraham tradition that were incorporated into the work of the Yahwist. The first stratum is reflected in Gen. 12:1, 4a*, 6a, 7, 10–20; 13:1*–2; 16:1–3a, 4–9, 11ab, 12; 18:1a, 10–14; 21:2, 6–7.[2] It consists of three episodes in the life of the patriarch set within a rather loose framework. The first story, the trip of Abraham and Sarah to Egypt (12:10–20), does not contain any reflections of a divine promise, so it does not come into consideration here.

In his work on patriarchal promises, Westermann made much of the fact that both Genesis 16 and 18:1–15 contain the promise of a son, and he identified this as the oldest form of divine promise and one in which the promise was the central theme or goal of the narrative.[3] Now it should be noted in the case of Genesis 16 that the point of the angel's announcement is not the promise of a child, for Hagar is already pregnant, but the destiny of the child corresponding to that of the Ishmaelites. It is an ethnographic etiology. The remark about numerous offspring in 16:10 is an obvious addition of a promise theme that does not belong to the original.[4]

The second narrative, in 18:1a, 10–14; 21:2, 6–7, is a story about

246

the wondrous birth of a child through special divine intervention.[5] This type of story is very widespread both within the Old Testament itself and outside of it. Westermann cites Ugaritic parallels to support an early provenience for such stories in the patriarchal tradition, but that is hardly necessary.[6] This kind of birth story has no direct connection with the development of the other patriarchal promises but was simply part of the traditional material taken over by the later writer, the Yahwist. The form, as Westermann himself points out, has to do most often with the mother — Sarah and Hagar are the central figures in the stories — which makes it even less likely that it is related to the promises to the ancestor.

These three stories seem to have been held together by a loose framework to which at least 13:1–2, 18 belong and that suggest a certain wandering or itinerary within the land. For this reason it seems possible that 12:1, 4a, 6a, and 7 are also part of it. The altar building would be parallel to 13:18 and symbolically establish Abraham's connection with the two centers of the future nations: Shechem and Hebron. If this is the case, then the oldest level of the Abraham tradition that we can identify already had the shape of an antiquarian tradition of the travels and founding of the nation by the ancestor. This would also form the oldest basis for the tradition of a direct gift of land to the patriarch.

The second pre-Yahwistic expansion of the tradition that is reflected in 20:1–17; 21:25–26, 28–31a, having to do with Abraham's sojourn at Gerar, does not contain any reference to the patriarchal promises.[7] But it does contain a remark that is important for the larger discussion. In 20:13, Abraham makes this statement to Abimelech: "When God caused me to wander from my father's house. . . ." This remark would seem to reflect 12:1 and the following journeys of the patriarchs as well as the recognition of the motif of heroes and ancestors who were compelled by the gods to leave their homeland in order to found new nations. In the process, they put themselves constantly at risk until they founded new states and homelands.[8]

In his recent treatment of Genesis 20, Blum has assigned this text to the latest phase of the development of the Abraham tradition, even as late as the Hellenistic times.[9] This would make it not only post-J, according to our terminology, but even post-P. The key to Blum's position lies in his analysis of 21:22–34 as a sequel to chapter 20.[10] Blum takes 21:22–24, 27, 34 as the appropriate sequel to the earlier episode and the rest as a later expansion. Such a text division is problematic, for it is difficult to see how 21:32 can be separated from vs. 22, 27, and 34. Verse 33 also hangs in limbo. Yet it is only if one accepts Blum's source division and the connection of 21:22–24 with chapter 20 that one can argue, as Blum does, for the dependence of chapter 20 on chapter 26.[11] Blum's view raises a number of further questions:

1. The unit 21:25–26, 28–32 becomes a later Hellenistic (?) expansion. Does this also depend upon the story of the well's dispute in chapter 26? And when is v. 33 attached to all of this?

2. Both Gen. 26:15 and 26:18 refer back to chapter 21 and are regarded as later connections, but they would have to come after the latest expansion of chapter 21. Does 26:1–2 also belong to these very late glosses?

The whole proposal becomes so implausible and complex that I must revert to my earlier analysis.[12]

The Yahwist and the Promises

Hoftijzer had identified Genesis 15 as the one text in which the divine promises of land and numerous progeny were integral to the narrative.[13] The other texts that he grouped together with Genesis 15 were all considered to be redactional additions.[14] What we must now consider is the status of the various texts that relate to this group. Do they all belong together on the same compositional level, or are they related to a series of redactional layers in the composition of the patriarchal stories? With the possible exception of Genesis 15, are they all merely additions to the narratives in which they are now placed?

Genesis 15

Although it has been argued since the time of Alt that within this chapter lay the oldest remnants of one or more of the promise themes — either having to do with progeny, 15:1–6 or with the promise of land, vs. 7–21 — the latest discussion of this text has almost entirely given way to the view that the chapter as a whole is a late construction and that it is scarcely possible to isolate any part of it as reflecting an early promise tradition. One recent attempt by Emerton to isolate 15:7-11, 17-18 as belonging to a somewhat older period than the rest does not seem very convincing.[15] Emerton must admit that v. 7 is exilic in its present form, so the original form of the divine statement must have been different. By contrast, Rendtorff and Blum make no attempt to find an older level in the text and regard it as Dtr.[16] There seems to be no need to dispute any longer that the text, in spite of a certain awkwardness of style, is a unity.[17] It brings together the theme of numerous offspring through the heir (vs. 2-4) and the inheritance of the land as divine gift (vs. 7-8).

If we may assume that the two birth stories of Ishmael and Isaac belong to the older pre-Yahwist tradition as argued above, then the theme of childlessness expressed in vs. 2-3 is directly dependent upon these stories and anticipates them in the Yahwist's arrangement.[18] But J has made an important shift in emphasis from the barrenness of the matriarch and her plight[19]— the basic form of the ancestral tradition — to that of the patriarch and his problem of having a son as heir. Westermann has compared this story of the need for a son with the accounts in the Ugaritic texts about how King Keret was bereft of his family and how the god El granted him offspring and a family in place of the old one.[20] This story from Ugarit is not about ancestors but about the problem of the heir to the throne and dynastic succession. Its comparison with Genesis 15 suggests that the latter has shifted from the story type dealing with ancestry to the ancestor as king.[21] This is confirmed by the language of the text at a number of points. The first is in the salvation oracle (*Heilsorakel*) that Abraham receives, v. 1, with its offer of "reward," equivalent to the spoils of war. The royal *Sitz im Leben* of such an oracle is quite clear.[22] The second indication of royal ideology is in the language regarding Abraham's offspring; that is, that the heir would be someone "born from his own body" (v. 4). This same language occurs in the dynastic promise to David: "I will raise up your offspring after you, who shall come forth from your body, and I will establish his kingdom" (2 Sam. 7:12). The third example is in the remarks about inheritance, who will succeed to Abraham's household, which has its closest analogue in the dynastic promise of a "sure house" forever (2 Sam. 7:16).[23]

The subject of inheritance leads first to the divine promise of numerous progeny and then to the promise of inheritance/possession of the land. So closely are these two themes intertwined that it has been a mistake in the past for scholars to try to separate them.

In a recent study, Rendtorff has called attention to the importance of the use of the verb yrš, "to inherit," "to possess," in this text.[24] The use of this concept of "taking possession" of the land is very characteristic of Dtr and is most often associated with the conquest of the land by the Israelites after coming out of Egypt.[25] However, Ezek. 33:24 suggests an alternative tradition that came into prominence in the exilic period in which a claim to the land is made through Abraham. The inhabitants left in the land of Israel use the argument: "Abraham was only one when he inherited (yrš imperf. qal) the land. But we are now many; to us the land is given as a possession." The same use of yrš in the qal with Abraham as subject and the land as object occurs in Gen. 15:7–8. The descendants of Abraham, "the many," are making unconditional claims to the land through their forefather. But this is opposed by Ezekiel on the basis, as in the Dtr tradition, that possession of the land is conditional, even though this position is formulated in Ezekiel's own language.

This connection between numerous progeny and possession/inheritance of the land is referred to again in Ezek. 36:1–15, now in a positive tone as a restoration after the exile. Yahweh promises to bless the land with fruitfulness and the inhabitants with numerous offspring. Likewise, in Isa. 54:1–3 the "barren one" is promised offspring and great increase in order that Israel's "seed" will fill the land and "possess" the nations. And again in Isa. 65:9 God promises that the "seed" of Jacob and the "heir" of Judah will possess the land and dwell in it as God's chosen ones (see also Jer. 49:1–2). All of these texts point both to the unity of theme between the two halves of Genesis 15 and the close association between the descendants of the forefathers and land possession in the exilic period.

What is the relationship of God's declaration of righteousness (v. 6) and the possession of the land? As we noted above in Ezek.

33:24ff., the prophet declares that without righteousness there can be no claim to possession of the land. This is clearly the heritage of the Dtr land-theology.[26] Obedience to the law comes before possession of the land. So in Genesis 15, before the covenant confirming Abraham's possession of the land, he is declared to be righteous ($ṣᵉdāqâ$). In Isa. 60:21a, the same declaration of righteousness is made in connection with possessing the land: "My people, all of them, are righteous ($ṣaddîqîm$). They will possess the land forever."

The land-promise theme is directly related to that of the patriarch's travels under divine guidance and impulse from a distant land (15:7). As stated above, this same tradition seems to be reflected in the older story of Gen. 20:13. The idea of an ancestor traveling from some distant region, preferably an older civilization, to take possession of a new land and found a new nation is so common in the western antiquarian tradition that it cannot be regarded as merely secondary here. The land that is promised is given in terms of both the geographic extent[27] and the nations to be dispossessed. Only a great and numerous people can possess such a large region.

The promise, confirmed by a most solemn covenant, relates explicitly (and unconditionally) to the land but implicitly also to the creation of the nation as the descendants who will inherit it. Yet the question remains, Why is the covenant connected with the land-promise in particular, whereas in Genesis 17 (P) the emphasis has shifted to the numerous offspring? We have already argued above that in the prior land-theology of Dtn/Dtr, JerDtr, and Ezekiel, the promise of land to the "fathers" as a solemn covenant was made to the exodus generation. When this promise theme was transferred to the patriarchs, it was natural to retain the close connection between land and covenant even though the promise of nationhood and numerous offspring had become a new and pressing concern.

Genesis 15 is an ideological and theological text with only a minimum of narrative about events in the patriarch's life. From this we turn to other texts in which the story element is more predominant and the question of the relationship of promise texts to their context more difficult to decide.

Gen. 12:1-9

The introduction to the Abraham story in Gen. 12:1-9 (with the exception of the Priestly texts, vs. 4b, 5) should first of all be considered as a unit. We have already offered some reasons for believing that part of this unit belongs to the earlier level of the tradition; that is, the notion of a divine impulse to send Abraham forth from his homeland to found a new nation. This would include the divine command in v. 1, Abraham's obedience in v. 4a (alone, without Lot), his arrival in the land at the holy place of Shechem in v. 6a, Yahweh's appearance to him to promise him the land, and Abraham's response by building an altar, v. 7. If 13:18 is to be regarded as the original introduction to the pre-Yahwist story in 18:1ff., then we have an interesting parallel in which, in the older tradition, Abraham is associated with the two ancient centers of the two kingdoms, Shechem in the north and Hebron in the south. At the one he receives the gift of the new land and at the other the gift of progeny. Together they constitute the basic etiology of the nation.[28]

It is the very nature of antiquarian ancestor traditions to establish the presence of the forefathers at national centers, reinforced by theophanies. The Yahwist has taken up this traditional structure and expanded the themes of the land grant and the promise of progeny to make them the dominant themes of his work. He does this by including in the introduction of the Abraham story, after the divine command, his own version of the themes as divine promises.[29] The promise of nationhood corresponds to that of progeny, but in addition God promises a great name, blessing or prosperity, and a means of blessing to other nations. These promises now provide the motivation for obedience to the divine command and create the thematic unity for the Yahwist's treatment of the patriarchal stories. It also provides a link with the primeval history in its reference to "all the families of the earth."[30]

The divine promise in Gen. 12:2-3 calls for some comment because its meaning is not entirely clear and therefore very much debated.[31] It states: "I will make of you a great nation and will bless you and make your name great so that it will be a means of blessing. I will surely bless those who bless you but those who curse you I will curse. Thus all the families of the earth will bless themselves through you."[32] What is important for understanding this promise of blessing is that all of the elements in it belong closely together. Thus the deity's blessing and curse on others is directly related to Abraham's state of blessedness, and the means by which "the families of the earth" bless themselves is through the great name.[33] This is not a haphazard collection of statements but a theme with a quite specific *Sitz im Leben.*

It is now quite widely recognized that the language used in this promise speech is drawn from royal ideology. The reference to the deity giving to the king a great name is found in Nathan's oracle to David, 2 Sam. 7:9: "I will make for you a great name, like the name of the great ones of the earth."[34] In the royal psalms the king is both the object of blessing by God and the people, but also the means of blessing to others.[35] The most striking parallel, however, is that of Ps. 72:17, which may be reconstructed with the help of the Greek text, and reads: "May his name be blest for ever, his name endure as long as the sun; and may all the families of the earth bless themselves by him, all nations esteem him blessed."[36] This text gives the same close connection between the great name and blessing, as well as the use of the name in blessing for others, that is found in Gen. 12:2–3. So similar is the language and thought that Gen. 12:2–3 must derive from the royal ideology of Jerusalem in general, if not this text is particular.[37]

Although many scholars have seen a reference to royalty in the notion of the "great name" and in being a mediator of blessing to the nation, there is still a strong tendency to link it with the Davidic-Solomonic era. This is based, first, on the argument that the designation "great nation" is only appropriate as a reference to the kingdoms of David and Solomon. It would not have been used in any later time.[38] The fact is, however, that this usage can appear in texts generally acknowledged as late. In the "golden calf" episode, God says to Moses: "But of you I will make a great nation" (Ex. 32:10b; cf. Deut. 9:14b). In Deut. 4:6–8, a late Deuteronomistic text, Israel is described as a "great nation" in comparison with other nations. There is no reason to believe that the author had the Davidic period specifically in mind.

A second argument for the Davidic-Solomonic dating of Gen. 12:2–3, recently put forward by Berge, is that the phrase "all the families of the earth" (כל משפחת האדמה) has a meaning that reflects the particular social context of that era and no other.[39] It is not to be confused with the parallel phrase "all the nations of the earth" (כל גויי הארץ), as in 18:18; 22:18; 26:4, which he takes to be late Dtr additions reflecting revisions of J's thought. Berge proposes that the term "family" (משפחה) refers to small group-ings of people, "clans," and that the "land" (אדמה) is the "cultivated land of Palestine."[40] This suggests to him that the people of Abraham, represented by the "great nation" of David, are to be the mediators of blessing to the small non-Israelite communities under its sphere of influence. This highly restricted and specialized meaning makes sense only during the early Solomonic period, as he understands it.

This suggestion, however, does not stand up to close scrutiny. Another use of the phrase "all the families of the earth" occurs in Amos 3:2: "'You only have I known of all the families of the earth, therefore I will punish you for all your iniquities.'" The circum-stances of Amos's day were far different from those of David, and Israel is here regarded as one of those "families" of the earth. Because Amos regularly compares Israel with the other nations, it makes the best sense to understand the term "family" here as a synonym for nation. This is also supported by other prophetic texts where "family" is used as a parallel and synonym for "nation": Jer. 10:25; Ezek. 20:32; Nahum 3:4; Zech. 14:16–19.[41] As we have seen above, the Greek text of Ps. 72:17b, which also uses "all the families of the earth," contains the phrase "all nations" in the next parallel line.[42]

If the language of Gen. 12:3b is derived directly from royal ideology, as suggested by Ps. 72:17, then how did it function in its original *Sitz im Leben*?[43] This can be clarified by a particular example from the Assyrian royal ideology. In the so-called Rassam cylinder of Ashurbanipal's annals, there is an account of how the god Assur revealed the name of Ashurbanipal in a dream to Gyges, king of Lydia.[44] This revelation suggested that Gyges should sub-mit to Ashurbanipal's lordship, but also that by means of invok-ing the king's name he would have victory over his enemies. When Gyges complied with this revelation, he was most successful. However, when he neglected to show deference to the Assyrian king and "hardened his heart," siding with Assyria's enemies, then

Ashurbanipal invoked a curse upon Gyges. The latter's fortunes were now reversed, and he was defeated by the Cimmerians, "whom he had (previously) trodden underfoot, by calling upon my name." This text clearly reflects the view that the gods bless those who hold the great king in honor, but those who do not regard him highly are cursed. Even invoking the name of the king may lead to success or blessing.

The story is told for the sole purpose of suggesting the greatness of Ashurbanipal and how distant kings could make use of his great name for their own benefit. Similarly, Psalm 72, which clearly reflects Mesopotamian influence, presents the notion that the greatness and prosperity of the king are evidence of his blessed status with the deity, which can lead to blessings for the nations who recognize and glorify the name of the Judean king. This does not portray the monarchy at a specific time in its history. It is ideology, the wish expressed at the royal coronation. In similar fashion, Gen. 12:2–3, which appropriates this ideology, does not represent any historical reality. And Gen. 12:3b does not have in mind any more specific groups than does Ps. 72:17b. But whereas in Egypt and Mesopotamia, from which all the parallels are drawn, it is consistently the king who is the mediator of such blessing, in J it has become Abraham and his offspring.

Contrary to Berge's view, the terminology of Gen. 12:2–3 is not specific to the Davidic-Solomonic age; nor is it to be distinguished from those texts that have slightly different wording, such as "all the nations of the earth." To suggest that on this basis they should be dated four hundred years later is quite unreasonable. They all belong together. Schmid has convincingly argued that because the language is clearly original to royalty it could only be separated from this *Sitz im Leben* and applied to the people as a whole after the demise of the monarchy.[45]

Schmid likewise examines the idea of blessing as promise and concludes that it can only be a rather late development in Israelite thought, as reflected in the D/Dtr literature.[46] However, an important difference is that whereas in Deuteronomy[47] the blessing is understood as a result of obedience to the law, in the Yahwist in Genesis it has no such connection. It is a divine benefaction along side of the promises of numerous offspring and the land. Only in one place are the promises as a whole conditioned by "doing what is right and just" (18:19). So the promise of blessing represents a post-Dtr development.[48]

Although the original command may not have been regarded as a "call,"[49] there is little doubt that the addition of the promises does interpret the divine action in this way. This is so, first, because Abraham is immediately regarded as the recipient of special status among the nations and a special relationship with the deity of blessing and protection; and second, because the language used of Abraham is that drawn from royal ideology, the "call" is not that of a prophet[50] but the special election of the king. The same language in 2 Sam. 7:9, which speaks of God giving David a great name, occurs precisely in the context of David's calling and election. Furthermore, in Isa. 41:8–10 Abraham's call is also regarded as his election, and the prophet concludes the saying by invoking a royal salvation oracle, which he applies to Israel, Abraham's offspring.[51] This same act of calling can be used of Second Isaiah in reference to Yahweh's election of Cyrus as his anointed: "that you may know that it is I, Yahweh, the God of Israel, who have called you by your name" (Isa. 45:3, see also 45:4). It will be clear in the following discussion that the Yahwist has democratized the royal ideology by applying it to the forefather of the people, just as we find it in Second Isaiah.[52]

The call of Abraham is put by the Yahwist in the context of a migration from Mesopotamia in 11:28–31. As we have seen above, with this combined genealogy and itinerary the Yahwist sets his own account in a much broader perspective. Thus into the journeys of Abraham he includes Lot, the forefather of Israel's neighbors, the Moabites and the Ammonites.[53] The addition of Lot creates a complication for the promise of land in 12:7, which completes the divine command in v. 1 in the earlier tradition. Thus the Yahwist cannot spell out this promise in detail until after Abraham's separation from Lot in chapter 13. The episode with Lot must be built into the earlier itinerary by including Bethel as another important altar site to which Abraham will return after his trip to Egypt, just as Jacob does before and after his trip to Mesopotamia (28:10ff.; 35:1–7). The Yahwist imitates the altar building of Gen. 12:7 in v. 8 but with the significant addition that Abraham "called on the name of Yahweh." This use of the altar as primarily a place of prayer is also reflected in the Dtr prayer of Solomon at the altar in 1 Kings 8:29ff.[54] The building of altars also signified the taking possession of the land. It is reflected in the conquest tradition in late Dtr texts or additions such as Josh. 8:30–34; Deut. 27:1–10; cf. 12:1ff.

The references to the Canaanites in 12:6 and to Canaanites and Perizzites in 13:7 as the original population of the land is a contribution of J. This feature of distinguishing the newcomers from the autochthonous peoples is typical of western antiquarian traditions.

The Abraham-Lot Story

The Abraham-Lot story is contained in Genesis 12*, 13, 18, and 19.[55] I will not repeat here the argument presented in an earlier work for the position that Genesis 13, 18, and 19 belong to the same literary source, the Yahwist.[56] Although some traditio-historical studies attempted to see a number of separate stories or versions within these chapters, the recent tendency, as reflected in the work of Blum,[57] not only brings them together again but argues that they compose the oldest level and nucleus of the Abraham tradition. His analysis, however, differs in certain important respects from mine and represents issues that are quite basic to the larger study. They have to do, first, with Genesis 18.

Blum argues that 18:1–15, 16* is a fine example of Hebrew narrative art that tells about the announcement and birth of Isaac and so constitutes a kind of "etiology of Israel."[58] He admits that the story in its present form is incomplete but does not wish to accept the fact that any part of Gen. 21:1–7 might belong originally to this account. Yet everything argues in favor of just this possibility. With Gunkel, Westermann, and myself,[59] he recognizes that the closest biblical parallel to this account is 2 Kings 4:8–17, which tells of how Elisha promised the Shunammite woman a son and, in spite of her doubts, she had the child exactly as predicted. I earlier argued that Gen. 21:2, 6–7 immediately followed the announcement in Gen. 18:14, just as we have the statement in 2 Kings 17.[60] In fact, their verbal correspondence is remarkably similar.

Gen. 18:14b; 21:2	*2 Kings 4:16a, 17*
למועד אשוב אליך כעת חיה	למועד הזה כעת חיה
ולשרה בן	אתי חבקת בן

ותהר האשה ותלד בן   ותהר ותלד שרה . . . בן
למועד הזה כעת חיה אשר דבר   מועד אשר דבר אתו אלהים
אליה אלישע

The fact that 21:6–7 continues the wordplay on the name Isaac to mean "laughter," as we have it in 18:12–14 (15), points in the same direction of a unified story about Isaac's birth.[61]

But if 18:10–14 was actually part of a story that told of the birth itself a year later, then this poses a serious problem for Blum's analysis because it means that 18:16ff. could not have been the original continuation of the story. Yet it is equally clear that the close verbal similarity between 18:1–8 and 19:1–8 and the way in which the events are carefully structured as part of a sequence means that they cannot be viewed as separate compositions. How is one to account for this? Because Blum ignores the necessary ending to the birth story, he can make the birth announcement merely part of the larger story of Sodom. But how could the "etiology of Israel" — the announcement of Isaac's birth — be treated only as an incidental detail loosely connected to a quite different kind of story? That seems to me very doubtful.

The alternative is to see the older birth story used as a point of departure for a quite different tale about Sodom by postponing the fulfillment of the promise to a later point in the larger account.[62] The clue to multiple layers in the text of 18:1–15 has always been in the fluctuation between singular and plural in reference to the divine visitors. Blum dismisses this by arguing on stylistic grounds that the divine announcement in 18:10ff. could only come from Yahweh himself. But the divine commands in chapter 19 come from both angelic figures, so this seems a rather weak argument. It may be that in the original account of the birth story only Yahweh himself appeared as a divine stranger who was entertained by the aged couple, as in the story of Samson's birth in Judges 13. The increase in the numbers of divine visitors has significance only as it relates to the story of the destruction of Sodom.

The story of Sodom does not belong to the earliest, but only to the subsequent, development of the Abraham tradition. Its focus is on Israel's neighbors and not on the origins of Israel itself. This greatly expanded secondary level I have identified with the Yahwist. This immediately places an altogether different perspective on the material in 18:16ff., which makes the connection of the earlier episode with the Sodom story explicit. Scholars have been reluctant to assign very much of this section to the earliest form of the Sodom tradition, and the recent study of Blum is no exception.[63] He attributes to it only 18:16, 20–22a, and possibly 33b, but his distinguishing these verses from the rest is not literary. Against this position it can be argued that the same terminology is used throughout the divine speech in 18:20–32 and by the angelic figures in 19:12–17. This consistency cannot be so easily ignored. Furthermore, it is difficult to imagine why the divine announcement of the destruction is made to Abraham if no response is expected. Why would an author double the divine visits merely to announce judgment twice? Such a treatment of the motif of heavenly visitation is quite exceptional and must have some additional purpose, as the present account suggests. Finally, the fact is that three men visit Abraham, but only two of them proceed to Sodom. That fits with all the other evidence that points to a careful composition, but it also means that Yahweh remains behind to conduct the dialogue with Abraham.

The purpose of the visitation is to make Abraham a party to the deliberations of the divine council.[64] The motif of the heavenly inspection tour often includes the element of prior deliberation; only here Abraham is given a special role in the divine council not unlike that of a prophetic figure who intercedes for his people to spare them from judgment.[65] This issue of whether the righteous could deflect the judgment of God from falling upon the wicked within a people or community was of paramount importance in the exilic period, as seen in Ezekiel and Second Isaiah.[66]

If one admits all of 18:20–32 as belonging to the Sodom story, there seems little reason to deny 18:17–19 as well. It is true that these verses include some formulas and clichés that seem easily to brand them as redactional and Deuteronomistic; but the passage in question also demonstrates narrative skill, and there is some point to their inclusion. The speech opens with a soliloquy that seeks to justify why the deity is revealing his plans to Abraham, who is otherwise not threatened or directly involved.[67] The reason is twofold, that Abraham and his offspring are to have a relationship to the other nations as a means of blessing and that the destruction of Sodom might be a means of persuasion toward obedience to Yahweh, a reflection of the fact that the memory of Sodom and Gomorrah was often invoked as a warning by the later prophets. The most obvious reason, that of the presence of Lot in Sodom, is not mentioned, and it is not explicitly referred to by Abraham in his subsequent appeal in 18:23ff. All the parts in the section 18:16–32 fit together, and there is no reason, on literary grounds, to exclude any of it from the author, the Yahwist.

The account of Lot's separation from Abraham in Genesis 13 has little point as a self-contained story. It belongs to the Sodom story and accounts for Lot's presence in the city away from Abraham his kinsman.[68] But this introduction to the larger story also cannot stand alone. Scholars who attempt to isolate the Lot tradition as an early layer of the Abraham story must concede that in Genesis 13 there is no suitable beginning. The statement in v. 5, "And Lot, who went with Abram, also had flocks . . . ," presupposes some prior information about Abraham's possessions and about their travels together. This is given in Gen. 12:1–9, 13:1–4, which cannot all be dismissed as redactional or part of other traditions separate from the Lot story.[69] As indicated above, the Lot story is an antiquarian composition in which the genealogy and itinerary from Haran to Canaan together with Abraham, their separation, and Lot's eventual settlement in the eastern plateau of Moab and Ammon is the necessary framework for the whole tradition. The legendary destruction of Sodom and Gomorrah is fitted in with some ingenuity. Only in the case of the received tradition of Gen. 12:10–20 in written form in which Lot plays no role was an adjustment needed to accommodate the story of the trip to Egypt. The place where the separation of the two patriarchs occurs would also seem to be important, but this is not given within 13:5–12. Bethel, mentioned only in 13:3–4, is entirely appropriate as the midpoint in the land from which Lot's choice is made. The story of Lot in chapter 13 cannot, in fact, be isolated from the larger narrative context of J any more than in the case of Genesis 18–19.

It is necessary now to consider the place of 13:14–17 in the story of Lot. Many commentators have regarded it as secondary, and the recent study of Blum is no exception.[70] Nevertheless, the unit is particularly appropriate in its present context. It makes the connection directly with the preceding events, "After Lot had separated from him" (v. 14, cf. v. 11b),[71] and it recognizes the appropriateness of the vantage point, vs. 14–15. Even when there is the apparent contradiction that what Abraham saw to the east would include the same region that Lot had just chosen, the end of the story makes it clear that such a tension in the promise was only temporary. The episode of the separation would have ended on a rather strange note if there had been no response to Abraham's magnanimity. The divine word seems to recognize this gesture of Abraham with the assurance of his own great destiny. Although the land gift is made to Abraham when he first arrives in Canaan (12:6), it is only after Lot separates from Abraham and Lot becomes a single people that the full scope of the promise of land and numerous progeny is spelled out and in which it is construed as future promise.

In the case of 13:14–17, there is no decisive argument for or against the position that regards it as a redactional addition to the text. What will be decisive is if there are other parts of the same literary stratum that do include the promises themes in a genuine fashion within the narrative action itself.

Gen. 22:1–19

In my earlier study of this chapter, I argued for the unity of this story, including the verses on the promises in vs. 15–18, which are usually regarded as a redactional addition. Since publication of that work, the position on this chapter has shifted considerably, most notably in the works of Westermann and Blum, and these call for some further discussion here.[72] Let me, first, summarize my own view of this account.

The story of the near-sacrifice of Isaac may rest upon a rather common and widespread motif in which a hero, often at the command of a deity, is forced to sacrifice his own son or daughter. In the case of the story of Agamemnon's sacrifice of Iphigenia, two versions were known, the one in which she was actually slain and the other in which she was rescued by the deity and an animal put in her place.[73] This story motif has been considerably modified by the narrator into a narrative that deals with the divine testing of the patriarch and the corresponding struggle of faith by the patriarch. These two complementary themes now dominate the whole structure of the narrative. Another theme has to do with the sacred place to which the deity directs the activity of the patriarch and in which the action takes place. Although it has the form of an etiology in v. 14 and has often misled scholars into viewing this as the goal and conclusion of the story, the resemblance is misleading and constitutes only a supporting role to the theme of the providence of God, which is the basis of Abraham's faith.

The recent treatments of Westermann and Blum[74] have also agreed with the view that the testing theme, and with it Abraham's obedience and trust, is primary, and there is no real etiology in v. 14.[75] The real point at issue here is whether vs. 15–18 are secondary or necessary to the theme of testing and obedience. Both Westermann and Blum argue that they are secondary and that the story is quite complete without them. Westermann rejects vs. 15–18 because they do not use the same narrative style as the rest of the story. He states: "There are only a few texts in Gen. 12–50 which are so easily recognizable as an addition."[76] Blum also follows him in this judgment[77] and adds to this further arguments that suggest that vs. 15–18 belong to a Dtr redaction.[78]

This argument of style would have some weight if it could be shown, as others have tried, that 22:1–14, 19 is an independent and self-contained story. But neither Westermann nor Blum wishes to pursue such an argument. The statement in 22:1a, "It happened after these things that God tested Abraham," not only links it with the larger context but also allows the narrator to intrude into the account and immediately provides us with the key to interpreting the events. But unlike the prologue to Job, the information here about testing is not part of the story itself. In telling the story about the divine testing of the ancestor, Abraham, the narrator allows the action to run its course according to the received form of the story up to the rescue and the animal substitution. Only in the manner of the rescue — the voice from heaven and the nonmiraculous replacing of the youth by the animal — is there a reference back to the particular shaping of the story by the narrator as a divine testing: "Now I know that you fear God since you have not withheld your son, your only one, from me" (v. 12). But the theological significance of the patriarchal testing is not exhausted by the story itself, as if the episode could have been told in this way without suggesting any further consequences. The author did not want to interrupt the drama of the story itself by a long divine speech, so he did the only other thing possible. He added his theological reflections by means of a second divine appearance. It is an addition to the story in that it breaks the narrative style and does not affect the action, but it is still by the same author who introduced and shaped the episode as a divine testing.

This theme of divine testing cannot be separated from the dominant treatment given to the theme of God's testing Israel in the Deuteronomic literature.[79] The test is one of obedience to God and his commands. DtrH indicates that the fathers of Israel in the wilderness and at the time of conquest and early settlement failed this test, with consequences for later generations.[80] But this author in Genesis 22 asserts that the forefather Abraham passed the test "with flying colors," and he now makes Abraham's obedience have important consequences for the way in which the promises will be extended to his offspring. Because of Abraham's obedience his offspring will be blessed. And to make this point even more strongly, the next two divine appearances, both to the first offspring Isaac, reiterate the theme that the blessings are extended to the next generation because of Abraham's obedience (26:5, 24).

The parallel with DtrH goes beyond just the notion of testing to include the consequence of one person's obedience for subsequent generations. In 1 Kings 11:13, 32–34, it is stated that part of the kingdom—Judah and Jerusalem—would always remain under the rule of a son of David "for the sake of David, my servant—who kept my commandments and my statutes" (v. 34). The obedience of David was the direct cause and guarantee of the dynastic linear succession of his household, and in the same way Abraham's obedience is regarded as guaranteeing the numerous offspring of Israel: "for the sake of Abraham, my servant" (26:24), "because Abraham obeyed my voice and kept my charge, my commandments, my statutes and my laws" (26:5; cf. 22:18). The language and ideas are so close that this theme of the testing and obedience of Abraham must be directly related to the whole Dtr complex of ideas. This is the case even if it is not explicitly stated that God tested David. The idea of the test is certainly implied in the case of Solomon with the divine warning in 1 Kings 9:1–9 and also in the case of Jeroboam in 1 Kings 11:37–39.[81] Thus the theme of testing, which is basic to Gen. 22:1–14, cannot be separated from the consequences in the divine blessing of vs. 15–18.[82]

Gen. 21:8–21

My conclusions regarding the place of the promises in Genesis 22 may be confirmed by an analysis of 21:8–21. This unit clearly presupposes a direct continuity with the birth story to which it is attached and also the earlier episode of the expulsion of Hagar, her return, and her subsequent giving birth to Ishmael. In this episode, the issue becomes which son will gain possession (*yrš*) of the land as the primary heir of Abraham. This contest of wills is resolved by a divine appearance to Abraham that confirms the desire of Sarah for her son through whom the chosen line of Abraham's posterity is to be named. But the assurance that Ishmael will also become a nation provides sufficient assurance for Abraham to let the child and his mother go. In the second scene, when the angel of God comes to rescue the child, this same promise of becoming a nation is restated (v. 18). This promise is confirmed in v. 20 by pointing to his ultimate destiny as a people of the desert. The subject matter of this whole unit is so completely centered on the two separate but parallel destinies of the offspring of Abraham that the promises theme cannot be regarded as secondary to the story.

The theme in 21:8–21 corresponds directly to that of Gen. 15:1–6 in that it has to do with Abraham's heir. Here it is no longer a matter of the lack of offspring but of a decision that must be made between the two sons. The model for this story is not that of the proliferation of offspring by the ancestor to become forefather to various peoples, but the royal model of the heir to the kingdom, as we saw in Genesis 15. As in a monarchy, only one can be the heir, and the struggle within Abraham's family resembles that of a royal harem with the principal wife asserting her claim over her rival. It is significant that the object of the verb *yrš* is not stated because the implied object, the land, is still just a matter of promise, so that one must render the imperfect in the durative sense, "be the heir."[83] That this royal model lies behind the structuring of the episode is confirmed by the divine speech "for in

Isaac will your descendants ("seed") be called." This cannot mean simply that future generations will speak of Abraham's offspring only through Isaac, as Lohfink suggests,[84] because the story clearly recognizes that all the Ishmaelites are the offspring of Abraham. The "calling" refers to Isaac's election, as it does in Isa. 41:8–9, and therefore to his special status as the heir of Abraham's calling in Gen. 12:1–3.

The text also combines the notion of expulsion (*grš*) with that of inheritance (*yrš*), just as it does in the J references to the conquest.[85] This is intended as an anticipation of the conquest theme with its expulsion of the nations and its possession of the land. It is noteworthy that the nations in Gen. 15:19 list three nomadic peoples similar to the Ishmaelites in addition to the traditional seven from the Dtr tradition.[86]

Now this episode in the life of Abraham and Isaac fits closely together with that of chapter 22 not only in the clear sequence of events but also in the way in which the two stories are told. This is particularly true in the case of the two scenes in which the angel of God/Yahweh calls from heaven to rescue the child from death (21:17; 22:11). After the divine speech in the first story, God opens Hagar's eyes so that she sees the well of water and is able to give her child something to drink (21:19). In the second story, Abraham lifts up his eyes and sees the ram and sacrifices it in place of Isaac. In both stories, Abraham also rises early to make preparations for a journey, either that of Hagar (21:14) or his own (22:3). These similarities point strongly to common authorship. But if in the case of the first story the narrator could include a reference to the divine promises within the episode itself, that makes it very likely that the references to the promises in the second story also belong to the same author even though they were placed in a second speech by the angel of God.[87]

Genesis 24

The basic unity of the chapter has been affirmed by recent studies, so there is no need to debate the issue of a diversity of sources. Only at the end of the account has the narrative been adjusted to fit with the present context. As Blum has pointed out,[88] the story seems to presuppose that Abraham has died during the course of the servant's mission, so Isaac is now the head of the household. It also suggests that Rebekah was placed in the tent of Isaac's mother, Sarah, before the actual marriage (v. 67).[89] This means that Sarah was still alive, and the story of Sarah's death and burial in chapter 23 as well as the subsequent marriage of Abraham to Keturah in 25:1ff. are secondary additions. The immediate sequel would be 25:11.

The story in Genesis 24 fits closely with the other two in the series about Isaac, but at the same time it looks back on the whole life of Abraham. The speeches of Abraham and of his servant recapitulate Abraham's call from his homeland and the divine promise of a new land, his great blessing by God, and the birth of Isaac in his old age to whom he has left everything as inheritance. The story itself is about the proper continuity of the line through the acquisition of wife and family. All of this relates directly to the concerns of the divine promises.[90] In addition to this there is the theme of the angel of God and his role in the story of providing divine guidance and providence.[91] It is true that in this case the angel never makes his appearance or is actually heard, but his guidance is merely observed in the circumstances that befall the servant. It is the "accidental" meeting of the right woman at the well that is viewed as the angel's intervention in the same way that Abraham saw the ram and that Hagar saw the well of water.

The story also stands in close connection with the genealogy of 22:20–24. That genealogy provides the information about the family of Abraham in Aram-Naharaim to which the servant is sent and about Rebekah's family in particular. The story reiterates this genealogical connection frequently in vs. 15, 24, and 47. It also furnishes the additional information about the relationship of Laban as brother to Rebekah and gives him a prominent place in anticipation of his further role in the Jacob story. In keeping with these genealogical notices is the itinerary notice of 24:62, which makes a connection with 25:11 and the larger context.

There is no need to seek in this story of chapter 24 a "simple family narrative" based upon some genealogical note that may go back to the "patriarchal period," as Westermann proposes.[92] The fact that the motif of encountering an eligible bride at a well occurs elsewhere in Gen. 29:1–14, and Ex. 2:15b–22 as a stock scene says nothing about the story's antiquity.[93] Nor is this just a family story built on a genealogical note but a narrative that is built upon the whole genealogical structure, developed by the narrator, of the interrelationship between the two peoples. The theme of divine guidance has in view not just the acquiring of a suitable wife for Isaac but the whole destiny of the peoples involved and relates to the theme that begins with Abraham's call and continues throughout the Yahwist's entire account. Although the Yahwist adopts a more discursive style with long speeches in this story, there is no reason to attribute it to a different source.

M. Rose has called attention to the messenger form that dominates the chapter in the doubling of the schema:[94]

A. Introduction to the situation	vs. 1f.	vs. 34–36
B. Commission	vs. 3f.	vs. 37f.
C. Objection	v. 5	v. 39
D. Strengthening of the commission/ assurance of divine assistance	vs. 6ff.	v. 40
E. Signs/confirmation	vs. 12–21	vs. 42–48

Rose finds the closest parallel to this schema in 2 Kings 18:19–35 in the speeches of the Rabshakeh before the walls of Jerusalem in which the form also occurs twice. It is found in the story of the negotiations between Saul and David concerning the latter's marriage to the king's daughters in 1 Sam. 18:17–27 as well as in extrabiblical examples.[95] What these parallels signify is that this messenger form is the *royal* commissioning of an ambassador or other important emissary, and the *Sitz im Leben* of the form is the court. In the literary use of the form in Genesis 24, Abraham's household is being treated as if he were a king. This is further strengthened by the title that the servant bears as the "senior servant of his house, who had charge of all his property" (v. 2)[96] and also by the entourage of ten camels laden with royal gifts. The servant has the full powers of negotiation even in the matter of the son's marriage.

Genesis 26

Genesis 26 represents the complete "collection" of the Isaac traditions. In the earlier stories in chapters 21, 22, and 24, he functions passively as the son of Abraham, and in the following story in chapter 27 (see also 25:19ff.) he serves as the father of Jacob and Esau. In my earlier treatment of this chapter, I argued that no older traditions lay behind the Yahwist narrator and that he simply constructed a life of Isaac based upon similar episodes in the life of Abraham.[97] The first episode of the threat to the patriarch's wife in vs. 1–11 is a rather tame version of the two stories in Gen. 12:10–20 and chapter 20, with elements drawn from each.[98] The tension between Isaac's *herdsmen* and those of Abimelech resembles the story of Abraham and Lot and their separation in chapter 13, whereas the controversy between Isaac's *servants* and those of Abimelech over wells reflects the story of the controversy over the well in 21:25–26, 28–31a. The fact that the earlier story mentions only one well in dispute does not constitute a major problem. Because the earlier story mentions seven lambs as witnesses of ownership, a later narrator may have interpreted the number as the number of wells in dispute with only the last one, Beersheba, "Well of Seven/Oath," mentioned specifically. The references to Abraham in 26:15 and 26:18 do not need to be regarded as secondary glosses any more than is the mention of Abraham in 26:1. The covenant between Isaac and Abimelech in vs. 26–31 is by the same hand that added the covenant between Abraham and Abimelech in 21:22–24, 27, 31b–32, as is apparent by the almost identical language of the two versions. The story of covenant making that reflects an addition to 21:22ff. belongs to the basic narrative of chapter 26. This whole life of Isaac is a rather pale reflection of the life of Abraham, and one can scarcely find in it any evidence of older traditions.

One argument used by Westermann for treating it in isolation from the rest of the larger context of patriarchal stories is that the story knows nothing of the birth and life of the twins Jacob and Esau.[99] But such a change misunderstands the narrator's purpose. What the author needs is a life of Isaac, and the stories he imitates from the life of Abraham make no reference to children either. Nor is it any objection that the two stories in 21:31 and 26:33 offer two different etiologies for Beersheba. The author allows for this by indicating that the former wells of Abraham had been filled in by the Philistines, so they were redug and presumably renamed by Isaac. We also know from Greek historical works that authors often recorded a number of etiologies for the same place.

Hellanicus lists four different etiologies for the Areopagus in Athens.[100]

In Genesis 26, the divine promises play a distinct role in the narrative itself, so that the narrator of the Isaac story and the author of the promises are one and the same. Not only is the divine command to dwell in Gerar part of Isaac's motivation, but the references to divine blessing and to the promise of divine accompaniment are taken up in vs. 12–16 in Isaac's prosperity and might and in Abimelech's desire for a covenant: "We see plainly that Yahweh is with you" (v. 28) and "you are now blessed of Yahweh" (v. 29). The divine appearance to Isaac at Beersheba provides the motivation for the construction of the altar (cf. Gen. 12:7) and the last well story.

The place of the promises within this chapter betrays some differences. It is generally held that 26:3b, 4–5 is a later expansion of the promises to Isaac for two primary reasons: (1) these verses depend so obviously upon those of 22:15–18, which are also judged to be a later addition (see above), and (2) the language of vs. 3b–5 is very reminiscent of Dtr phraseology, and this was totally incompatible with an early dating of J. Neither of these reasons is particularly cogent for the present study, because it is argued that 22:15–18 is not an expansion of the earlier story and all the promises are equally of late date.

The promises contained in 26:24 are dealt with in various ways. Gunkel, followed by Westermann, takes vs. 24–25a as a later addition on the rather weak grounds that the pitching of the tent should precede the building of an altar.[101] Skinner disputes any such interpolation, regards them as original, and points to the theme of altar building in the J source elsewhere.[102] Blum wants to separate v. 24 from v. 25a and make v. 24 a later addition together with vs. 3b–5,[103] although the divine appearance and altar building seem to go well together.[104] Blum notes the fact that v. 24 contains the *whrbyty 't zr'k* as in v. 4 and *b'bwr 'brhm 'bdy* parallel to v. 5. But what Blum fails to note is that v. 24 begins the promises series with *ky 'tk 'nki wbrktyk*, which is almost identical to *w'hyh 'mk w'brkk*, v. 3a, which is part of the original account according to his view! It seems to me that v. 24 is meant to be a shorter version of vs. 3–5 and argues for a unity of vs. 3–5 with v. 24 by the same hand. Note also that v. 24 is immediately followed by the covenant with

Abimelech in which Abimelech asserts: "We see plainly that Yahweh is with you. . . . You are now the blessed of Yahweh" (vs. 28, 29). The same *reference* to the abiding presence of God for protection and blessing is also found in 21:22 but with the additional *reference* to the posterity of the covenant partners and to the land (21:23). The author of these units on covenant is the author of the blessings.

In the case of Abraham's covenant with Abimelech in Gen. 21:22–32 and its mirror image in Isaac's covenant with the same king in 26:26–31, the scenes resemble that of peace treaties between potentates of two nations. In both cases, the treaties are negotiated after disputes between the two groups have been resolved. The image of the patriarch as king is not reflected in the earlier stories of Abraham's dealings with Pharaoh in Gen. 12:10–20 nor with Abimelech in chapter 20 (where he is specifically described as a prophet). Like Abraham in Genesis 24, Isaac is also described as rich, powerful, and the head of a great household (26:12–14, 16).

Conclusion

What we have seen throughout the Yahwist's treatment of Abraham and Isaac is the transformation of the patriarch from that of wandering nomadic forefather to royalty, even though he has neither throne nor kingdom. Royal ideology is reflected in the "call" in Gen. 12:1–3, in the promise of an heir and covenant of chapter 15, in the designation of Isaac as the chosen heir in 21:8ff., in Abraham's "merit" in 22:15–17, in the provisions for Isaac's marriage in chapter 24, and in Abraham's and Isaac's relations with Abimelech in 21:22ff. and 26:26ff. The consistent use of royal ideology for the patriarchs, especially Abraham, cannot be fortuitous nor assigned to different levels in the tradition.[105]

The interpretation of this royal ideology in the Abraham story in the past has been to view the stories as a legitimation of the monarchy under David and Solomon. But this is unlikely because there is no effort in the biblical tradition to make a linear connection between the patriarchs and David until very late. It seems preferable to view the purpose of this use of royal terminology and characteristics as a democratization of the royal ideology in the exilic period. The lateness of the texts also confirms this interpretation.

There is another possible reason for the application of royal attributes to the patriarch, and this has to do with the genre of historiography itself. It is a clearly attested fact that in the ancient Near East historiographic forms and historical texts of many kinds have to do primarily with kings and their deeds. To transform antiquarian traditions about ancestors into a history may well have influenced the use of such elements of royal ideology by the Yahwist.

NOTES

1. Van Seters, *Abraham.*
2. Except the references to Lot.
3. Westermann, *The Promises to the Fathers,* pp. 11–15, 132–137; idem, *Genesis 12–36,* pp. 232–249; 274–275.
4. See Van Seters, *Abraham,* pp. 192–196.
5. See my earlier discussion in *Abraham,* pp. 202–208. On its relationship to the Sodom and Gomorrah story, see below.
6. Westermann, *The Promises to the Fathers,* pp. 170–176.
7. See the discussion in Van Seters, *Abraham,* pp. 171–175.
8. See West, *Hesiodic Catalogue of Women,* p. 58.
9. Blum, *Die Komposition,* pp. 405–410.
10. Ibid., pp. 411–413.
11. Cf. Van Seters, *Abraham,* pp. 183–191.
12. See also Westermann, *Genesis 12–36,* pp. 161, 319, for support of my position.
13. J. Hoftijzer, *Die Verheissungen an die drei Erzväter,* 1956.
14. Although this claim was somewhat complicated by Westermann's introduction of the "promise of a son" theme and its role in Genesis 16 and 18:1–15, these stories belong to a wholly different level of the Abraham tradition and do not concern the treatment of the promises in J.
15. Emerton, "The Origin of the Promises to the Patriarchs." Emerton dates it to the seventh century!
16. Rendtorff, "Genesis 15"; Blum, *Die Komposition,* pp. 362–383. See also M. Anbar, "Genesis 15: A Conflation of Two Deuteronomic Narratives," *JBL* 101 (1982), 39–55; and H. H. Schmid, "Gerechtigkeit und Glaube: Genesis 15,1–6 und sein biblisch-theologischer Kontext," *EvT* 40 (1980), 396–420.
17. Van Seters, *Abraham,* pp. 249–249; see also recently Ha, *Genesis 15,* with his extensive discussion of the question of the chapter's unity.
18. It is possible that a "servant of the household" (*bn byt*) may reflect the story of chapter 16, although the status of Ishmael was more than is implied by this term. See Van Seters, *Abraham,* pp. 18–19.
19. See also Gen. 25:21ff.; 30:1ff.
20. Westermann, *The Promises to the Fathers,* pp. 165–186. See also R. S. Hendel, *The Epic of the Patriarch,* HSM 42 (1987), pp. 37–59. The effort at establishing parallels in these studies seems a little desperate. The fact is that there are no

extant royal birth stories in the Old Testament of the type suggested here. The birth of Solomon, 2 Sam. 12:24–25, hardly counts as such.

21.   Westermann's attempt to use the Ugaritic texts to confirm the antiquity of the theme of the promise of a son rather obscures its real significance. The *older*, nonroyal tradition centered on the ancestress is being reshaped by the royal ideology. This criticism also applies to Hendel.

22.   Schmid, *Der sogenannte Jahwist*, pp. 121f.; Van Seters, *Abraham*, p. 254; as first pointed out by O. Kaiser, "Traditionsgeschichtliche Untersuchung von Genesis 15," *ZAW* 70 (1958), 107–127.

23.   The curious reference to the steward, Eliezer of Damascus, as a possible heir is surely reminiscent of the fact that the vassal Aramean state of Hadadezer in David's day later came to dominate Israelite politics. The author may have intended such a foreshadowing.

24.   Rendtorff, "Genesis 15."

25.   See N. Lohfink, article *yrš* *TWAT* III, 953–985; and Römer, *Israels Väter*, pp. 36–39.

26.   See Perlitt, "Motive und Schichten." See pp. 228–230, 240–241 above.

27.   This corresponds to the ideal of royal imperial control but was never the actual bounds of the Davidic-Solomonic kingdom as many have suggested.

28.   See the discussion in Blum, *Die Komposition*, pp. 331ff. There is no need to regard the two itinerary notices of Shechem and Hebron as secondary to the earlier tradition of the patriarch. Blum takes the itinerary notices and references to altar building and tree planting in 12:6–8; 13:18; 21:33; 26:23–25 as all on the same diachronic level (p. 335). But those in the Jacob story (33:18, 20; 35:6–7) belong to an earlier level. This scheme is based entirely upon the priority he gives to the Jacob traditions over the Abraham traditions, which I do not find convincing.

29.   The latest treatment of this text in detail is Berge, *Die Zeit des Jahwisten*. He gives an extensive review of the literature on pp. 11–15.

30.   It is perhaps true that too much has been made of this connection in the past (see O. H. Steck, "Genesis 12,1–3"). More important is the continuous genealogy, as I have argued above.

31.   For recent discussion of the text with literature, see Westermann, *Genesis 12–36*, pp. 145–152; E. Ruprecht, "Vorgegebene Tradition und theologische Gestaltung in Genesis XII 1–3," *VT* 29 (1979), 171–188; Berge, *Die Zeit des Jahwisten*, pp. 11–76.

32.   The grammatical structure of this text has frequently been discussed. The divine promises, expressed in first person precative forms, depend upon the imperative in v. 1, so that they follow only as a consequence of this act of obedience. The only serious textual problem is whether to retain the imperative of *hyh* in v. 2b, as most commentators do, and construe it as consequence or result, "so that you will be a blessing." The parallels, e.g., Zech. 8:13, are not decisive, and I prefer to read *waw consecutive* perfect, which is closer to the structure of v. 3.

33.   Cf. Gen. 48:20.

34.   See also 2 Sam. 8:13; 1 Kings 1:47.

35.   Psalm 21:4, 7; Psalm 72 passim.

36.   See BHS notes.

37.   Contra Berge, *Die Zeit des Jahwisten,* pp. 259–271, esp. p. 271. Because Berge rejects any connection between the Jerusalem royal ideology and J, Berge leaves totally unexplained how J would have picked up his notions about general Near Eastern conceptions of kingship and why he would have been eager to apply them to the patriarchs.

38.   Westermann, *Genesis 12–36,* p. 150; E. Ruprecht, "Der traditionsgeschichtliche Hintergrund der Gestaltung in Genesis XII 1–3," *VT* 29 (1979), 460–461; Berge, *Die Zeit des Jahwisten,* pp. 55, 72f.

39.   Berge, *Die Zeit des Jahwisten,* pp. 55–76.

40.   Berge's rendering of *mšpht* is *vorpolitische Einheiten* (in ibid., p. 62). I do not know how to make any sense out of this term. How could one ever recognize such groups? The examples of "families" of the Canaanites listed in the Table of Nations, Gen. 10:15–18, are either well-known city-states or groups elsewhere identified as "nations." The term *'ădāmâ* is rendered by *palästinischen Kulturlandes* (ibid., p. 72). As a geographic region, this is an anachronism. When *'dmh* means "farmland," it does not have any specific geographic area in mind.

41.   Berge (ibid., pp. 57–59) discusses all of these texts and yet attempts to explain away the obvious.

42.   This text is not given its due in Berge (ibid., pp. 268f.) because he chooses to ignore the Greek as the superior text.

43.   Ruprecht has not found any Near Eastern parallels to Gen. 12:3b. He thus states: "But nowhere does it speak of a task of the king to bring blessing and prosperity to other peoples. The king is the dispenser of blessing only within, to his own people" ("Der traditionsgeschichtliche," *VT* 29:463).

44.   D. D. Luckenbill, *Ancient Records of Assyria and Babylonia,* II, paras. 784–785, pp. 297–298.

45.   Schmid, *Der sogenannte Jahwist,* pp. 133–136; Van Seters, *Abraham,* pp. 274–278; Blum, *Die Komposition,* pp. 349–359. Cf. Berge, in n. 29 above.

46.   Schmid, *Der sogenannte Jahwist,* pp. 136–138; see also Van Seters, *Abraham,* pp. 272–274.

47.   Above all, Deuteronomy 28; also 7:12ff.; 15:10, 18; 16:15.

48.   Cf. Berge, *Die Zeit des Jahwisten,* pp. 273–310. Even with his minimalist view of J, he cannot account for the form of future blessing in Gen. 12:2–3.

49.   Cf. Gen. 20:13.

50.   See Westermann, *Genesis 12–36,* p. 148. Westermann limits the notion of "calling" entirely to the prophetic call, but that is clearly not the case.

51.   Hosea uses the same language of "calling" to speak of Israel's election in the exodus: "Out of Egypt I called my son" (11:1).

52.   Contra Berge, *Die Zeit des Jahwisten,* pp. 259–270. See Van Seters, *Abraham,* pp. 274–277.

53.   More below.

54.   See the remarks in Schmid, *Der sogenannte Jahwist,* p. 147; and Blum, *Die Komposition,* pp. 334ff.

55.   We may leave aside Genesis 14 as a later addition.

56.   See Van Seters, *Abraham,* pp. 209–226.

274   THE PATRIARCHS

57.   Blum, *Die Komposition,* pp. 273–297.

58.   Ibid., pp. 273–280.

59.   Gunkel, *Genesis,* p. 197; Westermann, *The Promises to the Fathers,* pp. 134–137; Van Seters, *Abraham,* pp. 204–206.

60.   Blum points to the correspondence between Genesis 17 and 21:1–3, but this only demonstrates the fact that the P writer relied heavily upon the previous account for his terminology, as we have so often seen to be the case.

61.   Westermann (*Genesis 12–36,* p. 331; and *Promises to the Fathers,* p. 137) acknowledges the connection between Gen. 21:1–7 and chapter 18 but confuses the issue badly by misunderstanding the nature of the Priestly redaction in 21:1–7.

62.   Westermann (*Genesis 12–36,* p. 275) seems to acknowledge that "the scene in vv. 1b–8 does not necessarily belong to the older form. It is likely that in the course of transmission the narrative of the promise (and birth) of a child as deliverance from distress was joined with a narrative variant." But this vague concession does not address the literary question of how the two sources were combined.

63.   Blum, *Die Komposition,* pp. 282–283, 400–405; see also Westermann, *Genesis 12–36,* pp. 285–286.

64.   Van Seters, *Abraham,* pp. 212–215.

65.   On the role of prophet as intercessor, see S. Balentine, "The Prophet as Intercessor: A Reassessment," *JBL* 103 (1984), 161–173.

66.   See esp. Ezek. 14:12–23; Isaiah 53; and the discussion of Blum, *Die Komposition,* pp. 403–405. See also von Rad, *Genesis,* pp. 211–215.

67.   The use of divine soliloquy is rather rare, but it also occurs in the Yahwist's story of the flood in Gen. 6:5–7 as an introduction to judgment. See it also in the creation story, Gen. 2:18, in the fall story, 3:22, and in the Tower of Babel story, 11:6–7.

68.   See also Blum, *Die Komposition,* p. 284.

69.   Ibid., p. 286.

70.   Ibid., pp. 290–291. See also Westermann, *Genesis 12–36,* pp. 178–179.

71.   The verb *prd,* "to separate," reflects the theme of the distribution of humankind, as in the Table of Nations, Gen. 10:5, 32. Although both texts are ascribed to P, 10:5 may well rest upon a J original (see above, pp. 174–175). See also Gen. 25:23.

72.   Westermann, *Genesis 12–36,* pp. 354–356; Blum, *Die Komposition,* pp. 320–331. Note that both Westermann and Blum accept my criticisms of the earlier works of R. Kilian, *Isaaks Opferung. Zur Überlieferungsgeschichte von Gen 22,* SBS 44, 1970; and H. G. Reventlow, *Opfere deinen Sohn. Eine Auslegung von Genesis 22,* BS 53, 1968. See Van Seters, *Abraham,* pp. 228–229; and more recently T. Veijola, "Das Opfer des Abraham—Paradigma des Glaubens aus dem nachexilischen Zeitalter," *ZTK* 85 (1988), 129–164, esp. 149ff.

73.   See Van Seters, *Abraham,* p. 233, for reference. Note also that the latter version occurs in the *Catalogue* (see West, *Hesiodic Catalogue of Women,* p. 134).

74.   See n. 72 above.

75.   Westermann believes that v. 14b is secondary and possibly corrupt.

76.   Westermann, *Genesis 12–36,* p. 363.

77. Blum, *Die Komposition,* p. 320.

78. Ibid., pp. 363ff. See also Westermann, n. 72 above; and Veijola, "Das Opfer des Abraham," *ZTK* 85:159.

79. See Van Seters, *Abraham,* p. 239; also references in Blum, *Die Komposition,* p. 329; Westermann, *Genesis 12–36,* p. 356; and Veijola, "Das Opfer des Abraham," *ZTK* 85:150ff.

80. Deut. 8:2–16; Judg. 2:22; 3:1–4.

81. Although Westermann regards 22:1–14, 19 and 15–18 to be by two different authors, he still sees the same kind of Deuteronomic influence in both parts of the narrative and dates both to the same time period. To me this division is quite unnecessary.

82. Veijola ("Das Opfer des Abraham") interprets the story, without vs. 15–18, as a late postexilic story about the testing of a righteous man in the spirit of the Chronicler's piety. But what has Abraham gained for all his anguish? Nothing, since his son is simply returned to him. That hardly seems like an adequate expression of this kind of piety.

83. On the development of the durative sense in the exilic period, see N. Lohfink, "Die Bedeutungen von hebr. *jrš qal* und *hif,*" *BZ* 27 (1983), p. 24.

84. Ibid., p. 16.

85. See Van Seters, *Abraham,* p. 201; contra Lohfink, "Die Bedeutungen," *BZ* 27:31. The use of *grš* in Ex. 34:11; Josh. 24:12, 18; Judg. 6:9 (cf. Lev. 18:24; 20:23 HC) does not point to an earlier, but rather a later, use than *yrš*.

86. See Van Seters, *Abraham,* p. 266.

87. Veijola ("Das Opfer des Abraham") does not take into consideration the extensive similarities between 21:8–21 and 22:1–19. Since the promise is basic to the rescue of Ishmael in the first story, it is also basic to the rescue of Isaac in the second.

88. Blum, *Die Komposition,* pp. 383ff.

89. So ibid., p. 384. The remark in v. 67b must then be understood to mean "Isaac was comforted after the death of his father." See also BHS.

90. The verbal similarity between 24:60b and 22:17b leads Blum to assign the chapter to a D-redactional level of the tradition later than the other Isaac stories. Because I do not regard 22:15–18 as an addition to the story in 22:14, 19, this notion of a D redaction is quite unnecessary.

91. See Van Seters, *Abraham,* pp. 247f.

92. Westermann, *Genesis 12–36,* p. 383.

93. Note also the motif of hospitality similar to Genesis 18–19.

94. Rose, *Deuteronomist und Jahwist,* pp. 132–142.

95. See also the example cited by S. B. Parker, "The Historical Composition of KRT and the Cult of El," *ZAW* 89 (1977), 161–175. But this example must be seen in the context of the others.

96. See the title of Joseph in Gen. 45:8, 26.

97. Van Seters, *Abraham,* pp. 183–192.

98. A recent defense of this position is offered by Berge, *Die Zeit des Jahwisten,* pp. 93–114.

99. Westermann, *Genesis 12-36*, pp. 423-424; following Gunkel, *Genesis*, pp. 299-300.

100. See Pearson, *Local Historians*, pp. 15-17.

101. Gunkel, *Genesis*, p. 303; Westermann, *Genesis 12-36*, pp. 427f.

102. Skinner, *Genesis*, p. 366.

103. Blum, *Die Komposition*, pp. 301-304; so also Berge, *Die Zeit des Jahwisten*, pp. 75-93, 116-118. For Berge, this creates the strange result that he has a promise text, Gen. 12:2-3, that is original to the Abraham stories and another in Gen. 28:13-15 that belongs to the Jacob tradition, but none in the Isaac story. That hardly seems likely in view of the reference to the God of Isaac in 28:13.

104. See Gen. 12:7-8; 13:18; 18:1; 46:1-4.

105. Blum attributes these texts to several different levels of the tradition's development. This is also the case in the recent study by Berge, *Die Zeit des Jahwisten*.

15
THE JACOB STORY

The Pre-Yahwist Tradition of Jacob

As with the Abraham tradition, the story of Jacob and his sons contains a number of independent narratives that can be identified as belonging to a stage of the tradition prior to their integration by the Yahwist into the larger history of the patriarchs. Some of these are obvious, as in the case of the story of the rape of Dinah in Genesis 34 and the tradition about Judah in Genesis 38. Others are not so clear and demand more detailed discussion. For the present, I will merely sketch in broad outline the pre-Yahwist tradition of Jacob and his sons, by which I mean the stage before it became part of the patriarchal history as a whole.

The story of the birth and rivalry of the eponymous ancestors of Jacob and Esau in Gen. 25:21–34 would appear to belong to the same genre of folktale as that of the births of Ishmael and Isaac in the Abraham tradition. The similarity even includes the fact that in both stories the ancestress is barren until the deity intervenes to make the woman fruitful. The unit in Gen. 25:21–34 is largely independent of the following story of Jacob, although the question of how it has been integrated into the larger whole and what its relationship is to the parallel text of chapter 27 will be explored below.

More difficult to assess is the story of Laban and Jacob in Gen. 29–31.[1] There is some evidence of an older level of the story in the location "the land of the people of the east" (29:1) compared with the later placing of Laban's home in Haran. This same tension in geography is also evident in the account of the boundary markers between Laban, the Aramean, and Jacob (31:44–54).[2] But attempts to separate the older story from the later one are very difficult and tentative at best. The story has certainly been modified at a number of points to fit with the larger Jacob story.[3]

Embedded within the Laban-Jacob story is the genealogy of the sons of Jacob, Gen. 29:31–30:34, which in content and narrative character seems so entirely foreign to its larger context. This suggests a quite independent origin. To this also belongs the account of Benjamin's birth in 35:16b–18.

The story of the rape of Dinah in Genesis 34 is connected at its beginning with the genealogy. It deals with relations between the original population of the land, the eponymous ancestor Shechem and his countrymen, and the newcomers, the sons of Jacob. Whether or not it was originally a story of conquest and settlement of the region by the Israelites, so typical of the stories found in antiquarian folklore, cannot be decided for certain from the present form of the story. With its integration into the larger Jacob story, the episode leads instead to a migration from Shechem to Bethel (34:30–35:5).[4]

The problems of Genesis 34 call for some additional comment here. Scholars have long observed a certain unevenness in the text and have attempted various solutions. A recent proposal by B. Edele suggests that the text is a unified story by the Yahwist critical of the actions of Simeon and Levi to which a later author/ editor has added some remarks to mitigate the criticism and justify the slaughter of the inhabitants of Shechem.[5] These additions can be identified in vv. 5, 13b, 27–29, and 31, to which I would also add v. 7b. The activity of plundering and the description of the booty corresponds so closely to that of Num. 31:9–11, 32–41 (P) that the additions may be attributed to P. This means that Gen. 34:30 was followed directly by 35:1–5 as the continuation of Jacob's travels.

The story of Judah in Genesis 38 also reflects a separate tradition that may have some loose connection with Genesis 34. It suggests that whereas the other brothers settled in the north (Shechem), Judah migrated south and established himself in his final patrimony. On the other hand, it fits badly with the idea that Jacob had already migrated with his family into the southern region, as suggested in the itinerary of 35:19. The story portrays relations between Judah, the newcomer, and the local indigenous population with whom he intermarries, in contrast to the situation in chapter 34. The story goes on to deal with the subsequent descendants of Judah, the clans of the southern region.

There are also a few short units dealing with etiologies of cult sites and place names: 28:10–22; 32:2–3, and 32:22–32. These have all been integrated into the larger whole, but not without some modification, especially in the case of 28:10–22. To these story units we will return below for more detailed analysis.

It is not too difficult to see in these pre-Yahwist stories a collection of themes and interests having to do with the genealogical origins of peoples, tribes, and clans, interspersed with anecdotes and short stories about relations between the ancestors and their neighbors and rivals or the original population, the establishment of territorial claims and settlement, the etiology of ethnic characteristics and ways of life, and so forth. All of these are typical of the antiquarian folk-tradition. In form and content and in style of presentation, they are quite similar to the same pre-Yahwistic material in the Abraham story discussed above.

An exception to this type of pre-Yahwistic folk-tradition is the Joseph novella. There is good reason to believe that the story in Genesis 37, 39–50 developed as an independent composition through more than one stage, quite separate from the rest of the Jacob story.[6] Unlike the other pre-Yahwist stories, it is not concerned with tribal origins or other features of antiquarian interest. Joseph is the subject of a "wisdom" novella about the working out of divine providence in the affairs of men. The fact that the Yahwist had both the Joseph story and the story of Judah (Genesis 38) as sources for his own work led to the awkward juxtaposition of the one story as a digression within the other.

The additions by which the Yahwist integrated the Joseph story into his history of the patriarchs were not very extensive and will be discussed below. For the Yahwist, the Joseph story is an indispensable link in the history because it connects the patriarchs with the story of the exodus and accounts for the Israelite presence in Egypt. But it was not composed as a novella for this purpose and could have envisaged only a temporary stay by the sons of Jacob during the course of the famine, just as we have it in the case of Abraham in Gen. 12:10–20.

In none of the pre-Yahwistic traditions about Jacob does the theme of the divine promises of land and progeny play a role. On the contrary, the family of Jacob begins to proliferate immediately and to become firmly established in the land. At the pre-Yahwist level, the whole patriarchal tradition could constitute a migration/settlement tradition with accompanying genealogies, quite independent from the exodus tradition. This confirms the observations made above[7] that the tradition about the eponymous ancestors was originally quite independent from the land-promise tradition as reflected in Deuteronomy.

Birthright and Blessing

The Jacob story begins in Gen. 25:19–34 with the account of his birth, alongside that of his brother and rival, Esau, and their growth to early manhood. This unit raises a whole set of issues that become important for the larger analysis of the Jacob story, for the nature of the Yahwist's work in Genesis as a whole, and for literary criticism of the Pentateuch. At the very outset, one is faced with the curious problem of Genesis 26—a life of Isaac—interrupting what would appear to be the more obvious sequel to chapter 25 in chapter 27. Leaving aside this problem for the moment, there remains the more pressing question of the relationship of the two narrative units 25:19–34 and chapter 27 to each other. Can they be regarded as independent pieces and at least in some respects doublets? Do they belong to different sources, or are they different traditions brought together by one source or author, the Yahwist? What, in turn, is the relationship of both texts to the larger story of Jacob and to the structures and themes of the patriarchal stories as a whole?

These questions have been addressed in the past by the documentary hypothesis, but this approach cannot take us very far, especially when the presence of E in either piece is strongly disputed and when parts of both units have long been attributed to the Yahwist. The focus, instead, has been on tradition-history to elucidate the materials behind the present text together with a composition history of their present form and combination, as reflected in the recent works of Westermann, Blum, and Otto.[8]

Let us begin our analysis of 25:19–34 with some observations on the usual source division of this unit. Verses 19–20 and 26b are easily identified as belonging to P with its *tôlĕdōt* formula and chronology, as in vs. 12–18. The dependence of these verses on the older material in vs. 21ff. is so obvious that Westermann prefers to speak of R (= redactor) and to credit him with the composition of the whole unit,[9] but that is hardly necessary and would make the relationship between 25:19–34 and chapter 27 very difficult to explain, as we will see below. If P is dependent upon and an addition to J, then there is no problem of accounting for these verses here.

Once vs. 19–20 have been reckoned as later additions, then v. 21 is a problem because it does not contain an appropriate beginning. However, it was immediately preceded by 25:11: "After the death of Abraham God blessed Isaac his son. And Isaac dwelt at Beerlahairoi. . . . And Isaac prayed to Yahweh for his wife." In spite of the use of Elohim for the deity in v. 11, it belongs to the same author as v. 21. This makes a smooth transition, coming as it does soon after the story of Rebekah's marriage to Isaac in chapter 24. For the rest, the text of vs. 21–34, with the exception of v. 26b (P) and v. 28[10] offers a unified text in the style of etiological anecdotes that resist divisions into smaller units. In spite of this, Westermann divides the text form-critically into vs. 19–28 and vs. 29–34.[11] The former, without vs. 22–23, he compares with 11:27–32 as an introduction to the Jacob story corresponding to the introduction to the Abraham story. But once the P verses are removed, the only similarity is in the barrenness of both Sarah and Rebekah. They have little else in common.

Close parallels in story form in the patriarchal stories are (1) the story of Isaac's birth in 18:1, 10–14; 21:2–7, (2) the story of Lot's daughters and the origin of the Moabites and the Ammonites, (3) the series of etiological anecdotes accounting for the birth of the sons of Jacob, and (4) the birth of the sons of Judah, Perez, and Zerah in Gen. 38:27–30. Furthermore, in the Greek tradition, as reflected in the *Hesiodic Catalogue of Women,* there is a similar etiological anecdote in which the twin sons of Phokos, Krisos, and Panopeus (corresponding to the place-names Krisa and Panopeus in Phocis) struggle with each other in the womb of their mother as a portent of their later rivalry.[12] What we have in 25:21–34 is a very common and widespread folk-tradition at the pre-Yahwistic level of composition.

This portrayal of the origins of two neighboring peoples is

not restricted to the divine oracle of vs. 22–23, as Westermann suggests, and which he wishes to regard as secondary. Not only does the above Greek example speak against this, but there are clear allusions in the rest of the unit as well.[13] The description of Esau as "red," *'admônî,* and "hairy," *śē'ār,* is surely meant to reflect the place-names Edom and Seir. This is also true of the second part, 25:29–34, which in v. 30 seeks to derive the name Edom from Esau's great desire for Jacob's lentil soup, *hā'ādōm.*[14] It is true, as Westermann points out, that this part of the story has some resemblance to that of Cain and Abel, but in neither case are we dealing with origin of civilization myths. It is more likely that some comparison is suggested here between Edomites and Israelites and their respective ways of life.

When we come to the question of the relationship of 25:21–34 to chapter 27 and to the story of Jacob as a whole, there is a seeming paradox. On the one hand it is recognized that the characters of Jacob and Esau, especially the latter, are quite different in the two stories, so that 25:27–34 and chapter 27 hardly seem to be from the same hand. Yet there are, on the other hand, a lot of cross-references between the two stories that must be accounted for. This has led von Rad to suggest that 25:21–28 has been put together from various traditional materials as an introduction to the rest of the Jacob story.[15]

This way of stating the problem of the relationship between the two units, however, is somewhat misleading. Only v. 28, which states Isaac's preference for Esau and Rebekah's for Jacob, anticipates the story in chapter 27 so clearly that it must be by the same hand. But v. 28 also has no role in the present context. Once this verse is identified as an addition, then the rest of the material stands entirely on its own and does not lead to anything else in the Jacob story. It must be viewed as a set of etiological anecdotes in the antiquarian tradition that sought to account for the origins, interrelationships, and characteristics of the two peoples, the Edomites and the Israelites, from the perspective of the latter. Although Israel clearly regarded Edom as the older nation, it also viewed its own land as superior territory, and the sale of the birthright was an explanation by way of folklore to account fully for this.[16]

When the Yahwist took up this tradition, he made the

connection with his Abraham story and his larger themes in the introductory verse, 25:11. The content of the divine blessing in this verse is not made explicit but is meant to anticipate, perhaps, the blessing in chapter 26. Within the unit of 25:21–34, however, the usual themes of the Yahwist do not intrude even when one might have expected them, as in the case of Rebekah's barrenness. Instead, the story focuses entirely on Rebekah's plight and not on that of the divine promise, such as we have it in chapter 15. This suggests that the Yahwist did very little to reshape this particular unit of tradition as he received it.[17]

The compositional history of Genesis 27 is, I believe, altogether different. After some efforts in the earlier period of research to divide the chapter into the two sources, J and E, this has been largely abandoned.[18] Most now see the story as a unity with the possible exception of a few verses and the ending in vs. 41–45. But the argument for the exclusion of the ending based on the conviction that the rest of the story was originally independent is very weak and not supported by the evidence.[19]

1. The argument used by Westermann, that the form of the story is a family saga and therefore vs. 29 and 40 must be excluded, does not carry any weight because this genre is nowhere appropriate to the stories of Genesis.

2. The transition in v. 41 with Esau's reaction to his father's words and the subsequent preparations for Jacob's flight is entirely suitable to the whole and shows no marks of secondary expansion.

3. The most telling argument against viewing chapter 27 as an independent story lies in the number of cross-references to the earlier unit in 25:21–34.[20] The clear reference back to the earlier story in 27:36 ("Esau said, 'Is he not rightly named Jacob? For he has supplanted me these two times. He took away my birthright; and behold, now he has taken away my blessing'") cannot be viewed as an addition but is integral to the account. The conclusion is clear. The account in chapter 27 is subsequent to, and dependent upon, 25:21–34.[21]

The relationship of the two stories, however, must be pursued further. All the essential features in chapter 27 are derived from details in the earlier unit and creatively shaped into a new and parallel episode.[22] The element of rivalry between the two brothers is dependent upon the remarks about the way the two fetuses struggled in the womb and about Jacob's getting the better of Esau in the matter of the birthright. This rivalry in chapter 25 is meant to be primarily a portent of the future of the nations. But in chapter 27 the parents are also included, so that it is portrayed as part of their life in the family. In chapter 25, Esau is quite blasé and disinterested in his birthright. But in chapter 27, Jacob's actions are interpreted as acts of deception, and the matter of the blessing is then construed as a parallel event on this motive. Jacob's name is even reinterpreted to mean "supplanter" (27:36) to describe his character instead of the play on "heel" in the earlier story (25:26). The occupations of the two sons as hunter and tent dweller representing two separate peoples and their way of life (25:27) is construed in chapter 27 as merely the difference between the nature or disposition of two children still within the one family, the one a manly adventurer and the other a soft stay-at-home. The treatment of the etiological detail that Esau at birth was like a "hairy mantel" (25:25) receives special treatment in chapter 27, where Jacob is actually made to wear parts of hairy clothing so that he will physically resemble his brother and fool his blind father. The figurative description has been construed in a quite literal way.

Many exegetes have commented on the interesting correspondence between the *běkōrâ*, "birthright," and the *běrākâ*, "blessing," which certainly seems to reflect a play on the assonance between the two. But a number of scholars, most recently Westermann, continue to draw quite wrong conclusions about this fact.[23] The two are *not* the same; a blessing cannot confer on a son any legal claim to inheritance or any other right over the preferential claim of the firstborn son. The story in chapter 27 recognizes that Jacob has already obtained by other means Esau's firstborn share (25:29–34; 27:36).

In contrast to the legal right of the firstborn, the blessing can deal only with such matters as future prosperity, fertility, and prowess over one's foes. Isaac meant to confer all of these on Esau because he was his favorite, not because he was the firstborn. The blessing could be thought of as divided in various "portions" of unequal force or potency, as in the case of Jacob's blessing of his sons and grandsons (Genesis 48 and 49). But in this story, Isaac had intended to spend it all on Esau. Instead, by deception he gives it all to Jacob. What Esau then ends up with is a sort of curse—the lack of blessing—with only the modicum of some mitigation in 27:40.[24]

To suppose, as Westermann does, that this particular blessing actually resembles a social ritual of the primitive patriarchal period is most unlikely. One can hardly imagine the institutionalizing of deathbed scenes. Blessings may be given in many different situations but especially at partings.[25] Thus Rebekah is blessed by her family (24:60) when she departs from her mother's home for marriage and life in a new land. Isaac, in P, blesses Jacob when he departs for Paddan-Aram (28:1–4). The deathbed is, of course, the final parting. It also serves as a most obvious *literary* setting for blessing or other kinds of speech making. It can hardly be used to define the limits or nature of chapter 27 as an independent, primitive tradition, as Westermann does.

The content of the blessings (27:29, 40) also corresponds to the content of the oracle in 25:23 in that in both cases they relate to the future nations of the two ancestors. This is inconvenient for Westermann's view, so he eliminates all these references as additions. But as we saw in the case of 25:19–34, this is hardly possible, and I would argue that chapter 27 merely takes this theme over from chapter 25. That a blessing could be construed as the equivalent of an oracle about the future destiny of a people may also be seen in the Balaam oracles (Numbers 23–24).

What is also noteworthy is that the cross-references and parallels between chapters 25 and 27 are not just limited to the birthright episode in 25:27–34, as one might expect if it were a case of independent story variants. Elements in chapter 27 relate also to the quite different episodic unit in 25:21–26a, so the whole of 25:21–34 must have been known to the author of chapter 27. Consequently, Genesis 27 is not an independent story unit because its very composition is based upon the earlier materials of 25:21–34.

Furthermore, unlike chapter 25, chapter 27 stands in a very close relationship to the rest of the Jacob story and constitutes its introduction.[26] It provides the reason for Jacob's flight and his long stay with Laban in Mesopotamia. And it also sets the stage for his later reconciliation to Esau and return to the land of Canaan. At the same time, the reference to Rebekah's family in Haran recalls the earlier genealogical connections and the story of Rebekah's marriage in chapter 24, which seems to be clearly presupposed. We will consider this chapter's place in the larger form of the Jacob story below.

The subject of Genesis 27 is the patriarchal blessing, just as the birthright is the central focus in 25:27–34. Now it is unreasonable to suppose that the account would have said nothing about the content of the blessing, and it is hard to imagine any content more appropriate to the story of ancestors than what we have in the poetry. For if the story were merely about one son who was a hunter and the other a shepherd, then any blessing strictly appropriate to the life of the one would be useless to the other. What is always in view is their larger destinies, the national and territorial states that they ultimately represent. In 25:27–34, Esau cares nothing for the future, the birthright, only for his present state, whereas in chapter 27 Esau cares passionately for the future, the blessing, and for what Jacob has done to deprive him of it.

The blessings of chapter 27, as expressions of national destinies, fit with those of the rest of the Yahwist's work.[27] This deserves a somewhat closer form-critical examination. The opening assertion in v. 27b, "See, the smell of my son is as the smell of the field which Yahweh has blessed!" although not part of the blessing itself, would seem to be a further confirmation of earlier statements about Yahweh's blessing of Isaac in 25:11 and 26:12. The actual blessing in vs. 28–29 consists of the following components:

1. The blessing for prosperity and fertility of the land;
2. Superiority over other neighboring states;
3. A curse for those who curse Israel and a blessing for those who bless her.

Let us now compare the form of this blessing with other examples of blessings in J. In the brief blessing of Rebekah in 24:60, two of these components are present: the blessing of fertility in producing numerous offspring and superiority over one's enemies. Likewise in the blessing of the sons of Jacob in Genesis 49, the two extended blessings of Judah and Joseph both contain these two elements. In the blessing of Judah, vs. 8–12, the order of items is changed with the emphasis first on Judah's military prowess and superiority over his brother-tribes. This is expressed in very similar language to Isaac's blessing: "Your father's sons shall bow down before you" (v. 8), "May your mother's sons bow down to you" (27:29).[28] The blessing concludes with language reflecting the fertility of the land. In the blessing of Joseph, vs. 22–26, the two themes of prosperity/fertility and political/military prowess are somewhat mixed; but in the version in Deut. 33:13–17 the order is clear, with the emphasis on the fertility of the land, then political superiority ("prince among his brothers"), followed by his military prowess. But the most striking parallel to Gen. 27:28–29 is the blessing in the Balaam oracle of Num. 24:5–9 in which all the components are present in the same order: (1) prosperity and fertility of the land, vs. 5–7a, (2) political and military superiority, vs. 7b–9, (3) the blessing and curse formula (v. 9b).[29]

Ever since M. Noth attempted to use the tribal blessings of Genesis 49 and Deuteronomy 33 as evidence for an early tribal league and the premonarchic history of Israel, there has been a tendency to characterize the tribal sayings as a distinct form of primitive tradition.[30] To the extent that the sayings reflect some royal ideology or interest, this is usually regarded as secondary. Although questions recently raised about Noth's whole sociological reconstruction of a tribal league[31] call for a reappraisal of these traditions used to support it, that is not the concern here. The two blessings of Judah and Joseph cannot be taken as typical of the genre of tribal sayings; they are sayings composed to reflect the monarchies of Israel and Judah.

Another form of blessing that comes into consideration here is the blessing for the king, as in Psalm 72, which contains all the basic components of the patriarchal form outlined above. It emphasizes a wish for the prosperity and fertility of the realm (vs. 3, 6–7, 15–16), superiority over other nations and his enemies (vs. 8–11),[32] and the element of expressing blessings on the king by men and nations (vs. 15, 17). In addition, there are some other elements that are more peculiar to the role of the king.[33] It would appear that the various components of these blessings are original to the royal ideology and that tribal blessings of Judah and Joseph, which are made up of such components, borrow directly from royal prototypes. It is doubtful that the tribal blessings of Judah and Joseph and such forms as in Gen. 27:28–29 have any other origin than the *literary* imitation of royal blessings.[34]

This conclusion supports the view, expressed above, that the blessing of Abraham in Gen. 12:2–3 is also modeled on royal ideology with a strong similarity to Psalm 72. The fact that the same blessing and curse formula occurs in Gen. 12:3a and 27:29b is not accidental and points to common authorship.

It remains to address one final issue in this context and that is the placing of chapter 26 in the Jacob story. It is easy enough to invoke a redactor for this purpose, but that hardly solves the problem. As I have argued above,[35] this chapter has all the marks of the Yahwist's work in creating a "life of Isaac." The question is, Why did J not try to place the unit early in Isaac's life before the birth of the children? The answer must be that the material in 25:21–34 came to J as a block of tradition that he wished to keep close to chapter 24 and not to interrupt with his own material in chapter 26. Furthermore, chapter 26 also gave some space between the stories of 25:21–34 and J's own imitation of them in chapter 27.[36]

In my book on Abraham, I argued that the Yahwist took preexisting stories, such as the wife/sister motif or the flight of Hagar, and developed his own parallel episodes of these stories. The same appears to be the case here in the Jacob story. It demonstrates how J developed and expanded the Pentateuchal tradition and gave to it his own perspective and thematic concerns.

Jacob at Bethel: Gen. 28:10–22

The revelation to Jacob at Bethel calls for rather close analysis, so a translation of the text might be helpful to guide the subsequent argument.

10. Jacob set out from Beersheba and traveled toward Haran.
11. He came upon a certain place and spent the night there because the sun had already set. He took one of the stones of the place, set it as a headrest, and lay down to sleep in that place.
12. He dreamed that there was a staircase set up on earth with its top reaching the heavens and that there were angels of God going up and down on it.
13. Yahweh was standing beside him and said, "I am Yahweh, the God of Abraham, your forefather, and the God of Isaac. The ground upon which you are lying I will give to you and to your descendants.
14. Your descendants will be like the dust of the earth and will expand to the west and to the east, to the north and to the south; by you and by your descendants will all the families of the earth bless themselves.
15. I will be with you to protect you wherever you go and restore you to this land. For I will not abandon you until I have done what I have promised you."

16. Then Jacob awoke from sleep and said, "Surely Yahweh is in this place and I was not aware of it."
17. He was afraid, saying, "What an awesome place is this. This is none other than the house of God and the gateway to heaven."
18. Jacob rose early in the morning and took the stone that he had used for a headrest, set it up as a sacred pillar, and poured oil on top of it.
19. He named the place Bethel, but formerly the name of the town was Luz.
20. Jacob made a vow, saying, "If God will be with me and protect me on my journey and give me food to eat and clothes to wear,
21. so that I return safely to my father's house, then Yahweh will be my God.
22. This stone that I have set up as a sacred marker will be the house of God, and I will tithe a tenth of all that you give to me."

This text is a parade example among biblical scholars for the division of sources into J and E and for the identification of a self-contained unit of tradition within the larger whole. I will not take the time here to review the extensive debate on the analysis of this text but will focus primarily upon the recent detailed studies of de Pury, Berge, and Blum.[37] De Pury follows the classical approach of trying to find, by the use of the divine names Yahweh and Elohim, a division into two independent variants.[38] This yields the result: J = vs. 10, 13–16, 19a; E = vs. 10–12, 17–18, 20–22a (22b?), with v. 19b as redactional. But this division becomes rather difficult to make for the following reasons:

1. Both sources must share the introduction in v. 10 and perhaps also the statement in v. 16a, "And Jacob awoke from his sleep . . ."

2. The divine speech in vs. 13–15 (J) seems to go very closely with the vow in vs. 20–22 (E), with the latter even making reference to Yahweh (v. 21), which would demand a change in the name by a redactor.

3. It is hard to see how vs. 17–18 can be separated from v. 19a as its logical conclusion. But this would leave J without any reference to the cult etiology. It is only because de Pury insists that vs. 20ff. must go with v. 18 that v. 19 becomes an interruption.

4. On this division, J is clearly fragmentary because something of the information of v. 11 would need to be supplied to make sense.

5. What also makes de Pury's source analysis suspect is his form-critical discussion elsewhere in his study that must select elements from both J and E to reconstitute the form of the original *Vorlage*. It seems more reasonable to me to use form-criticism as

a basis to identify the literary unity in the first instance.[39] To the form-critical question we will return below.

A recent modification of de Pury's division is that of Berge.[40] He omits v. 19a from J but adds v. 11aα and argues that vs. 10, 11aα, 13–16 is a self-contained narrative. Whether such a story has an adequate ending may be disputed. But what is new about this proposal is the effort to separate v. 11aα from what follows to fill the obvious gap in J between v. 10 and v. 13. Berge's argument for doing so is that his study of the usage of the verb *lûn*, "to spend the night," suggests to him that the series of actions that follow it in v. 11 ("he took one of the stones . . . he set it as a headrest and he lay down in that place") should more appropriately come before "to spend the night."[41] But none of his examples demonstrate that a verb like *škb*, "to lie down," could ever precede *lûn* and the example of Ruth 3:13, where the more general command: "Remain the night" (*lînî hallaylᵉlâ*) is followed by the more specific request: "Lie down until morning" (*šikbî 'ad-habbōqer*).[42] I can find no objection against the arrangement of the narrative in Gen. 28:11. What is rather common among the examples cited by Berge is the sequence: *lûn* ("to spend the night") . . . *škm* ("to rise early"). Thus one would expect v. 18 to belong to the same source as v. 11, but in this case Berge places them in different sources. Furthermore, the reference to Jacob "waking," in v. 16, must depend upon a reference to his "dreaming," in v. 12. The verb *lûn* by itself does not include the notion of rest or sleep.[43] Thus Berge has not been able to demonstrate that v. 11 must be the conflation of two different sources.

In the interests of establishing an independent J text, Berge has considerable trouble clarifying the nature of the E source. Parts of it, such as the angelic vision of v. 12, are construed as remnants of an old tradition, but the vow in vs. 20–22 seems so clearly reflective of v. 15 that they are possible secondary sources. The literary analysis has become highly suspect.

Westermann deliberately abandoned a source division within the texts on the grounds that the unit seems to consist of an original story having to do with the revelation of a sacred place, in vs. 10–12, 16–19, and two later expansions, vs. 13–15, and 20–22.[44] Blum, in his study of Gen. 28:10–22, follows Westermann's lead and develops it at length.[45] Starting from the position that the unit contains an independent tradition about Jacob, he identifies all those elements that make reference to the wider context, such as vs. 10, 13–15, 20–22, and then examines the thick literary structure of the rest (vs. 11–13a, 16–19a). He identifies a series of closely knit elements, such as these:

a. temporal:

v. 11: "when the sun had set"	v. 18: "in the morning"

b. the actions of Jacob:

v. 11: "he spent the night"	v. 18: "he arose early"
"he lay down to sleep"	
"he placed the stone	
as a headrest"	v. 18: "he set it up as a sacred pillar"

c. the emphasis on "the place" throughout (vs. 11, 16, 17, 19)

d. the identification of the heavenly staircase (v. 12) as the "gateway to heaven" (v. 17).

All of these interweaving structures do not seem to be present in the divine speech of vs. 13–15 or the vow of vs. 20–22. Blum's conclusion is to identify vs. 11–13aα, 16–19a as an original literary unity and to regard the other verses as a later expansion of the original.

One problem with Blum's literary analysis is that he takes the reference to Yahweh in v. 13aα as original even though the meaning of the text *ʿālāyw*, "above it (the ladder)" or "beside him (Jacob)," is very obscure. It is also doubtful that Yahweh would appear to Jacob without speaking to him.[46] This would be unprecedented in the OT. And how was Jacob able to identify this numinous presence, v. 16, without the deity making his identity quite clear, as in the parallel Exodus 3? The fact is that from the viewpoint of the work's structure, the first speech of Jacob in v. 16 is quite awkward. It would be much more effective if the text simply stated: "Then Jacob awoke from his sleep and was afraid and said . . ." This would also eliminate the need for a reference to Yahweh in v. 13aα. These observations may be confirmed by a look at form-critical aspects of the text.

Blum identifies the original tradition unit as a "cult foundation legend" — an etiology of the sanctuary at Bethel traced back to the ancestor of the people. This suggestion also goes back to Westermann, who cites the parallel in Gen. 32:2–3, where we have the following similarities: (1) in both cases, the events take place in the course of a journey, (2) Jacob encounters "angels of God," (3) Jacob gives a similar response, using the demonstrative "This is . . ." (*zeh*), and (4) Jacob names the place.[47] It may further be noted that the introduction to both stories, Gen. 28:10 and 32:1, belong to the larger story into which they have been integrated. Finally, Gen. 32:2–3 does not make any mention of Yahweh together with the angels.

If we accept the view, as seems quite reasonable, that we have in Gen. 28:10–22 a cult etiology that has been modified by later additions, then the earliest form of this tradition would be reflected in vs. 11–12, 16aα, 17–19a. The introductory connection in v. 10, the whole of Yahweh's appearance and speech in vs. 13–15, and Jacob's vow in vs. 20–22 represent a later addition. The first speech of Jacob in v. 16aβ,b was used to tie the divine speech to the older story. The fact that v. 13 begins with *wᵉhinnēh* is a way of making the speech of Yahweh part of the previous series in v. 12. It also explains the vagueness of the description in v. 13aα. Similarly, the reference to "this place" in v. 16 is an imitation of the same phrase in v. 17, but it has the effect of making the remark in v. 17 anti-climactic.

For Blum's traditio-historical approach, it is necessary to see a number of different compositional reworkings or additions to the cult etiology in 28:10–22.[48] This is an important issue for our own understanding of the Yahwist, so it must be considered in some detail. The first redactional addition that Blum identifies is 28:20–22. It is this material that allows for the integration of this separate cult etiology into the larger Jacob story (*Jakob-erzählung*). The vows of Jacob clearly have reference to his travels in foreign lands and to his return. Blum even sees in the sentence "so that I return to my father's house in peace" (v. 21a) a specific reference to his reconciliation with his brother Esau. That may be forced, for on his return his brother was no longer part of his father's household but dwelt quite apart in another region. But the reference to the rest of the story is clear enough.

However, Blum has some difficulty with the statement in v. 21b, "then Yahweh shall be my God." He associates this with those covenantal declarations in which Israel makes free choice of Yahweh, and compares this with such Dtr texts as Deut. 26:16ff. and Josh. 24:14ff. Such a possibility would fit badly with his general scheme, so he regards this as a later addition to the vows. In support of this he points out that it does not fit smoothly with the previous verses, because one would have expected in the protasis of v. 20: "If Yahweh will be with me . . ." followed by "then Yahweh will be my God" (v. 21b), and not just "If God will be with me . . ." as in the present text.

But this position is rather weak for the following reasons:

1. The text in v. 20 cannot mean any god but a specific deity, Yahweh; and because we have already argued that the use of Elohim for Yahweh is quite regular and indiscriminate in J, its use here is of little consequence.

2. If Yahweh is already mentioned in v. 16 as the one who was revealed to Jacob (so Blum), then the deity to whom the vow is made is entirely clear from the context, and the author may have used Elohim to correspond with *beth Ĕlōhîm* in v. 22.

3. The declaration that Yahweh will be his god fits very well with the statement that he will also build a house for him and offer tithes. The three statements in the apodosis go so well together that it is hard to imagine the first as a later gloss.

4. The *maṣṣēbâ* (v. 22) that is set up is taken over from v. 18 but seems to be reinterpreted here as a marker and witness stone for some future action. It is noteworthy that in Joshua 24, after the people declare that Yahweh will be their God (vs. 18, 21, 24), Joshua also sets up a great stone in the sanctuary as a witness to what the people have said (vs. 26–27). The two scenes have been constructed in very similar fashion.

The vows in 28:20–22 also raise the question of their relationship to the earlier divine appearance that evoked them. It is most obvious to see them as a response to the divine promise in 28:15: "Behold, I will be with you and protect you wherever you go and bring you back to this land." But Blum argues that this statement is far less specific than that of Jacob's vow, which adds to this "and give me bread to eat and clothes to wear."[49] Yet that can hardly be a reason to see a different author here. Blum also notes that "my father's house" (v. 21) has a different connotation than "this land" (v. 15) and makes much of this distinction. However, in the call of Abraham in 12:1, three entities are grouped together "from your land (*m'rṣk*)," "from your kindred (*mmwltk*)," and "from your father's house (*mbyt 'byk*)." And elsewhere in the Jacob story we find in 31:3: "to the land of your fathers" and "to your kindred"; in 31:13: "to the land of your kindred"; in 32:10: "to your land" and "to your kindred." One can put very little weight in such variation in terminology. To suppose that the author would include a vow just because Jacob had seen a vision of angels hardly seems credible. The divine speech cannot be separated from the vow.[50] The real reason why Blum cannot take these texts together is that 28:15 also contains the statement "for I will not leave you until I have done what I have promised you." This language is reminiscent of statements in Dtr sources that reflect the exilic hope of a return and the prophecy-fulfillment pattern. Blum has collected numerous examples of parallels to demonstrate clearly that this phraseology is Dtr and exilic.[51] But objection on these grounds is no more acceptable than in the case of 28:21b.

Blum also wishes to separate 28:15 from 28:13–14, which he identifies as part of the pre-Deuteronomic composition of the patriarchal history.[52] The parallels between 28:13–14 and 13:14–17 of the Abraham story are so close that a connection can hardly be denied. In both cases, the promises are tied to the immediate context, here by the reference to "the land on which you are lying" (v. 13). However, even in these verses, v. 14b is regarded as a secondary expansion, because the theme of the nations/families of the earth blessing themselves by the name of Jacob/Israel is attested as a common exilic theme. Yet Blum does not wish to identify the redactor of v. 14b with that of v. 15. What we are left with is the view that, in addition to the original cult legend of vs. 11–12 (13aα, 16) 17–19a, there are no less than four subsequent redactions: (1) 20, 21b–22; (2) 13a–14a; (3) 10(?), 14b, 19b (?); (4) 15, 21a.

I can find no adequate justification in Blum's arguments for such a scheme, and I see no reason why these four redactions cannot be viewed as all belonging to the same source, the Yahwist. My arguments for the unity of all the secondary additions are the following:

1. Genesis 28:16aβ,b, the first speech of Jacob, does not belong to the oldest account. It does not fit well with v. 17, and it presupposes both Yahweh's appearance and self-identification. Therefore, v. 13aα does not belong to the oldest account as well.

2. The vow in 28:20–22 does not stand alone, especially if v. 16aβ,b belongs to vs. 13–15, but must presuppose a divine appearance and promise such as occurs in 28:15. The speech and vow all go together.[53]

3. There seems to me little justification for splitting up the divine speech into different sources. Such a division rests entirely upon the acceptance of Rendtorff's traditio-historical differentiation within the levels of the promises themes that we completely reject.

For these reasons I regard all the additions to the earlier cult etiology as belonging to the same author, the Yahwist. This includes the itinerary statement in v. 10, which ties the episode into the larger story; the divine speech in vs. 13–15; the speech of Jacob in v. 16aβ,b, which is a way of recognizing Yahweh's appearance in Jacob's reaction; the antiquarian notice about the earlier identity of Bethel as Luz in v. 19b; and Jacob's vows in vs. 20–22.

Gen. 28:10–22 and the Literary Horizon of the Jacob Story

Once the secondary additions to 28:10–22 are identified as the work of the Yahwist and once the way in which he takes up and transforms the earlier traditions of the cult legend are recognized, then a number of other texts scattered throughout the rest of the Jacob story also come into consideration. Such texts are these: 31:3, 13; 32:10–13; 35:1–7. These refer back in one form or another to this episode in 28:10–22 and become pivotal for the Yahwist's interpretation of the whole account.[54]

In 31:3, 13, in which a divine appearance provides the motivation for Jacob's return, there is a direct reference back to 28:10–22, to both the theophany and the vow together. This comes at a critical stage in Jacob's adventures. Although some have argued that 31:3 does not fit so firmly in its context, the fact is that 31:2–3 seems merely to anticipate the longer explanation and theophany account by Jacob in 31:5–13, and this double motivation of ill treatment by Laban together with divine command is confirmed by the remarks of Jacob's wives (31:14–16). To these references can be added the divine appearances to Laban in 31:24, 29, 42 and the remarks about "the god of my/your father," "the god of Abraham," "the fear of Isaac," and so forth, in 31:5, 29, 42, 53. The obvious conclusion to be drawn from this is that the Yahwist has largely shaped the present narrative.

The matter of 32:10–13 is more difficult to judge because it can more easily be isolated from its context. But the fact that one can move from v. 9 to v. 14 and omit the prayer is little justification by itself for regarding it as secondary. Because Jacob attributes his prosperity to the deity in 33:5, 10, 11, this would support its place in the narrative. The prayer has also been shaped in vs. 11–12 to give it a connection to the immediate context as well as a reference back to the command of the deity to return to his own land and place of birth. The fact that the prayer has a close parallel with that of David's prayer in 2 Sam. 7:18–29 and also with that of Solomon in 1 Kings 3:5ff.[55] is hardly reason to regard it as part of a later D-revision.

The end of Jacob's journey is reflected in Gen. 35:1–7. It presents a divine command to go to Bethel and build an altar to the deity who had appeared to him when he fled from Esau (28:10–22) and thus completes the cycle of events. Blum argues that there is a certain lack of correspondence between the building of an altar (v. 7) and the vow in 28:22 to build a temple and pay tithes, and on this basis attributes the two units to different sources.[56] Yet Blum also recognizes that the vow of 28:22 was not intended as something that the patriarch himself would actually do but was a reference to the later temple worship at Bethel. In that case, there is no difficulty with the fact that Jacob builds only an altar as an anticipation of the later cultic installations and their support.

The unit, 35:1–7, builds onto, or presupposes, the previous episodes in the Jacob story. In addition to the flight from Esau, it seems also to have in mind the theft of gods by Rachel (31:19, 30–35) and the slaughter of the Shechemites in chapter 34. The latter appears to be an independent tradition that is fitted into the larger story by making it an episode in Jacob's itinerary with connective links in 33:18aα,b, 19; 34:30; 35:5.

The Form of the Jacob Story and Its Relationship to Chapter 28

One of the great merits of de Pury's study on the Jacob story is to raise the question of its overall form. Beginning from the position that the divine promises and the vows are basic to the narrative as a whole, de Pury argues that they cannot be complete within the episode itself in chapter 28 but must be part of a larger account by which they reach their fulfillment.[57] This larger form of narrative he characterizes as the "geste de Jacob." The limits of this work are thus governed by the determination of the features of this genre. At this point, de Pury is critical of Gunkel, who allowed for only small units with a single episode and did not take into consideration the kind of hero cycle story that includes various scenes and locations in this *geste patriarchale*. When de Pury speaks of a cycle, he does not mean just a collection of isolated units but a work in which the whole series of events forms and completes an arc of tension from beginning to end. The story of deception at the beginning, chapter 27, demands to be completed by the episodes that result from it in the reconciliation and return.

De Pury also attacks the notion that the stories need a specific *Haftpunkt* in which they are to be located.[58] This leads to the erroneous separation of the Cisjordan narratives from the Trans-jordanian ones. The travels of the hero are not just redactional seams between stories but part of the nature of the stories themselves. In the "cyclic" type of story, the *return* of the hero is crucial for the denouement. In the "linear" type, the departure leads to the *arrival* of the hero in a new region (as in the Abraham story). The Jacob story represents a clear example of the cyclic model with a large part being played out in a foreign region.

De Pury carries through his form-critical observations by finding evidence of its form in both the J and E sources of the Jacob story as he divides it. Although we have offered reasons earlier to question such a source division, the form-critical obser-vations themselves are worth pursuing. De Pury's primary example of a hero cycle is drawn from Arabic sources as collected by Litt-mann, but the pattern is also evident in the classical sources of Greece. This may be seen in the story of the sons of Abas in Apol-lodorus, *Bibliotheca* II, 2.1:

> And Abas had twin sons Acrisius and Proetus by Aglaia, daughter of Mantineus. These two quarrelled with each other while they were still in the womb, and when they were grown up they waged war for the kingdom, and in the course of the war they were the first to invent shields. And Acrisius gained the mastery and drove Proetus from Argos; and Proetus went to Lycia to the court of Iobates . . . and married his daughter. . . . His father-in-law restored him to his own land with an army of Lycians, and

he occupied Tiryns, which the Cyclopes had fortified for him. They divided the whole of the Argive territory between them and settled in it.[59]

If we accept the plausibility of this suggestion of the story's form, the question that must then be answered is the relationship of this larger story structure to the other traditional elements that have been identified within it. We have argued above that chapter 27 is a composition by the Yahwist, based upon the older tradition in 25:21–34, but it is also essential to the larger story form. Similarly, it was J who added the divine promise and the vows to the cult etiology in 28:10–22. Therefore it was the Yahwist who created this *geste patriarchale*. He did so by using a familiar story model into which he attempted to fit a range of traditional pieces about the forefather Jacob. Both the story model and the historiographic technique are common to antiquarian historiography, as the above quotation makes clear.

The Promise Theme in the Jacob Story

It is appropriate here to make some remarks about the divine promises to Jacob and their relationship to the larger perspective of the Yahwist. Of the various promise texts, the most important is Gen. 28:13–15. The divine speech begins with the self-identification formula: "I am Yahweh, the God of Abraham, your forefather, and the God of Isaac." This relates back to, and affirms, the revelations to Isaac in 26:3–5, 24 and even repeats the same formula, v. 24: "I am the God of Abraham, your father."[60] It also emphasizes the continuity in the divine promise through the three generations of ancestors. This title will be extended further to include Jacob for all the later descendants. This means that the revelation to Moses in Ex. 3:6: "I am the God of your forefather, the God of Abraham, the God of Isaac, and the God of Jacob," belongs to this same literary horizon.[61] In all cases, this title for deity is bound up with the patriarchal promises.[62]

The title "God of my/your father" with or without the patriarchal names becomes an important theme and mark of authorship in the Jacob story. It is especially prominent in the account of Jacob's return from Laban to his own region. This can be seen in Jacob's discussion with his wives about his return. In 31:5 he refers to the deity as "the God of my father," but in v. 13 as "the

God of Bethel," so the two are clearly identical.[63] Later Laban admits
to Jacob God's divine protection by disclosing a revelation from
"the God of your father" (31:29); and in Jacob's speech of self-
justification following Laban's search of his goods, he refers to "the
God of my father, the God of Abraham and the Fear of Isaac" (v. 42,
see also v. 53). In Jacob's prayer, 32:10, he refers to the deity as "God
of my father Abraham and God of my father Isaac."[64]

The significance of this usage was obscured by A. Alt's thesis
that the God of the Fathers religion belonged to a primitive level
of the patriarchal traditions.[65] In no case, however, is this "God
of my/your father" formula found in any pre-Yahwistic strata of
the Jacob traditions. The formula "God of your fathers" does occur
in late editorial levels of Dtr, but even here one must not assume
that the reference is to the patriarchs.[66] The title of the deity that
uses the patriarchal names is rare and late outside of the Tetrateuch.
This fact is not consistent with the view that the title belongs to
several layers of authorship and redaction in the Pentateuch over
several centuries while remaining absent from such a large corpus
of historical and prophetic literature. In my view, all these texts
that use the "God of my/your father" formula in the Jacob story
belong to the same post-Dtr Yahwist.[67]

The content of the promises in 28:13b–14 is a reiteration of
the promises to Abraham, drawn from 12:2–3 and 13:14–17. The
land-promise: "The land upon which you lie I will give to you and
to your descendants" (v. 13b) is made to fit the particular setting
of the theophany. In the same way, God's promise of land to
Abraham is related to his viewing the land from Bethel: "All the
land which you see I will give to you and to your descendants
forever" (13:15). The promise of numerous progeny to Jacob: "and
your descendants shall be like the dust of the earth" (28:14aα) also
parallels the similar comparison with "the dust of the earth" in
13:16a. However, this theme of increase is developed differently
in the two texts. Jacob is told that his offspring will "spread abroad
(*prṣ*) to the west and the east, to the north and the south" (v. 14aβ),
but in 13:14 the four cardinal compass points are connected with
the land-promise. A striking parallel to the text in 28:14, however,
may be seen in Isa. 54:1–3, which speaks of the restoration of Israel
to numerous offspring. The imagery seems to reflect that of the
tent-dwelling forefathers who are told that their numbers will lead

to an expansion of their territories: "For you will spread abroad (*prṣ*) to the right and to the left" (v. 3a). The similarity cannot be fortuitous.[68]

The final element of the patriarchal promises theme: "By you and by your descendants shall all the families of the earth bless themselves" (28:14b) is virtually identical to that of 12:3b, except with the addition of the reference to "descendants" at the end of the verse.[69] I have already discussed above the significance of this expression within the royal ideology of Jerusalem and will not repeat that here.

The last part of the divine speech moves in quite a new direction and gives to Jacob the promise of divine presence and guidance on his journey and restoration in the land. This is closely related to the circumstances of the story and constitutes an important theme within it, to which we will return below. There are, however, two important issues that must be addressed. First, the promise of divine presence is confirmed by the further statement: "For I will not leave you until I have done that about which I have spoken to you" (28:15b). As Blum has shown,[70] this phraseology is so characteristic of Dtr language that it must be understood in that context. It is used primarily in terms of the fulfillment of the land-promise and the establishment of Israel as God's people or the fulfillment of God's promises to David. This means that the author of Genesis 28 also has in mind the larger destiny of the people. He is not merely thinking of Jacob's return but is associating that prospect with the people's own return from exile. One can hardly avoid the conclusion that Jacob's adventure is being used as a paradigm for the exilic period and the people's experiences at that time.

The second problem has to do with the vow of Jacob in 28:20–22. The same theme of divine presence is expressed differently, so that either it belongs to another source or there must be some special point to presenting the theme in this form. If the divine promise has in view the people as a whole primarily, then the vow is more particularly the expression of personal piety within the religious realm. With the vow, Jacob becomes the paradigm of the individual Israelite faced with the crisis of exile. The phrase "so that I return to my father's house in peace" surely has a poignancy for those displaced by war. But it is especially the declaration "then Yahweh will be my God" that expresses the need for individual commitment in the exilic age. This is also the theme of Joshua 24 in which each household is challenged to choose Yahweh as God and to serve him on the basis of all the good that he has done the people. Elsewhere I have argued that this text reflects the exilic period and also belongs to J.[71]

The interpretation of v. 22 is more obscure. On the one hand it clearly builds upon the etiology of the Bethel sanctuary and the stone marker as the "house of God." But the intention of the vow is to shift the meaning of Jacob's anointing of the *mṣbh* to some future event. The "pillar" of stone now becomes a marker of a future commitment to build a temple, just like the stone of witness in Josh. 24:27. This reinterpretation could have in mind the Jerusalem temple and its restoration under the guise of this Bethel = "house of God."[72] The reference to the voluntary tithe in support of such a temple has in view the exilic community, because it has no relevance within the story itself. It is a specific Deuteronomic institution that arose out of centralization of worship and that has been given a new understanding and place in exilic religion.

The theme of divine presence is prominent in the Jacob story, particularly when it deals with Jacob's return from Mesopotamia, either as a reference to the promise of Yahweh (28:15) or as Jacob's vow (28:20–22), or a combination of both. Thus, in Gen. 31:3 Yahweh summons Jacob to return home with a reminder of his promise (= 28:15), whereas in 31:13 God refers to Jacob's vow (= 28:20–22). Jacob himself identifies the acquisition of his wealth with God's presence (31:5, 42), in keeping with his vow, but he uses the formula "God of my father" from the divine promises. It is likely that all the texts that speak of divine protection and presence and that attribute Jacob's wealth to the deity are part of the same revision to emphasize this theme.

The same is true of the prayer of Jacob in 32:10–13, which does not use the divine presence formula but the closely related idea "I will do you good" (vs. 10, 13). This can be seen when the divine command of 31:3 is quoted in Jacob's prayer in 32:10.

31:3	*32:10*
Return to the land of your fathers and to your kindred and I will be with you.	Return to your country and to your kindred, and I will do you good.

Jacob's quotation of the deity in 32:13 does not repeat exactly that of 28:13–15 but is a loose paraphrase drawing elements from various other promise texts. Although the phrase, "I will do you good" corresponds to the divine presence formula of 28:15, the comparison "as the sand on the seashore" comes from 22:17; but the inability to count the descendants corresponds to the statement in 13:16, "if one can count the dust of the earth, your descendants can also be counted." This lack of precision in quotation does not signify a difference in authorship. Ancients did not feel the same compulsion as do moderns toward exact quotation, even of public documents.[73] And when it is a case of the same author, the variety is simply a matter of literary style.

The theme of divine presence is taken up again when Jacob resolves to return to Bethel, "that I may make there an altar to the God who answered me in the day of my distress and has been with me wherever I have gone" (35:3). The reference is to the revelation by God and to the context of the flight from Esau (see also v. 7), but the building of the altar and the use of Elohim is the fulfillment of the vow. It brings to a fitting conclusion the Jacob adventure, begun in chapter 27. There is no need to attribute any of it to a redactor.[74]

The formula to express the promise of divine presence and guidance (*Beistandsformel*) is not used of Abraham, but it is used of Isaac in 26:3 in combination with that of the promise of blessing. The two are virtually identical. Thus, in the patriarch's dealings with Abimelech, king of Gerar, the king acknowledges to Abraham: "God is with you in all that you do" (21:22), and to Isaac: "We see clearly that Yahweh has been with you" (26:28). This is a recognition of God's blessing, and in both cases it leads to a treaty between the patriarch and the foreign ruler. Likewise, when Abraham sends his servant on a journey to distant kin to get a wife for his son, he assures his servant of divine guidance (24:7, 40). The servant subsequently acknowledges that it is the "God of my master Abraham" who has given him guidance on his mission (vs. 27, 48, 56).[75] It is clear that the whole story in chapter 24 is about the way in which God has been with Abraham and guides and protects his whole household.[76]

The divine presence formula is also used of Ishmael in 21:20 by virtue of the fact that he is a son of Abraham. It does not relate to any particular episode but to the fact that his whole life was under divine protection: "God was with the boy and he grew up."

There is considerable debate about the origin and *Sitz im Leben* of the promise of divine presence formula (*Beistandsformel*) in the patriarchal stories. It is not restricted to these texts but is used of Moses and his mission, the divine presence in the wilderness, and of Joshua in the conquest of the land. It also functions as a prominent theme in the story of David's rise to power and the divine promise to David through Nathan (2 Samuel 7). This theme extends the usage into the story of Solomon. This means that the biblical usage covers the whole range of possible settings from nomadic to royal. Is there any way of deciding which is the original and which is secondary?

The discussion of the formula in Genesis has been dominated in the past by the search for nomadic roots in the patriarchal traditions.[77] Although no comparative material relevant to a nomadic *Sitz im Leben* has been suggested because of the very nature of such an illiterate social context, it has been freely conjectured that the promise of divine guidance and protection by the personal deity would be most appropriate for nomadic groups moving to new pasture lands and in constant contact with threatening foreign groups. This form of nomadic piety became extended to other aspects of Israelite life after the settlement, such as that of the monarchy.[78]

With the demise of the nomadic "God of the fathers" thesis of Alt, there has been a radical reappraisal of this proposal. It becomes much more likely that the divine presence formula is derived from a royal militaristic context. It is one of the dominant themes of DtrH's portrayal of David (1 Sam. 16:18; 18:12, 14, 28; 20:13; 2 Sam. 5:10; 7:3, 9) as a way of accounting for all David's military success but also for divine favor and protection in a broader sense, especially in his struggle with Saul.[79] The divine presence appears to be a particular quality of royalty, and it leads to close relations between David and Hiram, king of Tyre (2 Sam. 5:10–11) and also between Solomon and Hiram (1 Kings 5:15ff.).

It is not difficult to understand why the same formulaic language of the *Beistandsformel* is used with Joshua (Josh. 1:5, 17; 3:7). The whole of the DtrH conquest narrative is modeled on that of a military expedition by a great king, and the Assyrian kings in particular.[80] The comparison with Moses, "as I was with Moses . . . ," is primarily with his victorious campaign against the eastern kings of Transjordan. The promise of divine presence in Josh. 1:5 stands within the context of a "confidence-inspiring oracle" (*Heilsorakel*) before a military campaign and so suggests comparison with Assyrian royal inscriptions.

It is common for the royal inscriptions of Esarhaddon and Ashurbanipal to include a reference to such an oracle in which the deity promises divine presence before a military adventure.[81] The language of these texts emphasizes the presence of the deity and divine guidance: "I will go before you and behind you"; "Sixty great gods are standing together with me (Bel) and protect you, the god Sin is at your right, the god Shamash at your left"; "Fear not, O king, . . . I have not abandoned you"; "wherever you go, I shall go with you." There are many expressions of divine protection: "I am your protector, your gracious leader am I"; "my mercy is your shield." There may also be a pledge to keep the divine promise: "This is the word of Ninlil herself for the king, 'Fear not, O Ashurbanipal! Now as I have spoken, it will come to pass; I shall grant it to you.'" It seems quite likely that DtrH has derived this formulaic language of the divine presence from this particular foreign *Sitz im Leben*.

In the case of Gen. 28:15 it should now be quite clear that the language of divine presence and guidance, as well as the assurance of the fulfillment of all God's promises, matches exactly the language and concepts that we have outlined above. In addition, the notion that God's presence also gave Jacob protection against any possible harm from Laban fits the language of protection against one's enemies in the Assyrian texts. Furthermore, Jacob's relations with Laban parallel those of David with Saul at least to the degree that Laban recognizes that Yahweh is with Jacob and is prospering him (Gen. 30:27; cf. 1 Sam. 16:18–23), but this very success leads to jealousy and bad feeling between Jacob and Laban (Gen. 31:1–2, 4; 1 Sam. 18:12–16, 28). The relations of Abraham and Isaac with Abimelech also correspond closely to that of David and Solomon with Hiram, largely for the same reasons. The patriarchs are clearly understood as representing political states.

Berge has recently disallowed this comparison with the royal *Sitz im Leben* on the argument that Jacob's flight does not correspond to that of a military expedition. He prefers to view it as reflective of nomadic life, and therefore he explains the origins of the *Beistandsformel* entirely in these terms.[82] Apart from the fact that association of the *Beistandsformel* with nomadic religion is pure conjecture for which there is no evidence, Jacob's wandering does not make the scene nomadic. Jacob is in flight from his brother and must live in a foreign region for a time. But the same can be said of David in his flight from Saul. In fact, Jacob travels entirely alone, without flocks or family, to a city, Haran, in which he has relatives. His return is specifically to his own land and his father's house. How can any of this be said to reflect nomadic life and religion? The notion of an adventure in a foreign land is a genre quite common in antiquity and does not derive from nomadic life but from settled regions.[83] It often has to do with rival claims to the throne. This agrees well with the rivalry between Jacob over the blessing, which, as we have seen, is expressed in royal language.

The vow may also be understood as confirming this same conclusion. There is nothing in the vow that is nomadic except perhaps the vague reference to a journey, "and keep me in the way that I go." But that could apply to almost any situation. It is the promise to establish a cult with sanctuary and offerings for its support in the middle of the settled land as fulfillment of a vow that is noteworthy. This corresponds to the practice of royal dedications to the cult and temple building as a consequence of a victorious campaign, so common in Near Eastern inscriptions, especially Assyrian. Even in the Nathan oracle, David desires to build Yahweh a "house" after God has given him rest from all his enemies (2 Sam. 7:1–4). If Jacob returns home from his foreign adventure *in peace,* he will also dedicate a cult to the deity. Jacob's adventure does not reflect nomadic life but royal and heroic models.

As we have seen above, the language of the promises to Abraham is completely dominated by royal ideology, so it is not surprising to find it in the case of Jacob as well. Immediately preceding the promise of the divine presence is the remark "By you all the families of the earth will bless themselves." I have argued, with reference to an Assyrian royal inscription, that this reflects royal ideology. In that same Assyrian text, the Lydian king submits to Ashurbanipal's authority with the statement: "Thou art the king whom the gods have favored."[84]

This democratization of the royal *Beistandsformel* in terms of the patriarchs can also be seen in Second Isaiah. The prophet states in 41:8-10:

> But you, Israel, my servant,
>   Jacob whom I have chosen,
>   the offspring of Abraham, my friend;
> you whom I took from the ends of the earth,
>   and called from its farthest corners,
> saying to you, "You are my servant,
>   I have chosen you and not cast you off;
> fear not, for I am with you,
>   be not dismayed, for I am your God."

That this saying imitates the royal *Heilsorakel* with the *Beistandsformel* embedded in it is beyond dispute. Its association with Jacob, the offspring of Abraham, who represents the people in exile who like Jacob are promised a return from the distant land of Mesopotamia, makes the parallel with Gen. 28:15 so close that the texts must be related. Second Isaiah preaches a victory for Yahweh and a glorious return from exile for the people. There he will be their God; he will fulfill his word and restore Jerusalem and its sanctuary. Jacob is offered by the Yahwist as a paradigm for these same sentiments. It is also not too difficult to see how the militaristic aspect of the foreign adventure has become transformed in the process of adaptation to the patriarchal stories.

NOTES

1.   Compare the recent attempts by Eckart Otto, *Jakob in Sichem*, BWANT 110 (1979), pp. 47-67; Blum, *Die Komposition*, pp. 98-140.

2.   The idea of a territorial boundary marker between ancestors does not fit very well with a tradition of a later conquest of the kingdom of Bashan.

3.   Basic components of this older Jacob story seem to be reflected in Hosea 12. For the most recent treatment of this, see W. D. Whitt, "The Jacob Traditions in Hosea and their Relation to Genesis," *ZAW* 103 (1991), 18-43.

4.   For earlier discussion of this text see A. de Pury, "Genèse XXXIV et l'histoire," *RB* 66 (1969), 5-49; P. Kevers, "Étude littéraire de Genèse XXXIV," *RB* 87 (1980), 38-86; Westermann, *Genesis 12-36*, pp. 532-545; Blum, *Die Komposition*, pp. 210-223.

5.   B. Edele, "A Diachronic Analysis of Genesis 34," to appear in a forthcoming issue of *Vetus Testamentum*. I am indebted to this study for my observations here.

6.   Discussion of the Joseph story and its place in the Yahwist's work will be taken up below.

7.   See chapter 13 above.

8.   Westermann, *Genesis 12–36,* pp. 405–419, 431–444; Blum, *Die Komposition,* pp. 66–88. See also Eckart Otto, *Jakob in Sichem,* pp. 17–88, esp. pp. 24–40.

9.   Westermann, *Genesis 12–36,* pp. 411–412.

10.   See below.

11.   So also Eckart Otto, *Jakob in Sichem,* pp. 24–35.

12.   See West, *Hesiodic Catalogue of Women,* p. 68; and a similar story in Apollodorus, *Bibliotheca,* 2.2.1ff., as observed by Skinner, *Genesis, p.* 359.

13.   So also Blum, *Die Komposition,* pp. 67ff.

14.   Westermann's attempt to strike the verse as secondary seems arbitrary.

15.   Von Rad, *Genesis,* p. 265.

16.   Westermann's interpretation of these episodes as "family stories" quite misses the point.

17.   See also Genesis 16.

18.   See Noth, *A History of Pentateuchal Traditions,* p. 29 n. 93; cf. von Rad, *Genesis,* p. 276.

19.   Westermann, *Genesis 12–36,* p. 435; and Blum, *Die Komposition,* pp. 86f. Eckart Otto, *Jakob in Sichem,* pp. 24–32, argues for a basic unity for 27:1–45, including the flight to Mesopotamia.

20.   An observation made by Blum, *Die Komposition,* pp. 68ff., although he does not draw the obvious conclusion. Cf. Eckart Otto, *Jakob in Sichem,* pp. 28–32.

21.   This is also the conclusion of Otto. See note above.

22.   Von Rad, in *Genesis,* p. 266, interprets the story in chapter 25 in the light of chapter 27, but that hardly seems legitimate when investigating their tradition-history.

23.   Westermann, *The Promises to the Fathers,* pp. 76–81.

24.   In this way Esau's "blessing" is not unlike the curses of the primeval history that emphasize both physical hardships and servitude but with some mitigation. See above, pp. 139–140.

25.   See also Westermann, *Genesis 12–36,* p. 436.

26.   Cf. von Rad, *Genesis,* p. 265, who interprets 25:21–28 as an introduction to the Jacob story, but that is hardly the case. Eckart Otto (*Jakob in Sichem,* p. 32) understands 27:1–45 as "eine vorquellenschriftliche Redaktion" of the Jacob tradition (= Noth's G), meant to combine the Esau cycle with the Laban cycle.

27.   Berge, *Die Zeit des Jahwisten,* pp. 119–146, has made an extensive study of the blessing in Gen. 27:27b–29 but with little attention to the broader relationship of chapter 27 to chapter 25. His conclusions are quite different from those proposed here.

28.   The change from "father's" to "mother's" is directly related to the story context in which Jacob is the favorite of Rebekah.

29.   See H. Rouillard, *La péricope de Balaam (Nombres 22–24)* (1985), pp. 345–388. Her attempt to divide this blessing into two parts does not commend itself.

30.   M. Noth, *The History of Israel,* 2nd ed. (1960), pp. 85–97.

31.   De Geus, *The Tribes of Israel.*

32.   Note the similarity of language:

Gen. 27:29	*Ps. 72:11*
יעבדוך עמים	וישתחוו לו כל מלכים
וישתחו לך לאמים	כל גוים יעבדוהו

33.   See also the texts in Amos 9:11-15 and Micah 5:1ff. Blum, *Die Komposition,* p. 193, does not do justice to this connection with royal ideology. See Rouillard's exilic dating of the parallel in Num. 24:3-9 (*La péricope,* pp. 387-388).

34.   Berge's recent study of Isaac's blessing (see n. 25 above), which he regards as belonging to the Yahwist, dismisses the similarity to royal language as traditional from the older "Canaanite" culture. This royal terminology J combined with a traditional element out of the tribal sayings (the reference to the submission of "brothers" and "mother's sons") that originally referred to the relationship of Israelite tribes to each other. J used it in his story to reflect the relationship of Israel as a whole to the non-Israelite nations (pp. 142f.). The argument is too forced, because the language of the Isaac blessing does not reflect a single element of tribal sayings, only royal language, as it does in Gen. 49:8-12 and 49:22-26.

35.   See pp. 267-270; also Van Seters, *Abraham,* p. 190.

36.   Some scholars have suggested that the episode in chapter 26 should be thought of as coming during Rebekah's period of barrenness. But placement here would have been a problem because the barrenness would have reflected badly on Isaac, as it did in the case of Abimelech in Gen. 20:18 as divine punishment, and it would have been a denial of the divine blessing suggested in 26:12ff. So the Yahwist could not put it in that spot.

37.   De Pury, *Promesse divine,* pp. 32-45, 345-470; Berge, *Die Zeit des Jahwisten,* pp. 145-194; Blum, *Die Komposition,* pp. 7-35, 88-98, 152-164. See also Eckart Otto, *Jakob in Sichem,* pp. 67-82.

38.   De Pury, *Promesse divine,* pp. 32-45.

39.   See de Pury's statement, *Promesse divine,* p. 449:

> Le récit primitif était ainsi plus "complet" que ne le sont la version yahviste et les fragments de la version élohiste preserves en Gen 28. On constate donc, non sans un certain étonnement, que le récit compile par RJE est reste plus proche du récit original que ne sont, pris isolement, les fragments des versions yahviste et élohiste preserves en son sein.

This result is surely a very unlikely one and suggests that the method of source division is at fault.

The approach of Eckart Otto (*Jakob in Sichem,* pp. 67-72) is similar. He divides the text into two sources, J and E, but then reverts to an older tradition for his traditio-historical discussion. This includes vs. 11-19 to which he regards vs. 20-22 as a secondary addition. A critique of this is implicit in what follows.

40.   Berge, *Die Zeit des Jahwisten,* pp. 147-170. Berge's study contains a current review of the earlier discussion on this text.

41.   See ibid., pp. 150-154.

42.   Other texts that suggest that a series of actions could follow the general statement about "spending the night" are Gen. 19:2-4; 32:21ff.; Judg. 19:9 and passim.

43.   Contra Berge, *Die Zeit des Jahwisten,* p. 160.

44.   Westermann, *Genesis 12-36,* p. 453.

45.   Blum, *Die Komposition,* pp. 7-35. See also R. Rendtorff, "Jacob in Bethel. Beobachtungen zum Aufbau und zur Quellenfrage in Gen. 28,10-22," *ZAW* 94 (1982), 511-523.

46.   See also de Pury, *Promesse divine,* pp. 376–379.
47.   Westermann, *Genesis 12–36,* p. 452; see also Blum, *Die Komposition,* pp. 140–142. Blum's other examples of the form in Exodus 3 and 2 Samuel 24 (p. 28) are not so persuasive.
48.   Blum, *Die Komposition,* pp. 88–98.
49.   Ibid., pp. 163–164.
50.   This is the same conclusion to which de Pury comes on the form-critical level, in spite of his attempt to divide the text into J and E. See *Promesse divine,* pp. 434–446.
51.   Blum, *Die Komposition,* pp. 159, 164. See 1 Kings 8:34; Jer. 16:15; 24:6; 29:10, 14.
52.   Blum, *Die Komposition,* p. 158, 290–297.
53.   I do not accept Westermann's statement (*Genesis 12–36,* p. 453) that a divine promise cannot also be the condition of a vow.
54.   Berge (*Die Zeit des Jahwisten,* pp. 175–183) assigns these texts to various sources based upon his source division of 28:10–22. So also Eckart Otto, *Jakob in Sichem,* pp. 35–40. Blum (*Die Komposition,* pp. 35–45, 152–164) ascribes them to different redactional levels, based on the distinctions he has identified in 28:13–15 and 20–22.
55.   See Blum, *Die Komposition,* pp. 155–157.
56.   Ibid., pp. 62–65. In this he follows Eckart Otto (*Jakob in Sichem,* pp. 72–77), who constructs a separate Bethel tradition in 35:1–7 independent from 28:10–22, both primitive etiologies.
57.   De Pury, *Promesse divine,* p. 473.
58.   See de Pury's critique of Noth, ibid., p. 515.
59.   Cited from J. G. Frazer, *Apollodorus,* I, p. 145; and his comment in n. 4. See also Pausanias ii.16.2, ii.25.7. The voyage of the Argonauts is also a cyclic tale of adventure. On the motif of the twins struggling in the womb, see also West, *Hesiodic Catalogue of Women,* p. 68.
60.   Berge, in *Die Zeit des Jahwisten,* pp. 77–93, 116–118, regards the promises in Genesis 26 as very late but otherwise has no explanation for the use of the formula that includes Isaac in what is for him the much earlier text of 28:13.
61.   See also Gen. 46:2–3.
62.   For recent discussion on the development of the title "God of the Fathers" = "God of the Patriarchs," see Römer, *Israels Väter,* pp. 337–352.
63.   Attempts at source division in 31:4–16 are completely defeated by this combination. Cf. Westermann, *Genesis 12–36,* pp. 490–492; Berge, *Die Zeit des Jahwisten,* pp. 178–183; Blum, *Die Komposition,* pp. 117–132.
64.   On the usage in the Joseph story, see below.
65.   Alt, *Der Gott der Väter.* For a critique, see recently H. Vorländer, *Mein Gott. Die Vorstellungen vom persönlichen Gott im Alten Testament,* AOAT 23, 1975; M. Kockert, *Vätergott und Väterverheissungen. Eine Auseinandersetzung mit Albrecht Alt und seinen Erben,* FRLANT 142, 1988.
66.   See the study of Römer in n. 60 above.
67.   Although Römer (in *Israels Väter*) does not deal with the texts of Genesis, his examination of the use of "fathers" in the rest of the Old Testament would strongly support this conclusion.

68.   See Van Seters, *Abraham,* p. 277. Cf. Berge, *Die Zeit des Jahwisten,* p. 258.

69.   The final word, *wbzrʿk,* is often considered as a harmonizing scribal addition. So also in BHS. Given the variety of expression in J, that is not altogether necessary.

70.   Blum, *Die Komposition,* pp. 159ff. But this is not by itself a reason to consider v. 15b as an addition. Berge, *Die Zeit des Jahwisten,* pp. 167–168, 223–225, tries to explain away as much of the similarity to Dtr as possible.

71.   J. Van Seters, "Joshua 24 and the Problem of Tradition in the Old Testament," in *The Shelter of Elyon,* JSOT SS 31 (1984), pp. 139–158.

72.   Perhaps the Yahwist was not committed to the view that the rebuilt temple had to be in Jerusalem.

73.   See Thomas, *Oral Tradition and Written Record,* pp. 45–60.

74.   See Blum, *Die Komposition,* pp. 61–65; Eckart Otto, *Jakob in Sichem,* pp. 72–76. I cannot support Otto's effort to find an independent Bethel cult-etiology in 35:1–7.

75.   The phrase "God of my master Abraham" is intended as an equivalent of "God of my father Abraham," as we have it in the Jacob story.

76.   See von Rad, *Genesis,* pp. 159–160. Cf. Westermann, *Genesis 12–36,* pp. 383–384. Westermann's arguments against attributing Genesis 24 to J because the latter is 10–9th century is not persuasive.

77.   See Berge, *Die Zeit des Jahwisten,* pp. 195–203, for a review of the older discussion.

78.   This is the view of Berge, ibid., 203–227, following V. Maag, "Malkut JHWH," in *Congress Volume Oxford,* SVT 7 (1960), pp. 129–153; H. D. Preuss, ". . . ich will mit dir sein," *ZAW* 80 (1968), 161ff.; see also T. W. Mann, *Divine Presence and Guidance in Israelite Tradition,* 1977.

79.   See Van Seters, *In Search of History,* pp. 265–266.

80.   See ibid., pp. 324–331; and J. Van Seters, "Joshua's Conquest of Canaan and Near Eastern Historiography," *SJOT* 2 (1990), 1–12.

81.   See *ANET,* pp. 449–451.

82.   Berge, *Die Zeit des Jahwisten,* pp. 216–225.

83.   In the *Catalogue of Women,* fr. 19a, we are told that Zeus sent his son, the hero Sarpedon, to Troy to lead the Lycian forces against the Greeks. It further states: "Zeus . . . sent him forth from heaven a star, showing tokens for the return of his dear son . . . for well he (Sarpedon) knew in his heart that the sign was indeed from Zeus." Quoted from Evelyn-White, *Hesiod,* p. 603.

84.   Luckenbill, *Ancient Records of Assyria and Babylonia,* II, para. 785, p. 298. On the notion of "spreading abroad" cf. para. 659E, p. 253.

16
JACOB
AND THE STORY OF
JOSEPH

Introduction

It is not my purpose to investigate the literary history and composition of the Joseph story, Genesis 37, 39–50. Nor will I attempt to review the extensive literature that has developed on this subject in recent years.[1] Since the time of Wellhausen,[2] the various doublets and tensions within the story have made it a prime example for the division of sources into parallel J and E versions. At the same time, the form-critical approach of Gunkel and Gressmann suggested that the Joseph story was in the nature of a short story or novella, a literary product quite different from the *Sagen* traditions of the patriarchs.[3] This gave rise to the view by subsequent scholars that the original Joseph story was a unity separate from the rest of the traditions of Abraham to Jacob. The Joseph story had its own history of development in which there were some revisions and expansions. Thus, for instance, an earlier form of the story in which Reuben plays a dominant role as the older brother has been revised by a later hand to give Judah a more prominent place.[4] The episode of Joseph's temptation by Potiphar's wife in chapter 39 is also frequently considered as an expansion of the earlier story.[5]

Although there are still a few advocates of the older source division of the Joseph story,[6] the view that the Joseph story should be viewed as a literary work of separate origin and development prior to its integration into the Pentateuch has become the dominant view and will be followed here. Nothing in our previous investigation in Genesis has given any reason to support the

311

division of the pre-Priestly material into J and E sources, and current research on the Joseph story points to a further retreat in this area as well. Nor is Noth's position, that the Joseph story was composed to bridge the gap between the patriarchal traditions and the sojourn in Egypt,[7] any longer viewed as a satisfactory explanation.[8] Once the "original" story is identified, it appears to have an independence from the rest of the Pentateuch. Its nature as a "wisdom" novella means that it was not concerned to reflect tribal or national history and the future destiny of the descendants of the ancestors.

Yet there remains to be addressed an issue that is most important for this study, and that is the relationship of the Joseph story to the Yahwist's account of the patriarch, Jacob. There are a plethora of recent studies that address this question in one way or another. I will not review them all here,[9] but will use the presentation of Westermann as my point of departure.[10] Westermann advocates the view that the Jacob story originally explained how the sons of Jacob went to Egypt without the use of the Joseph story. This Jacob story consisted of some parts of Genesis 37 and 46–50 and told of how Jacob went down to Egypt and found his lost son there. Westermann argues "that the Joseph story in the stricter sense is an insertion into the Jacob story, that it arose independently of it, and that it was artistically interwoven with it in chs. 37 and 46–47."[11]

Closer scrutiny, however, discloses a host of unresolved problems.[12] Westermann suggests that Genesis 38 and 49 were late insertions into the Jacob story before its connection with the Joseph story.[13] But the addition of chapter 38, a Judean tradition, to the Jacob story, as Westermann understands it, would have had the effect of denying that Judah had any part in the Egyptian sojourn and exodus because he is not mentioned as being in Egypt outside of the Joseph story. This would seem to exclude Judah from the whole exodus tradition prior to the introduction of the Joseph story into it. Because most scholars regard the Joseph story as having a northern provenience, this would be a most curious development.[14]

Westermann suggests that Genesis 37 contains a quite separate and original Jacob story alongside the Joseph story. The evidence for this can be seen in the doubling of names and doublets:

Israel/Jacob, Ishmaelites/Midianites, and Reuben/Judah, and in various other tensions in the story. But Westermann attempts no literary separation in this chapter to extract a Jacob story alongside of the Joseph story. Where then is the evidence for a separate story about how Jacob travels to Egypt to find his lost son? He further asserts that the Joseph story has no adequate introduction and therefore is dependent upon the Jacob story for its exposition. On this basis, Westermann argues that the Joseph story is an expansion of the Jacob story by the author himself.[15] Yet Westermann insists that the story of Joseph is an independent literary composition that was inserted secondarily into the work of J.[16] It seems that he would like to have it both ways. Furthermore, it has often been pointed out that there are too many contradictions between the details of the Joseph story and the preceding Jacob story to view the one as dependent upon the other for its setting and information.[17]

Westermann never actually tells us what the conclusion of the Jacob story would have looked like prior to the inclusion of the Joseph story. In fact, apart from pieces in chapters 46–50 attributed to either the Joseph story or to the Priestly Writer, all the rest of the material consists of additions made by a redactor (not J) to the combined Joseph-Jacob stories.[18] The conclusion of J has virtually disappeared. How, then, does one get from this state of affairs to the statement in Ex. 1:8, widely attributed to J: "Now there arose a new king in Egypt who did not know Joseph"?

Westermann first explains the repetition of the reconciliation theme in 50:15–21, which has its true place at the story's climax in 45:5–8, as the attempt by the author of the Joseph story to integrate his story more closely with that of the Jacob story.[19] By the end of his commentary, however, the Jacob story has disappeared, so the same text, 50:15–21, is now attributed to a redactor who repeated the scene after amalgamating the Joseph story with all the Jacob traditions.[20] This addition is followed, in Westermann's view,[21] by two more additions in the epilogue of 50:22–26, all by different authors.

In conclusion, Westermann has failed to demonstrate that a Jacob story existed prior to, and alongside of, the Joseph story. All the pieces that do not belong to the Joseph story are viewed as additions to the Joseph story by later redactors, whatever their origin. No comprehensive historiographic method or design lies behind these additions. They are haphazard and individual additions for the most part. The relationship of the Joseph story to the patriarchal traditions and the rest of the Pentateuch is not adequately addressed. For us this includes three questions:

1. What is the Yahwist's ending of the Jacob story?
2. What served, in J, as the bridge from the patriarchs to the story of the sojourn in Egypt and the exodus?
3. How much of the so-called additions to the Joseph story, not attributed to P, belong to J?

A recent study by W. Dietrich[22] presents a substantial modification of Westermann's position that would seem to address some of the weaknesses of his position. Dietrich accepts the view that the Joseph story is an independent work separate from the other Pentateuchal sources. He takes seriously the tensions between it and the Jacob tradition; therefore, it cannot be viewed as an addition to the Jacob story as Westermann held. Instead, Dietrich proposes two versions of the Joseph story, an earlier version and a later revision. The early version had only rudimentary knowledge of a tradition about the sons of Jacob; its author used his imagination to fill in the details. A second author expanded the work, without correcting or disturbing most of the older version, to take into account the broader Pentateuchal material, both with respect to the patriarchs and to the sojourn in Egypt. It is this author that understood the Joseph story as the bridge from the patriarchs to the exodus. It provides the justification for the sojourn in Egypt as the salvation of God and adds the Joseph story to the "national epic" dealing with Israel's origins and early history.

This "reviser" (*Bearbeiter*) can be identified and his additions isolated in much the same way that earlier scholars made their source division, by means of doublets and double names. In particular, it is the reviser who is responsible for bringing the figure of Judah to the fore as the one to replace Reuben and to give to him a status corresponding to that of Joseph. This encourages Dietrich to follow a political interpretation of the Joseph story, a northern origin for the early story, and a provenience in Judah shortly after the fall the Northern Kingdom for the revision.[23]

Although this study addresses a number of problems observed above in Westermann's treatment, some difficulties still remain.

The first problem with Dietrich's view is that the criteria for assigning materials to the "reviser" seem debatable. Genesis 39 and some harmonizing glosses in chapter 40 have often been viewed as a later addition, but they have little in common with the other "additions."[24] Dietrich also regards all of the texts referring to Judah as the reviser's work, but this seems to create havoc with the climax to the Joseph story by the removal of Judah's speech in 44:18–34. Dietrich, however, retains the passage in 44:14–16 but removes the two references to Judah from these texts.[25] This seems to me quite arbitrary.

The earlier position by Redford regarding the Judah-expansion is to suggest that in chapters 43 and 44 the name of Judah, with a few additional revisions, was substituted for that of Reuben.[26] This would keep much more of the story intact. This means that the same could be said for the use of Israel for Jacob, because the alternation of the names Jacob/Israel outside of the Joseph story does not constitute a criterion for the division of sources.

Dietrich also says very little about the extent of the Jacob tradition prior to the activity of the reviser of the Joseph story. Some texts, like 41:50–52 and 48:8–20, were apparently based upon the Jacob tradition and integrated into the story by the reviser. So they are listed as part of his work.[27] But Dietrich seems less certain about what to do with 46:1–5 and 50:24–25, which he excludes from the reviser's version. What is even more curious is that Dietrich supposes that the statement in Ex. 1:8 about the "new king in Egypt who did not know Joseph" could exist as part of an older "J" tradition corpus before the work of the reviser and presumably quite independent of the early Joseph story as well.[28] Yet nothing else in the Jacob tradition could suggest such a comment, and it could hardly be made "out of the blue."

Dietrich's study recognizes the fact that the Joseph story in its present revised form plays an important role in the historiography of the Pentateuch. Its failure, in my view, is that this fact is not understood within the wider context of the historiography of the Yahwist, both within Genesis and in its connections with Exodus. By ignoring the Yahwist, all the questions posed at the end of our examination of Westermann still remain unanswered.

Blum's contribution to the discussion is that he is primarily concerned with the relationship of the Joseph story to the Jacob traditions as he understands their compositional development.[29] As we have seen above, he does not use the source division categories of the documentary hypothesis, so there is no question of a prior J source, but instead a multileveled Jacob tradition. For Blum the Joseph story is an independent literary work[30] into which various pieces have been fitted: Genesis 38; 41:50–52; 46:1–5a; 48; 49; 50:22–26. Although chapter 38 represents an older independent tradition that has been fitted in with some editorial adjustments,[31] the rest are later redactional additions belonging to various levels of composition. Thus 41:50–52 and 48* reflect an independent northern tradition that was added to the Joseph story before the combination with the southern traditions of chapters 38 and 49. Those texts that have a more obvious connection with the larger patriarchal tradition and the exodus (46:1–5a; 50:22–26; Ex. 1:6, 8) are part of the later post-Dtr redaction of the Pentateuch as a whole.[32]

Blum's major departures from Westermann are these: (1) Because the connection between the patriarchal tradition and the exodus is relatively late, there is no need to construct an early Jacob tradition that contains an explanation for how the Israelites arrived in Egypt. (2) The Joseph story was not an addition to a parallel Jacob story but was taken up as a way of expanding the Jacob tradition. These differences overcome a number of the problems with Westermann's presentation, mentioned above. Yet some basic difficulties with Blum's traditio-historical reconstruction remain. First, his views on the development of the Joseph story within the Jacob tradition are acceptable only if his previous reconstruction of the Jacob tradition is accepted. Thus the episode in 48:1–2, 8–22 is regarded as complementing that of chapter 27 and bringing a closure to an early stage of the Jacob tradition's expansion. But we have argued above that Genesis 27 belongs to J and therefore to the final prepriestly composition of the Pentateuch. Second, Blum has not taken seriously the historiographic aspect of the Joseph story within the Pentateuch, as pointed out by Dietrich. Thus, according to Blum's scheme, the historiographic structure of the Pentateuch is an accident of successive redactions and revisions of various blocks of tradition that result in the historical continuum from the patriarchs, through several generations, to the exodus and beyond. This is a legacy of the method of Noth and Rendtorff, and the premise of this entire study is that such an explanation is unacceptable.

My own view of the matter follows basically from the analysis of Redford.[33] However, I do not find his "Genesis editor" very useful. It contains P material primarily, which we can set aside for the purpose of this study, and some texts that I attribute to J, which we will consider below. The Joseph story was a literary composition quite independent originally from the other patriarchal traditions.[34] The tradition about Judah in chapter 38 was another separate tradition of origin. The two were combined by an antiquarian historian, the Yahwist. This combination necessitated the quite conscious introduction of Judah into the Joseph story for two reasons. First, if Judah was not mentioned by name in the Joseph story, then the clear impression would have been given, based on chapter 38 alone, that this tribe did not participate in the exodus. For the Yahwist's national tradition such a view was not tolerable. Second, it was necessary also to give Judah a role of leadership among his brethren to reflect the obvious political reality of the Judean monarchy and Judah's place in the national tradition.[35]

There is no need to assume that such a revision was very extensive. In some instances, as in chapter 37, a doublet to the role of Reuben was created, but in most other cases it is quite likely that Judah's name was merely substituted for that of Reuben. J may have substituted the name of Israel for Jacob in some instances, but this name alternation cannot be used as a means of source division.[36] In addition to these changes, J may have embellished the original story at some points.[37] I do not believe that chapter 39 was a part of his work. It appears much more like the addition of a didactic tale similar to the addition of the man of God from Judah story in 1 Kings 13.[38]

The outline of the pre-Yahwistic Joseph story seems fairly clear up to chapter 45. But the amount of the story in chapters 46–50 is very much disputed. I would conjecture the following ending:

1. Jacob goes to Egypt, where Joseph comes to meet him in an emotional reunion. Pharaoh offers Joseph's family the best of the land of Egypt. They are settled in the "land of Rameses," where Joseph supplies them with food (46:1aα, 5b, 28–30; 47:5–6a, 11–12).[39]

2. As the time of his death approaches, Jacob summons Joseph and has him swear that he will bury him in the land of Canaan, not in Egypt (47:29–31).

3. Jacob dies, is mourned by Joseph and embalmed. He is then taken by Joseph and an entourage of Egyptians and buried in Canaan. Joseph returns and remains with his brothers in Egypt (50:1–7, 14, 22a).

To this story ending the Yahwist has added some embellishments. First, the references to the land of Goshen (45:10; 46:28, 34; 47:1, 4, 6; 50:8) and the justification for settling in this region, in 46:31–47:4, are J's anticipation of the exodus sojourn. This may be the same location as the "land of Rameses" but is perhaps a later name for that region.[40] The story of the enslavement of the Egyptians by Joseph in 47:13–26 may be an etiological midrash inspired by the remarks in 41:53ff. Because J has strong etiological interests, this could well belong to him. It creates a certain ironic contrast to the later enslavement of the Israelites in Egypt in Exodus 1. It also contrasts with the remarks in 50:18ff. The etiology on the place-name, Abel-mizraim in 50:8–11, may also belong to J.

The Yahwist's contribution to the historiography of the Pentateuch, however, is to be seen primarily in the blocks of material that are usually ascribed to the Jacob tradition: 41:50–52; 46:1–5a; 48:1–2, 8–22; (49); 50:22–26. It is to these texts that I will now turn.

The Promises: Gen. 46:1–5a

The themes of this unit: (1) the itinerary and the reference to sacred place, (2) the protection and guidance by the god of the father, (3) the promise of becoming a great nation (in Egypt), and (4) the anticipation of the exodus, are all lacking from the Joseph story up to this point, as is the particular mode of divine revelation by the direct address of the deity. On the other hand, the author skillfully ties his itinerary into what precedes in 46:1a and takes up the item about the wagons sent for transport by Pharaoh (45:21ff.) in the transitional verse in 46:5b. The remark that Joseph's hand shall close Jacob's eyes (46:4) also is a touching allusion to the events of the larger story anticipating Jacob's death.[41]

This unit looks back on the previous patriarchal history, but the connections are not merely "redactional" repetition. They are part of the larger design that we have attributed to the Yahwist. The itinerary is part of a progressive series that follows the pattern of the earlier itinerary notices but in the case of Jacob moves deliberately toward Egypt. The location of Jacob in Hebron (37:14)[42] fits very well as part of this itinerary with 35:1–8, 16–22 and 46:1a. The reference to Beersheba makes a connection with Isaac's previous abode there and his construction of an altar (26:24–25). It is presumably on that altar that Jacob is thought to offer sacrifices to the God of his father, Isaac, who had appeared to him there. This also provides a contrast between the command of the deity to Isaac not to go down to Egypt (26:2) with the encouragement of the deity to do so in this instance.[43]

The divine name, "the God ($h\bar{a}$'$\bar{e}l$), the God of Isaac" combines the two forms of the divine name used in the other Jacob narratives, that is, "the God ($h\bar{a}$'$\bar{e}l$), the God of Bethel" (31:13; cf. 35:1) and "Yahweh, the God of Isaac your father" (28:13; 32:10). This also completes the circle of the divine appearance at the beginning of Jacob's journeys in chapter 28:13, where Yahweh, the God of the fathers, appeared to him at Bethel. In other respects, this text also closely resembles those of Gen. 31:11, 13, 17, in which Jacob takes his leave of Aram-Naharim for Canaan under divine command and guidance.[44] It is scarcely possible to attribute these various texts either to different sources (on the basis of the use of Elohim here in place of Yahweh) or even to different levels in the redaction of the tradition.[45]

The unit in 46:3b–4a also makes a direct connection with the history of the Exodus and therefore with a much larger unity than the patriarchal history alone.[46] It can hardly be separated from the nocturnal vision to Abraham, 15:13–16, in which the sojourn and exodus are predicted. Here it is made quite explicit that the patriarch is to become a great nation *in Egypt.*[47] It is for this reason that Westermann wishes to regard this particular unit as rather late in the formation of the whole.[48] Westermann also points to the rather late usage of the idea of "visions of the night," מראת הלילה, to represent a revelation that is in fact not visual but verbal, as found in Ezekiel (Ezek. 1:1; 8:3; 40:2; 43:3). This usage also occurs in DtrH in 2 Sam. 7:17, in which the divine promise to David through Nathan is described as a vision, חזיון, that comes to him at night, v. 4.

The fact that this text has the same literary horizon of exilic texts that we have already seen in all the other closely related Yahwist promise texts confirms the view that they all belong together to the exilic period.[49] The Yahwist has embedded this thematic promise text within the Joseph story, making reference to the immediate story context ("Joseph's hand shall close your eyes") with the larger ideological concerns. This is the same technique we observed in 26:2–3 and 28:13–15. Furthermore, his prediction of the exodus, like that of Gen. 15:13–16, provides a connection with the following major block of tradition. Like 15:13–16, it is a theodicy of the exodus and is similar to the justification of Jacob's sojourn in Mesopotamia in 28:15. All of them point, in turn, to the exile and suggest a promise of God's divine presence with his people there.

Joseph's Genealogy: Gen. 48:1–2, 8–22; 41:50–52

Genesis 48 has long been regarded as an expansion of the Joseph story. In the previous episode, it tells of Jacob's imminent death and the extraction of an oath by Jacob/Israel from Joseph to be buried in his own country. It would be most natural to interpret 47:31b as a reference to his death and to take chapter 50 as its continuation.[50] The rather vague connection "after these things," which J also uses elsewhere, and the device of having Jacob "revive" and sit up in bed (48:2) is the author's way of incorporating a deathbed blessing into the narrative. The remarks by Jacob in vs. 3–7 can be clearly identified as an expansion by P and so left aside from consideration. It is obvious, however, that P has before him J's narrative of the Jacob story. The remarks in vs. 5ff. are simply a more explicit doublet for the reference to adoption in v. 12.

The remaining J text (48:1–2, 8–22) has been anticipated by an earlier addition to the Joseph story in 41:50–52. This is not just an isolated etiological appendix but part of the larger scheme to account for all the tribes of Israel. The birth notice in 41:50–52 complements the series in 29:31–34; 35:16–18, but it belongs to quite a different form. It closely resembles in style and circumstances the naming of Moses' two sons (Ex. 2:22; 18:3–4). In the case of Joseph, the king of Egypt gives him the wife of the priest of Heliopolis (41:45); she bears him two sons. Moses, in the foreign land of Midian, is given a daughter by the priest of Midian; she bears him two sons. The naming formula is also identical in both cases. This same pattern is found again in DtrH, in the notice about Hadad (1 Kings 11:18–20) in which Hadad takes refuge in Egypt, is befriended by the king of Egypt and given a wife who bears him a son whom he names (but without an etymological etiology). This is a historiographic genre that the Yahwist has borrowed and used in the Joseph story to imitate historical texts.

The scene of the aged patriarch who is blind or near-blind offering a blessing to his offspring on his deathbed is quite similar to, and perhaps modeled on, Isaac's blessing of Jacob and Esau in Genesis 27. The two scenes form an inclusio or frame for the Jacob story as a whole. In both cases, the younger receives the preferred blessing. A number of scholars would like to restrict the blessing in the original account to 48:20.[51] Their reasons are (1) that v. 17 follows v. 14 directly, (2) that Joseph's protest comes too late after the blessing of vs. 15–16, and (3) that the blessing in v. 20 is in the most appropriate location after the remarks of v. 19. But this argument is rather weak because it is much more likely that an expansion would be made to v. 20 than to break up a closely knit unit. It is preferable to interpret Joseph's protest as interrupting the blessing. The remarks of Jacob in v. 19 are more appropriate as an expansion of the blessing in v. 16 than if they were preceded by no blessing at all. It is in this way that the familiar themes of numerous progeny, becoming great peoples or nations and being a means of blessing, are brought out in a colorful way. What is also apparent is that this primary blessing is given to the first son of Rachel, the favorite wife, probably because the tribes of the house of Joseph represent Israel politically more than all the rest of the tribes.

The content of the blessing is significant because it has in view the whole of the patriarchal history of Abraham, Isaac, and Jacob, in particular laying stress on the theme of divine guidance and providence throughout their journeying. The theme of divine accompaniment (*Beistandsformel*) is a major theme in the Jacob story, as we have seen above.[52] This guidance, as symbolized in the "angel" (v. 16), recalls not only the concrete appearances of this figure in the life of Abraham but the particular use of this term in chapter 24 as the expression of divine guidance. It occurs again with this meaning in Ex. 23:20ff.; 32:34; 33:2. The rather distinctive phrase, to be called by the name of the patriarchs in the sense of perpetuating the name and lineage, also recalls the statement in 21:12, "in Isaac shall your descendants be called." That text also goes on to suggest in v. 13 (see also v. 18) that both of Abraham's sons will become nations, but the younger one will be the greater. Such a combination of the same themes in 48:16, 19 is not the fortuitous result of redactional addition but the work of the same author, J.

The statements by Jacob/Israel in 48:21–22 are regarded by a number of scholars as either appendages[53] or redactional additions.[54] But this seems rather arbitrary, particularly for v. 21. On the one hand, it completes the thought of divine guidance and safekeeping reflected in vs. 15–16 and projects this into the future; and on the other, it repeats this theme as expressed in 46:1–4 and clearly belongs to the same source. The language is similar to that of 28:15 and the theme of divine presence in the Jacob story. The reason for treating it as secondary is that it envisages the larger history of the exodus, but by itself that argument becomes entirely circular. The matter of v. 22 is more difficult to decide, partly because the meaning is obscure[55] but also because it does not seem to correspond very well with the story about Shechem in chapter 34 or any suggestion of any other military activity by Jacob alone in the Jacob story. Yet that may be placing too stringent a requirement upon an etiological remark. It may simply be an anecdote alluding to a variant tradition that relates Jacob to Shechem.

The Blessing of Jacob: Genesis 49

The blessing of Jacob in chapter 49 is another addition to the Joseph story, but its attribution to a particular source is difficult. It is not necessary to engage in an extensive study of this text and its parallels in Deuteronomy 33 and Judges 5. The framework in vs. 1a and 28–33 contains language that is particularly appropriate to P. This would mean that after the addition of chapter 48 by J there would be no appropriate transition to the scene in 50:1ff, which presupposes some statement about Jacob's death. Some scholars have noted that the phrase "he drew up his feet into the bed" corresponds to the remark in 48:2 that suggests that J's account of Jacob's death has been taken up into the P statement in 49:33.

Joseph's Farewell: Gen. 50:15–21, 22–26

The scene of Joseph's second reconciliation with his brothers deserves some consideration here. There is a marked difference of opinion as to whether it should be regarded as part of the Joseph story or viewed as a later addition.[56] In my view, the statement is anticlimactic and not original to the Joseph story. It contains some important differences from the earlier scene in chapters 44–45. The appeal for forgiveness is made on the supposed command of their father, which is a rather desperate and thinly veiled ruse,[57] and on an appeal to the "God of your father." This is a common title in the Jacob story (see also 46:3) but never otherwise used in the Joseph story. It clearly points to J as the author. The voluntary submission to Joseph, "We are your servants," is different from the unwitting obeisance to Joseph as the unrecognized Egyptian vizier. This suggests much more directly a political interpretation.[58] But Joseph's reply, "Am I in the place of God?" can be understood only as a disclaimer to the rights of kingship as exercised by a single individual to rule over one's brethren and a rejection of the royal ideology that indeed placed the king as a god over his people.

The most important difference, however, comes with the explanation of divine providence in the event of Jacob's enslavement in Egypt. In 45:5, Joseph tells his brothers: "For God sent me before you to preserve life" (see also v. 7), but in 50:20, Joseph states: "As for you, you meant evil against me; but God meant it for good, to keep many people alive, as they are today." The first statement has in view the story with its crisis of famine: "There are yet five years (of famine)." But in the second, that situation has passed, and now the perspective is the larger destiny of the people of Israel, the "many people . . . as they are today." This has now become a theodicy and justification for the sojourn in Egypt. This leads on to the final scene in 50:22–26.

The unit in 50:22–26 is also closely connected with 48:21 and 46:1–4 in its clear reference to the exodus. In addition, the theme of Joseph's bones being transported back to the homeland is mentioned again in Ex. 13:19 and Josh. 24:32 as a conscious link between major blocks of material. In addition to this, there is the remark in 50:23 about the offspring of Joseph to the third generation. There is also the remark that the sons of Machir were born upon Joseph's knees, which can only mean that they were given tribal status along with Ephraim and Manasseh.[59] This accounts for yet another "tribe" in Israel. The remark must be compared with that of Gen. 30:3, where Rachel's maid bears her children upon Rachel's knees so that they become her own. The text of 50:23 thus belongs closely to this complex of anecdotes in J about the Israelite tribes and is not merely an appendage.[60]

Conclusion

From this examination of the Joseph story we may conclude that this narrative came to the Yahwist as a separate piece of literature that he incorporated into his larger history. He made a number of additions to it that were primarily for the purpose of extending the lineage to include the Joseph tribes and to establish the Israelites in Egypt. The most problematic addition was the tradition about Judah and his offspring in chapter 38. Judah's traditions of origin had no connection with the exodus/conquest tradition, which was Israelite in the more limited sense. It was the Yahwist who effected the integration of Judah into this larger national identity tradition, hence Judah's enhanced role in the Joseph story.

The Yahwist also extends the promises by reaffirmation to Jacob (46:1-4) and then from Jacob to his offspring, particularly to the house of Joseph (48:1-2, 8-22). But of even more importance, it is the Yahwist who used the Joseph story and his additions to it to establish the continuity between the patriarchal traditions and the traditions of the sojourn in Egypt and the exodus. But that is the subject of another volume.

NOTES

1.   G. W. Coats, *From Canaan to Egypt*, CBQ MS 4, 1976; H. Donner, *Die literarische Gestalt der alttestamentlichen Josephsgeschichte*, SHAW.PH 2, 1976; W. Dietrich, *Die Josephserzählung als Novelle und Geschichtsschreibung*, BTS 14, 1989; W. L. Humphreys, *Joseph and His Family: A Literary Study*, 1988; von Rad, *Genesis*; D. B. Redford, *A Study of the Biblical Story of Joseph (Genesis 37–50)*, SVT 20, 1970; W. Rudolph, "Die Josephsgeschichte," in P. Volz and W. Rudolph, *Der Elohist als Erzähler—ein Irrweg*

der Pentateuchkritik?, BZAW 63 (1933), pp. 143–183; L. Ruppert, *Die Josephserzählung der Genesis*, SANT 11, 1965; L. Schmidt, *Literarische Studien zur Josephsgeschichte*, BZAW 167 (1986), pp. 120–297, 307–310; H. C. Schmitt, *Die nichtpriesterliche Josephsgeschichte*, BZAW 154, 1980; H. Seebass, *Geschichtliche Zeit und theonome Tradition in der Joseph–Erzählung*, 1978; Westermann, *Genesis 37–50;* R. N. Whybray, "The Joseph Story and Pentateuchal Criticism," *VT* 18 (1968), 522–528. For additional bibliography, see Westermann's commentary.

2. Wellhausen, *Die Composition*, p. 52.

3. See Westermann, *Genesis 37–50*, p. 18.

4. See esp. Redford's influential study (n. 1 above); see also Dietrich. Schmitt (*Die nichtpriesterliche Josephsgeschichte*) advocates the view that the Judah version was the earliest and the Reuben revision much later. It is hard to follow him in this.

5. Redford, *The Biblical Story of Joseph*, pp. 147–148, makes it a later addition. He is followed by Humphreys, *Joseph*, pp. 201–204; and Dietrich, *Die Josephserzählung*, pp. 29–30. This position is disputed by Coats, *From Canaan to Egypt*, pp. 28–32; and Westermann, *Genesis 37–50*, p. 60.

6. See the works of Ruppert, Seebass, Schmidt, and Schmitt in n. 1 above.

7. See Noth, *A History of Pentateuchal Traditions*, pp. 208–213.

8. See Westermann, *Genesis 37–50*, p. 18.

9. In addition to the works in n. 1 above, see also Blum, *Die Komposition*, pp. 229–263.

10. Westermann, *Genesis 37–50*, pp. 22–27.

11. Ibid., p. 23.

12. We follow the arguments in order as set out in ibid., pp. 22ff.

13. Cf. Blum, *Die Komposition*, pp. 244–245, who sees chapter 38 as an addition to the Joseph story in which Gen. 37:32–33 has been modified to resemble 38:25–26.

14. It is true that Westermann dates the Joseph story to the time of David and Solomon, but that hardly lessens the problem because for him the Joseph story stands outside of the work of J (*Genesis 37–50*, p. 28). This would virtually exclude Judah from J's national tradition, also dated by Westermann to the Davidic/Solomonic period!

15. Ibid., p. 23.

16. Ibid., p. 28.

17. See Redford, *The Biblical Story of Joseph*, pp. 247f.; Humphreys, *Joseph*, p. 195; and Dietrich, *Die Josephserzählung*, p. 45.

18. Westermann, *Genesis 37–50*, pp. 211–214.

19. Ibid., pp. 23f.

20. Ibid., p. 204.

21. Ibid., p. 208.

22. See n. 1 above. Dietrich's literary analysis closely resembles the basic features of Redford's study.

23. Dietrich, *Die Josephserzählung*, pp. 60–66, 76–77.

24. Redford, *The Biblical Story of Joseph*, pp. 182–183, does not attribute chapter 39 to the Judah-expansion in his chart but makes it a later addition. However, he does allow for the possibility.

25. Dietrich, *Die Josephserzählung,* pp. 53–55.
26. Redford, *The Biblical Story of Joseph,* p. 179.
27. Dietrich, *Die Josephserzählung,* pp. 44, 68.
28. Ibid., p. 47.
29. Blum, *Die Komposition,* pp. 229–257.
30. It consists of Genesis 37*; 39–45; 46:5b, 28–33; 47*; 50:1–11, 14–21.
31. Blum, *Die Komposition,* pp. 244–245.
32. Ibid., pp. 259, 398.
33. See the summary of Redford's source analysis in *The Biblical Story of Joseph,* pp. 182–186.
34. The prominence of Joseph may have nothing to do with an origin in the Northern Kingdom of Israel. The choice may have to do with the fact of Joseph and Benjamin as traditionally the youngest sons. There is no reason to see in the story some sociopolitical meaning in the domination of Joseph over his brothers.
35. For J, national and tribal identity is important in a way that it is not for the older Joseph story.
36. That has been a fundamental mistake in source division, based on the analogy of the use of the Elohim/Yahweh distinction. But both J and P alternate in their use of Israel/Jacob outside of the Joseph story.
37. Redford suggests a number of embellishments and glosses by the "Judah-expansion" = J. There is no need to debate each one here.
38. See A. Rofé, "Classes in the Prophetic Stories: Didactic Legenda and Parable," SVT 26 (1974), pp. 153–164.
39. This is the point at which Redford ends the original Joseph story.
40. The "land of Rameses" is the region in the neighborhood of the modern villages of Qantir and Faqus in the northeastern Delta, a very fertile agricultural area. J does not use this term in Exodus. He refers there to the *city* of Rameses, Ex. 1:11. See Dietrich, *Die Josephserzählung,* pp. 47–48.
41. So Westermann, *Genesis 37–50,* pp. 156–157.
42. This reference to Hebron speaks against any northern connection for the Joseph story. The coupling of Hebron with Shechem reflects the claim of the tribes to the whole land.
43. Berge, *Die Zeit des Jahwisten,* p. 207, also points to the same form of *Heilsorakel* used with the *Beistandsformel* as in 26:24 but denies that there is any connection between Genesis 26 and this text!
44. See Blum, *Die Komposition,* pp. 246–248.
45. Contra Blum. See Rendtorff, *Das überlieferungsgeschichtliche Problem des Pentateuch,* p. 111.
46. See Westermann, *Genesis 37–50,* p. 156. Berge, *Die Zeit des Jahwisten,* p. 207, follows Seebass and de Pury in seeing an old tradition in this text, but nothing argues in favor of such a suggestion.
47. This means that efforts to restrict the notion of "great nation" to the Davidic-Solomonic era are not supported by this text. See above, p. 253. Berge overlooks this text entirely in his discussion of *gôy gādôl.*
48. Westermann, *Genesis 37–50,* p. 155. So also Blum, *Die Komposition,* pp. 249, 298.

49.   Blum, *Die Komposition*, pp. 297–301, includes 12:1–3; 26:2–3; 31:13; and 46:3–4 as belonging to the same late redactional level. I would include the other promise texts discussed above as well.

50.   There is a similarity in the oath form used in 47:29 and that of 24:2f., 9, which might suggest that they are the work of the same author. In this case, however, I think that chapter 24 (J) is modeled on the Joseph story in 47:29ff.

51.   See Westermann, *Genesis 37–50*, pp. 188–191.

52.   See above, pp. 302–306. Berge's discussion of the *Beistandsformel* in the patriarchal texts, in *Die Zeit des Jahwisten*, pp. 195–227, gives no consideration to this text.

53.   Westermann, *Genesis 37–50*, p. 182; see also Skinner, *Genesis*, p. 507.

54.   Blum, *Die Komposition*, pp. 254, 257.

55.   See the discussion with literature in Westermann, *Genesis 37–50*, pp. 192–193.

56.   Redford, *The Biblical Story of Joseph*, pp. 163–164, 179, ascribes it to the "Judah"-expansion, whereas the first reconciliation scene belonged to the original story. Dietrich, *Die Josephserzählung*, p. 68, regards both scenes as part of the reviser's work. Westermann, *Genesis 37–50*, p. 204, assigns 50:15–21 to the redactor who combined the Joseph and Jacob stories. Blum, *Die Komposition*, p. 255, regards it as part of the original Joseph story.

57.   Compare the similar situation in the palace intrigue in 1 Kings 1:11ff. where Nathan the prophet concocts a promise about Solomon in order to save his own skin and that of Bathsheba.

58.   Cf. Dietrich, *Die Josephserzählung*, pp. 67–78, for his political interpretation.

59.   See Westermann, *Genesis 37–50*, p. 208.

60.   So Westermann, ibid., p. 208.

SUMMARY AND CONCLUSION

This study has argued that the Yahwist is an ancient historian. By Yahwist is meant the pre-Priestly corpus of the Pentateuch as a whole. In my earlier treatment of the Abraham tradition I seriously questioned the existence of a parallel E document, and in the present work I find no grounds for such a source in the Jacob traditions. What have sometimes been identified as E fragments are older sources used by the historian J. This historian is also a "redactor" of materials from a variety of works in the scribal tradition. The imposition of additional redactional layers, Dtr or otherwise, prior to the Priestly Writer is also unwarranted.

The Yahwist's history was an attempt to present an account of Israel's origins as a "vulgate" tradition[1] in a manner similar to other comparable works of ancient historiography, both in the classical world of Greece and Rome and the primeval traditions of Mesopotamia. Although the presence of etiological myths and legends may argue against its usefulness for modern historiography, that fact does not vitiate its place within the ancient genres of antiquarian "research" (*historia*). What seems abundantly clear from comparisons with the historiography of antiquity is that for ancient histories nothing in Genesis is particularly unusual or inappropriate.

There was a fundamental lack in earlier treatments of Genesis that this study seeks to address. Form-critical analysis of Genesis meant, in the first instance, following Gunkel, the identification of the form and character of the small units. But only very general assumptions were made about how these smaller units were collected and combined into a larger whole without ever adequately addressing the form-critical nature of the larger works. Von Rad's protest against this neglect and his search for the form of the Yahwist did not find an adequate solution, so matters remained as they were.[2] Most recently, concern for the "final form" has led to attempts to provide a diagrammatic scheme in which there is virtually no relationship between small units and the "final form." In such discussions, the "final form" belongs to no particular genre, no intellectual or traditio-historical *Sitz im Leben,* that could be clarified by comparative study and that would have a bearing upon the interpretation of the text.[3] Even when scholars spoke of authors or compositional redactions, the question of genre was scarcely given any further clarity. These were regarded as self-evident categories.

However, identifying the Yahwist as historian raises several important form-critical questions that cannot be ignored. The small units of myth and legend represent the historian's sources, and they constitute his attempt to preserve tradition. Most of the collecting and combining of independent units of tradition in Genesis is the work of the Yahwist. But his work is much more than a mere collection, *Sammlung,* the fixation in writing of a traditio-historical process. The structural arrangement of his material, the genealogical chronology, and the attempt at thematic unity go beyond the preservation of ancient lore. The inherited traditions become sources for the creation of the more comprehensive vulgate tradition. But the conception of corporate identity expressed by the whole work can impose a powerful influence on the traditions that are taken up into it. In this process, some material may be included with little change, some may be modified a little, and some may be radically transformed. Where there are gaps in the story from insufficient material, there may be wholesale invention.

Making these assumptions about the characteristics of the J source does not impose upon it our modern notions about historians and their intellectual activity. The Yahwist is an ancient historian of a particular type, so his work may be fruitfully compared with works of antiquity comparable in form and subject. The comparative studies of Greek and Mesopotamian traditions have laid out the evidence for judging J to be an antiquarian historian. The classical historians who dealt with national origins made use of much myth and legend as sources within genealogical chronologies similar to that of Genesis. They became the primary custodians for the articulation and preservation of the vulgate tradition of nations and states. That is why it seems to me that we cannot understand the compositional history of Genesis until we understand the important intellectual and literary activity of ancient historiography in all its diversity.

For the primeval history of Genesis 2–11, I have argued that the Yahwist had access to both eastern and western antiquarian traditions. Their integration with each other posed some problems not hitherto recognized. Thus the attempt by some to make the flood story the end of the primeval history places one-sided emphasis on the Mesopotamian component. The union of mortals with the "sons of the gods" and the subsequent Table of Nations (= the genealogy of heroes and ancestors) comprise the western tradition into which the flood has been fitted by J. This combination of diverse traditions reflects the Yahwist's historiographic skills. It is also true to say that the story of Creation and Fall represents the greatest degree of creativity and flexibility by the Yahwist within the primeval history and therefore also the highest level of ideological and thematic concern. But there is no unit that has not received some modification to the traditional sources that the Yahwist has taken up.

The primary modification of the traditions throughout the primeval history has been in terms of the theological theme of sin and judgment ("crime and punishment"). That which serves as the unifying factor in the national history of Israel, that is, the people's sin and the divine judgment, is extended to the universal domain of God's rule in the Yahwist's history.[4] It is no longer the particular ethic of a national code reflected in Deuteronomy but a universal morality that is in view, and this constantly informs the Yahwist's perspective throughout Genesis. Yahweh is both the creator of all humanity but also its judge. If the DtrH corresponds to the nationalistic, prophetic view of Israel's history up to the exile, then the Yahwist is more akin to the broader universalistic concerns of Second Isaiah.

The primeval traditions have also been modified to fit a genealogical framework. The genealogical chronology is so basic to early Greek historiography, especially the *Genealogies,* that its comparable function of framing units of tradition in J is best explained in the same way. Because this device encompasses not only Genesis 2–11 but also the whole of Genesis in a complex segmented structure, there is good reason to believe that the same literary work extends throughout Genesis. By contrast, there is no such genealogical structure in DtrH. For the monarchy, DtrH uses the king lists as a framework, and for the period of the Judges, a generational succession of unrelated leaders. It is, however, precisely with this type of primeval and ancestral history that such a form of genealogical chronology is so important. Nothing in this genre of historiography would suggest any break between the primeval age and the time of the nation's eponymous ancestors.

This *archaiologia* or "prologue" has, as its purpose, to account for the origins of Israel and its neighbors. The idea that an ancestor or founding hero migrates from one region and civilization to a new land to begin a nation there is very basic to this type of origin tradition, as we have seen. The Yahwist's sources contained such stories, and some, such as that of Judah in Genesis 38, are easily recognized as distinct legends. But they have been brought together into a common origin tradition and integrated by means of the divine promises of land and nationhood. The promise of land to the fathers was originally made to the generation of the Egyptian sojourn and exodus as an anticipation of their deliverance and the conquest of Canaan. It was conditioned by the Horeb covenant. As I have argued above, it was the Yahwist's innovation to transfer this promise theme to the patriarchs and thus make the patriarchal origins the "prologue" of the exodus/conquest tradition and transform the national tradition's sense of identity.

The multiple promises of land and nationhood work as an effective means of integrating the traditions of Abraham and Jacob. Isaac is made the link between the two, and his story is invented as a copy of the life of Abraham. The genealogical sequence of Abraham, Isaac, and Jacob already existed in the tradition, but this was combined with the promises to transform the God of the fathers into the God of Abraham, Isaac, and Jacob. As I have tried to show, so pervasive is this complex historiographic framework of promises and genealogy that once it is removed along with all the compositional pieces that are integral to it, there is no extensive compositional stratum left.

Because the evidence points convincingly to a post-Dtr period for the development of the complex promise theme in Genesis, there is no need to conjecture a series of compositional stages, as Blum has done.[5] The Yahwist compiled his work in the full knowledge of the national tradition of DtrH. He wrote his history as a suitable prologue to DtrH, including for the first time the traditions of the patriarchs.[6] He also provided for the national tradition a broader universal context.

The Yahwist's history was a product of the exilic period. The notion that a period of very rudimentary literacy, such as must have been the case in the Solomonic age, could have produced an extensive and complex piece of historiography is hardly tenable. By contrast, the exilic period was a time when Judean intellectual traditions were open to strong foreign influence, and this alone accounts for the Babylonian materials reflected in the primeval history. The challenge of the larger world of the diaspora is evident throughout the work. It called for a transformation from a national religion of the land of Israel to a world religion in which the chosen people and the Promised Land continued to have a destiny beyond the crisis of the state's demise.[7]

Although the work is didactic and theological, it is intended as a history and should not be read as allegory. It is true that some texts reflect the special concern of the exilic age, such as Jacob's flight to Mesopotamia with the promise of divine guidance and protection there and the theme of his return. But such instances of direct comparison are rather limited and not unusual in historical works of antiquity. What is more important for the author is the principle that origin discloses character and destiny.[8] The nature of a hero's or ancestor's birth reveals his future greatness. It is the historian's task to render an account of the traditions about the nation's origins, but to do so in a way that will also reveal its special nature and destiny. Second Isaiah makes abundantly clear that this is precisely the impact that this presentation had upon the exilic community in Babylon.

I have called the Yahwist's work in Genesis a "prologue to history." In ancient historiography, the "prologue" or *archaiologia* set forth the ancient background for the historical work, and in doing so it often laid down the principles by which the history was to be understood. By his presentation of the origins of

humanity and that of the people's ancestry, the Y
a radical revision and reinterpretation of the na

NOTES

1. I use the term *vulgate* rather than *canonical* because the la
entirely different activity, that of recognition by a much later gr
antiquity and authority. On the use of *vulgate,* see above pp. 34–38.
2. Von Rad's treatment of the Yahwist led to interest in J as theologian more
than historian, which ultimately resulted in Rendtorff's protest on form-critical
and traditio-historical grounds. See Rendtorff, "Der 'Jahwist' als Theologe?"
3. So Coats, *Genesis.*
4. Compare this theme in Herodotus's *Histories* and the discussion of it in Van
Seters, *In Search of History,* pp. 31–35.
5. In Blum, *Die Komposition.*
6. See also Rose, *Deuteronomist und Jahwist.*
7. See H. H. Schmid, "Vers un théologie du Pentateuque," in *Le Pentateuque en
question,* ed. A. de Pury (1989), pp. 374–379.
8. Compare the prophetic use of history.

BIBLIOGRAPHY

Ackroyd, P. R. "Hosea and Jacob." *VT* 13 (1963), 245–257.

Albright, W. F. "The Babylonian Matter in the Predeuteronomic Primeval History (JE) in Genesis 1–11." *JBL* 58 (1939), 87–103.

Alonso-Schökel, L. "Sapiential and Covenant Themes in Genesis 2–3." *Theological Digest* 13 (1965), 3–10.

Alster, B. "The Paradigmatic Character of Mesopotamian Heroes." *RA* 68 (1974), 49–60.

Alt, A. *Der Gott der Väter* (1929) = *Kleine Schriften zur Geschichte des Volkes Israel.* Vol. 1, pp. 1–78. Munich, 1953.

Aly, W. *Volksmärchen, Sage und Novelle bei Herodot und seinen Zeitgenossen: Eine Untersuchung über die volkstümlichen Elemente der altgriechischen Prosaerzählung.* Göttingen, 1921.

Anbar, M. "Genesis 15: A Conflation of Two Deuteronomic Narratives." *JBL* 101 (1982), 39–55.

Anderson, B. W. "From Analysis to Synthesis: The Interpretation of Genesis 1–11." *JBL* 97 (1978), 28–39.

Attridge, H. W., and R. A. Oden. *Philo of Byblos: The Phoenician History.* CBQ MS 9. Washington, D.C., 1981.

Balentine, S. "The Prophet as Intercessor: A Reassessment." *JBL* 103 (1984), 161–173.

Bartelmus, R. *Heroentum in Israel und seine Umwelt.* ATANT 65. Zurich, 1979.

Baumgarten, A. I. *The Phoenician History of Philo of Byblos: A Commentary.* Leiden, 1981.

Begrich, J. "Die Paradieserzählung. Eine literargeschichtliche Studie." *ZAW* 50 (1932), 93–116.

Berge, K. *Die Zeit des Jahwisten, Ein Beitrag zur Datierung jahwistischer Vätertexte.* BZAW 186. Berlin and New York, 1990.

Bernhardt, K.-H. "Zur Bedeutung der Schöpfungsvorstellung für die Religion Israels im vorexilischer Zeit." *TLZ* 85 (1960), 821–824.

Bickerman, E. "Origines Gentium." *Classical Philology* 47 (1952), 65–81.

Biddle, M. E. *A Redaction History of Jeremiah 2:1–4:2.* ATANT 77. Zurich, 1990.

Blum, E. *Die Komposition der Vätergeschichte.* WMANT 57. Neukirchen-Vluyn, 1984.

———. *Studien zur Komposition des Pentateuch.* BZAW 189. Berlin and New York, 1990.

Blundell, S. *The Origins of Civilization in Greek and Roman Thought.* London, 1986.

Böhl, F. de Liagre, and H. A. Brongers. "Weltschöpfungsgedanken in Alt-Israel." *Persica* 7 (1975/78), 69–136.

Bonner, S. "The Importance of a Diachronic Approach: The Case of Genesis-Kings." *CBQ* 51 (1989), 195–208.

Bost, H. "La tour de Babel. Genèse 11,1–9." In *La ville dans le Proche-Orient ancien.* Les Cahiers du CEPOA 1. Edited by A. de Pury, pp. 231–237. Leuven, 1983.

Breebaart, A. B. "Weltgeschichte als Thema der antiken Geschichts-schreibung." *Acta Historica Nederlandica* 1 (1966), 1–19.

Brekelmans, C. H. W. "Die sogenannten deuteronomistischen Elemente in Gen.–Num. Ein Beitrag zur Vorgeschichte des Deuteronomiums." SVT 15, pp. 90–96. Leiden, 1966.

Brueggemann, W. "From Dust to Kingship." *ZAW* 84 (1972), 1–18.

Budde, K. *Die biblische Paradiesgeschichte.* BZAW 60. Giessen, 1932.

Burkert, W. *Structure and History in Greek Mythology and Ritual.* Berkeley, 1979.

Burstein, S. M. *The Babyloniaca of Berossus.* SANE 1/5. Malibu, 1978.

Cagni, L. *The Poem of Erra.* SANE 1/3. Malibu, 1977.

Cassuto, U. *A Commentary on the Book of Genesis.* Part 1: *From Adam to Noah (Genesis I–VI,8).* Part 2: *From Noah to Abraham (Genesis VI,9–IX,32).* Jerusalem, 1961–64.

Childs, B. S. *Myth and Reality in the Old Testament.* SBT 1/27. London, 1960.

———. "The Etiological Tale Re-examined." *VT* 24 (1974), 387–397.

Clark, W. M. "The Animal Series in Primeval History." *VT* 18 (1968), 433–449.

——. "A Legal Background to the Yahwist's Use of 'Good and Evil' in Genesis 2–3." *JBL* 88 (1969), 266–278.

——. "The Flood and the Structure of the Pre-patriarchal History." *ZAW* 83 (1971), 184–211.

Clifford, R. J. "Cosmogonies in the Ugaritic Texts and in the Bible." *Orientalia* 53 (1984), 183–201.

Clines, D. J. A. "The Tree of Knowledge and the Law of Yahweh." *VT* 24 (1974), 8–14.

——. *The Theme of the Pentateuch.* JSOT SS 10. Sheffield, 1978.

Coats, G. W. "The God of Death: Power and Obedience in the Primeval History." *Int* 29 (1975), 227–239.

——. *From Canaan to Egypt.* CBQ MS 4. Washington, D.C., 1976.

——. *Genesis with an Introduction to Narrative Literature.* FOTL 1. Grand Rapids, 1983.

Coote, R. B. "Hosea XII." *VT* 21 (1971), 389–402.

Cross, F. M. *Canaanite Myth and Hebrew Epic: Essays in the History of the Religion of Israel.* Cambridge, Mass., 1973.

——. "The Epic Traditions of Early Israel: Epic Narrative and the Reconstruction of Early Israelite Institutions." In *The Poet and the Historian.* HSS 26. Edited by R. E. Friedman, pp. 13–39. Chico, Calif., 1983.

Crüsemann, F. "Die Eigenständigkeit der Urgeschichte. Ein Beitrag zur Diskussion um den 'Jahwisten.'" In *Die Botschaft und die Boten, Festschrift für H. W. Wolff.* Edited by J. Jeremias and L. Perlitt, pp. 11–29. Neukirchen-Vluyn, 1981.

Culley, R. C. *Studies in the Structure of Hebrew Narrative.* Philadelphia, 1976.

Dalley, S. *Myths from Mesopotamia.* Oxford, 1989.

Davies, G. I. "The Wilderness Itineraries: A Comparative Study." *Tyndale Bulletin* 25 (1974), 46–81.

——. *The Way of the Wilderness: A Geographical Study of the Wilderness Itineraries in the Old Testament.* Cambridge, 1979.

——. "The Wilderness Itineraries and the Composition of the Pentateuch." *VT* 33 (1983), 1–13.

Diedrich, F., *Die Ausspielungen auf die Jacob-Tradition in Hosea 12,1–13,3.* FzB 27. Würzburg, 1977.

Diepold, P. *Israels Land.* BWANT 95. Stuttgart, 1972.

Dietrich, W. "'Wo ist Dein Bruder?' Zu Tradition und Intention von Genesis 4." In *Beiträge zur Alttestamentlichen Theologie, Festschrift für W. Zimmerli.* Edited by H. Donner et al., pp. 94–111. Göttingen, 1977.

———. *Die Josephserzählung als Novelle und Geschichtsschreibung.* BTS 14. Neukirchen-Vluyn, 1989.

Dijk, J. van. "Le motif cosmique dans la pensée sumérienne." *Ac Or* 28 (1964/65), 1–59.

———. "Existe-t-il un 'poème de la création' sumérien?" *Kramer Anniversary Volume.* AOAT 25, pp. 125–133. Neukirchen-Vluyn, 1976.

———. *LUGAL UD ME-LAM-bi NIR-GAL. Le récit épique et didactique des travaux de Ninurta, du déluge et de la nouvelle-création.* Bd. 1 and 2. Leiden, 1983.

Dodds, E. R. *The Ancient Concept of Progress and Other Essays on Greek Literature and Belief.* Oxford, 1973.

Donner, H. *Die literarische Gestalt der alttestamentlichen Josephsgeschichte.* SHAW.PH 2. Heidelberg, 1976.

Drews, R. *The Greek Accounts of Eastern History.* Washington, D.C., 1973.

Ebach, J. *Weltentstehung und Kulturentwicklung bei Philo von Byblos.* BWANT 108. Stuttgart, 1979.

Eisenstadt, S. N. "Intellectuals and Tradition." *Daedalus* (1972), 1–20.

Eissfeldt, O. *The Old Testament: An Introduction.* New York, 1965.

Ellis, P. F. *The Yahwist.* Notre Dame, Ind., 1960.

Emerton, J. A. "The Origin of the Promises to the Patriarchs in the Older Sources of the Book of Genesis." *VT* 32 (1982), 14–32.

———. "The Priestly Writer in Genesis." *JTS* 39 (1988), 381–400.

Evelyn-White, H. G. *Hesiod: The Homeric Hymns and Homerica.* LCL. Cambridge, Mass., 1936.

Finkelstein, J. J. "The Antediluvian Kings." *JCS* 17 (1963), 39–51.

———. "The Genealogy of the Hammurapi Dynasty." *JCS* 20 (1966), 95–118.

Finley, M. I. "Myth, Memory and History." In *The Use and Abuse of History,* pp. 11–33. New York, 1971.

———. *Ancient History: Evidence and Models.* New York, 1986.

Fisher, E. "Gilgamesh and Genesis: The Flood Story in Context." *CBQ* 32 (1970), 392–403.

Fohrer, G. *Introduction to the Old Testament.* Nashville, 1968.

Fornara, C. W. *The Nature of History in Ancient Greece and Rome.* Berkeley, 1983.

Frankfort, H. *Kingship and the Gods.* Chicago, 1948.

Frazer, J. G. *Apollodoros. The Library.* 2 vols. LCL. Cambridge, Mass., and London, 1921.

Fretheim, T. E. *Creation, Fall, and Flood: Studies in Genesis 1–11.* Minneapolis, 1969.

Fritz, K. von. "Das Hesiodische in den Werken Hesiods." *Fondation Hardt pour l'étude de l'antiquité classique* 7 (1962), 3–47.

———. *Die griechische Geschichtsschreibung.* Vol. 1: *Von den Anfängen bis Thukydides. Text* and *Anmerkungen.* Berlin, 1967.

———. "Pandora, Prometheus und der Mythos von den Weltaltern." In *Schriften zur griechischen und römischen Verfassungsgeschichte und Verfassungstheorie,* pp. 24–59. Berlin, 1976.

Fritz, V. "'Solange die Erde steht' — vom Sinn der jahwistischen Fluterzählung in Gen 6–8." *ZAW* 94 (1982), 599–614.

Frymer-Kensky, T. "The Atrahasis Epic and Its Significance for Our Understanding of Genesis 1–9." *BA* 40 (1977), 147–155.

Fuss, W. *Die sogenannte Paradieserzählung. Aufbau, Herkunft und Theologische Bedeutung.* Gütersloh, 1968.

Galling, K. *Die Erwählungstraditionen Israels.* BZAW 48. Giessen, 1928.

Gardiner, A. H. *The Royal Canon of Turin.* Oxford, 1959.

Geller, M. J., "More Graeco-Babylonica." *ZA* 73 (1983), 114–20.

Gentile, B., and G. Cerri, "Written and Oral Communication in Greek Historiographical Thought." in *Communication Arts in the Ancient World.* Edited by E. A. Havelock and J. P. Hershbell, pp. 137–155. New York, 1978.

Gertner, M. "The Masorah and the Levites. (Appendix: An Attempt at an Interpretation of Hosea XII)." *VT* 10 (1960), 272–284.

Geus, C. H. J. de. *The Tribes of Israel: An Investigation into Some of the Presuppositions of Martin Noth's Amphictyony Hypothesis.* Assen and Amsterdam, 1976.

Gigon, O. *Der Ursprung der griechischen Philosophie von Hesiod bis Parmenides.* Basel, 1945.

Good, E. M. "Hosea and the Jacob Tradition." *VT* 16 (1966), 137–151.

Goody, J. *The Logic of Writing and the Organization of Society.* Cambridge, 1986.

——. *The Interface Between the Written and the Oral*. Cambridge, 1987.

Goody, J., and I. Watt, eds. *Literacy in Traditional Societies*. Cambridge, 1968.

Grayson, A. K. *Assyrian and Babylonian Chronicles*. Locust Valley, N.Y., 1975.

Groningen, B. A. van. *In the Grip of the Past*. Leiden, 1953.

Gunkel, H. *Genesis, übersetzt und erklärt*. HKAT I/1. Göttingen, 1901; 3rd ed., 1910. See the introduction in English translation, *The Legends of Genesis*. Chicago, 1901; repr., New York, 1964.

Guthrie, W. K. C. *In the Beginning: Some Greek Views on the Origins of Life and the Early State of Man*. London, 1957.

Ha, J. *Genesis 15*. BZAW 181. Berlin and New York, 1989.

Haag, E. *Der Mensch am Anfang. Die alttestamentliche Paradiesvorstellung nach Genesis 2–3*. Trier, 1970.

Haag, H. "Die Komposition der Sündenfallerzählung." *Tübinger Theol. Quartalschrift* 146 (1966), 1–7.

Habel, N. C. "'Yahweh, Maker of Heaven and Earth': A Study in Tradition Criticism." *JBL* 91 (1972), 321–337.

Hallo, W. W. "Beginning and End of the Sumerian King List in the Nippur Recension." *JCS* 17 (1963), 52–57.

——. "Antediluvian Cities." *JCS* 23 (1970), 57–67.

Halpern, B. *The First Historians: The Hebrew Bible and History*. San Francisco, 1988.

Hanson, P. D. "Rebellion in Heaven, Azazel, and Euhemeristic Heroes in 1 Enoch 6–11." *JBL* 96 (1977), 195–233.

Haran, M. "Book Scrolls in Israel in Pre-Exilic Times." *JJS* 32 (1982), 161–173.

——. "On the Diffusion of Literacy and Schools in Ancient Israel." SVT 40, pp. 81–95. Leiden, 1988.

Harris, W. V. *Ancient Literacy*. Cambridge, Mass., 1989.

Hartog, F. "Écriture, généalogies, archives, histoire en Grèce ancienne." In *Histoire et conscience historique dans les civilizations du Proche-Orient ancien*. Les Cahiers du CEPOA 5. Edited by A. de Pury, pp. 121–132. Leuven, 1989.

Heidel, A. *The Gilgamesh Epic and Old Testament Parallels*. 2nd ed. Chicago, 1949.

——. *The Babylonian Genesis*. 2nd ed. Chicago, 1951.

Helck, H. W. *Untersuchungen zu Manetho und den ägyptischen Königs-listen.* Berlin, 1956.

Hendel, R. S. *The Epic of the Patriarch: The Jacob Cycle and the Narrative Traditions of Canaan and Israel.* HSM 42. Atlanta, 1987.

———. "Of Demigods and Deluge: Toward an Interpretation of Genesis 6:1–4." *JBL* 106 (1987), 13–26.

Herrmann, J. "Zu Genesis 9,18–27." *ZAW* 30 (1910), 127–131.

Hoftijzer, J. *Die Verheissungen an die drei Erzväter.* Leiden, 1956.

Hölscher, G. *Geschichtsschreibung in Israel: Untersuchung zum Jahwisten und Elohisten.* Rev. ed. Lund, 1952.

Hornung, E. *Geschichte als Fest. Zwei Vorträge zum Geschichtsbild der frühen Menschheit.* Darmstadt, 1966.

Humphreys, W. L. *Joseph and His Family: A Literary Study.* Columbia, S.C., 1988.

Hutter, M. "Adam als Gärtner und König (Gen 2,8.15)." *BZ* 30 (1986), 258–262.

Jacobsen, T. *The Sumerian King List.* Chicago, 1939.

———. *The Treasures of Darkness: A History of Mesopotamian Religion.* New Haven, 1976.

———. "The Eridu Genesis." *JBL* 100 (1981), 513–529.

———. *The Harab Myth.* SANE 2. Malibu, 1984.

———. *The Harps That Once . . . : Sumerian Poetry in Translation.* New Haven, 1987.

Jacoby, F. *Die Fragmente der griechischen Historiker.* Berlin, 1923–58.

———. "The First Athenian Prose Writer." *Mnemosyne* 3rd series, vol. 13 (1947), 13–64. Also in *Abhandlungen zur griechischen Geschichtsschreibung von Felix Jacoby,* pp. 100–143. Leiden, 1956.

———. *Atthis: The Local Chronicles of Ancient Athens.* Oxford, 1949.

———. *Griechische Historiker.* Stuttgart, 1956.

Jansen, P. "Babylonischer Turm." *RLA* I, 384–386.

Jaros, K. "Bildmotive in der Paradieserzählung: Gedanken zur Botschaft von Genesis 2–3." *BLit* 50 (1978), 5–11.

———. "Die Motive der Heiligen Bäume und der Schlange in Genesis 2–3." *ZAW* 92 (1980), 204–215.

Jeremias, C. "Die Erzväter in der Verkündigen der Propheten." In *Beiträge zur Alttestamentlichen Theologie, Festschrift für W. Zimmerli.* Edited by H. Donner et al., pp. 206–222. Göttingen, 1977.

Joines, K. R. "The Serpent in Genesis 3." *ZAW* 87 (1975), 1–11.

Junge, F. "Zur Frühdatierung des sog. 'Denkmals memphitischer Theologie.'" *MDIK* 29 (1973), 195–204.

Kaiser, O. "Traditionsgeschichtliche Untersuchung von Genesis 15." *ZAW* 70 (1958), 107–27.

Kevers, P. "Étude littéraire de Genèse XXXIV." *RB* 87 (1980), 38–86.

Kienast, B. "Die Weisheit des Adapa von Eridu." In *Symbolae Biblicae et Mesopotamicae Fr. M. Th. de Liagre Böhl Dedicatae*. Edited by M. A. Beek, et al., pp. 234–239, Leiden, 1973.

Kilian, R. *Isaaks Opferung. Zur Überlieferungsgeschichte von Genesis 22.* SBS 44. Stuttgart, 1970.

Kilmer, A. D. "The Mesopotamian Concept of Overpopulation and Its Solution as Reflected in the Mythology." *Orientalia* 41 (1972), 160–177.

Kirk, G. S. "The Structure and Aim of the Theogony." *Fondation Hardt pour l'étude de l'antiquité classique* 7 (1962), 63–95.

——. *Myth: Its Meaning and Function in Ancient and Other Cultures.* London and Berkeley, 1970.

——. *The Nature of Greek Myths.* Woodstock, N.Y., 1975.

Kirkpatrick, P. G. *The Old Testament and Folklore Study.* JSOT SS 62, 1988.

Kleingunther, A. *Protos Heuretes.* In Supplement to *Philologus* 26, no. 1 (1933), 1–155.

Klengel-Brandt, E. *Der Turm von Babylon. Legende und Geschichte eines Bauwerks.* Leipzig, 1982.

Klotchkoff, I. S. "The Late Babylonian List of Scholars." In *Gesellschaft und Kultur im alten Vorderasien.* Edited by H. Klengel, pp. 149–154. Berlin, 1982.

Koch, K. "Zur Geschichte der Erwählungsvorstellung in Israel." *ZAW* 67 (1955), 205–226.

Kockert, M. *Vätergott und Väterverheissungen. Eine Auseinandersetzung mit Albrecht Alt und seinen Erben.* FRLANT 142. Göttingen, 1988.

Komoroczy, G. "Berossus and the Mesopotamian Literature." *Ac Ant* 21 (1973), 125–152.

——. "Die mesopotamische Mythologie als System." *Oikumene* 4 (1983), 109–119.

Kraeling, E. G. "The Tower of Babel." *JAOS* 40 (1920), 276–281.

——. "The Earliest Hebrew Flood Story." *JBL* 66 (1947), 279–293.

———. "The Significance and Origin of Gen. 6:1–4." *JNES* 6 (1947), 193–208.

———. "Xisouthros, Deucalion and the Flood Traditions." *JAOS* 67 (1947), 177–183.

Kramer, S. N. "The 'Babel of Tongues': A Sumerian Version." *JAOS* 88 (1968), 108–111.

———. "The Sumerian Deluge Myth: Reviewed and Revised." *An St* 33 (1983), 115–121.

———. "Sumerian Mythology Reviewed and Revised." In *Biblical Archaeology Today. Proceedings of the International Congress on Biblical Archaeology, Jerusalem, April 1984*, pp. 286–298. Jerusalem, 1985.

Kramer, S. N., and J. Maier. *Myths of Enki, the Crafty God.* Oxford, 1989.

Kummel, H. M. "Bemerkungen zu den altorientalischen Berichten von der Menschenschöpfung." *WO* 7 (1973/74), 25–38.

Kutsch, E. *Verheissung und Gesetz.* BZAW 131. Berlin and New York, 1972.

———. "Die Paradieserzählung Genesis 2–3 und ihr Verfasser." In G. Braulik, ed., *Studien zum Pentateuch*, pp. 9–24. Vienna, 1977.

Labat, R., et al. *Les religions du proche-orient asiatique.* Paris, 1970.

Lambert, W. G. "Ancestors, Authors, and Canonicity." *JCS* 11 (1957), 1–14, 112.

———. "A New Look at the Babylonian Background of Genesis." *JTS* 16 (1965), 288–290.

———. "A New Fragment from a List of Antediluvian Kings and Marduk's Chariot." In *Symbolae ... Fr. M. Th. de Liagre Böhl Dedicatae.* Edited by M. A. Beek, et al., pp. 271–280. Leiden, 1973.

———."The Seed of Kingship." In *Le palais et la royauté. XXXe rencontre assyriologique internationale.* Edited by P. Garelli, pp. 427–440. Paris, 1974.

Lambert, W. G., and A. R. Millard. *Atra-Ḫasis: The Babylonian Story of the Flood.* London, 1969.

Lambert, W. G., and P. Walcot. "A New Babylonian Theogony and Hesiod." *Kadmos* 4 (1965), 64–72.

Latte, K. "Die Anfänge der griechischen Geschichtsschreibung." *Fondation Hardt pour l'étude de l'antiquité classique* 4 (1952), 3–20.

Lemche, N. P. *Early Israel.* SVT 37. Leiden, 1985.

Lichtheim, M. *Ancient Egyptian Literature: A Book of Readings.* 3 vols. Berkeley, Los Angeles, and London, 1973–80.

Loewenstamm, S. E. "The Flood." In *Comparative Studies in Biblical and Ancient Oriental Literature.* AOAT 204, pp. 93–121. Neukirchen-Vluyn, 1980.

———. "Die Wasser der biblischen Sintflut: Ihr Hereinbrechen und ihr Verschwinden." *VT* 34 (1984), 179–194.

Lohfink, N. *Das Hauptgebot. Eine Untersuchung literarischer Einleitungsfragen zu Dtn 5–11.* AB 20. Rome, 1963.

———. "Die Erzählung vom Sündenfall." In *Das Siegeslied am Schilfmeer,* pp. 81–101. Frankfurt, 1965.

———. "Genesis 2–3 as 'Historical Etiology.'" *Theological Digest* 13 (1965), 11–17. Also in *Scholia* 38 (1963), 321–334.

———. "*yrš.*" In *TWAT* III, pp. 953–985.

———. "Die Bedeutungen von hebr. *jrš qal* und *hif.*" *BZ* 27 (1983), 14–33.

Long, B. O. *The Problem of Etiological Narrative in the Old Testament.* BZAW 108. Berlin, 1968.

Longman, T. *Fictional Akkadian Autobiography: A Genetic and Comparative Study.* Winona Lake, Ind., 1991.

Loretz, O. "Ugarit-Texte und israelitische Religionsgeschichte. Zu F. M. Cross, Canaanite Myth and Hebrew Epic." *UF* 6 (1967), 241–248.

———. *Schöpfung und Mythos: Mensch und Welt nach den Anfangskapiteln der Genesis.* Stuttgart, 1968.

Lovejoy, A. O., and G. Boas. *Primitivism and Related Ideas in Antiquity.* New York, 1965.

Luckenbill, D. D. *Ancient Records of Assyria and Babylonia.* 2 vols. Chicago, 1926–27.

Maag, V. "Malkut JHWH." In *Congress Volume Oxford.* SVT 7, pp. 129–153. Leiden, 1960.

McCarter, P. K. "The River Ordeal in Israelite Literature." *HTR* 66 (1973), 403–412.

McKane, W. Review of R. Rendtorff, *Das überlieferungsgeschichtliche Problem des Pentateuch. VT* 28 (1978), 371–382.

———. *Jeremiah.* ICC, vol. 1. Edinburgh, 1986.

McKenzie, J. L. "The Literary Characteristics of Genesis 2–3." In *Myths and Realities: Studies in Biblical Theology,* pp. 146–181. Milwaukee, 1963.

Maeda, T. "Notes on the Sumerian King List." *Oriento* 25 (1982), 106–117.

Mann, T. W. *Divine Presence and Guidance in Israelite Tradition.* Baltimore, 1977.

Matous, L. "Die Urgeschichte der Menschheit im Atrahasis-Epos und in der Genesis." *Ar Or* 37 (1969), 1–7.

May, H. G. "The King in the Garden of Eden: A Study of Ezekiel 28:12–19." In *Israel's Prophetic Heritage: Essays in Honor of James Muilenburg.* Edited by B. W. Anderson and W. Harrelson, pp. 166–176. New York, 1962.

Mayer, W. R. "Ein Mythos von der Erschaffung des Menschen und des Königs." *Orientalia* 56 (1987), 55–68.

Mayes, A. D. H. *Deuteronomy: New Century Bible Commentary.* London, 1979.

———. *The Story of Israel Between Settlement and Exile.* London, 1983.

Mays, J. L. *Hosea.* Philadelphia, 1969.

Meyer, E. *Die Israeliten und ihre Nachbarstamme.* Halle, 1906.

Michalowski, P. "History as Charter: Some Observations on the Sumerian King List." *JAOS* 103 (1983), 237–248.

Milik, J. T. *The Book of Enoch: Aramaic Fragments of Qumran Cave 4.* Oxford, 1976.

Millard, A. R. "The Etymology of Eden." *VT* 34 (1984), 103–106.

——— "An Assessment of the Evidence of Writing in Ancient Israel." In *Biblical Archaeology Today, Proceedings of the International Congress on Biblical Archaeology, Jerusalem, April 1984,* pp. 301–312. Jerusalem, 1985.

Miller, J. M. "The Descendants of Cain: Notes on Genesis 4." *ZAW* 86 (1974), 164–174.

Miller, P. D. "Eridu, Dunnu, and Babel: A Study in Comparative Mythology." *HAR* 9 (1985), 227–251.

Momigliano, A. "Ancient History and the Antiquarian." In *Studies in Historiography,* pp. 1–39. London, 1966.

———. "Historiography on Written Tradition and Historiography on Oral Tradition." In *Studies in Historiography,* pp. 211–220. London, 1966.

———. "Tradition and the Classical Historian." In *Essays in Ancient and Modern Historiography,* pp. 161–177. Middletown, Conn., 1977.

——. "Greek Historiography." In *History and Theory* 19 (1978), 1–28.

——. "The Historians of the Classical World and Their Audiences." In *Sesto Contributo Alla Storia Degli Studi Classici e del Mondo Antico,* vol. 1, pp. 361–376. Rome, 1980.

——. "History and Biography." In *The Legacy of Greece*. Edited by M. I. Finley, pp. 155–184. Oxford, 1981.

——. "The Origins of Universal History." In *The Poet and the Historian*. Edited by R. E. Friedman, pp. 133–154. Chico, Calif., 1983.

Moran, W. L. "The Creation of Man in Atrahasis I 192–248." *BASOR* 200 (1970), 48–56.

——. "Atrahasis: The Babylonian Story of the Flood." *Biblica* 52 (1971), 51–61.

Mowinckel, S. "Israelite Historiography." *ASTI* 2 (1963), 4–26.

Müller, H.-P. "Mythische Elemente in der jahwistischen Schöpfungs-erzählung." *ZTK* 69 (1972), 259–289.

——. "Das Motiv für die Sintflut." *ZAW* 97 (1985), 295–316.

——. "Eine neue babylonisch Menschenschöpfungserzählung im Licht Keilschriftlicher und biblischer Parallelen — Zur Wirklichkeitsauffassung im Mythos." *Orientalia* 58 (1989), 61–85.

Naidoff, B. D. "A Man to Work the Soil: A New Interpretation of Genesis 2–3." *JAOS* 5 (1978), 2–14.

Neveu, L. *Avant Abraham (Genèse I–XI). Recherches sur des procédés de composition bibliques*. Paris, 1984.

Nicholson, E. W. *Deuteronomy and Tradition*. Oxford, 1967.

——. *God and His People: Covenant and Theology in the Old Testament*. Oxford, 1986.

Nielsen, E. "Creation and the Fall of Man: A Cross-Disciplinary Investigation." *HUCA* 43 (1972), 1–22.

Noth, M. *The History of Israel*. 2nd ed. New York, 1960.

——. *Das zweite Buch Mose. Exodus*. ATD 5. Göttingen, 1958. = *Exodus*. London, 1962.

——. *Überlieferungsgeschichte des Pentateuch*. Stuttgart, 1948. = *A History of Pentateuchal Traditions*. Translated by B. W. Anderson. Englewood Cliffs, N.J., 1972.

——. *Überlieferungsgeschichtliche Studien*. Halle, 1943. = *The Deuteronomistic History*. JSOT SS 15. Sheffield, 1981.

Notter, V. *Biblischer Schöpfungsbericht und ägyptische Schöpfungsmythen*. SBS 68. Stuttgart, 1974.

Oberforcher, R. *Die Flutprologe als Kompositionsschlüssel der biblischen Urgeschichte. Ein Beitrag zur Redaktionskritik.* Innsbruck, 1981.

Oberhuber, K. "Ein Versuch zum Verständnis von Atra-Hasis I 223 und I 1." In *"Wenn nicht jetzt, wann dann?" Aufsätze für Hans-Joachim Kraus.* Edited by H. G. Geyer et al., pp. 279–281. Neukirchen-Vluyn, 1983.

Oded, B. "The Table of Nations (Genesis 10): A Socio-cultural Approach." *ZAW* 98 (1986), 14–31.

Oden, R. A. *Studies in Lucian's De Syria Dea.* HSM 15. Missoula, Mont., 1977.

———. "Divine Aspirations in Atrahasis and in Genesis 1–11." *ZAW* 93 (1981), 197–216.

———. *The Bible Without Theology.* San Francisco, 1987.

Ohler, A. "Die biblische Deutung des Mythos. Zur Auslegung von Genesis 1–3." *ThR* 66 (1970), 177–184.

Oppenheim, A. L. "On Royal Gardens in Mesopotamia." *JNES* 24 (1965), 328–333.

Otto, Eberhard. "Geschichtsbild und Geschichtsschreibung in Ägypten." *WO* 3 (1966), 161–176.

Otto, Eckart. "Jakob in Bethel." *ZAW* 88 (1976), 165–190.

———. *Jakob in Sichem.* BWANT 110. Stuttgart, 1979.

Parker, S. B. "The Historical Composition of KRT and the Cult of El." *ZAW* 89 (1977), 161–175.

Pearson, L. *The Early Ionian Historians.* Oxford, 1939.

———. *The Local Historians of Attica.* APA MS 11. Philadelphia, 1942.

Perlitt, L. *Bundestheologie im Alten Testament.* WMANT 36. Neukirchen-Vluyn, 1969.

———. "Motive und Schichten der Landtheologie im Deuteronomium." In *Das Land Israel in biblischer Zeit.* Edited by G. Strecker, pp. 46–58. Göttingen, 1983.

Petersen, D. L. "The Yahwist on the Flood." *VT* 26 (1976), 438–446.

———. "Genesis 6:1–4: Yahweh and the Organization of the Cosmos." *JSOT* 13 (1979), 47–64.

Pettinato, G. "Die Bestrafung des Menschengeschlechts durch die Sinflut: Die erste Tafel des Atramhasis-Epos eröffnet eine neue Einsicht in die Motivation dieser Strafe." *Orientalia* 37 (1968), 165–200.

———. *Das altorientalische Menschenbild und die sumerischen und akkadischen Schöpfungsmythen.* Heidelberg, 1971.

Poebel, A. *Historical and Grammatical Texts.* Philadelphia, 1914.

Pope, M. H. *El in the Ugaritic Texts.* SVT 2. Leiden, 1955.

Preuss, H. D. ". . . ich will mit dir sein." *ZAW* 80 (1968), 139–173.

Pury, A. de. "Genèse XXXIV et l'histoire." *RB* 66 (1969), 5–49.

———. *Promesse divine et légende culturelle dans le cycle de Jacob: Genèse 28 et les traditions patriarchales.* 2 vols. Paris, 1975.

Pury, A. de, and T. Römer. "Le pentateuque en question: position du problème et brève histoire de la recherche." In *Le pentateuque en question.* Edited by A. de Pury, pp. 9–80. Geneva, 1989.

Rad, G. von. *Old Testament Theology.* Vol. 1. New York, 1962.

———. *Das formgeschichtliche Problem des Hexateuchs.* BWANT 4,26 (1938). = "The Form-Critical Problem of the Hexateuch." In *The Problem of the Hexateuch and Other Essays.* Translated by E. W. T. Dicken, pp. 1–78. Edinburgh and London, 1966.

———. *Genesis: A Commentary.* Rev. ed. Translated by J. H. Marks. Philadelphia, 1972.

Redford, D. B. *A Study of the Biblical Story of Joseph (Genesis 37–50).* SVT 20, 1970.

———. *Pharaonic King-Lists, Annals and Day-Books.* Mississauga, Ont., 1986.

Reiner, E. "The Etiological Myth of the 'Seven Sages.'" *Orientalia* 30 (1961), 1–11.

Rendtorff, R. "Genesis 8,21 und die Urgeschichte des Jahwisten." *KuD* 7 (1961), 69–78.

———. "Hermeneutische Probleme der biblischen Urgeschichte." In *Festschrift für Friedrich Smend,* pp. 19–29. Berlin, 1963.

———. *Das überlieferungsgeschichtliche Problem des Pentateuch.* BZAW 147. Berlin, 1977.

———. "Der 'Jahwist' als Theologe? Zum Dilemma der Pentateuchkritik." SVT 28, pp. 159–166. Leiden, 1975. = "The 'Yahwist' as Theologian? The Dilemma of Pentateuchal Criticism." *JSOT* 3 (1977), 2–10.

———. "Genesis 15 im Rahmen der theologischen Bearbeitung der Vätergeschichten." In *Werden und Wirken des Alten Testaments: Festschrift für C. Westermann.* Edited by R. Albertz, pp. 74–81. Göttingen/Neukirchen-Vluyn, 1980.

———. "Jacob in Bethel. Beobachtungen zum Aufbau und zur Quellenfrage in Genesis 28,10–22." *ZAW* 94 (1982), 511–523.

———. *The Old Testament: An Introduction.* Philadelphia, 1985.

Reventlow, H. G. *Opfere deinen Sohn, Eine Auslegung von Genesis 22.* BS 53. Neukirchen-Vluyn, 1968.

Richter, W. "Urgeschichte und Hoftheologie." *BZ* 10 (1966), 96–105.

Rofé, A. "Classes in the Prophetic Stories: Didactic Legenda and Parable." SVT 26, pp. 153–164. Leiden, 1974.

———. "The History of the Cities of Refuge in Biblical Law." *Studies in Bible. Scrip Hier* 21 (1986), 205–239.

Rogerson, J. W. *Myth in Old Testament Interpretation.* BZAW 134. Berlin, 1974.

Römer, T. "Israël et son histoire d'après l'historiographie deuteronomiste." *ETR* 61 (1986), 1–19.

———. *Israels Väter: Untersuchungen zur Vaterthematik im Deuteronomium und in der deuteronomistischen Tradition.* OBO 99. Freiburg, Switzerland, and Göttingen, 1990.

Rose, M. *Deuteronomist und Jahwist: Untersuchungen zu den Berührungspunkten beider Literaturwerke.* ATANT 67. Zurich, 1981.

Rosenmeyer, T. G. "Hesiod and Historiography (Erga 106–201)." *Hermes* 83 (1957), 257–285.

Rost, L. "Noah der Weinbauer." In *Das kleine Credo und andere Studien zum Alten Testament,* pp. 44–53. Heidelberg, 1965.

Rouillard, H. *La péricope de Balaam (Nombres 22–24).* Paris, 1985.

Rudolph, W. "Die Josephsgeschichte." In P. Volz and W. Rudolph, *Der Elohist als Erzähler — ein Irrweg der Pentateuchkritik?* BZAW 63, pp. 143–183. Berlin, 1933.

Ruppert, L. *Die Josephserzählung der Genesis.* SANT 11. Munich, 1965.

———. "Die Sündenfallerzählung (Genesis 3) in vorjahwistischer Tradition und Interpretation." *BZ* 15 (1971), 185–202.

———. "Herkunft und Bedeutung der Jacob-Tradition bei Hosea." *Biblica* 52 (1971), 488–504.

Ruprecht, E. "Der traditionsgeschichtliche Hintergrund der Gestaltung in Genesis XII 1–3." *VT* 29 (1979), 444–464.

———. "Vorgegebene Tradition und theologische Gestaltung in Genesis XII 1–3." *VT* 29 (1979), 171–188.

Rüterswörden, U. "Kanaanäisch-städtische Mythologie im Werk des Jahwisten. Eine Notiz zu Genesis 4." *BN* 1 (1976), 19–23.

Scharbert, J. "Quellen und Redaktion in Gen. 2:4b–4:16." *BZ* 18 (1974), 45–64.

———. *Genesis 1–11.* Die neue Echter Bibel. Würzburg, 1983.

Schmid, H. H. *Der sogenannte Jahwist. Beobachtungen und Fragen zur Pentateuchforschung.* Zurich, 1976.

——. "Gerechtigkeit und Glaube: Genesis 15,1–6 und sein biblisch-theologischer Kontext." *EvT* 40 (1980), 396–420.

——. "Vers une théologie du Pentateuque." In *Le Pentateuque en question.* Edited by A. de Pury, pp. 374–379. Geneva, 1989.

Schmidt, L. "Überlegungen zum Jahwisten." *EvT* 37 (1977), 230–247.

——. *Literarische Studien zur Josephsgeschichte.* BZAW 167, pp. 120–297, 307–310. Berlin and New York, 1986.

Schmidt, W. H. *Die Schöpfungsgeschichte der Priesterschrift. Zur Überlieferungsgeschichte von Gen. 1,1–2,4a und 2,4b–3,24.* WMANT 17. 2nd ed. Neukirchen-Vluyn, 1967.

Schmitt, H. C. *Die nichtpriesterliche Josephsgeschichte.* BZAW 154. Berlin and New York, 1980.

Schulte, H. *Die Entstehung der Geschichtsschreibung im alten Israel.* BZAW 128. Berlin, 1972.

Seebass, H. *Geschichtliche Zeit und theonome Tradition in der Joseph-Erzählung.* Gutersloh, 1978.

Seux, M.-J. *Épithètes royales akkadiennes et sumériennes.* Paris, 1967.

——. *La Création du monde et de l'homme d'après les textes du Proche-Orient ancien.* Paris, 1981.

Seybold, K. "Der Turmbau zu Babel. Zur Entstehung von Gen. 11,1–9." *VT* 26 (1976), 453–479.

Shils, E. "Intellectuals, Traditions, and the Traditions of Intellectuals: Some Preliminary Considerations." *Daedalus* (1972), 21–34.

——. *Tradition.* Chicago, 1981.

Simoons-Vermeer, R. E. "The Mesopotamian Flood Stories: A Comparison and Interpretation." *Numen* 21 (1974), 17–34.

Skinner, J. *A Critical and Exegetical Commentary on Genesis.* ICC. 2nd ed. Edinburgh, 1930.

Skweres, D. E. *Die Rückverweise im Buch Deuteronomium.* AB 79. Rome, 1979.

Soden, W. von. "Etemenanki von Asarhaddon: Nach der Erzählung vom Turmbau zu Babel und dem Erra-Mythos." *UF* 3 (1971), 253–264.

——. "Der Mensch bescheidet sich nicht." *Symbolae . . . Böhl Dedicatae.* Edited by M. A. Beek et al., pp. 349–358. Leiden, 1973.

———. "Verschlüsselte Kritik an Salomo in der Urgeschichte des Jahwisten?" *WO* 7 (1974), 228–240.

———. "Die erste Tafel des altbabylonischen Atramhasis-Mythos. 'Haupttext' und Parallelversionen." *ZA* 68 (1978), 50–94.

———. "Konflikt und ihre Bewältigung in babylonischen Schöpfungs- und Fluterzählungen. Mit einer Teil-Übersetzung des Atramhasis-Mythos." *MDOG* 111 (1979), 1–33.

Soisalon-Soininen, I. "Die Urgeschichte im Geschichtswerk des Jahwisten." *Temenos* 6 (1970), 130–141.

Sollberger, E. "The Rulers of Lagaš." *JCS* 21 (1967), 279–291.

———. *The Babylonian Legend of the Flood.* London, 1971.

Solmsen, F. *Hesiod and Aeschylus.* Ithaca, 1949.

Speiser, E. A. *Genesis: The Anchor Bible.* Garden City, N.Y., 1964.

Starr, C. G. *Essays on Ancient History: A Selection of Articles and Reviews.* Leiden, 1979.

Steck, O. H. "Die Paradieserzählung: Eine Auslegung von Genesis 2,4b–3,24." In *Wahrnehmungen Gottes im Alten Testament. Gesammelte Studien,* pp. 9–116. Munich, 1982.

———. "Genesis 12,1–3 und die Urgeschichte des Jahwisten." In *Wahrnehmungen Gottes im Alten Testament. Gesammelte Studien,* pp. 117–148. Munich, 1982.

Tengström, S. *Die Hexateucherzählung. Eine literaturgeschichtliche Studie.* CB OTS 7. Uppsala, 1976.

———. *Die Toledotformel und die literarische Struktur der priesterlichen Erweiterungsgeschichte im Pentateuch.* CB OTS 17. Uppsala, 1982.

Thomas, R. *Oral Tradition and Written Record in Classical Athens.* Cambridge, 1989.

Thrade, K. "Erfinder II." In *Reallexikon für Antike und Christentum.* Vol. 5, pp. 1191–1278. Stuttgart, 1950.

———. "Das Lob des Erfinders" *Rheinisches Museum für Philologie* 105 (1962), 158–188.

Tigay, J. *The Evolution of the Gilgamesh Epic.* Philadelphia, 1982.

Ühlinger, C. *Weltreich und "eine Rede": Eine neue Deutung der sogenannte Turmbauerzählung (Gen 11,1–9).* OBO 101. Freiburg, Switzerland, 1990.

Unger, E. "Babylon." *RLA* I, 364–366.

———. *Babylon, Die heilige Stadt nach der Beschreibung der Babylonier.* Berlin and Leipzig, 1931.

VanderKam, J. C. *Enoch and the Growth of the Apocalyptic Tradition.* CBQ MS 16, 1984.

Van Seters, J. "Confessional Reformulation in the Exilic Period." *VT* 22 (1972), 448–459.

——. *Abraham in History and Tradition.* New Haven, 1975.

——. "Recent Studies on the Pentateuch: A Crisis in Method." *JAOS* 99 (1979), 663–673.

——. *In Search of History.* New Haven, 1983.

——. "Joshua 24 and the Problem of Tradition in the Old Testament." In *The Shelter of Elyon.* JSOT SS 31, pp. 139–158. Sheffield, 1984.

——. *Der Jahwist als Historiker.* ThSt 134. Zurich, 1987.

——. "'Comparing Scripture with Scripture': Some Observations on the Sinai Pericope of Exodus 19–24." In *Canon, Theology and Old Testament Interpretation.* Edited by G. M. Tucker, D. L. Petersen, and R. R. Wilson, pp. 111–130. Philadelphia, 1988.

——. "The Primeval Histories of Greece and Israel Compared." *ZAW* 100 (1988), 1–22.

——. "The Creation of Man and the Creation of the King." *ZAW* 101 (1989), 333–342.

——. "Myth and History: The Problem of Origins." In *Histoire et conscience historique dans les civilizations du Proche-Orient ancien.* Les Cahiers du CEPOA 5. Edited by A. de Pury, pp. 49–61. Leuven, 1989.

——. "Tradition and History: History as National Tradition." In *Histoire et conscience historique dans les civilizations du Proche-Orient ancien.* Les Cahiers du CEPOA 5. Edited by A. de Pury, pp. 63–74. Leuven, 1989.

——. "Joshua's Conquest of Canaan and Near Eastern Historiography." *SJOT* 1990, no. 2, pp. 1–12.

Veijola, T. "Das Opfer des Abraham—Paradigma des Glaubens aus dem nachexilischen Zeitalter." *ZTK* 85 (1988), 129–164.

Verdin, H. "Hérodote historien? quelques interpretations récentes." *L'Antiquité Classique* 44 (1975), 668–685.

Vernant, J.-P. *Myth and Society in Ancient Greece.* London, 1982.

Veyne, P. *Did the Greeks Believe in Their Myths?* Chicago, 1988.

Vollmer, J. *Geschichtliche Rüchblicke und Motive in der Prophetie des Amos, Hosea und Jesaja.* BZAW 119. Berlin and New York, 1971.

Vorländer, H. *Mein Gott. Die Vorstellungen vom persönlichen Gott im Alten Testament.* AOAT 23. Neukirchen-Vluyn, 1975.

Vriezen, T. C. *Die Erwählung Israels nach dem Alten Testament.* Zurich, 1953.

Wallace, H. N. *The Eden Narrative.* HSM 32. Atlanta, 1985.

Walton, J. "The Antediluvian Section of the Sumerian King List and Genesis 5." *BA* 44 (1981), 207–208.

Warner, S. "The Alphabet: An Innovation and Its Diffusion." *VT* 30 (1980), 81–90.

Wellhausen, J. *Prolegomena to the History of Ancient Israel.* Edinburgh, 1885.

———. *Die Composition des Hexateuchs und der historischen Bücher des Alten Testaments.* 3rd ed. Berlin, 1899.

West, M. L. *Hesiod: Works and Days.* Oxford, 1978.

———. *The Hesiodic Catalogue of Women: Its Nature, Structure, and Origins.* Oxford, 1985.

Westermann, C. "Der Mensch im Urgeschehen." *KuD* 13 (1967), 231–246.

———. "Arten der Erzählung in der Genesis." *Forschung am Alten Testament.* TB 24 (1964), 9–91. = *The Promises to the Fathers.* Philadelphia, 1976.

———. *Genesis.* Biblischer Kommentar I/1–3. Neukirchen-Vluyn, 1974–82. English translation, *Genesis 1–11, Genesis 12–36, Genesis 37–50.* Translated by J. J. Scullion. Minneapolis, 1984–86.

Whitt, W. D. "The Jacob Traditions in Hosea and their Relations to Genesis." *ZAW* 103 (1991), 18–43.

Whybray, R. N. "The Joseph Story and Pentateuchal Criticism." *VT* 18 (1968), 522–528.

———. *The Making of the Pentateuch: A Methodological Study.* JSOT SS 53. Sheffield, 1987.

Wilson, R. R. *Genealogy and History in the Biblical World.* New Haven, 1977.

———. "The Death of the King of Tyre: The Editorial History of Ezekiel 28." In *Love and Death in the Ancient Near East: Essays in Honor of Marvin H. Pope.* Edited by J. H. Marks, pp. 211–218. Guilford, 1987.

Winnett, F. V. "The Arabian Genealogies in the Book of Genesis." In *Translating and Understanding the Old Testament: In Honor of*

H. G. May. Edited by H. T. Frank and W. L. Reed, pp. 171–196. Nashville/New York, 1970.

Wiseman, D. J. "Mesopotamian Gardens." *An St* 33 (1983), 137–144.

———. *Nebuchadrezzar and Babylon.* Oxford, 1985.

Wolff, H. W. *Hosea.* Hermeneia. Philadelphia, 1974.

Wyatt, N. "Interpreting the Creation and Fall Story in Genesis 2–3." *ZAW* 93 (1981), 11–21.

———. "Where Did Jacob Dream His Dream?" *SJOT* 1990, no. 2, 44–57.

Yeivin, S. "Administration." In *World History of the Jewish People.* Vol. 4/2, *The Age of the Monarchies: Culture and Society.* Edited by A. Malamat, pp. 147–171. Jerusalem, 1979.

Zenger, E. "Beobachtungen zur Komposition und Theologie der jahwistischen Urgeschichte." In *Dynamik im Wort. FS aus Anlass des 50 jährigen Bestehens des Kath. Bibelwerks in Deutschland,* pp. 35–54. Stuttgart, 1983.

Zimmerli, W. "Das Gottesrecht bei den Propheten Amos, Hosea und Jesaja." In *Werden und Wirken des Alten Testaments, Festschrift für C. Westermann.* Edited by R. Albertz, pp. 220–228. Göttingen, 1980.

———. "The 'Land' in the Pre-Exilic and Early Post-Exilic Prophets." In *Understanding the Word. Essays in Honor of B. W. Anderson.* Edited by J. T. Butler et al. JSOT SS 37, pp. 245–262. Sheffield, 1985.

INDEX OF SCRIPTURE

INDEX OF SUBJECTS